Sulla

Sulla

A Dictator Reconsidered

Lynda Telford

Pen & Sword
MILITARY

First published in Great Britain in 2014 by
Pen & Sword Military
an imprint of
Pen & Sword Books Ltd
47 Church Street
Barnsley
South Yorkshire
S70 2AS

ISBN 978 1 78303 048 4

A CIP catalogue record for this book is available from the British
Library

Typeset in Ehrhardt by
Mac Style, Bridlington, East Yorkshire
Printed and bound in the UK by CPI Group (UK) Ltd, Croydon,
CRO 4YY

Pen & Sword Books Ltd incorporates the imprints of Pen & Sword
Archaeology, Atlas, Aviation, Battleground, Discovery, Family History,
History, Maritime, Military, Naval, Politics, Railways, Select,
Social History, Transport, True Crime, and Claymore Press,
Frontline Books, Leo Cooper, Praetorian Press, Remember When,
Seaforth Publishing and Wharncliffe.

For a complete list of Pen & Sword titles please contact
PEN & SWORD BOOKS LIMITED
47 Church Street, Barnsley, South Yorkshire, S70 2AS, England
E-mail: enquiries@pen-and-sword.co.uk
Website: www.pen-and-sword.co.uk

Contents

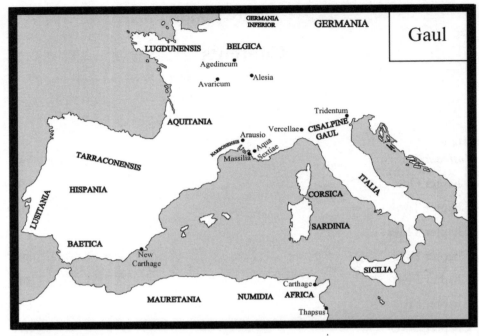

Map 1: Gaul.

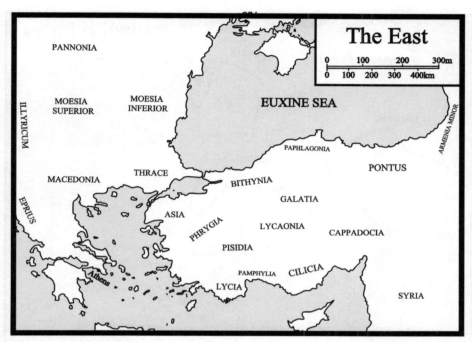

Map 2: The East.

Map 3: Italian States.

Introduction

The last 150 years of the Roman Republic undoubtedly produced some of the greatest men who have ever lived. Across the stage of the then known world walked, within a relatively short space of time, men whose names still ring aloud their glory and their achievements.

They ranged from the Brothers Gracchi, who struggled and had to die for the cause of land reform, or fairer distribution of the Italian lands, which had become the private sinecure of wealthy landowners. This control of the *ager publica* by several of the great families, using slave gangs to work the land, was to the detriment of the original small farmers who might otherwise have produced a modest prosperity for their own class. Even more, they would also have bred families of their own, and those children would in various ways advance the cause of Rome. Naturally, the great reforming brothers met with opposition from those who benefited most from the *latifundia*, and they were eventually destroyed, but their legacy of land reform lived on to be raised again in later years when land was required for veterans of the wars.

Next there was the great Gaius Marius. He not only reshaped the Roman army into something that a modern day soldier might still recognize, but started his brilliant rise by being successful against Jugurtha. He was also able to turn aside the hordes of the Germanic peoples, who were desperate to descend on southern Europe in the hope of better lands and a more equable climate. These people, many hundreds of thousands of them, represented a very real threat to Rome and the Roman way of life. When they were finally turned aside and the survivors eventually made their way towards the lands of the Belgae, seeking refuge, the stay-at-homes in Rome became aware that Gaius Marius, though a man of no birth, had saved them. He was capable not only of showing the old families that he was one of their greatest generals, but was beloved by those who swung the votes, and thereby became Consul for an unprecedented seven times.

Then followed my subject, Lucius Cornelius Sulla. He started life with the great advantage of Patrician birth, but also the huge disadvantage of lack of sufficient wealth to support that birth, and to help him make the expected ascent of the cursus honorum to which his Patrician blood entitled him.

There was also Pompey – Gnaeus Pompeius Magnus. He saw himself as the greatest man in Rome and, despite his youth, very nearly proved it to be so.

Then Caesar himself, another Patrician, who managed to do the impossible, in making himself Dictator for Life, but who had to pay for his presumption by the loss of that life.

Also walking the Roman stage at that time were Crassus and Cato, Brutus and Cicero and the scandalous young Publius Clodius Pulcher and his equally scandalous sister Clodia, together with his delectable wife Fulvia. She was a descendant of the Gracchi and first married P. Clodius, then Curio, then finally Marcus Antonius, who was Gaius Julius Caesar's second cousin and who expected to be his heir – an expectation which, sadly for him, failed to materialize.

Exciting though these people are, who all have a tale to tell us, it is a very great mistake to look upon them, or indeed any historical character, with twenty-first century eyes, or to judge them by twenty-first century standards. They lived in a very different time when people had to make their decisions according to more brutal rules, which demanded more brutal reactions in return. They were often forced into situations we would probably be unable to cope with, therefore trying to understand their motives with minds blinded by modern considerations is a futile exercise.

This account does not pretend to be a military or political history of the period, nor do I believe that it needs to be. There are many such accounts already written by people who are experts in those fields. What the work does hope to do is to show this one man, Lucius Cornelius Sulla, as a real and living person. Not just as a figurehead of the Roman state, a name in a history book, a general, a politician, a dictator, or a murderer, though at various times in his life he became all of those things.

I believe he was a very able and competent man. This was at a time when Rome was rich in such men, but many, indeed most, of them failed to put Rome's needs before their own. Yet Sulla, whose actions sometimes had to become extreme, was fundamentally a decent man, whose first love was always for Rome. I believe that he has had a very 'bad press' and is not at all appreciated as he should be, nor does his life attract the sympathy and understanding given to other men of his time. Men of status and power were often compelled to deal with situations similar to his and were just as ruthless when they needed to be.

They too, often performed or instigated acts which have stained their names, and very few of them could claim to be free of this taint. Indeed, in the context of the time, it would hardly be possible for any man to live as a soldier and politician without at some time being obliged to stain his hands with the blood of those who fought against him or opposed him politically. This was the world in which they lived. However, other men have done this and been more easily forgiven for it.

Caesar was not exempt from extreme acts during his years as a general, yet he is still revered. He was not only responsible for horrific slaughters in Gaul, but some histories actually fail to mention Thapsus, on 6 April 46 BC. On that occasion, fighting the supporters of Pompey's sons, his men massacred 10,000 of the defeated side, while they were trying to surrender! After the massacre was over, he then executed Lucius Afranius, who had been Consul, along with Sulla's son Faustus. These were, of course, not savages or barbarians, but fellow Romans. I fail to see how anything done by Sulla compares with that action, which is actually glossed over in many books dealing with the period.

Gaius Marius suffered a series of strokes, which seriously affected his mental capacities. After his second stroke he became almost a monster of cruelty, destroying all those who defied him, friend and foe alike, but he is still openly referred to as the 'great' Gaius Marius!

Sulla, however, is always referred to in histories of the period in a very different way. Writers feel free to admire his ability as a general, or refer to the perfectly sensible laws he promulgated when he achieved power, or even to describe the affection in which he was held by those who knew him well and served him for years. Some writers indulge themselves with blaming him for every cruelty and debauchery, often without producing evidence, and even with the fairest of them there seems to be always a 'but' to qualify any praise of him.

Corruption and greed were as rife in the Republic as in any other time in history, and those who put the interests of their State first have always been in a minority. Unfortunately, due to the opposition, jealousy and short-sightedness of others, Sulla was several times forced into actions which have since defined him in a way which might well have surprised him, and which have certainly stained his name for ever.

For Sulla truly loved Rome. Not, as many men did, for what she could give back to her sons, in power, prestige and wealth, but for herself. Sulla believed in her implicitly. He believed that she was a mother to her citizens and a mistress to be served. When he was finally able to do so, after a long struggle, he promulgated laws which were not only in many ways models of common sense, but incorporated the reforms he believed essential to Rome's prosperity and economic recovery. These were necessary after the decades of wars had leached her of all her resources.

Sulla fought with distinction in those wars, with Gaius Marius against the Germanic peoples, who were still trying to find a new homeland, and against Jugurtha, whose capture he accomplished. He also had to fight the Italians themselves, who resented the idea of Rome's pre-eminence and the unfairness with which they were treated as allies of Rome. The resulting conflict dragged on for years. During that time he was awarded the Corona Graminea outside the walls of Nola, and conquered Pompeii which then became known as Colonia

Cornelia Veneria Pompeianorum or Sulla's Colony of Venus. But by then the State was bankrupt and tottering.

Trying to find solutions to this, Sulla also found himself up against those men who resented him and whose self-interest prevented them not only from helping to rebuild and restore Rome but also from sharing his vision of a new security and prosperity. Certainly he grew to hate and deeply resent the bankers and loan sharks, in a predicament which has many all too familiar references to the present day. The 'money-men' who, though still personally unbelievably rich, expected him to fight again in the East, yet were not prepared to put their hands into their ample pockets and provide the funds. They wanted him out of the way, ostensibly to acquire for Rome (or for themselves) any riches that might be available. But they had no interest in the fact that he had to go without ships, funds or equipment, which he had to find by taking the battle to Greece.

It should be remembered that before Caesar won his Corona Civica, Sulla had earned the Corona Graminea, or Grass Crown, the highest of all Roman military honours. Before Caesar crossed the Rubicon and marched on Rome, calling himself Dictator, Sulla had already been there. He had done it all before. Not for the usual six months' duration, awarded by the Senate when necessity arose and they found themselves driven into a corner, but taken by him into his own hands for as long as he considered necessary, in order to reorganize and rectify the State's many problems. That he was obliged to take extreme measures in order to attain these ends has tended to blight the effects of his achievements in the eyes of many historians.

His hatred of the Ordo Equestor, whose members persisted in thwarting his every attempt, defined his actions upon his return. Rome was by this time on her knees and Sulla was determined to end the appalling self-seeking amongst the knightly class, refill Rome's empty treasuries, rebuild her rotting temples, and put her back on her feet.

He eliminated those many enemies who were intent on preventing his success and who disbelieved his claims to put Rome's welfare first, accustomed as they were to considering only their own. He is greatly criticized for giving increased powers to the Senate and reducing the power of the Tribunes. These were necessary reforms for the time and to claim that he advanced the patricians at the cost of the plebians is a gross over-simplification. Sulla tried to strengthen the Senate, certainly not because of any love for its members, who were only too often his own enemies, but because he was aware that it needed strength to rule an empire that was already becoming unwieldy. He reduced the powers of the Tribunes because they had the power of veto. This enormous power, given to a group of people who had proved themselves to be eminently bribable, was a great danger to reform. Any man who wished to block a new move simply had to 'buy' a Tribune and that man would then veto whatever he was paid to oppose. The result was that any action against people with a vested interest could not even be discussed and no real work could ever be achieved. Sulla, in preventing these all too common abuses, allowed the work of reforming the state to proceed.

His actions taken against the Ordo Equestor and the Senators who persisted in opposing him were in line with this. Firstly, they would never stand aside and allow him to make the reforms that were desperately needed. Secondly, the money for restructuring and rebuilding a shattered Rome had to come from somewhere! Rome would need to have vast sums of money before she could become financially solvent again. Sulla always showed that he believed strongly that such a terrible burden should not be thrust onto the ordinary people, and neither could he put it upon those people who had served and supported him, demonstrating their loyalty with their lives.

The members of the Ordo Equestor had waxed fat under the administrations of Marius, Cinna and Carbo. Now it was their turn to pay the price and pay they did. Not only did their lives become forfeit, their fortunes were used to replenish the empty treasuries of Rome and help to rebuild her prosperity.

However, he did not use the money from all their confiscated estates for his own enrichment, as another man might easily have been tempted to do. Even though he had never been a wealthy man in the way his contemporaries were and when wealth was still a very necessary adjunct to status. (It is interesting to note that while Sulla put the confiscated monies back into Rome's treasuries, it was Caesar who was to later take it all back out again!) Sulla made and enforced new laws in an attempt to simplify the political system and prevent the corruption that was endemic within the state, just as he tried to ensure a future stability.

When all this was finished, in the space of just over two years, he did what nobody had ever expected him to do, or believed that he would dare to do. He laid down the supreme power and retired to the country.

No man ever voluntarily set down such power as he had held. Those men who had not expected Sulla to behave in such a way were judging him only by their own lesser standards. They would certainly not have laid down the Dictator's power, if they had ever managed to acquire it, if only for fear of the retribution of their enemies. Caesar did not, when his own turn came. He simply could not afford to, knowing that if he did step down they would all turn and rend him. Eventually, he had to declare himself Dictator in Perpetuity, and this was far too close to the status of the old kings for anyone's comfort and satisfaction. (Was there not the slight but definite idea in his mind that of all men he had the best right to be a king?) Whatever his thoughts and ambitions at that time, Caesar had finally to be removed by assassination.

However, Sulla had kept his word. After doing what he considered necessary, he announced his retirement and stepped down, taking those who loved him with him. There were still many who did love him, despite the agonies of the past years.

Sulla had started his career as a man of great physical beauty. Such beauty, however, had its downside, especially in Rome. One the one hand, it was admired, but also greatly suspect. If a man was beautiful of face when a boy, he was considered a temptation to other men and always that suspicion of passive homosexuality clung to him. When that same man matured, he was then a temptation to women, and other men looked askance at him, wondering if they were being cuckolded. Either way, he might be considered to be a lightweight, not a proper Roman male.

Sulla proved beyond a doubt that, despite his unusual appearance, he was certainly no lightweight, though he did have lovers in plenty, male and female, plus wives and children. He was also possessed of that one elusive and most important thing, a great deal of charm. He had a wonderful capacity for making and keeping friends, and that ability does not sit happily with the idea that he was a crazy despot. Such people have cronies and sycophants, not true friends. Despite all his many faults, and he was a normal human being with human frailties, people who knew him intimately continued to respect and care for him.

Later in his life he contracted a terrible disease in Greece, which many historians think may have been scabies. However, the scabious plant, (Succisa pratensis), a commonly found blue wild flower, was used to treat that condition from earliest times, hence the name. But I prefer another possibility. If he suffered from shingles, the symptoms would be very similar. Shingles, (or post herpetic neuralgia), especially if it affects the face, can be a very debilitating ailment indeed. This disease is caused by the same virus as chickenpox, the Herpes Virus Type 3 and it produces the same rash and intense itching as scabies, which eventually leads to serious pain and permanent scarring. This would have had no possibility of treatment during his lifetime. Doctors even now find that in an older patient, the prognosis is far from good and there is more likelihood of not only intense, but continuing pain with little chance of relief.

Though neither of the suggested ailments is life threatening, the condition did destroy his looks completely. He must have suffered terribly, not only from the illness itself, causing him to tear in agony at the skin of his face in attempts to relieve the constant irritation, but it was probably at this time that he began to take refuge in wine. This may have blunted the continual discomfort of the skin disease that no doctor at that time could understand, although the resultant heavy drinking certainly helped to shorten his life. Furthermore, he then had to suffer the utter humiliation of finally returning to Rome, to face his enemies, knowing that his looks were completely wrecked, and that other people felt free to laugh at him. He was then described openly as having a complexion 'like mulberries sprinkled with oatmeal'.

His personal motto of 'no better friend, no worse enemy' speaks volumes of his feelings at this time. He did indeed become a terrible enemy to those who opposed him, but he still was, at the same time, the best and truest friend to those who were loyal to him. He repaid their faith and their loyalty gladly. These closest friends were often drawn from the lowest levels of Roman society, the actors, mimes and dancers who had been his preferred companions since youth, when his lack of personal funds prevented him from mixing in the circles to which his birth otherwise should have entitled him. I have seen these friends of his described as 'evildoers' and 'people sunk in every kind of debauchery'. Thankfully in our own time we can appreciate that poverty and low birth are not crimes and that those who suffer these indignities can still be decent people. These were largely the friends who retired with him, drawn from the outcasts of society, who did not judge him by his relative poverty, or by the evils he was supposed to have done, but by his true character, which they were in the best possible position to know.

These connections, some of them homosexual, are probably the reason why Sulla has not been a favourite of early twentieth century historians, at least in England. Thankfully, we are now able to see the real person behind the labels that certainly show only a very small part of this full and many-faceted character. He was a man who lived and struggled, won and lost, all within the bounds of Rome's greatest time, surrounded by a large number of the finest and most vibrant people who have ever lived.

This biography will seek to show Sulla as a brave, capable, devout man of his time. I feel strongly that he deserves a better understanding of his difficulties and an appreciation of his undoubted achievements. It is a great pity that most of those achievements were torn down after his death and Rome's society returned gladly enough to that from which he had tried to save it. He certainly intended to prevent the self-aggrandizement of those whose only interest was in their own greed. Few men lasted long in the political arena of Rome, though Sulla, in his eventual retirement, enjoyed a rounding off of his public life that was indeed unusual. He must have known that his health was failing and that he had only a short time left to live.

Other maligned historical characters have benefited from a modern rehabilitation of their reputations. Two favourites of mine, Anne Boleyn and Richard III have in recent years been looked at far more fairly. Eric Ives has done wonderful work in showing that Anne Boleyn was far more than just a greedy and ambitious good-time girl who got what she deserved for being nasty to Queen Catherine, who is often represented as a patient Griselda. David Starkey has also achieved a great deal with his research, which shows clearly that there is a lot more to their story than originally met the eye!

I have for many years been a member of the Richard III Society and have seen first-hand the excellent work that has been done, and is still being done, to put before the public the knowledge they need to evaluate King Richard differently. Every effort is made to focus more on what he was attempting to achieve, rather than the later Tudor 'monster' fairy stories that have been prevalent for so long.

I believe that it is now high time that Lucius Cornelius Sulla was looked at more equably. I am aware that mine may be something of a lone voice initially, and my theories regarding the reasons for his actions will undoubtedly be highly controversial, as a new opinion so often is. Nevertheless, I would welcome an opportunity to ask readers to reconsider the usual glib accounts of him and give him a fair hearing, as he undoubtedly deserves.

Chapter One

Born in Rome in 138 BC to a faded branch of a Patrician family, Lucius Cornelius Sulla's prospects did not appear particularly promising. He grew up, however, with a great determination to somehow live the kind of life to which his aristocratic birth entitled him, even if his lack of fortune seemed always to be in the way to prevent him from doing so. His life and rise to prominence was a series of struggles to achieve the position which, for other men, came easily and almost automatically.

For Sulla, everything he was to do was fraught with controversy and opposition. He always fought the opposition and often courted the controversy, forging a path for himself which sometimes had to ride roughshod over the opinions and interests of others. He never lost sight of the final goal, however, which was not only to have for himself the approbation and appreciation he felt deprived of, but to bring Rome herself back from the brink upon which she tottered. He always intended to try to make her strong, rich and all-powerful again, after the series of wars and disasters, which had all but bankrupted and destroyed her. Sulla's struggles and achievements, in order to be fully understood, need firstly to be seen against the background of the Rome into which he was born.

It needs to be remembered that Rome had finally taken over the whole Mediterranean area by the time of Sulla's birth and if the Mediterranean Sea was not yet called the 'Mare Nostrum' or Our Sea, the principle was already clear. The few states still retaining apparent independence from Rome only did so under Rome's sufferance.

This enviable situation had not, however, been achieved easily. The final stage of the Punic Wars had only been completed in 146 BC and had lasted, overall, for 118 years!

This lengthy conflict had caused Rome a world of loss and pain. For, prior to this time, it was Carthage, not Rome, who ruled the Middle Sea. It was Carthage who had built up a maritime and commercial empire able to spread its tentacles across the whole area, when Rome was nothing more than a struggling town surrounded by a muddy marsh.

Carthage was founded in 814 BC, traditionally by Dido, the daughter of a King of Tyre. It formed one of a series of Phoenician settlements stretching from Asia to Spain, but, although it became extensive, it was not aggressive. It was a trading, rather than a military, empire. Carthage took tribute from all the colonies around the Mediterranean, including, initially, Rome. Eventually, that great Phoenician society decided that its trading and mercantile families were too valuable economically to be risked in warfare, and it put its defence into the hands of mercenaries. The ruling class of Carthage were opposed to militarism, fearing that arming its citizens, or even its mercenaries, was dangerous, leading inevitably to democracy or a military coup. Therefore, they treated even their successful generals with little favour.

Carthage and Rome were, therefore, not strangers when they began their first conflict in 264 BC. Treaties had been negotiated and they show not only that Carthage was not really interested in anything but commerce, but that Rome was indifferent to it. When Rome, that little town on the Tiber, began to stretch her wings and look around her for conquests, Carthage was standing in her way. Unfortunately for Carthage, Rome was to prove to be very aggressive indeed.

Cicero tells us that there were three Punic Wars. The first was separated from the second by twenty-three years and the second from the third by fifty-two years, but they were still all a part of one struggle. At the end of the first, and longest, of these conflicts, and despite maritime disasters that practically bankrupted the emergent Rome, the Romans still built a new navy, albeit on Phoenician lines, when their first had been destroyed. This was in itself an achievement, for Rome was never primarily a naval power. The Consuls for that year – 242 to 241 BC – were Gaius Lutatius Catulus and Appius Postumius Albinus. The latter was not only Junior Consul for that year, but also Flamen Martialis, the head of the cult of Mars, the god of war, and he was forbidden to leave the city, so the command was entrusted to Gaius Lutatius Catulus.

Carthage belatedly realized her danger when an enormous convoy – 700 transports – descended on the coast near Lilybaeum in Sicily. Rome did not often need to be told anything twice, and was to prove to be the most efficient power ever known at learning from mistakes, before rapidly turning them to its advantage. Finally, in 241 BC a victory off the Aegates Islands allowed Rome to annex Sicily and make her very important grain-producing area the first Roman Province.

In 238 BC both Sardinia and Corsica were also annexed – in effect safeguarding Rome's back door and making it perfectly clear to the Carthaginians (if they still needed reminding), that Rome was here to stay. They were obliged to stand by and watch Sardinia and Corsica become Roman possessions.

In 223 BC successful Roman campaigns in Cisalpine Gaul led to colonies also being formed there and by 219 BC Hannibal, the son of the Carthaginian general Hamilcar Borca, took some new territory in Spain, at Saguntum. This action led, in the following year, to the start of the Second Punic War.

Before the ending of 217 BC Hannibal had crossed the Alps along with his thirty-seven elephants. His skill, along with a certain amount of Roman amateurishness, led to three defeats for Rome – at Ticinus and at Trebbia, culminating in the horrendous defeat at Cannae in 216 BC. Despite these victories and also despite Philip of Macedonia forming an alliance with Hannibal, few of Rome's allies decided to abandon her at that time, as might well have been expected. We know that Capua, Tarento and Syracuse did change sides, but Hannibal did not manage to capture Rome herself, even though at one time he was close enough to actually ride around the walls!

Keeping its head and showing immense courage, the Senate sent an army into Spain, to attack Hannibal's base there. After some defeats, Cornelius Scipio landed in 210 BC and by 206 BC had managed to oust the Carthaginians. Spain itself now became a Roman possession and was divided into two provinces.

Back in Italy, Rome was forced to institute a scorched-earth policy in order to deny Hannibal resources, and although this naturally caused a good deal of suffering and homelessness for the Italians caught up in it, the action succeeded in its objective. This displacement of farmers from their lands was, however, to cause further contention for Rome some time later. The then vacant areas were to be subsequently snapped up, not by the farmers and smallholders who had previously worked them for generations, but by rich families who were easily able to stock them with slave workers. This was eventually to lead to the conflict with the Brothers Gracchi and their supporters, who strenuously objected to the displacement of the farmers and their replacement by gangs designed only to enrich the new landholders.

In 204 BC Scipio landed in Africa, and Carthage was forced to recall Hannibal. At the battle of Zama in 202 BC Scipio defeated Hannibal and Carthage was obliged to suffer humiliation at the hands of Rome and see the end of its overseas power for good. This period, with the ending of the Second Punic War, was the most momentous in Rome's history. It now became obvious that Rome would rule the entire Mediterranean.

Rome had by now moved to the East, to fight Philip of Macedonia, who had joined forces with Carthage back in 214 BC when Rome had appeared to be doomed to failure. But by 205 BC, after almost nine years, the first Macedonian war petered out. However, Rome was to move against Philip again, five years later, when it was feared that he was regaining too much power. He was finally beaten decisively in 197 BC. In 191 BC Cisalpine Gaul was conquered by Rome and the following year the Seleucid King, Antiochus of Syria, was defeated at Magnesia and expelled. In 168 BC Perseus of Macedonia was defeated at Pydna and Macedonia also became a Roman dependency.

However, despite these obvious achievements the Third Punic War flared up in 149 BC and was to last until the final total destruction of Carthage in 146 BC.

Also at this time, the sack of Corinth, which was at that time the richest port in Greece, showed all too plainly that there was a new and worrying determination, and even a taste for brutality, becoming apparent in Rome's imperial expansion policy.

Rome's nobles were, of course, by now making vast fortunes. Many were returning from military triumphs or provincial governorships with huge amounts of booty, which had always been considered to be an acceptable perquisite of the job, or with shiploads of slaves for sale, the profits of which would help to extend their own family's affluence and influence. The destruction of Epirus alone had brought in 150,000 slaves to be sold in the markets of Rome. Many of these captives were well-educated people of decent background, and their arrival actually did a good deal for Roman society, in helping to spread a knowledge and appreciation of Greek culture.

However, on the other hand, it did nothing at all for the tens of thousands of newly impoverished Romans who had been forced off their ancestral lands during the Punic Wars. They now faced a very bleak future indeed, being not only homeless and unemployed in Rome, but becoming aware that the newly arrived Greek slaves were about to take from under their noses what work was still available.

The years 136 to 132 BC were to see the first Sicilian slave war. Also during this time, Tiberius Sempronius Gracchus fought his private battle over the distribution of the *ager publicus*. This public land, originally leased to small farmers and worked by their families, had gradually been taken over by the rich landowners who found it far easier and more profitable to have it worked by slave gangs. These unfortunates would be kept in squalid conditions and worked to death in order to increase the profits of their owner. It was far more cost effective to simply replace slaves who proved unable to continue than to allow the land to be restored to the small farmers who had previously leased it and had to wait for the smaller profits. However, the small farmers, while living and working on the leased land, had provided Rome with more than meat and vegetables. They also provided her with their children. With daughters able to marry and breed further generations and sons not only to farm the land but also to man the Legions. This had, for generations, been the backbone of Rome's prosperity and the Roman still entertained a sentimental attachment to the idea of the simple country life. It did not, however, stop him from profiting hugely from the suffering of the poor farmers who were now enduring the poverty and humiliation of being unable to find work to feed their families.

Tiberius Gracchus had become disgusted by this process and had determined that the ager publicus should be returned to those families who had always worked it. Of course, by setting himself up as a champion of land reform in this way, he naturally faced great opposition from the money-men who liked things just as they were, and saw no reason at all to change back to the old ways. His campaign over the *latifundia* eventually became a battle against the Senate over their foreign policy and turned most of the conservative minded senators against him to such an extent that he and 300 of his supporters were finally killed. Unfortunately, his younger brother, Gaius Sempronius Gracchus, nine years his junior, was to take up his elder brother's cause in his turn, and was also to lose his life in that struggle in 122 BC.

It is a curious example of the Roman psyche that, although these young men were both killed, along with their supporters, while in opposition to the status quo, their names were not reviled. Indeed, they became a kind of symbol of the Roman spirit. Their mother, Cornelia, went down in Roman history as the perfect example of the Roman matron, due to her ability to withstand and surmount the agony of losing her two fine sons in that way. Of course, she was a Patrician and she was also still very rich. This naturally meant that Cornelia, 'Mother of the Gracchi', would always have an enviable place in Society, and an enormous amount of respect, so long as she exhibited the correct dignity and stoicism considered suitable to the noble women of a military race.

During these upheavals, in Rome, in 138 BC, only eight years after the end of the Third and final Punic War, and two years before the beginning of the Sicilian slave war, was born Lucius Cornelius Sulla.

He was born into a Patrician family, which had previously provided Rome with a Dictator (Publius Cornelius Rufinus way back in 334 BC) and whose son, Publius Cornelius Rufus, became Consul in 290 and was prominent in the Samnite Wars. Around 285 BC he had become Dictator, like his father, and was then Consul again in 277. Despite a good military record, his career came to an abrupt end in 276 BC when he was found to be in possession of rather more silver plate than was allowed by the sumptuary laws then in force and he was ignominiously expelled from the Senate.

It was, for some considerable time, fashionable to applaud a certain simplicity of living, and the suggestion that Rome had once been the height of perfection in achieving this standard was gained by occasional purges and by punishing any who attempted to singularize himself above his peers. This attitude may well have been as hypocritical then as it is now. However, hypocritical or not, being found to have acquired more precious metal than was permitted served to eclipse the family politically for some time to come.

One of his sons, Publius Cornelius Sulla, was elected Flamen Dialis around the year 250 BC. Although on the face of it this was considered to be a great honour, it was in actual fact an appalling restriction on normal living for the man (and his wife) whom were appointed as the priest and priestess. An appointment for life, it effectively prevented the man from pursuing any kind of political or military career. This in itself, in a military society, set him apart from his peers in a way not altogether to be envied.

He and his wife would not be permitted normal foods, for instance with restrictions even on the kind of bread they were allowed to eat. The Romans were a people who loved their bread, as the number of bakeries in each town testified. A great deal of effort was put into getting the right kind of crisped crust, to the extent that baking bread at home became most unusual. Having to conform to such dietary rules were not the only restrictions on the Flamen and Flaminia. They were not allowed to wear certain types of clothing, with the result that the Flamen could not even have buckles or similar fasteners on his shoes, which was a part of the prohibition stating that he could not touch steel. This of course prevented him from ever being involved in a military career, along with the further rule that he could not witness a death. He and his wife must both be Patricians and must have had no previous wife or husband, another restriction not always easy to conform to at a time when divorce was common.

These taboos sometimes led to ironical amusement for the Romans, who were supposed to have said that 'every day is a holiday' for the Flamen, due to his inability to take any real part in normal life. However, the restrictions can only have been irksome in the extreme for the holder of the office, even while the honour of being related to a Flamen devolved upon his family.

The son of the Flamen Dialis was to become Praetor in 212 BC and his son, another Publius Cornelius Sulla, also reached this position in 186. This man was to become the grandfather of Lucius Cornelius Sulla.

Very little is known about Sulla's own father except that he married twice and his second wife seems to have been a woman who had a considerable amount of money of her own. This was one day to prove significant. However, the family into which Lucius Cornelius was born in Rome, in 138 BC had not actually risen above the rank of Praetor for several generations. Although this had originally been the title of the senior magistrate who replaced the kings, it had become an office of second in command. The number of Praetors had gradually risen from one man serving alone, to six by 197 BC when two were sent to Spain to govern the two new provinces there. It would, eventually, be obliged to be extended far further than that, as the empire expanded over the years to come and officials were needed to carry Roman authority to new territories.

However, by the time of Sulla's birth, his family had sunk somewhat down the social scale, due to a serious depletion of funds. Wealth, in Rome, was absolutely essential and the fact that a man had achieved high office could sometimes result in the eventual loss of status for his entire family, due to the amounts of cash needed to fund the position. Each magisterial position required a certain level of financial standing to back it, along with a great deal of free spending once it was achieved. Unfortunately it was the lack of this necessity which was to prevent the young Lucius Cornelius from taking up the position in the level of Rome's society to which his birth might otherwise have been considered an entitlement.

He was born into a world where war and turmoil were the norm and a society in which birth and wealth would open the doors to power and advancement for its possessor. Equally, lack of either of these essential commodities would just as easily close those doors to him for good, despite any natural ability in learning or military skill he may have had, which might have otherwise been considered useful to Rome.

A Patrician had to be seen to be a Patrician, and a certain amount of free-handedness was obligatory. Without it he would be unable to make the necessary friends, or enrol the necessary clients, who would be expected to accompany any important (or seemingly important) man about his daily business. This entourage, continually following him about, was the visible sign of the up and coming man without which he would not be taken as a serious contender for any political position. It was the mark of his popularity and the visible number of his clients showed his power and supposed influence.

Finally, without money even the lowest position would be impossible for him. It is a fact that although on the face of it any man in a republic is supposed to be considered equal to any other and can aspire to greatness on ability alone; in reality all political life requires vast sums of money. This is not only to achieve high office but also to oil the wheels once there. Any hopeful without money available to him, either his own or someone else's, is definitely surplus to requirements.

It was in this eminently practical and essentially heartless world that the young and ambitious Lucius Cornelius Sulla would have to struggle to find his place.

Chapter Two

Poverty is, of course, relative. The young Lucius Cornelius was not in danger of starvation, and was, so far as we can tell, given the usual education of the Roman male of status. This may well have been due to his stepmother, who seems to have been a generous woman and fond of the boy. We cannot be sure whether he had siblings, but there were certainly relatives from other branches of the family.[1] However, there is no evidence that these relatives ever did anything to help the young Sulla and so, apart from his father, who seemed to be a lightweight, and the stepmother, who was eventually to prove to be a lifesaver, he was on his own.

At what point in his life his mother died (or was divorced) and the stepmother became a fixture is likewise lost to us. It was, in any case, usual for a boy to be largely brought up by slaves in his youngest days, so any lack of maternal affection would be something he shared with most of his contemporaries. It is noteworthy that in Roman society it was considered to be a sign of being absolutely at the bottom of the social ladder if one did not own a single slave. Even in a very modest household there would be slaves available, even if only one or two, to deal with domestic matters and raise the children. Female slaves were cheaper than male servants and most of the work in an average house would be on a domestic level, so it is fair to assume that Sulla's family owned some servants.

A boy would be given lessons in the home until the age of six or seven years. He would be expected to speak Latin correctly, with a good accent, and likewise Greek. It was considered to be the mark of a boor if a man were not fluent in Greek. Indeed 'an Italian with no Greek' was an epithet often thrown at Gaius Marius in his early days, although he did in fact speak Greek well. Perhaps it was merely that his accent was faulty.

At around the age of seven, a boy would leave the hands of the women and come under the influence of his father, though what little we know of Sulla's father does not give us any confidence in his ability to teach an intelligent and precocious boy. He has even been referred to as a drunk. Whatever the truth of his home life, Sulla was taught the necessary rudiments, either by a private tutor paid for by his stepmother, or perhaps by attending one of the open-air schools with other pupils, for a small fee. A skilled slave or freedman was often given the responsibility of teaching the young children, though for those households of limited funds it was always possible to share a tutor between families. Naturally, a highly skilled tutor could fetch a fantastic price – the grammaticus called Lutatius Daphnis was sold twice, before his manumission, each time fetching the incredible sum of 700,000 sesterces![2] Obviously far beyond the resources of Sulla's family. In a rich family a paedagogus would live in the household and be a sort of companion to the boy, escorting him to school if he attended one outside the home, or otherwise teaching the boy himself. This would doubtless also exceed Sulla's family's means. But some sort of education suitable to his rank was found for him. Education for boys generally came in three stages, primary, which included reading and writing in both Greek and Latin, and basic arithmetic, while secondary education dealt with literature, grammar and syntax.

By the time he was thirteen or fourteen he would be considered ready to pass into the hands of a rhetor. This was his higher education and consisted of rhetoric, or instilling fluency of speech and clever argument, in order to fit him for a political career. In the future, his style of speech, or indeed his dramatic ability to pose and posture while speaking, could have a great effect on those who heard him. A style of his own might make all the difference between being merely mediocre or becoming an eloquent and inspiring speaker capable of stirring the hearts of his audience and carrying them along with him. Naturally, such a gift would be a great boon to the political orator. Law would also be fundamental to the training of any young man expected to take his place in the public life of Rome. Once he had completed his formal training, he would then be expected to see the law in practice and learn all he could from the great speakers of his day. We have, however, no evidence to suggest that there was any form of examination which the pupil was eventually expected to pass. Naturally enough, a decent education was then, as now, considered to be essential to any future success in life, and educated parents, who might be expected to provide an intellectual atmosphere in the home, along with the necessary encouragement, were prized. We cannot know whether the young Sulla received any encouragement from his father, or what kind of atmosphere he lived in while at home. Hopefully, his stepmother provided some stability for him, for her fondness for him prompted her to leave him what was left of her fortune when she died.[3]

Once his formal education was completed, however, Sulla would have found himself out on a limb. By birth Patrician, he would normally have been expected to find his friends among the other young men who were of the same rank, living in Rome, and looking forward to taking their eventual place in the great scheme of things. In short, his peers were able to look forward to budding careers in public life, military campaigns and the essential rise along the Cursus

Honorum, which would bring them to the highest office and the most important status for a Roman male. But all of that took money.

When he reached his teens, at a time when other young men of his class found life in all its fascination and excitement beginning to open up for them, Sulla's situation was made even worse by the death of his father. He inherited nothing. He was now reduced to a very real personal poverty, which certainly prevented him from pursuing even basic friendships with those of his own class. That he was able to rent a small ground floor apartment may well have been due to the kindness and generosity of his stepmother, for so far as we know he had no other income. It has been suggested that because he had this 'back-up' and was able to afford to eat and clothe himself and have a roof, however modest, over his head, that he was not in real poverty. But real poverty to a Patrician who had his way to make is a very different thing to the kind of poverty suffered by a working man who might be grateful to have anything at all. By the standards of Sulla's world he was very poor indeed.

This situation must have been humiliating in the extreme for a young man who had not only intelligence and good birth, but also ability and ambition. It prevented him from making any attempt at a political or military career, and from forming with his peers the sort of useful contacts he would need in the future. However, all young people need some kind of companionship, and being denied the ability to join in with the other young men of his class due to his obvious lack of funds drove Sulla to find friends elsewhere.

Rome was an essentially pragmatic society in which any citizen who could not hold his own would be likely to be trampled under. Sulla, despite education, charm, good looks and good birth, did not have the cash to fund the entertainments of the other young bloods, so they had no interest at all in befriending one who could not keep up with them, and certainly could not pay his way. That they all knew about his poverty would have added to the shame he suffered. Perhaps desperate for company, he found his way to the 'other side of town' where he met up with a lower class of people in the sort of places that Patrician youths did not usually frequent.

At first, of course, there must have been considerable hesitation, due to the natural dislike of ordinary people from being patronized by the equivalent of upper class 'hooray henrys', intent merely on slumming. Eventually, though, these people, otherwise considered to be the absolute dregs of society, from the theatres, the gladiator schools, the taverns and the brothels, learned that the lonely and very attractive young man was genuinely looking for friends and actually liked them for themselves. It may have taken a little time, but they did come to trust him and to realize that he was prepared to be friendly without harbouring any ulterior motive.

They must have been a very refreshing change for him too, with their open acceptance and free and easy ways. It was from these people, dancers, mimes, actors and prostitutes, along with a sprinkling of drag queens and drunks, that Sulla acquired a taste for the exotic and the bizarre which never left him. His attachment to them was considered, later in his life, to show a disgraceful lack of taste and discrimination. He never cared. Those people, the lowest of the low in Roman society, had been the only ones who had befriended him when he was desperate for friendship and when the people of his own class, knowing his situation, chose to avoid him. It was from that experience that he learned loyalty and a disregard for class opinion, while at the same time he still certainly felt the same pride of birth inside himself that any other Patrician would. It was to make for a very interesting mixture and provide two of the facets of his character. On the one hand, his great pride in his status, his ancestors and his natural ambition, with a firm determination to somehow make good and astound all the people who had so cruelly disregarded him. On the other, there were the temptations of the flesh, to which all young men are subject, along with the excitement of being with people who had no status to lose and no limits or boundaries within their own world, together with a very colourful and stimulating, if disreputable, lifestyle.

These were the people who welcomed him for himself. Sulla in his youth had a natural charm along with a great deal of physical beauty, with a very white skin, pale eyes and reddish-gold hair, which attracted both men and women to him. He was also good-natured and had the enviable knack of making and keeping friends, so they asked nothing more of him. They did not care that he had no money, nor had they. He showed that he was happy to join in with their unsophisticated amusements, and indeed we are told that he had a fine singing voice and was able to write not only plays but also rude farces. He took to their world like a duck to water and in a real sense never left it.

It says a very great deal for Sulla as a man, and was enormously to his credit, that even when life had changed completely for him and he had become not only famous but very powerful, holding the world in his hands, he did not forget those old friends. He also never forgot that the people he should have been able to turn to, the people of his own class, had ignored and abandoned him when it seemed that he would never be of any worth. It had taught him the most valuable lesson in life, that friendship and real loyalty do not depend on wealth or equal status. His most significant relationships would rightly always be with those people who had accepted him when nobody else would. Later, he would allow them the most blatant liberties, seek out their company, and show his everlasting gratitude to them, with a total disregard of what anyone else thought about it.

Thankfully, in our own time, we are enlightened enough to know that being poor and of low birth is not a crime and that ordinary and uneducated people can still be reliable and decent. Sulla certainly knew it, even though most eminent Romans did not. It has been written, and sadly all too frequently by otherwise sensible men, that he and all of his friends were evil and totally debauched. Evil is a very strong word to apply to people who are merely low born and uneducated, while debauchery can stretch all the way from a mere drunken frolic to absolute corruption and every possible vice. Corruption and vice were certainly not confined to the lower orders in Rome and such extravagant statements may unfortunately say far more about those writers who believe them, than they do about either Sulla or his low-born but loyal friends.

It must have been at this time that he first indulged in homosexual relationships. One of these, with the actor/mime named Metrobius was to become the most valuable and long-lasting relationship of his life. Even as an ageing and sick man, he still claimed that he loved Metrobius and always had. Naturally, in the Roman world, hypocrisy was king. For a man who wished for a political or military career to openly admit that he loved other men, even if he loved women also, was disastrous. Not that there were not plenty of homosexual and bisexual men in Rome at that time. Of course there were. But they pretended. They kept their opinions to themselves and indulged in their tastes only when others of their class could not see them. They visited Greece, where their most private proclivities were more acceptable, and tried to control, or hide, their impulses when at home. This caused even Sulla, as things changed for him, to be obliged to spend less time with Metrobius than he might have wished. It would have destroyed his early career, when he finally achieved it, to have admitted that the actor/drag queen was his lover, and necessary to him, though later on when he had more power to speak his mind openly he was more frank.

This probably also goes a long way towards explaining why history has always been so unkind and in many ways grossly unfair to Sulla. Later on, even Caesar would be stained by the mere suggestion that he had been involved in a homosexual relationship, which he always firmly denied. Until quite recently, the idea that a great man could have same-sex lovers was anathema, and that he could at the same time be a great general, a great fighter, a good leader and generally a decent and well-intentioned person was laughable and quite incredible. Perhaps this is the real reason why every possible evil has been attributed to him. Not because he was any worse than any other man of his time, but that he decided to be more honest, to his own detriment.

Eventually, however, like all other men of his time, he would have to marry. Marriage was a Roman essential. The choice of the bride was vital and a man's relationship with his wife was of interest not only to the married pair but also to their families and all their contacts. A Roman male was considered ripe for marriage by the age of fourteen and a girl by the age of twelve. However, in the days of the later Republic it was becoming more usual for a girl to be saved until about sixteen or sometimes seventeen before actually living with a husband, who was usually older. This was due to the need for children. It was considered unsafe for a very young girl to become a mother, as the health and strength of the children she bore would be likely to be compromised. When the five-year census was taken, it was always asked of a married man not only whether he had children, but also whether he intended to have them, with the strong emphasis that he and his wife were expected to do their duty. It is interesting to note that barrenness of a woman was a fault for which her husband could divorce her without having to return her dowry!

Of course, children were necessary to repopulate the Roman world, but as time went on it became not only unfashionable but also uneconomic for well-born families to have too many children. Many found that putting several sons through the necessary training and then funding a career for them became impossible, not to mention suitable dowries for daughters to make sure that they married the right sort of husbands. Excess children could either be adopted out, once they became adolescent, often to another branch of the family or social equals, or simply exposed if the family could not afford to raise them.

Exposed children, left out to die, might be taken up by anyone who wanted them, either to adopt or to train as slaves when older. Of course, in the higher levels of society, there were also attempts at contraception, some sensible and some ridiculous, to solve the problem of too many expensive births. On the other hand a man could always turn to the slaves and leave his wife alone. If his wife did not wish to be left alone, she also might turn to the slaves, or even find a lover outside the house, but for her this was far more dangerous. If found out she would face divorce and the loss of her children as well as social disgrace. It is intriguing to realize that the Roman ideal of the married woman is startlingly similar to the Victorian one. She is meant to be quiet and obedient, produce children and be a helpmeet to her husband. Also to turn a blind eye to her husband's faults and affairs, while having none of her own. Of course, real life is never like that, and the example of Fulvia Nobilioris shows that even during the days of the later Republic a woman of spirit could triumph over the oppressions of marriage, and live life on her own terms, at least for a time. That lady was married originally to the scandalous Clodius Pulcher, who was responsible for the gate-crashing of the Bona Dea celebrations (an important women-only event, which he attended dressed as a singing girl, to general social and religious horror). Later she married Curio, and later still Marcus Antonius, before he became involved with the Egyptian queen. Her life may ultimately not have been completely successful, but at least it was exciting and got her out of the house, which must have made her the envy of many less daring ladies.

Of course many men, including Sulla, had mistresses. This sort of relationship would not be presumed to affect the marriage in any way and the wife, if she knew of it, would be obliged to turn a blind eye. What went on outside of the doors of the home was not considered to be her concern. We know that the young Sulla had had a love affair with a Greek woman named Nicopolis, who was some years older than he was. In fact, exactly the sort of relationship many sensible fathers wanted for their sons before they found them the right sort of girl to marry.

The right sort of marriage, of course, would be the sort that would advance the family, and this applied both to men and women. By Sulla's day, the old form of marriage, known as *confarreatio*, which was almost indissoluble, was giving way to a rather more open form, which meant that divorce was possible for either party. Of course, if a woman managed to divorce her husband, it would again mean leaving behind her children, therefore it was rather less usual for her to make the attempt. Strictly speaking, a father or even a brother, being the paterfamilias, could divorce a woman from her husband if he considered that the match had done nothing for the advancement of their family, and they might more profitably marry her elsewhere. A son who did not manage to advance the cause of his family, or any young married woman who failed to influence her husband on her family's behalf, were both equally discredited.

Once the partners were chosen, though, it was supposed to be a happy time. The ceremony would include the new wife, after dedicating her childhood dolls to Venus, wearing the bride's flame coloured veil and being carried over the threshold of her husband's house before being offered bowls of fire and water. Through these she would lightly pass her right hand, to signify that she was now mistress of the house. The house would be provided by the husband, together with all its contents, so if they did divorce, the wife would lose everything except her personal items and be reduced to returning to her parental home, or the house of a brother if her parents were deceased. In certain circumstances her dowry would then be returned to her paternal family.

For Sulla, the choice of the right wife was of vital importance. Firstly, of course, there was his chronic lack of money to consider, therefore none of the great families would be willing to hand over a daughter to a life of poverty with a man who would be unable to make anything of himself or his children. On the other hand, Sulla himself would not have wished to disgrace himself by marrying a woman of lower birth than his own, resulting in a real dilemma for him. This problem was solved, however, in a surprising way for Plutarch tells us that Sulla actually managed to marry a Julia![4]

This amazing stroke of luck needs some explanation. The Julian clan were particularly highly born and every bit as conscious of their status as Sulla himself. They were also just as poor. This family would in the near future produce Gaius Julius Caesar. He was another man so conscious of his birth that he was suspected (perhaps rightly) of intending to make himself into a king. They claimed their descent from no less than the Goddess Venus, through her son Aeneas, a Prince of the Royal Trojan house. Suffice to say that if anyone in Rome had any claim at all to a kingship, the Julians must have thought that they did. Unfortunately, like many other great families, they had found that keeping up the expenses of political office did nothing at all for their finances, and they had not succeeded in keeping their coffers filled as well as they might have hoped.

The family home, also no doubt once perfectly pleasant, had gradually changed in status. Over the years the area it occupied had become completely built up, until it was eventually surrounded on all sides by an area known as the Suburra, which was to become the poorest and most insalubrious place in the whole of Rome. It was famous as a den of thieves and a polyglot ghetto for every type of immigrant. Not at all the sort of place to walk about unattended. Caesar was later to turn a disadvantage into an advantage by claiming that this start in life had given him the common touch.

It has been said of the Julians that they were in the habit of making strange marriages, which might not strictly be the case, as their marital relationships up to that time seem to have been normal enough. What they were obliged to do was face facts, and realize that they could not continue as they were. They had sons to find money for, to kick-start careers and daughters to find suitable husbands for. They did this initially by befriending Gaius Marius.

Gaius Marius, who was eventually to manage what no other man ever did by becoming Consul for a record seven times, was at this point in his life stuck in the same rut as Lucius Cornelius Sulla, but for the opposite reasons. He was from Arpinum, therefore he wasn't considered to be Roman at all, merely an Italian. That was the first strike against him. The second was that he was not of noble birth, and so all doors were shut firmly in his face, preventing him moving onward and upward. On the plus side, however, he was already a famous and most capable general. He was also extremely rich.

He already had a wife, though they appear to have been childless. He was by then of middle age, but he must have been in every way just as frustrated as Sulla by the glass ceiling which prevented him from reaching the position he expected and knew he deserved. He may well have thought by then that he would never get any further in life and that time was running out for him.

At some point, however, before Sulla's own first marriage, he had struck up a friendship with the Senator Gaius Julius Caesar. This man had two sons, Sextus and Gaius, to provide for, along with a daughter, naturally named Julia. A marriage was arranged between Gaius Marius and the daughter of Gaius Julius Caesar, whom he happily enough divorced his first wife to make room for. Exactly what financial agreement was made between the Marius and Julius families to forward this match, we will never know. It does seem obvious that Gaius Marius had married his Julia in order to give himself the necessary aristocratic relatives whose connections could open doors for him and enable him to make his mark politically.

The Julian clan, in their turn, would benefit a great deal financially, probably by Gaius Marius helping his new young brothers-in-law along the Cursus Honorum. It is exactly the sort of arrangement that has been tried and tested in selling social standing for hard cash, and has gone on for centuries, benefiting both sides.

It also benefited Sulla. What is done once is more easily done again and the Julian family may have decided that with a little backing the young man of good birth might finally make something of himself, or perhaps even that Gaius Marius, the family's new financial benefactor, might be of help.

Was his first wife another daughter of the Senator, or was she a niece? Both relationships have been suggested and either way it would have given Sulla a wife of the right lineage with whom to start a family of his own.[5] Certainly if Sulla's Julia were indeed a younger sister of the Julia married to Gaius Marius, it would have been a very great help to him. Almost equally so if she were a sister of Caesar Strabo, of another branch of the family, which is also a possibility. (Surely the rich man would feel duty bound to help out a young in-law just as he did his own wife's brothers?) It would also go a very long way towards explaining the very strong, indeed intimate bond, which developed between Sulla and Gaius Marius, a bond of trust and friendship lasting for many years. They were to go on campaign together very successfully and they worked well with each other. If they were actually brothers-in-law it would help to explain how Sulla suddenly got his great opportunity after so long in limbo. Whatever the exact relationship between those two men, whose lives were eventually to diverge so dramatically, it was for a considerable time a close, genuine and fruitful one.

However, the waiting must have seemed to be very long, and it must have been during this period that he first became a parent. We know for certain that he had a daughter with his first wife, naturally enough named Cornelia, for it is recorded that this young woman was eventually married to the son of Quintus Pompeius Rufus, when Pompeius later became a political ally of Sulla's.

We do not know how many children were lost to Sulla and his first wife, but given the appalling statistics of infant death at the time, it can be safely assumed that little Cornelia was not their only child. However, there is a very intriguing suggestion that Sulla may have also fathered a legitimate son at around this time. This would have been a very important event for any man who had a prestigious family name to pass on.

The very nature of a child's birth into the home was fraught with symbolism. From the father taking the child in his arms when it was first presented to him, by which he showed he accepted it into the household, to the registering of its birth at the Tablinium or tax office. That would have been a proud moment for anyone, in the case of a firstborn son.

There were also other ceremonies to perform, not least of which would be the giving of a coin to the Goddess Juno Lucina, to also register his birth at her temple. For Sulla, there would be yet another even more important place to show his gratitude. This would be at the temple of his personal favourite among the goddesses, Fortuna. He always said that he believed in her implicitly and relied upon her to aid him in his endeavours. He was later to declare that he had always considered himself to be one of Fortuna's favourite sons. Her temple was situated grandly on the Capitol, next to Jupiter Optimus Maximus himself and looked down over the Forum. In her guise of Fortuna Primogenia she would be very important for the safeguarding of the precious firstborn son.

It has been said that the Romans were a very religious people, due to the number of gods they worshipped. Certainly they had a god or goddess for everything, from important matters like births and deaths, (Juno Lucina and Venus Libitina), or Juventas (coming of age of Roman citizen males) and Bellona (foreign wars). Through every possible requirement, Juno Moneta (for timely warnings) or Venus Erucina (for prostitutes), and Janus (protector of doorways and beginnings and ends). Down to what were the very oldest gods, the numinae, bodiless and faceless, mere spiritual essences, such as Ops (Rome's plenty), Fides (faith) and Mens (proper Roman thinking).

Whether or not it is true that they had faith in all of them, they were certainly superstitious. Perhaps in their very need for a god or goddess to cover every eventuality, they show that they did not really believe in any of them very much. Their acceptance of any and every deity sometimes seems more like a frenetic hedging of one's bets than any real belief. However, we do know that Sulla believed in Fortuna, and believed that she guided and helped him in his struggles. Perhaps that is true religion after all.

The suggestion that Sulla had a son who was also born about this time is taken from his own words, much later in life, when he recounted his prophetic dreams. He reported that he had seen his dead son, along with a later wife, Caecilia Metella Dalmatica, also by then deceased. He said that the boy had called to him, beckoning him and asking his father to join him and his stepmother, where they could be happy together. For the boy to have been of such an age must have meant that he died while approaching adolescence, which would probably have been a great grief to his father. Certainly, with the mortality rate being so high, the loss of babies was something that every family would sooner or later have to deal with, and it would be necessary for parents to put on a brave face when it happened, often more than once. However, the loss of a promising son just when he was growing up into a man and becoming an interesting and intelligent individual in his own right would be for his father a very different thing. We cannot know how Sulla felt about it, but it is only fair to assume, given Sulla's proud attachment to his own, that it affected him a great deal.

However, such losses were for the future and Sulla was approaching thirty before things really started to happen for him. Normally, a young nobleman was required to have done ten years military service before he could stand for his first public office. However, by Sulla's time it had become acceptable for a man to stand for election to a quaestorship once he had reached the age of thirty. He now had, and what's more he also now had enough money to permit him to stand. A short time earlier his devoted stepmother had died and he inherited what was left of her fortune. Furthermore, his erstwhile mistress, Nicopolis, then died, after making him her heir.[6] His famous charm and good looks had certainly stood him in good stead with the ladies.

He was duly elected to the quaestorship for 107 BC and was eventually assigned service under the new Consul Gaius Marius, (obviously the world had now opened up for him too), who was to go to North Africa. Gaius Marius was being sent to deal with King Jugurtha of Numidia, who had been causing problems for Rome in the area now known as Algeria. It was hoped that a general of the calibre of Gaius Marius would be able to turn his astonishing talents to the problem and settle it once and for all.

Lucius Cornelius Sulla, if now not actually wealthy, was at least finally able to hold his own with his peers and was newly elected to his first public office. Despite his total lack of any military experience, he was to go with Gaius Marius. The relationship between them may well have had some influence in the matter of the appointment, but Gaius Marius was also very far from being a fool. He had to deal with a difficult and important matter in North Africa. The position he was taking up was certainly no sinecure. It is also certain that such a competent general would not have wanted with him, necessarily in a position of trust, a young man who had apparently done little for years except spend his time with actors and dancers, even in order to do a favour for the in-laws. Not, that is, unless he could see something more in the young man, other than that he was just another upper-class wastrel. In fact, his new quaestor was to prove to be very useful indeed.

At last, Sulla was on his way.

Chapter Three

The North Africa campaign involved an area once a part of the Carthaginian empire. Once that empire was vanquished, at the end of the third Punic War, the coastal part of North Africa became the Roman Africa Province. This covered the portion of land now known as Tunisia. To the west of this, now known as Algeria, was the Kingdom of Numidia.

King Micipsa of Numidia, son of Massinissa, had been the ruler of the area since the end of the Third Punic War and he had died in 118 BC. His kingdom was then divided between his heirs. Two of these were obvious heirs, being his legitimate sons, Prince Hiempsal and Prince Adherbal. But dividing the kingdom between those two was not enough, they had to share it with a man who on the face of it had no legitimate claim at all. This was a man named Jugurtha. He was a half-cousin of theirs, being the illegitimate son of King Micipsa's brother, Prince Mastanbal, and been more or less adopted by Micipsa.[1]

Prince Jugurtha had served initially with the Roman army in Spain, where he made many useful contacts and several friendships, which were to stand him in very good stead for the future. One of these friendships, surprising enough, was with Gaius Marius himself, who had been a cadet with Jugurtha in Spain, many years before.[2]

These contacts with important people in Rome may well have helped him to acquire a place in the rather unusual division of the kingdom after the death of his uncle, King Micipsa. However, there is also a suggestion that Jugurtha was actually the people's choice. He was probably a decade or so older than the other two heirs, and possessed a definite strength of character, which they appeared to lack, therefore Jugurtha was generally far more popular than they were.[3] Adherbal had a reputation for weakness and Hiempsal was hot-tempered and rash, therefore neither seemed ideal on their own. Jugurtha at that time was thought to be handsome and possessed of the martial appearance that was considered to be the attribute of a true king. However, whatever it was that prompted Jugurtha's rise to the shared rule of Numidia, it had not taken into account his extremely reckless and ruthless nature. As might have been expected from such an arrangement, quarrels quickly arose between the joint rulers and Jugurtha equally quickly arranged the deaths of the two legitimate heirs, his cousins Hiempsal and Adherbal, to ensure that he was able to achieve sole rule over Numidia.

Still his contacts held good and despite his actions Rome allowed him to hang on grimly, though he did face some strong opposition from certain elements in the Senate. At least, his contacts in Rome helped him to continue a fairly undisturbed rule until 112 BC. Then he recklessly and foolishly allowed his troops to kill a large number of Italian traders, who were based in Numidia, and who were reported to have spoken out in favour of the murdered legitimate heirs.

Rome could no longer allow the situation to continue as it had done, without some show of correction on its part towards Jugurtha, so war was declared against Numidia in 111 BC. This only proved to be a very short campaign, with no definite outcome. A peace treaty between Numidia and Rome was swiftly agreed, and this also caused something of an outcry in Rome. There were open accusations that bribery on Jugurtha's part had protected him from getting his just deserts, which may well have been true.[4] An inquiry was decided upon and Jugurtha was obliged to travel to Rome to be questioned about his activities in Numidia, after being granted a safe-conduct in order to make the journey.

Once in Rome, as a crowned king, he would not have been allowed to stay within the pomerium, as that would infringe the authority of the Senate. A house would have been found for him, where he would have lived in some comfort and luxury, while the commission of inquiry was organized. However, even while staying outside Rome, ostensibly under house arrest, he still managed to arrange the assassination of yet another Prince of the Numidian royal house, a man named Massiva. Despite the sudden and suspicious death of yet another contender for his throne, this time actually in Rome itself, he was still not formally punished. In fact, he soon returned home, after which the on-off campaign between Rome and Numidia resumed.

Command of this campaign had been given initially to the Consul Spurius Postumius Albinus, but he eventually returned to Rome, with nothing achieved, leaving his brother Aulus Postumius Albinus in charge. He also proved to be ineffectual, and indeed made the situation far worse, resulting in him being totally overwhelmed by Jugurtha and the Romans being driven out of Numidia completely for a time. There were again the now usual accusations of bribery and another commission was appointed to investigate.

The war against Jugurtha was then entrusted to Quintus Caecilius Metellus. Gaius Marius and Publius Rutilius Rufus went with him as his Legates. Unfortunately, Metellus and Gaius Marius were unable to get on well together, although initially Metellus prosecuted the war well. He was, in fact, eventually to be awarded a Triumph for his work in Numidia and be granted the right to use the extra cognomen of Numidicus for his achievements on the campaign.

In 109 BC he routed Jugurtha in a pitched battle at the River Muthul, but unfortunately even this success brought no final result, so over the winter of 109/108 BC Metellus instituted a scorched earth policy over the countryside in another effort to subdue Numidia.

By the year 107 BC King Jugurtha was looking around for help in his difficulties, firstly to the Gaetuli nomads, and then to his father-in-law King Bocchus of Mauretania. This must indeed have been a desperate need, for Bocchus is said to have disliked and distrusted his son-in-law.[5] In fact, his ambivalent attitude towards Jugurtha was to result in Rome's final success against him, but that was not yet.

The relationship between Metellus and Gaius Marius, however, was becoming more acrimonious. Gaius Marius had by then decided to return to Rome in order to stand for the Consulship himself. His marriage to a Julia had, of course, given him the social backing he needed to rise up the political ladder. Due entirely to his impressive marriage, he had become a possible somebody, instead of remaining a rich but unacceptable nobody, and he must then have felt that the time was right for him to make his mark. Metellus, naturally enough, did not wish him to do so, and put every possible obstacle in his way to prevent him from leaving Numidia and reaching Rome in time to stand. Eventually, however, Gaius Marius did succeed in returning to Rome in time for the elections, and ran for the Consulship in 108 BC. He was to achieve his first success in this, and was to take office in 107 BC as Junior Consul, with Lucius Cassius Longinus as the Senior Consul. It was the start of an amazing run of power for him.

As soon as Gaius Marius took over as Consul, he had the Plebian Assembly take the command of the campaign away from Metellus Numidicus.[6] The command of the campaign was then transferred to him. This gave him the opportunity to put into operation a major change to the army of Rome that he had doubtless had in mind for some time. There had always been property qualifications for the Legions. This stemmed from the idea that only men of a certain standing could be considered suitable to fight for Rome. This was a purely financial consideration, for a soldier who had a family who were able to supply him with his armour, his clothing and other necessaries was saving Rome the huge cost of equipping him at the state's expense.

Below the usual five classes, from which the soldiery of Rome was normally drawn, was the Capite Censi, or Head Count. These were absolutely at the bottom of the social strata, too poor to be considered a part of even the lowest of the numbered classes. They were people with no money, no property, and certainly no possibility of providing themselves with even the most basic equipment in order to serve with the Legions.[7]

Gaius Marius, after long experience of seeing the use and the losses of troops, had realized that volunteers were becoming rather thin on the ground and the result of this was that the necessary numbers would not in the future be available. Certainly not when Rome's provinces were expanding and the legions would be required to go further and further afield as time went on.

Until then, it was the farmers and small businessmen who had provided sons for the legions, proudly equipping them for service. However, now that they were required to go further afield, they were finding that a man might be absent from home for many months or even years. This left farms and businesses unattended, and families with their future children unsired, so even the future generations of soldiers for Rome would be put at risk. Then, when a man had finished a tour of duty, he would be quite likely to be called up again almost immediately, as one of the levies, which would have to be instituted because of the lack of volunteers for yet another campaign elsewhere. Not only a highly unsatisfactory situation, it was one that was potentially damaging. Simply, Rome was running out of men to fulfil the army's needs.

Gaius Marius' idea was perfectly straightforward. Rome should use the immense numbers of head count men. Naturally, this suggestion caused howls of dissent in the Senate for fear that Rome would be obliged to provide for all these penniless people. Not only was there a severe financial outlay to be considered, but it was firmly believed that these men would not be able to be trained to make decent soldiers. It had always been taken for granted that the head count people were not only indigent but largely useless.

However, Gaius Marius was determined to push through his brilliant new idea, and after a good deal of argument and opposition a law was finally passed. This empowered the Consuls in office to call for volunteers among the usually ignored capite censi, who would then be provided for and trained at the expense of the state. This was the beginning of the reorganization of the Roman army for which Gaius Marius was to become justly famous.[8] Not only was he to use otherwise unused resources of men, but he was also determined to streamline the forces he had at his disposal.

Until Marius' time, any young officer might be expected to turn up for his army service complete with servants and mule-carts to carry and attend to his personal effects. Likewise, soldiers also tended to collect possessions, which were then transported along the route of a march, following the men. Marius realized that a legion was only as swift as its slowest component, and that the long trains of baggage carts were not only a target for an enemy, but were a drag on the entire legion. He instituted new rules whereby the men carried their own equipment and necessaries, very much on the lines of the packs now carried by modern soldiers. From then on, only a certain number of carts per legion would be allowed, in order to transport the bulkier, heavier and less easily managed items. This eventually gave the foot soldiers the partially humorous name of 'Marius' Mules', because they were now obliged to carry almost all their own tools and weapons, without resource to the cumbersome baggage trains they had previously been used to.

His common sense ideas were a great advance and volunteers flocked to enlist. For once the lowest of the low in Rome had a purpose, other than just being a nuisance to be controlled. Gaius Marius was to show that these people were capable of being just as loyal to Rome as men who had their own property to defend, and that they could also be trained to make equally effective soldiers. These were the men who were to fight with him not only in Numidia, but also later with great success against the Germanic threat.

Lucius Cornelius Sulla, as Questor to Gaius Marius, was not immediately sent to Africa. He was first to be entrusted by Marius with the gathering of a cavalry force from Latium and the Italian Allies. This was a responsible position to be given to a young man without experience, although it was usual for a commander to treat his junior officers in a paternal and encouraging manner, even while putting them through their paces. However, it would seem that in this case Gaius Marius simply judged Sulla to be capable of performing the task well and was again to be proved correct in his assessment of him.[9]

Back in North Africa, Gaius Marius had some successes against Jugurtha, but initially continued the war much as his predecessor had done, by fortifying as many positions as he possibly could. Nothing very much seemed to have changed at first. On the other hand, Jugurtha was conducting far more of a guerilla war, which is always difficult to guard against, especially when one's troops are trained quite differently. There was, however, one set battle near to Cirta, which was resoundly won by Gaius Marius.

While these initial confrontations were taking place, King Bocchus of Mauretania was doing his best to avoid taking any definite stand. He claimed to Marius that he had no wish to engage him in a battle, and emphasized that his position was very difficult due to his relationship with Jugurtha. Bocchus obviously did not want to be involved in a long drawn out struggle with Rome that he could not possibly win and he was very reluctant indeed to give in to pressure. However, by the end of 107 BC Marius had decided to make a determined and dramatic effort against Jugurtha. He managed an intense march across the desert and succeeded in capturing the heavily fortified town of Capsa. This was a far greater achievement than any he had managed so far, and with that success in hand he was able to return fairly peacefully to his winter quarters near to Cirta.

By the following spring Jugurtha was obliged to realize that he was now very much on the defensive due to Gaius Marius' conduct of the war. The continued pressure had left him with a reduced ability to manoeuvre, as well as with very much reduced territory under his control. Next, Marius decided to attack a fortress on the Mulucha, not only to show the necessary military might to subdue the king, but also because of reports that there was a great deal of treasure stored there. This region bordered on Mauretania, so it might also have been hoped that movement so close to the border would help King Boccus to finally make up his mind that engaging himself against Rome on behalf of his son-in-law would be a foolish and futile gesture.

It was while Marius was engaged with the siege of this fortress that Sulla arrived, together with the cavalry that he had been busy gathering while in Italy.

Sulla's appearance with the necessary cavalry was welcome not only due to the useful men he brought with him. He also brought friendship for Marius, with whom he got on very well indeed. What's more, it was soon clear that he got on very well indeed with the legionaries too. He was courteous to everyone, charming and friendly from highest to lowest. He quickly became known as the man who was prepared to do anyone a favour, without looking for one in return. He was also unfailingly enthusiastic, which is always a helpful and usually a contagious attitude, and far easier for anyone to work with than its opposite. It is worthy of note that this admirable attitude never altered, and that for the rest of his career with the army he retained an optimistic, hard-working and cheerful approach to whatever duties were assigned to him.

It is an interesting and creditable facet of Sulla's character that his famous charm, hitherto used only on his friends and associates, could be easily transferred to the people he had to work with. This is no doubt the reason for the unfailing affection in which the men he commanded were always to hold him and why they admired and respected him so greatly.[10] Furthermore, he also had the common sense not to labour the point to his superiors, so that it did not appear to them that he was too obviously courting the popularity of the troops. No doubt Marius was pleased by this time at the success of his subordinate, without needing to fear that the young man's cheerful and obliging attitude was a cover for any ulterior motive on his part.

Marius then succeeded in capturing Jugurtha's fortress and the treasure-trove with it. Unfortunately, the success of the operation had had the opposite effect on Bocchus to that either expected or wanted. He had certainly been alarmed by the close encounter he had had with the Romans working so near to his borders, but instead of it causing him to decide to stand alongside Rome, he took fright completely. Jugurtha had also been busy establishing a faction of his own, on which he had spent a great deal of money and effort.

Jugurtha's people must have worked hard to influence Bocchus' decision, but their work paid off. Bocchus, thoroughly alarmed at the idea of being caught up in the fray, actually came down on the side of his son-in-law, despite his dislike of him. He did, however, exact a good price for his proposed affiliation – he wanted one third of Jugurtha's kingdom, when the war against Rome was finally won! Whether Jugurtha ever had any intention of paying his father-in-law such a substantial reward for his co-operation is highly unlikely, but it might have been expedient to promise him almost anything at that point, in order to secure his assistance. Better that he should fight on Jugurtha's side for the time being, than that he should go over to Rome.

To add to Marius' discomfiture, news then arrived that Jugurtha, in a new and determined action, had managed to recapture Cirta. It was by then approaching winter and a great deal had to be done to settle the situation safely, before they would be in any position to retreat to their winter camp on the coast.

Just to the west of Setif, the Romans were taken by surprise by a joint attack of the forces of Jugurtha and Bocchus. For once, Gaius Marius was unprepared for action and in the melee all that could be done was to form defensive circles. The attack was pressed fiercely by the attacking Gaetulian and Moorish cavalries and for a time Marius' main force found itself besieged on one smallish hill, while Sulla and his men were on the defensive on another even smaller hill nearby.

The attackers, thinking that they had the Romans well in hand and that they would be quite unable to make any real move, considered the matter completed, and began to celebrate their supposed victory prematurely. Fortunately for Marius and Sulla, by dawn they were in no position to defend themselves from any kind of counter-attack. Not only were most of them asleep, but they were also generally drunk. It was at this point that Gaius Marius and Sulla attacked them from their respective hillsides, sweeping down on their foolishly unsuspecting besiegers. The astonished Jugurthan forces were easily and completely routed by the combined effort.

The march to the coast was then resumed, with every attempt being made to defend the lines. Marius had no intention of being taken by surprise a second time, although a further attack was, of course, expected. Not far from Cirta, it came, and Sulla was the first to make contact with the enemy. He attacked in close order and charged by squadrons while Marius engaged Jugurtha's forces. Meanwhile, Bocchus then arrived to assist his son-in-law by an attack on the rear.

Hoping to make a swift end, Jugurtha decided on a feint, and called out that he had just killed Gaius Marius. For a short time his lie was successful and the Romans were thrown into confusion, but Sulla, who had just returned from his own successful pursuit of the enemy, then threw his forces against Bocchus. Shortly after this, Marius, also successful, was then able to turn his attention to coming to Sulla's aid, after which the defeat of the enemy was assured. King Bocchus fled and Jugurtha also managed to escape from the field, although their combined defeat at the hands of Marius and Sulla, yet again, must have been a most unpleasant surprise. After this, the rest of the march was incident free. When they approached Cirta it was very sensibly surrendered to them unconditionally.

This further defeat by the Romans had, however, caused Bocchus, ever-vacillating, to reconsider his position again and five days after the defeat he sent an envoy to Marius to ask him to begin negotiations for a truce. It had become obvious even to him that Jugurtha had to be captured and handed over in order to end the conflict. Bocchus now appeared to be willing to work with the Romans in order to achieve this, although he was still reluctant to risk himself for nothing. Again, he exacted a high price for his proposed assistance – this time he asked for the whole of Numidia!

Marius decided to send two envoys to discuss the matter. As might be expected, one of these was the new rising star, Sulla. The other was Aulus Manlius. Strangely enough, at the meeting between Sulla and King Bocchus, the two men took a decided liking to each other and a friendship was struck which was eventually to have a very beneficial effect on the course of the war. Sulla, although obliged to converse through an interpreter with the king, was still able to exercise enough charm to interest and intrigue Bocchus.[11] Despite the obvious difficulties of making themselves understood through others, a good deal of harmony managed to grow between them, which accord was to bode very well for their negotiations in the future.

Unfortunately, it was still not quite enough at that time to persuade Bocchus to take the final, and perhaps for him perilous, step of throwing in his lot with Rome, and he still found it extremely difficult to make up his mind to any final decision.

Gaius Marius sensibly decided to let the matter rest for the time being, and before long Bocchus was reconsidering again. He must have been in a very difficult position indeed, which may shed some light on his chronic inability to make up his mind at this point. On the one hand, he had a son-on-law who, however much disliked personally, was still very powerful and even dangerous and was, moreover, one of his own people. On the other hand, the Romans, however charming they may have been individually, and whatever promises they might make to him, were at best foreigners from a totally different culture to his own. It may have seemed to him that whichever side he decided to choose, it would inevitably turn out the wrong decision for him and for Mauretania. Hence his caution.

However, some of the king's counsellors now spoke in favour of Rome, and he may well have considered that he did have at least one true friend in the Roman camp – Sulla.

He finally sent envoys to have initial talks with him, and they were very well received, despite having been attacked by bandits on the way to the meeting, during which skirmish they had been relieved of their credentials.[12] They must have been shaken and disarranged, as well as fearful about their reception, but Sulla welcomed them with every courtesy and respect. When Bocchus heard details of their gracious treatment and acceptance by Sulla, he was even further reassured that he was making the right move, in seriously considering abandoning the cause of his son-in-law.

The main requirement of the talks, which were then arranged to take place, was fairly obvious. Bocchus would have to do everything in his power to deliver Jugurtha into the hands of the Romans, in order to end the war. Whether such an action would actually invest Bocchus with the whole of Numidia might have been open to doubt, but what was not open to doubt was that the Romans did not intend to go home. They obviously had no intention of giving in, or letting the matter rest, and if Bocchus did not help them to capture Jugurtha then the war would continue to drag on. Marius, showing great confidence in Sulla, then put the negotiations entirely into his hands, actually making him an envoy with plenipotentiary powers. This was a huge step forward for Sulla, who had so recently been 'the new boy', but he stepped up to the mark admirably.

It has to be reiterated that Sulla, far from being just a messenger, was now a key player and in a position of very real power. It was in his hands to bring the matter, already of too long duration, to a swift end, and both sides were now looking to him to finalize it. By becoming friendly with Bocchus personally, and by treating his ambassadors with civility and courtesy, he had paved the way for them to listen to what he had to say with real consideration. It was an unprecedented situation. Sulla was now a diplomat of genuine skill and the full responsibility for the outcome of the proposed talks rested with him.

Also, it must be remembered that Sulla was still taking up a position of great personal risk. Bocchus, though at that moment apparently friendly and conciliatory, had already proved that he was capable of changing his mind repeatedly and without warning. Sulla could very easily have been riding into a trap, and he must have been fully aware of it. Nevertheless, he arranged to travel to the meeting with his escort of horsemen.

He can hardly have been too surprised, while on the journey, to be approached by a party of barbarian cavalry, although their appearance may still have caused some dismay. Was this the trap he was half expecting? It turned out to be a man named Volux, who said he was one of the sons of Bocchus, and claimed that he had been sent by his father to escort Sulla. He was then informed that Bocchus had feared that if Jugurtha managed to capture Sulla, it would ruin everything, hence the need for the extra escort.

An overnight camp was made, and then Volux told Sulla that he had heard that Jugurtha himself was in the area – not more than two miles distant! He made the suggestion that it might be safer for them to creep away from the area in the dark.[13] Hearing this, Sulla's own men were incensed and wanted to have Volux killed, believing that he had indeed led them into a trap, although Volux strenuously denied it. Sulla then angrily ordered Volux to leave the Roman camp on the grounds that he had deliberately led them into danger.

Volux, however, begged that Sulla continue to trust him. He claimed that Jugurtha was now heavily reliant upon his father King Bocchus, and for that reason would not attempt anything against Sulla while he was in the presence of Bocchus' son. Therefore, while Sulla was still escorted by Bocchus' men, he was safe from any attempted attack. He then made a rather startling suggestion. Volux said that he and Sulla should personally put the matter to the test, by riding together through Jugurtha's camp openly, in full view of everyone. He claimed that Jugurtha would not dare to make any move against them.

This was, of course, the most preposterous idea, full of enormous risks. It would be the easiest thing in the world for Volux to later claim that they had been attacked and could not defend themselves, or that he was unable to prevent Sulla's capture. However, on hearing the suggestion, which many men would have refused out of hand, Sulla's reckless side came into play. It was just the sort of all-or-nothing throw that he would make more than once in his career, relying on his luck to go with him, and he made it then. To the utter dismay and amazement of his own escort, he actually agreed to Volux's challenging suggestion. King Jugurtha, probably more astonished than helpless, was obliged to watch while Sulla and his escort rode through his camp without interference.

It may well have been true that Jugurtha had always intended to attempt the capture of Sulla at that time, but the daring action had rather taken the wind out of his sails, and the Roman envoys and escorts were able to continue on their way without further incident.

Bocchus now arranged to meet with both sides, although nothing was decided at the first public meeting. Sulla was apparently unwilling to discuss the matter before the man sent by Jugurtha to represent him. The official meeting was initially postponed for ten days, pending a decision about Jugurtha's envoy, although later that same night Sulla and Bocchus had private talks. Whatever accommodations may have then been suggested, it was made perfectly clear to Bocchus, by Sulla, that only the surrender of Jugurtha would now be enough to satisfy Rome and settle the matter once and for all. To this Bocchus finally, though doubtless reluctantly, was forced to agree.

Jugurtha had not, of course, turned up in person at that meeting and the next discussion concentrated on finding a way to tempt him back into their orbit in order to effect his capture. It was finally agreed that Jugurtha would be told that peace terms were in the offing, which might bring him within range of such a capture, in the hope of favourable negotiations. However, when a conciliatory meeting was suggested to Jugurtha by Bocchus, yet another idea was put forward. Jugurtha's own proposal was that a peace conference should indeed be held, but this time with the intention that Sulla would be the one captured during it!

Bocchus now appears to have been playing both sides against the middle, for he apparently told the envoys of both Jugurtha and the Romans that he agreed to their proposals. Perhaps he really was still undecided, and honestly did not know which way to turn. He seemed to be genuinely confused and probably had a sleepless night or two, while he struggled to make his final decision. Perhaps, also, his personal liking and respect for Sulla may well have had a part to play in the way that vital final decision went. However, it was just as likely that he simply realized that Rome was not going to give in until they had Jugurtha, and that he would also be likely suffer for it eventually, if he betrayed them too obviously.

So, on the appointed day, Jugurtha arrived with a small escort. Bocchus met him, but standing alongside him was Sulla. At a given signal, armed men appeared who easily captured Jugurtha and handed him over to Sulla officially, as his prisoner. It would be natural for Sulla to reflect, as he took possession of this king, that the matter could only too easily have gone the other way. Whatever his thoughts were at that time, Sulla then took Jugurtha to Marius as a trophy.

This action marked the end of the Jugurthine War. Bocchus was rewarded for his treachery to his son-in-law by the title of 'friend and ally' of Rome. He might well have preferred the other part of his bounty, for he was then also awarded that part of Numidia that Jugurtha had originally promised him would be his.[14]

Gaius Marius returned to Rome and Sulla went with him. Marius was granted a Triumph which took place on 1 January 104 BC. The captured King Jugurtha walked in Marius' triumph, as was usual, and was afterwards thrust into the Tullianum to be killed.

The execution of a captive, in such circumstances, was usually achieved by the victim being garroted. His body would then be left to rot in the dungeon under the Tullianum. We are told that in this case, Jugurtha was not strangled, but left there to starve to death, an agony he suffered for some time before succumbing.[15] This doubtless seems savage to modern eyes but it needs pointing out that at this time in Rome's history, the Romans did not really have any real concept of imprisonment as a form of punishment.

If one was convicted of a lesser offence, then one was likely to be exiled, being denied fire and water on the way, which suggested being denied the means to live normally. This exile was sometimes, in late Republican times, designated as being beyond the hundredth milestone from Rome. However, this was often not a great punishment, because that simply sent the person convicted down to the Bay of Naples, where most of the nobles had summer villas anyway. For a greater offence one could, of course, be killed. Either in the Tullianum, which at that time was all Rome had in the way of a prison, or by being thrown from the tarpeian rock, which hung from the capitol hill, and was a steep drop down onto other rocks below. This was used as a punishment on several occasions in the history of the Republic, but would not apply to a personage of such rank as Jugurtha.

However, Jugurtha was punished with the extreme of Roman justice available at that time and he may well have regretted that he did not meet with the sturdy slave responsible for the strangling of such prisoners once he was actually inside the Tullianum. Perhaps as a greater punishment for his intransigence, and the expense and trouble he had caused to Rome, he was finally to be denied the quicker death.

It was from this point, at the ending of the war and the triumph of Gaius Marius, that Sulla is often accused of turning against Gaius Marius. This being on the grounds that he is supposed to have thought that his action in capturing Jugurtha should have been far better rewarded. In fact, that he was resentful that Marius should take all the credit for the ending of the war and be given a Triumph for his part in it.

This suggestion is very unlikely, not only because Sulla and Marius continued to work together in amity for some time longer. Also, Sulla, as a junior officer, albeit one who had been granted unusually important powers during the conflict, would be fully aware that in any military engagement it was customary for the commanding officer to take the credit. He was certainly not stupid. He would know perfectly well that whatever a junior officer may have done to speed the conclusion, it would be his commander who would benefit from it. Any remark that may have been made to the contrary, at a much later date, was made in the light of a quite different political situation, when Gaius Marius and Sulla were unfortunately to find themselves on opposing sides. That situation was instigated by Marius, who foolishly expected to be given command of the forces in the East, even though his extremely precarious health at that time must have clearly shown him that he was not fitted for the position of command he wished to assume.

Sulla's growing resentment at the end of the Jugurthine War, which was no doubt genuine enough, was I believe not directed towards Gaius Marius at all, but towards the conflicting attitude with which he was received in Rome on his return. After such a piece of work as he had just achieved, during which he not only fought well but also used his diplomatic skills, and took considerable risks with his own life, he must have hoped that he might at least have received a little personal praise. It was generally not to be.

Although there was some popular enthusiasm for Sulla, he must have still felt that there was no real appreciation of the risks he had so freely taken, from the people who actually mattered. In short, still no real acceptance of him from those in the Senate. There was a feeling there, among too many of its members, that he was still persona non grata.

Sulla, even if subconsciously, and despite a show of indifference, may well have wanted and even needed their praise. They were, after all, supposed to be his own people and he had surely proved himself worthy by then.

What he did get, at one point, was accosted in the Forum by one of the nobles. This man, whose name escapes us, accused him openly to his face, of wrongdoing.

'There is something wrong about you, who have become rich, when your father left you nothing at all!' he declared to Sulla.[16]

What Sulla's reply may have been, if any, we are not told, but it is fair to assume that he must have looked at him in dismay. Perhaps he had stopped, seeing the man approach, hoping for an appreciative word, a metaphorical pat on the back, instead of which he was insulted in public. It is possible to feel sorry for Sulla at this point, and to wonder, as he may well have done, just what it would take for them to finally appreciate and acknowledge his efforts.

Whether Sulla's peers appreciated him or not, Marius obviously still did, and would use his services again. One other still did too, for King Bocchus is said to have donated a gilded equestrian statue of Sulla, to stand in the Forum, in recognition of his success.

In his opinion, it may have been a small price to pay for what Sulla had achieved and from which he had personally benefited so much.[17]

However, there would still be serious work for Sulla to do, along with Gaius Marius. The Germans had already long since started their southerly move towards Spain and Italy, in search of a new homeland and an easier and more equable climate. Commanders with the great capabilities such as they had shown would be obliged to do in Gaul what they had already done in Numidia. They would have to take over command of the armies before much longer, which had been failing miserably against the extraordinary new danger, and deal with the threat to Rome's safety properly.

Chapter Four

The southward movement of the various northern tribes was actually no new thing. People from as far away as Denmark, Jutland and Southern Scandinavia had been making their way south and east for several years, driven by the need to find a warmer and drier climate. Their own homelands had some time earlier become colder and wetter, preventing the effective production of the necessary crops and the ability of their livestock to properly thrive. Therefore their attempts to move towards a warmer zone were essential to the survival of their families and their tribal structures.

On their journeys, they were gradually joined by others who were experiencing similar problems. Naturally, in such circumstances, the fertile lands of France, eastern Spain, and Italy itself drew them like a magnet. They travelled with all that they possessed – their families, their animals, carts and tents, weapons and personal possessions of all kinds, for the simple reason was that they had no intention of turning back. They had nothing to go back to. A young warrior like Boiorix, born only a little time before the trek started, would have known no other kind of life than peripatetic instability, and that must have been true of almost all of the younger people on the march.

Rome was certainly aware for some considerable time that these people were on the move, occasionally fighting with other tribes whose lands they crossed, who were naturally enough less than welcoming, occasionally also assimilating with others, adding to their numbers as the years passed, but ever progressing. However, their move towards the northern lands bordering Italy had also come at a time when Rome had its collective mind on other things and was very busy elsewhere. Therefore, although Rome was aware of the movement of people, it is hardly surprising that the danger they represented should be slightly underestimated. Particularly so as the first engagement of what was to become a long-running conflict took place in a relatively quiet area for Rome at that time.

In the year 113 BC the Scordisci tribe had been soundly beaten by the travelling Cimbri and Teutones, led by Boiorix and Teutobod. The invaders then moved onwards, towards the Danube, halting near to Noreia, in Noricum, but the area was already occupied by the Taurisci people, who were allies of Rome. Attempts on their part to repel the invaders were unsuccessful, and therefore the Taurisci, in an effort to protect their lands, appealed to Rome itself for help.[1]

In the following year, 112 BC, King Jugurtha was making a nuisance of himself in Numidia, and allowing the massacre of Roman traders and businessmen. This forced the Senate to deal with him, occupying time and attention. At the same time, the then Consul Gnaeus Papirius Carbo was commissioned to lead an army to Noricum, to go to the aid of the Taurisci. On arriving in the area, he took up a good position on heights near to Aquileia. He no doubt expected a short and successful campaign and a swift return home.

Carbo then sent a message to Boiorix and Teutobod, the leaders, demanding that they and their followers leave the territory belonging to the Taurisci without delay. The Cimbri must have already heard plenty about the power of Rome, but it may have been the first time they had seen Roman legionaries in strength, and that sight, together with the position taken up by Carbo, must have caused them to reconsider their actions. They actually began to comply with Carbo's order.

Had the matter been left there, a terrible defeat for Rome might well have been avoided. Furthermore, a valuable lesson about the human vulnerability of Roman troops might also have been saved for a later time, without a great many Roman lives being wasted. However, despite the vast numbers of tribesman gathered there, later estimated at possibly 300,000, Gnaeus Papirius Carbo became over-confident. He may also have had his eyes set on a Triumph on his return to Rome. Whatever reasons he may have had for his next action, he decided to take further steps to teach the invading Cimbri and Teutones a salutary lesson.

He had arranged with their leaders that he would send guides to escort their people to the frontier. In reality, he was preparing an ambush for them and hoped that the guides he had arranged would lead them into it. However, the Cimbri became aware that he was plotting an action against them and, instead of obligingly moving away on his command, they decided to stand and fight, partly to test the famous power of Rome, partly also because they no longer had any permanent home to retire to.

An engagement took place between the tribes and the Romans not far from Noreia, in which the invaders, to everyone's surprise, completely overwhelmed the Legions and inflicted a devastating loss on them.[2] It is said that only the appearance of a violent storm, which was so heavy that the combatants were separated, prevented the total annihilation of the Roman army.[3] Even so, it was certainly terrible enough. Out of an estimated 30,000 Legionaries, probably 24,000 lost their lives. Carbo managed to escape from the field with the remnants of his troops, although the Cimbri at first believed that they had killed him, and boasted of it. Unfortunately, it had merely served to show the invaders that the Romans, despite their reputation, were actually far from infallible and could die just as easily as other men. It was a lesson that they were to remember and one which was in the future to cost Rome dear.

Carbo limped back to Rome, where he was impeached as Consul by the Senate, but although disgraced, he was not exiled. Rome now prepared as well as possible for the horror it believed must surely come, but to the general surprise, the invaders did not act on their success at Noreia. Instead of immediately moving towards Italy and making good their achievement against Carbo, they seemed to disappear! Instead of invading Italy, as had been expected and feared, they had turned west, and were then headed towards Gaul. But the postponement of further hostilities, for which Rome was very grateful, was indeed only a temporary respite. Noreia was to prove merely the opening engagement in a long drawn out war against the Germanic people, which had already resulted in an astonishing and resounding defeat for Rome and a very damaging dent in Rome's reputation as a military power.

Time moved on and the matter seemed to have eased. The next major event in the conflict with the migrating tribes did not happen until the Consulship of Marcus Junius Silanus, in 109 BC.

Marcus Junius Silanus was the first member of his family to achieve the Consulship. He became junior consul in 109 BC with Quintus Caecilius Metellus Numidicus as senior. As the difficulties with Jugurtha in Numidia were a continuing problem for Rome, Metellus was obliged to continue with his work in North Africa, leaving Silanus to deal with the Cimbri, who had resurfaced in Transalpine Gaul, not far from the Rhodanus River. The Cimbri were reported to have asked for a domicile on Roman territory in Gaul, but they were refused this concession by the Senate.[4] The stage was then set for another battle against them, this time led by Silanus. The position of the actual engagement is obscure, but it is known that in Gallia Transalpina, approximately 100 miles north of Arausio, the new Consul Silanus was defeated by the Cimbri, thus suffering another humiliation for both himself and for Rome at the hands of the invaders. Silanus survived the battle and was some time later to be accused of his failure in court, by the Tribune Gnaeus Domitius Ahenobarbus.[5] However, despite the former consul being acquitted, the whole episode did nothing whatever to boost the standing of the newly consular family.

Two years after the battle by the Rhodanus River, from which Marcus Junius Silanus had gained nothing but shame, the Germanic tribes found themselves in 107 BC living on land to the north and east of Tolosa in south-western Gaul. They had actually allied themselves with the Volcae Tectosages, the indigenous people of the area and, despite their seemingly inharmonious objectives, appeared to be settling there in amity.

Nonetheless, to Rome the affiliation of these people posed a serious threat to stability in the area and Lucius Cassius Longinus was sent to Gaul to deal with the matter.

Ironically, he was taking with him the legions that had served with Quintus Caecilius Metellus (now known as Metellus Numidicus) in North Africa. When Metellus had left Africa Province to allow Gaius Marius to take over, he had refused to allow his legions to stay to fight with Marius, thus forcing the new consul to raise his troops from the capite censi, with conspicuous success. Now those experienced legions which had previously served with Metellus in Numidia, close to 40,000 men, were in Gaul, about to face the combined forces of the Cimbri and the Volcae Tectosages, under the command of Lucius Cassius Longinus along with Gaius Popillius Laenas as his subordinate.

At first, all went well for Rome. Just outside Tolosa the combatants met and, despite the huge numbers of allied forces, Cassius Longinus beat them and they retreated in disorder, leaving behind a large number of baggage wagons, containing practically all their possessions.

Flushed with this success, the first for some time against these people, Cassius Longinus collected together all the wagons and booty, and proceeded to follow the retreating tribes. He followed them for over two weeks, slowed down by the huge baggage train, which he was reluctant to leave behind for fear of it being stolen by the local people. By the time he and his troops reached Burdigala, it was heavily fortified and the barbarians had been reinforced. Burdigala was not merely a fort, it was a heavily protected oppidum, which was a substantial stronghold, usually found on an easily defensible hilltop, and in this case it was large enough to hold the combined forces, together with their substantial reinforcements, which the Romans now faced.

Cassius Longinus camped just to the east of Burdigala, and when he decided to attack the oppidum itself he left the baggage wagons in camp, under the command of Popillius Laenas, who had a force of about five cohorts with him, approximately half a legion.

Cassius Longinus was very confident after his recent success, too confident, and apparently marched his troops towards Burdigala without tightening ranks or marching in squares. It is said that his lack of defensive measures even included failing to send out scouts ahead of the troops. Unfortunately, his lax behaviour was to exact the highest price possible, for he and his men were ambushed very successfully by the combined tribes and Cassius Longinus was killed, along with around 10,000 legionaries, struggling to defend themselves against the onslaught.[6]

The first that Popillius Laenas would have known about it, apart from hearing the sounds of ferocious battle carried downwind, was the sight of the few surviving Roman troops running for their lives, away from the pursuing hordes of tribesmen. If he was waiting for Cassius Longinus to reappear he was to be disappointed, for what arrived instead was a force of thousands upon thousands of Germans, triumphantly aggressive, quickly surrounding his camp. It must have been a terrifying sight, especially for a junior commander who only had five cohorts with him.

He had a swift and very painful decision to make. Was he to fight to the last man, and undoubtedly be killed, along with what men he had left? Or was he to surrender, in the vain hope of saving the lives of those men? He could hardly expect to save his own life either way in those circumstances, for the German barbarians were already earning a reputation for more than once making an example of the commanders of captured forces. It was rumoured that they had previously burned men alive in wicker cages – not an easy death to contemplate. But then, Popillius Laenas was a brave young man, and he was determined that if he could manage it, he would not allow his few troops to die needlessly, whatever was to happen to him.

He surrendered.[7]

To his amazement, and the amazement of his men, the barbarians allowed them to live. Their lives were spared, except that they were to suffer the great indignity of passing under the yoke before retiring from the field.[8] This was a punishment which had become too familiar to the Romans of latter years, and although it did not cause the deaths of the men subjected to it, it did kill their pride and the pride of Rome in particular. It was considered to be the most horrendous humiliation that any commander could be faced with. It was far better to have been killed honourably in battle!

The 'yoke' itself was usually simply a crosspiece made of spears, under which the defeated men would have to crouch to pass in a humble and degraded manner. It seems innocuous enough, but it can hardly be underestimated just how the men subjected to this dishonour would feel. Despite having saved the lives of his men by his timely surrender, Popillius Laenas knew perfectly well that by then being obliged to undergo the punishment of passing under the yoke, he would be held to be guilty of treason. He would more than likely have to pay for that indignity with his life, once he returned to Rome.

Gaius Popillius Laenas was not only a brave young man, but also one who came from an important and worthy background. He was the great-grandson of the hero of Alexandria, another Gaius Popillius Laenas, who many years before, as Consul, had been sent to Egypt at the request of the Ptolemy monarchs. Kings Philometor and Euergetes and their sister – Queen Cleopatra II – had asked the Senate to help them in their desperate need, after being invaded by King Antiochus IV of Syria who had cast greedy eyes on their territories. Gaius Popillius Laenas the Consul had then travelled to Alexandria with only his twelve lictors and a couple of clerks.

Completely undefended by any troops he had walked out of Alexandria until he met with the forces from Syria, with Antiochus at their head. Popillius Laenas had told the king of Syria that he must leave the area and 'go home', a demand which naturally enough met with derision. But Popillius Laenas insisted and despite many strong threats from the Syrian king, who naturally enough refused to take him seriously, he drew a circle in the sand, around the feet of the astonished king of Syria. He told the king that when he stepped out from the drawn circle, he should make sure that he was facing east, and reiterated his demand that the king should go home.

For some time they were at an impasse, with the king of Syria, backed by his numerous troops, facing the Consul, who was backed only by his twelve lictors. It must have seemed a very unequal contest indeed. However, when the king had stopped making threats and started to think properly he saw that although it would be perfectly easy for him to kill this one man and his twelve bodyguards, if he actually did so he would bring the whole retribution of Rome down on his head. He was not prepared to start a war with Rome. When he finally stepped out of the circle drawn by Popillius Laenas in the sand, he was indeed facing east, and he and his troops left for home.

It was a story that had gone down in folklore as portraying the courage and power of the Roman people and was told by Roman matrons to their children as a good example to emulate.[9]

This was the calibre of the young Popillius Laenas who now had two options, either to leave immediately for a voluntary exile, from which he would be unable to return. Or to go back to Rome and face a treason trial for surrendering and being forced to pass under the yoke. But to leave for voluntary exile was in itself an admission of guilt, and Popillius Laenus knew that he was innocent of treason. He decided to return to Rome and face trial, in the hope that he could at least put forward his point of view.

Once there, he found himself facing many people who wished to take the blame for the catastrophe from the shoulders of the deceased Cassius Longinus, where it properly belonged, and place it squarely on those of Popillius Laenas. He was eventually tried for treason in the Centuriate Assembly, but to everyone's amazement, probably even his own, his reasons were accepted. Perhaps his accusers remembered the stories of his ancestor and decided that the young man's courage was obvious. At any rate, he was declared innocent and acquitted.

In the year 106 BC the Consulship was in the hands of Quintus Servilius Caepio and Gaius Atilius Serranus. The Volcae Tectosages and the Germans they had befriended were still living in the area of Tolosa, and Servilius Caepio was given the command to march against them. He was authorized to use eight legions in an effort to show these people that opposition to Rome was still likely to provoke reprisals.[10]

However, because of recent losses in the field the required numbers of men proved very hard to find, and he was obliged to resort to press-ganging almost any able-bodied man of reasonable age in an effort to fulfil the requirements of the legions he was to take with him. Servilius Caepio had already been a praetor-governor in Further Spain, where he had done very well for himself, certainly financially. He no doubt expected that on this assignment he would also be able to do well.

Caepio's legions naturally enough walked the 1,000 miles or so from Campania to Narbo. Not that Roman soldiers usually minded a long trek, they were perfectly well used to walking and were equipped to do so as comfortably as possible. Probably far more comfortably than on a sea voyage, which though much quicker, was often far riskier. The average Roman soldier doubtless felt far safer on his own two feet than on the sea, at the mercy of wind and weather. The journey was made in a little over seventy days, which was not considered to be particularly quick as it averaged little more than fifteen miles a day. However, once in Narbo they were able to rest for a while, before setting off again along the coast towards Tolosa.

While they had been travelling, the Volcae Tectosages had quarrelled with their German guests, and had requested them to leave the area. Therefore once Caepio arrived he found that he was to be faced only by the local tribes, who in turn very sensibly decided that they did not want to engage with the newly arrived legions. Tolosa surrendered at once.

Doubtless Servilius Caepio was very pleased at not having to engage them in battle. He was probably also pleased about the Gold of Tolosa, which was popularly supposed to be hidden in the area, and about which he had heard while he was governor of Further Spain, three years previously.

The Gold of Tolosa was partly history and partly myth. Over 100 years previously, a Celtic king named Brennus had gone into Macedonia, down to Thessaly and into central Greece. It was said that he had then looted the three richest temples in the known world, Dodona at Epirus, Zeus of Olympia, and Apollo at Delphi. The plunder from these was said to have been brought back to Tolosa under the care of the Volcae Tectosages. They were supposed to have melted it all down and hidden it in the area.

Quintus Servilius Caepio was determined to find the Gold of Tolosa, if it did indeed exist. Searches of the area were made, at first without success. Eventually though it was found. The treasures looted from the temples had indeed been melted down into gold and silver bars. Once it was retrieved even a Caepio would have been stunned by the amount of wealth it represented. It was said to have amounted to 15,000 talents of gold and around 3,500 talents of silver. (A talent represented approximately 25 kg modern weight.) The whole treasure came to more than was stocked in the treasuries in Rome itself.

It was arranged that the plunder should be transported to Rome. Firstly the silver, then the gold, was to be shipped from Narbo. The silver did indeed make its way safely, and the wagons which had been used to transport it to the coast returned to collect the gold.

The gold, packed upon the wagons, was then to be escorted by a single cohort of legionaries. It was not considered necessary to use a larger protection force as the oppidum of Burdigala still held the Volcae Tectosages. They probably hoped that Servilius Caepio would attempt to make a foolish attack on it as Cassius Longinus had done, but Caepio was to be far more interested in transporting the gold to Rome.

Unfortunately, while the wagons laden with the bars of gold were still travelling towards the coast, they were attacked in force and very quickly overwhelmed. Not a single Roman of the cohort sent to protect it was left alive to explain what had happened, and all the gold was gone. It was never retrieved, although it was widely suspected that Servilius Caepio knew a good deal more about its disappearance than he would ever admit to. It is interesting to note that in the future the Servilia Caepios were famous for being as rich as Croesus, although they always denied having any hand in the disappearance of the Gold of Tolosa. It is, however, an unfortunate mark of the man himself that he should consider the gold and its recovery far more important than dealing with the barbarians he had been sent to subjugate.

In fact, the legions sent to deal with the Volcae Tectosages had done no fighting at all during the months they had been in Gaul. Caepio was then informed that he was to remain as governor of Gaul for another year. This was to prove a decisive and disastrous year for him and for Rome itself.

In 105 BC a further six more legions were raised in Rome, led by the new Consul Marcus Mallius Maximus, and they marched to Gaul to join Servilius Caepio.

Gaius Marius and Lucius Cornelius Sulla were at the same time still busy in North Africa, taking the Roman army to the borders of Mauretania, in an attempt to force King Bocchus to finally take their side in the battle against his son-in-law Jugurtha.

However, in Gaul, the stage was being set for one of the greatest tragedies Rome was to experience. The uneasy peace of the area was not to be maintained, as the migration of the Cimbri through Gaul had incited other tribes to stand against Rome. There was a temporary rebellion at Tolosa, which caused a mobilization of Roman troops into the area to contain the problem after a delegation of Aedui had asked Rome for protection. However, the movement of the local tribesmen was not the only difficulty that Caepio and his forces were to face. The arrival of Gnaeus Mallius Maximus was to prove to be the catalyst.

The senior consul for that year was actually Publius Rutilius Rufus. He was an experienced and highly decorated veteran, but for some reason did not take command of the campaign in Gaul as might have been expected. His junior colleague, Mallius Maximus, went instead. As Consul of the year, albeit junior consul, he outranked Servilius Caepio and should therefore have been considered the senior commander of the combined armies in Gaul. However, Servilius Caepio, as a Patrician was totally opposed to a 'new man' without his social standing and refused absolutely to take orders from his new commander. This stupidity and inability to work with Mallius Maximus forced the splitting of the available troops, which was to precipitate the disaster of the coming conflict.[11]

Gnaeus Mallius Maximus was supported by Marcus Aurelius Scaurus, who was an able and experienced Legate, but there was a general shortage of experienced centurions available for the campaign. Mallius Maximus also had his two sons with him, along with Sextus Julius Caesar, Marcus Livius Drusus and Quintus Servilius Caepio Junior. Another junior military tribune with them was Quintus Sertorius.

There were also three Allied Italian Legions present, the one sent by the Marsi being led by Quintus Poppaedius Silo. Having such an entourage and the accompanying baggage wagons, their progress was quite slow and by the time they reached the Rhodanus River, Servilius Caepio was already in the area.

Firm instructions had already been sent from Rome that Servilius Caepio was to subordinate himself to his new commander, which he still resolutely refused to do. Information was now passed on that the Germans were again on their way south, moving through the lands of the Allobroges. The Allobroges had always disliked the Romans, but now they decided that they disliked the Germans even more, and were certainly not prepared to share their land with these marauding travellers.

The Germans by this time consisted of over three quarters of a million people, now travelling down alongside the river. When Caepio heard this, he turned off at Nemausus and marched his army along the western bank, keeping the river between himself and the Germans. On the eastern bank of the river was a prosperous Roman trading town. Its name was Arausio.

Still on the western bank, now around ten miles north of Arausio, Servilius Caepio put his army into a strongly fortified camp. He was now waiting for Mallius Maximus to appear on the opposite bank of the river. Mallius Maximus duly appeared shortly after and made his camp on the edge of the river about five miles north of Arausio, therefore with the river as a part of his defence. He must have believed that the river was the greater part of his protection, but if he made that mistake, he was to make a greater one.

He then sent his cavalry, about 5,000 strong, to make another camp about thirty miles further north, in order to act as an advance guard. A final big mistake was to send his most experienced Legate, Marcus Aurelius Scaurus, with the cavalry. This merely deprived him of Scaurus' good advice at a time when he would desperately need it.

He possibly hoped that by showing the advancing Germans a well fortified Roman camp, complete with cavalry, well organized and well commanded, he would cause them to pause in their advance. It was quite likely his hope that they would then retreat back into central Gaul and not provoke battle at all.

However, he still had the problem of Servilius Caepio being camped on the other side of the river and refusing absolutely to join Mallius Maximus in the main camp. Not only were messages to him of no avail, but he replied to his commander with great disdain.[12]

Eventually, about midway through September, six senators arrived from Rome, hoping to mediate between the two commanders. Consul Publius Rutilius Rufus, still in Rome, had worked hard at sending the embassage, knowing that Caepio was likely to be obdurate. However, there was no really senior senator with it, the most noble of them being Marcus Aurelius Cotta. This man did his best to persuade Caepio to see sense and give in, but without success. In fact, the attempts made seemed to enrage him all the more, and he shortly moved further north, until he was some twenty miles above Mallius Maximus' camp.[13] This put him only ten miles or so south of the cavalry camp, although he did eventually cross to the other side of the river.

A day or so later, Aurelius Scaurus at the cavalry camp, met with a German treating party, who asked for a peaceful right of way through Gaul, on their way towards Spain. They were informed that they would not be allowed to travel through Roman territory, nor would they be allowed to settle in Spain, which was also Roman territory. They were, in fact, to try to return home, or wherever it was they originally came from. They were simply not welcome and could not hope to make a home in Spain. The Germans were obliged to ride away again, with no further chance of a peaceful treaty, empty handed.

The first engagement in the conflict then took place, when a group of cavalry under the command of Marcus Aurelius Scaurus met with an advance party of Cimbri. The Romans were overwhelmed and Scaurus was captured and taken before Boiorix. He told Boiorix proudly that he should turn back his people, before they were destroyed by the Romans. For this act of hauteur Marcus Aurelius Scaurus was then executed by Boiorix as an example. For a further day or two more the Germans stayed by the ruins of the cavalry camp, before once again starting to move southwards.

Caepio, meanwhile, had decided to try to attack the Cimbri himself, which he did on 6 October. However, his attack was ill-planned and hastily executed and his force was annihilated by the Cimbri defence.[14] To add insult to injury, Caepio had left his own camp only lightly defended while he made his ill-advised attack, and the Cimbri were then able to ransack it. Servilius Caepio actually escaped from the battle unhurt, although the vast majority of his men were killed. Estimates of the numbers lost go as high as 50,000 and Caepio is said to have escaped by crossing again to the opposite bank of the river in a boat.

The Cimbri then, with the great confidence given them by what seemed to be an easy victory, then attacked the force commanded by Mallius Maximus. Not wishing to be trapped in his camp, Mallius Maximus, on seeing them approach, went out and formed up his men facing the advancing tribesmen. His two sons were among his personal staff. Unfortunately, he and his men, despite every attempt, were to do no better against the overwhelming numbers of Germans and there was simply no way to hold off their advance.

The Romans were completely destroyed. Many of them tried to escape from the slaughter by swimming the river, but the Romans were never entirely happy with water, and encumbered as they were by armour, very few managed to save themselves in that way. The six senators who had tried to make Caepio see sense had already been sent across the river by boat before the engagement began. They were therefore safe, and able to take the full story back to Rome, but Mallius Maximus suffered the great grief of seeing both his sons killed during the battle.

Young Metellus Numidicus, when he realized that defeat was inevitable, hustled Mallius Maximus and his few surviving aides into a boat and thereby saved his commander's life.

It was generally Roman policy to spare the lives of defeated enemies, if only because strong and healthy captives were likely to bring high prices as slaves, but the Germans went among the wounded after the battle and killed anyone who did not already appear to be dead. It was soon all over. The barbarians then made their way back towards their waiting wagons and non-combatants.

It took several more days for the remaining few thousand survivors to reassemble from wherever they had managed to find safety, with Servilius Caepio among them. When he heard that Mallius Maximus had survived, though he was mourning the loss of his sons along with his army, and was sheltering in Arausio, Caepio decided to press on towards Rome. He was probably hoping to arrive there before Maximus, which was more than likely going to be the case, since Maximus, stunned with shock and grief, was unable to deal with matters quickly. Caepio could then put his side of the story first, and hopefully minimize the damage to his reputation.

Unfortunately, the story reached Rome ahead of him. The news of Arausio provoked horror and outrage, both among the people and also the Senate. It is only too easy to imagine what the response must have been when the news spread around Rome. General mourning was the order of the day, as very few families could have been without some relative or friend among the dead.

Some estimates state that the total number of Romans killed at Arausio was more than 80,000.[15] There were also reports that the 80,000 casualties only covered the actual soldiers and that half as many again of cavalry, auxiliaries and camp followers also died at Arausio on that day.[16] 6 October 105 BC was to mark Rome's worst military defeat. It easily equalled, if not exceeded, the slaughter suffered at Cannae during the Punic Wars.[17]

It cannot be wondered at that Caepio stood to take most of the blame for what happened, as if he had at least stayed within reasonable reach of the other forces there would have been some chance of them being able to defend themselves. However, Mallius Maximus was also at fault in splitting his forces and sending the cavalry north under Scaurus to a position where it could be of no help at all to the other camps.

It was said afterwards that Publius Rutilius Rufus would never have made the appalling blunders that Mallius Maximus did, and that certainly Servilius Caepio would not have so contemptuously refused to obey orders from Rutilius Rufus, in the way he did with Mallius Maximus. If Rutilius Rufus had been present, he might have managed the situation differently, even if only to recommend a strategic retreat. Shaming, but far less damaging than a catastrophic defeat. It was a line that Sulla would be obliged to take at Tridentum, after Catulus Caesar led the legionaries there into danger.

The arguments raged on in Rome over who was most at fault, though generally the bulk of the blame was understandably put upon the shoulders of Servilius Caepio. The following January he was arraigned in the Plebian Assembly by the Tribune of the Plebs, Gaius Norbanus. The official accusation was for 'loss of his army'. Feelings were quite naturally running high regarding the appalling losses at Arausio, but there must also have been some peripheral thought given to the still-missing Gold of Tolosa. The Senate, being Patrician, could not participate in the debates, but made their feelings clear by hectoring Norbanus. There was actually at one point a scuffle, but nevertheless a vote was finally given which condemned Caepio, at least regarding his behaviour at Arausio.

When a sentence was passed down, it was unusually severe. He was to be stripped of his citizenship, exiled 800 miles from Rome, and fined 15,000 talents of gold. (They must have thought that he had it safely tucked away somewhere, in order for them to fine him such an amount.) Quintus Servilius Caepio departed for exile at Smyrna, where he lived out his life in some luxury. The younger members of his family continued to live in comfort in Rome, therefore his condemnation was not ruinous and rumour must certainly have remained busy.

Meanwhile, it was said that the fields over which the battle had been fought were made so fertile by the human remains left to rot on them, that they were for many years after to produce a vastly higher yield of crops.[18]

After their astounding and relatively easy success at Arausio, the Cimbri then went on to clash with the Averni, and later were to set out for the Pyrenees instead of marching straight to Italy. Their way of thought and their erratic movements continued to be totally unpredictable to the Romans, who had expected to be attacked at home. However, the respite Rome received by their incomprehensible behaviour was desperately needed, as they were now left with a critical shortage of manpower, both of commanders of all ranks and among the legionaries themselves.[19] This difficulty in keeping up the quotas for the legions eventually led the Senate to be obliged to set aside the usual constraints on the number of times a man could be elected Consul.

Previously, it had been the norm for a period of ten years to have to pass before a man could stand for the consulship again. Due to the reverses suffered by Rome, and, it has to be said, the incompetent and ineffective commanders who had been in the field, this rule was abandoned. It was greatly to the advantage of Gaius Marius that it should be so, for he was then proposed for the supreme position in absentia and elected consul again, only three years after completing his first consulship.

Although this was undoubtedly a pleasure to him, it might not have come entirely as a surprise. While in North Africa, he had been told by a prophetess there that he would be elected Consul of Rome an unprecedented seven times.[20] Like many Romans, he was superstitious rather than actually religious and he was to show by his future actions that he believed implicitly in this prophecy and would allow it to dictate his future actions.

For the remainder of that disastrous year Marius and Sulla were engaged in North Africa, busy with the cleaning up operations necessary after the change of ruler in Numidia.

Granted, the duties imposed upon them were by then largely administrative, but there must have been some satisfaction in helping to organize the new Africa Province.

Prince Gouda had taken over as King of Numidia and he had a son, another Hiempsal, to take over from him in due course. King Bocchus of Mauretania seemed content with his newly enlarged territory, but there was still land to spare, which was to be used by Gaius Marius as rewards for his clientele, with land available also for his veterans when they would need to be discharged.

The new peacefulness of Africa Province would have been a cruel contrast to what had been going on in Gaul, reports of which would certainly have reached Marius and Sulla. It must have been very tempting for them to discuss how the matter would have been dealt with, had they been in command. When the news reached them that they were required to return to Rome, preparatory to being sent to Gaul to take over the situation there, it might have come as a relief. They must have been itching to get their hands on the matter and they were primarily fighting men after all.

Marius now prepared to deal with the matter in his usual efficient manner, appropriate to a man who was to become known, and actually saw himself, as a saviour of Rome.

In his eager preparations for tackling the Germanic threat, that had for so long rendered other commanders seemingly helpless, he was again assisted and supported by the man he already had good reason to be able to trust and rely on, his friend and protégé – the ever-useful Lucius Cornelius Sulla.

Chapter Five

The election of Gaius Marius to the Consulate 'in absentia' was a mandate of the people. It was to give him great confidence, not only to deal with the problems in Gaul, but also in his determination to eventually achieve the passing of an agrarian law. He needed this to confirm the rights of his veteran legions to take possession of land in North Africa, and eventually also in Gaul. As these men were capite censi, therefore without property of their own in Italy itself, it would not only give them a stake in Rome's future in the expanding Provinces, but would also take into those same Provinces an example of the industry and habits of Rome itself. It would usefully serve to show the local populace, in whichever country it was established, just how Roman life and culture really worked.

This type of cultural expansion was not, however, without its strong and powerful opponents. Many of Rome's famous families already had their financial interests in the Provinces and were getting very rich indeed by their use of the land. The Gracchi brothers had already done their best to force fairer divisions both at home in Italy and abroad, but without success.[1]

It is obvious that with a quickly expanding empire it was never going to be possible to keep all those disparate people under control by subjugation alone. It was far better to show those subject people that the Roman way could work to their advantage too, and to gradually get them to appreciate it and assimilate with Roman ideas. Later, after the Social Wars, it would be seen as the only way forward, and generally it would work very well, with the areas concerned priding themselves on becoming 'sophisticated' and Romanized. Of course, it did not work everywhere, even then, with Judea as a prime example of stubborn intransigence, but it did serve to carry Roman thinking out to the empire and helped Rome to change the way the original barbarians behaved. This, of course, not only 'civilized' them but also made them easier to control.

However, in the early days of the Gracchi brothers' struggles and then Gaius Marius' requirement of land for his veterans, the Senators and their supporters saw no reason to educate or sophisticate those barbarians. They actually did not want them to become civilized, if it meant that they would then consider themselves in any way the equal of a pure Roman citizen. They were very much concerned that sending Roman legionaries out to live with, marry with and breed with the subject peoples, would only result in a bastardized form of Roman and a subsequent dilution of everything that constituted proper Roman thinking. That Gaius Marius was prepared to try to push through such a demand at this point was a measure of his courage and self-belief, and the knowledge of how necessary it would be. However, he would not be able to do it alone.

Despite the fact that he had been made Consul in an unusual way, with the support of the People, was in his opponent's eyes only a mark of the desperation of Rome in the face of a threat it had so far been unable to deal with satisfactorily. It certainly did not mean that the new Consul was going to be welcomed with open arms by the Senators. This showed itself all too clearly right from the beginning, because many men of position, usually only too eager to stand for election, did not on this occasion put themselves forward, as they generally preferred not to partner Gaius Marius in the Consulship. Therefore, instead of having the support of a strong Consular partner, Marius found himself with Gaius Flavius Fimbria as his Junior Consul. The Consulship began officially, of course, with Marius' Triumph on New Year's Day of 104 BC, during which King Jugurtha walked through Rome for the first and last time, shortly before ending his life in the Tullianum.[2]

While still in Rome Gaius Marius saw that he needed a spokesman to stand up for him in the Plebian Assembly, in order to start the long process of reserving some of the Roman public land for his veterans to settle on. The young Tribunes of the Plebs had recently been elected and amongst their number was a certain Lucius Marcius Phillipus. He and Gaius Marius came into contact with each other, after which Marcius Phillipus began to speak in favour of Marius' proposed agrarian bill. It would, of course, be taken for granted that Marius would make some financial arrangement with the Tribune in return for his services. This was the usual procedure of 'buying' oneself a Tribune of the Plebs. The difficulty of getting a bill passed was naturally commensurate with the price that would eventually have to be paid for its promotion. It needs to be remembered that only the Plebian Assembly had the power of veto against almost any action of the magistrates, or even that of any other Tribune. An elected Tribune of the Plebs could propose a bill, or veto one proposed by another, he could also legally veto any law about to be passed or any decree of the Senate. Within the Assembly he and his colleagues were all powerful. As Tribunes normally only served for one year, before using the Tribunate as a stepping stone up to higher office, they were generally keen to establish the beginnings of their fortune during their service. They usually did this by making themselves useful (in return for sufficient cash) to anyone who had a bill he needed pushing forward.

In the earlier Republic, it had been the rule that the Tribunes of the Plebs were not members of the Senate and could not progress to be. However, the Lex Atinia of 149 BC had ruled that any man elected as a Tribune of the Plebs then automatically became a member of the Senate.[3] It still remained, however, a very useful way for a young man to not only gain experience, but also gather enough money to help finance the early years of his career, although their power was, unfortunately, very often more obstructive than helpful. It would prove to be so, in the future, for Sulla.

However, despite the need for Gaius Marius and Sulla to deal with the problems in Gaul, Marius still felt strongly enough about the need for some system of reward for his troops, to spend some of his time, while still in Rome, in an attempt to settle the agrarian matter.

But there was another pressing problem which all of Rome would soon face. Troops, in themselves, were becoming all too scarce. It had already been acknowledged by Gaius Marius that the capite censi were by then very necessary to replenish the severe shortages in manpower and, despite his successes with them in Numidia, even he would find difficulty in raising enough troops to take with him to Gaul. Many of the troops used by Gaius Marius in North Africa had remained there, having a wish to retire in the Province.[4] Hence the need for land for them to retire to. Therefore he would be obliged to start his operations in Gaul by training an army of new and inexperienced men.

Unfortunately, there was an attitude of resistance growing amongst the Italian Allies which was to become stronger and more determined as time went on. Feelings were beginning to run very high in Italy by the end of Arausio year in 105 BC.

Quintus Poppaedius Silo had survived, but the Allied cavalry had largely perished at Arausio. The Allies had actually tried to bring a suit for damages against Caepio, for the appalling result of his foolish behaviour, but it failed and was thrown out by the Senate. This did not, however, prevent the Allies from becoming very angry at what they considered to be their shabby treatment by Rome.

The Paeligni, Picentines, Umbrians, Apulians, Lucanians, Etrurians, Marrucini and Vestini and the Samnites were all equally restive. They complained volubly that Rome was not only using all their propertied men for the wars but was taking them away for such long periods that their farms and businesses were being ruined by neglect. If they then survived and returned home, it was to find that they were in debt bondage to Roman landowners, and many of these men were then taken as slaves in payment for that debt, often ending up back in Africa, Sardinia or Sicily, when their farms were eventually confiscated. There was a general air of serious dissatisfaction.

The Social Wars were not to flare up yet, but by 91 BC they would explode into a conflict which would cause problems for Rome at home, even while she was already busy abroad.[5] Although the Julian Law would give some rights to the Italian Allies in 90 BC,[6] the Marsi would still prove to be a problem until 87 BC and Sulla would be obliged to deal with them too.[7]

But that was not yet. For once, time was on their side. The apparent disappearance of the Germanic tribes after Arausio had confused and worried everyone in Rome. Where would they appear next? To the regulated Roman mind the idea of not taking full advantage of their successes in Gaul by immediately moving on towards Italy was incomprehensible. However, the delay was just what Gaius Marius needed. He had an army full of new recruits and he needed time to train and organize them to face battle before long.

He also intended an overhaul of the system, which would enable him to introduce new weapons and give time for the men to become familiar with them, and also to change tactical units. In 104 BC he was able to also give them a little much-needed experience in subduing some of the Gallic tribes who had taken the opportunity of revolting after the dreadful defeat of Rome.[8]

Sulla was by this time in Gaul along with Gaius Marius, acting as his Legate. Also with them at that time was Quintus Sertorius, who was to prove to be another very courageous and clever member of Marius' staff. Sulla was active in preparing the new troops for action, however in the meantime he also led his men to finally subdue the Volcae Tectosages, at Tolosa. Their capital had been captured by Caepio, before the disaster of Arausio, but now was the time and opportunity to subdue them properly. Sulla took it, and succeeded so well that he also captured their chief, Copillus.[9]

Despite this success, Marius was still determined to try more diplomatic methods of bringing at least some of the tribes over to his side. We are told that Quintus Sertorius, who had shown an aptitude for learning one of the Celtic languages, undertook the mission of spying, disguising himself as one of the tribesmen, in order to learn their intentions.[10] Did he go alone? It seems that if anyone wished to disguise himself as a Celt, then Sulla, with his fair hair and complexion, would be ideal, certainly more likely to blend in with the enemy than the darker Sertorius. It would also appeal greatly to the more reckless side of his nature, to take part in such a daring action and infiltrate the tribe personally. However, as tempting as the idea is, we have no proof that he did take part in such an action, but he would certainly have known of it and perhaps even helped to arrange it. It seems that Sertorius and Sulla, at that stage in their lives, were something of a match for each other. Marius could hardly have hoped to better two such resourceful and daring officers.

In 103 BC Marius was Consul again, for the third time, with Lucius Aurelius Orestes as his consular partner. During this year Sulla once again showed his great abilities, in an action which turned out to be the most successful of the whole of Marius' campaign of diplomacy. He was to approach the Germanic Marsi in an attempt to separate them from the other barbarian tribes and persuade them that they would be more secure as friends and allies of Rome, rather than foes.[11] Once again, Sulla's undoubted talents were put to good use by Gaius Marius, and he was successful in convincing the Marsi to detach themselves from the other tribes.

After this, in 102 BC when Gaius Marius became Consul for the fourth time, came a separation between Gaius Marius and Sulla which is usually represented as being the result of jealousy between the two of them.[12] Marius' Consular partner on this occasion was Quintus Lutatius Catulus Caesar.

It is usually claimed that Sulla around that time then requested a transfer to the staff of Marius' new colleague Catulus. This is said to be because Sulla was resentful that Marius was not appreciative of his work so far and also because Catulus was a military nonentity under whose command Sulla would shine all the brighter. Also it is usually accepted that friction had arisen between Marius and Sulla, so that Marius was glad to be rid of him. However, I do not agree with this line of reasoning.

Gaius Marius and Sulla had worked exceedingly well together for several years by then, and Marius was not, at that time, the sort of man to express mere childish jealousy of a junior officer, however able or promising. The sending of Sulla to Catulus, constituting an apparent demotion, could only be read in those circumstances as an act of pique, bearing in mind that Sulla had on several occasions proved his ability, unless Marius had a very good reason for making such an arbitrary decision.[13] He had only recently made successful use of Sulla again and such a competent man as Marius would be all the more likely to be able to appreciate an officer who would never prove to be either lacklustre or a millstone around his neck. Neither would Sulla, at that time in his life, need to force himself forward. He had already proved himself and his abilities more than once and was about to do so again, in Gaul. No, it would be far more logical for Marius to have had a better reason for the action than merely wishing to be rid of Sulla.

That Gaius Marius and Sulla were, later on, to become bitter political enemies seems to have coloured general opinion and transposed actions which, I believe, were at the time not only perfectly innocent, but actually intended for the general good of the campaign.

Also, their eventual enmity and Sulla's much later writings on the matter were subject to hindsight and reflected in the light of the difficulties they were to later experience.[14] It is very easy indeed to transfer one's feelings to a previous occasion when looking back over time, and to forget or even ignore the situation as it actually was then, particularly when a once close relationship has become badly soured. It does not seem to me that their actions in 102 BC show any enmity at that point in their lives, quite the contrary.

It is, in my opinion, more logical to assume that Gaius Marius was already only too aware that Catulus was a far from competent commander and something of a military lightweight. Catulus was a Patrician to his fingertips, proud and also quite likely to be rather haughty. Marius would have to work with him, but he would not be able to trust or rely on him. It is perfectly possible that Gaius Marius could see the possibility of another situation like Arausio developing dangerously in the future, where the Patrician commander would refuse to work sensibly with the others.

What to do about it? The sensible thing, and Marius was an eminently sensible man, was to place with him another officer, in an attempt to guide him but also to be a brake on any gross errors of judgement that he might make. It would certainly need to be a man he could rely on and one whose ability and resource had already been proved. I firmly believe that this is exactly what Marius did. He had with him two very capable officers, in Sulla and Quintus Sertorius. Which one to choose? If he sent Sertorius to work with Catulus Caesar, then the 'Arausio situation' that Marius quite likely feared could easily come about. Catulus Caesar, that proud Patrician, was unlikely to allow himself to be guided by a mere Quintus Sertorius, another man of no family and no background. It might even inflame the very situation that Marius was trying to avoid.

Sulla, on the other hand, though officially outranked by the Consular Catulus, was still nearer to him socially. To such a man, such things mattered. They might, hopefully, be able to develop a friendly relationship, due to shared interests.[15] Catulus could still doubtless be haughty and unwilling to accept guidance, after all, Sulla was still not fully acceptable to the upper classes in Rome despite his military successes. On the other hand Sulla, with his undoubted diplomatic ability, would be perfectly capable of dealing with Catulus, and there was a chance that he might be able to offer good advice or, in the worst case, contain, or even curb, his commander's worst errors of judgement in the field. It would be a far more sensible action than that of keeping both of his good officers alongside him, yet leaving Catulus to wallow along making what mistakes he pleased.

Simply because Gaius Marius could not trust to the common sense of Catulus Caesar, he was obliged to put with him a man whose ability and common sense were beyond question. It is perfectly likely that Marius and Sulla discussed the situation and decided upon it between them. I do not accept that it showed any lack of appreciation of, or confidence in, Sulla on the part of Marius at that time. On Sulla's part, being another eminently sensible man, it would be obvious to him that he was again being put in a position of trust and responsibility, upon whom the success of the action would entirely depend. Before very long, Sulla would have been proved to be an adept at damage limitation, while with Catulus at Tridentum, which is probably exactly the role that Gaius Marius had in mind for him when the transfer was first made.[16]

It was at around this time that the Cimbri had returned from Spain, and were to attempt, with the Tigurini, to cross over into Italy. The precaution of placing an experienced and talented officer with Catulus was now all the more essential. It had showed his great confidence in Sulla, rather than the contrary, and Marius' foresight in using him in that way was shortly to prevent yet another disaster.

At that point, in early 102 BC, Catulus Caesar had the job of trying to prevent the advance of the Cimbri. He had travelled to the valley of the Athesis, to wait for, and hopefully stop, any further barbarian incursion.[17] Sulla, meanwhile was engaged in subduing other tribes in the region, in an attempt to prevent them from joining the German tribes and making the situation even worse. He rejoined his commander a little later in the year, prior to the move northwards.

It was Autumn before the Cimbri appeared. They were the most numerous of the tribes, possibly as many as 400,000 all together. Of the other tribes, the Cherusci claimed some sort of kinship with the Atuatuci, but there was an amount of ill-feeling between them and the Teutones and the Tigurini. Boiorix of the Cimbri, a man of ability and ambition, had managed to draw them all together, at least for a time, with the intention of invading Italy by travelling over the Alps. While this might seem to be an impossible task, the combined tribes had been travelling back and forth over the area for some time, and the terrain held no terrors for them at all.

Quintus Lutatius Catulus Caesar seemed to be another man with more confidence in his abilities than actual proof of them. It appears that it was then his decision to try to turn back the advancing Cimbri, by travelling up the Athesis to the east of Lake Benacus to meet them. High up the valley was a trading post named Tridentum.

Beyond Tridentum the valley narrowed considerably. If Catulus Caesar had any qualms at the idea of taking his troops into what constituted a narrow defile, he certainly showed nothing of them, and there is no evidence that at that point Sulla was able to make him reconsider his course of action. The Cimbri were, at that point, quite close to the Romans, and if Catulus intended to try to trap them in the narrowing valley, he cannot have fully realized that it was equally easy for those people to trap him in return. Presumably, they would be able to ascend the slopes alongside the valley and look down on, or even get ahead of, the moving Legions. Those Legions had already passed wide meadows on their way northwards, which would have been a far better situation for Roman military action. To try to be fair to Catulus, he was certainly heavily outnumbered by the Cimbri, and he may have thought that trapping them in a 'funnel' would give him an advantage.

There are few recorded details to give us any real idea what happened between Catulus and Sulla at that point. However, what seems to have happened is that Sulla, the far more experienced soldier, somehow managed to make Catulus realize the danger into which he had led his troops. It may well have been an argument that took some time to sink in to the commander's unwilling mind, but eventually there was no alternative but to order a strategic retreat, or face another catastrophic defeat.

By this time, however, the Cimbri had become fully aware of the Roman advance, and they decided to give chase. Sulla had Marcus Aemilius Scaurus Junior with him when the Cimbri overran the Samnite camp. Gnaeus Petreius, the Primus Pilus Centurion of the Samnites led a heroic charge to keep the advancing barbarians occupied long enough to give the rest of the men the opportunity to cross the river and escape. The Samnites attempted to get their men and wagons across the river and then tried to destroy the bridge over the Athesis to prevent the Cimbri following them. There were, of course, some losses but the situation, humiliating enough, was nothing like as bad as it might have been, had Sulla not been able to pressure Catulus into ordering the retreat.

Unfortunately, young Scaurus was not able to show the courage and resource of the Samnite Centurion, Gnaeus Patreius. It was reported afterwards that he was unable to give any orders and that his men were obliged to help him to get away. It may well have been his first engagement and unfortunately not all men are naturally blessed with instant heroism, perhaps he just froze. Whatever the reason, he would not be given a second chance and his lack of bravery was to be his downfall.

Catulus Caesar's troops were safely back in camp by the time Boiorix reached the plains beside the River Padus. Roman citizen and Latin Rights refugees were encouraged to leave the area for the time being, allowing the Cimbri to spread out over the area between Lake Benacus and the Padus itself. Sensibly, it was decided that this fertile area would engage their attentions for some time, at least long enough to give the Roman army time to regroup with Gaius Marius.

Unfortunately for young Marcus Aemilius Scaurus, he was then given the unenviable task of riding back to Rome with the official news for the Senate. He was the only child of Marcus Aemilius Scaurus, the Princeps Senatus, or Leader of the House.[18] His father, on hearing the news of his son's cowardice in the face of the enemy, refused to see him, and officially disowned him. Scaurus Junior then committed suicide. This left his betrothed, a young woman named Caecilia Metella Dalmatica, the niece of Quintus Metellus Numidicus, without a husband-to-be, and the Princeps Senatus soon decided to marry her himself, ignoring the difference in their ages. This young woman was to figure later in Sulla's life, when she became his third wife.[19]

The Cimbri were still comfortably occupying the pastures around the Padus River when their leader, Boiorix, heard of the defeat of the Teutones at Aquae Sextiae, under the command of Gaius Marius.

Approximately a quarter of a million Teutones had crossed the Druentia River, east of where it entered the Rhodanus, led by Teutobod. They spread out for miles, consisting of around 130,000 soldiers, the rest being made up of wagons, cattle, horses, and their women and children. The last group of wagons would be travelling many miles to the rear of the vanguard. Having the Ambrones standing with the Teutones gave Teutobod confidence and it appears that he intended to march on Massilia, on the coast, for supplies and rest, before travelling eastwards towards Italy, still scenting conquest.

The Roman fortress, heavily fortified, stood on a hill. The Ambrones first tried to tempt out the Romans, by catcalling and shouting insults, which were ignored. They then attacked the fortress, but the fortifications held and the Romans still seemed unimpressed.

The Teutones, led by Teutobod, then moved away towards Massilia, slightly to the south.[20] It took several days for their entire wagon train to clear the area of the fortress, but once it had done so, Gaius Marius moved with six over strength legions and crossed the river, taking up position on the south bank on a ridge, and there he dug in. Thirty thousand Ambrones found a Roman camp waiting for them, and they were obliged to attack it by running uphill.[21]

The Romans simply stepped out, over their ridge, to meet them, casting their pila to very good effect, killing the leading lines of the attackers easily.[22] They then drew their swords and waded in, in formation. Nearly all of the attacking Ambrones were killed but there were hardly any Roman casualties, so efficient was the manoeuvre. The action was over and done with very swiftly, after which the Romans piled up the barbarian dead as a rampart, and waited behind it for the Teutones to appear.[23]

While waiting, Gaius Marius took the precaution of sending Manius Aquillius slightly downstream with around 4,000 troops to cross the river. They were intended as an ambush, to fall on the barbarians from behind during the coming engagement.

When Teutobod and his army arrived, the first thing they saw was a rampart made up of the bodies of the dead Ambrones, behind which the Romans waited for them. It must have been a depressing sight particularly as, for once, the Romans were euphoric. They had succeeded in their first real achievement against the barbarians and were eager and ready for the coming fight with the Teutones.

However, the following day brought no action from the Germans and Marius may have had time to become a little concerned. The weather was very hot, which was to be a major factor in bringing added discomfort to the Germans, used as they were to a cooler and damper climate, but it would also cause the piled-up bodies of the Ambrones to begin to stink and rot all the quicker. Gaius Marius had no intention of keeping his position behind the rampart of corpses until they began to decompose, bringing germs and disease to his own men. He needed a decisive victory against the Germans, who remained camped on the far side of the river with Teutobod in command, and he was obliged to find a way to force them to take some action.

By the time another day had gone by, knowing that Manius Aquillius would have had plenty of time to get his ambush party into position, Marius decided to induce battle.

Firstly though, he would address his troops. This has always been a normal component of a battle plan, right up until medieval battles, where the commander, or King, would ride along the front of the waiting soldiers, wearing all his decorations, or his crown if he had one, in order to show himself to his gathered forces.[24] It is unlikely that many of the men could hear anything that was shouted at them by their commander at those times, but it was enough for them to see him, glittering in the sunlight, obviously fearless and eager for battle, and full of encouragement. It was a great morale booster, though in Marius' case on that particular day it would hardly be needed. The Romans were, for once, confident of victory over the barbarians due to their recent defeat of the Ambrones and, knowing that they were led by the best of commanders, would probably be eager to get on with it.

Gaius Marius' six legions moved slowly out of their camp and down the slope. Teutobod came out to meet them with his vanguard, which immediately fell under the unleashed Roman pila. It was to be a gruelling battle, for the Teutones were no cowards and they were now fighting for their survival. They kept on coming towards the Romans, thousand after thousand of them, but when it seemed that they could not be contained, Manius Aquillius and his 4,000 troops arrived at the German rear and slaughtered it.[25] The Teutones were thrown into confusion by the rearward attack and the battle became a rout. By the afternoon the vast majority of the Teutones were dead.

The reports said that around 37,000 superbly trained Romans had succeeded in defeating over 100,000 Germans in two engagements. Teutobod was said to be among the fallen.

There were around 17,000 surviving warriors, together with thousands of women and children who were to go into slavery. It was also later reported that several hundred of the German women committed suicide, rather than face a life of slavery, killing their children also.[26] The spoils from the sale of slaves were customarily for the General to keep, but in this case Gaius Marius donated the profits from the sales to his officers and soldiers. It was an act which was to add to the lustre of his name so far as his men were concerned.

Rome, on hearing the news of the triumph against the barbarians went wild with relief. The courageous Manius Aquillius was deputed to carry the good news and it must have been an immensely proud moment for him to face the Senators with such a good result, after Rome had had time to become very concerned about invasion. Gaius Marius, as an act of gratitude on the part of Rome, was again voted Senior Consul in absentia, for the following year, (101 BC), for his fourth Consulship, with Manius Aquillius as his Junior Consul. The Senate also voted for a three-day Thanksgiving, so great was the general relief at Rome's deliverance. The battle of Aquae Sextiae is still commemorated by the local name of the area, as Mont St. Victoire.[27]

Meanwhile, Boiorix and the Cimbri were still encamped by the Padus River. Boiorix had good reason to become depressed when the news reached him of the total defeat of his erstwhile allies the Ambrones and the Teutones by Gaius Marius. He was now alone with his Cimbri, as the Tigurini, the Marcomanni and the Cherusci had left him. He still had enough Cimbri to conquer Italy with, but the famed alliance of the tribes had fractured and dissolved.

Ironically, if he and his people had decided to stay in the region of the Padus, they might actually have been left in peace there by the Romans, and been able to form something of a new homeland there. It was an area where the rivers ran east to west, and they and the Apennines divided the land in Italian Gaul from the rest of Italy, making it an awkward and uneconomic area for Italy proper to use at that time. However, the land had been finally eaten clean by the vast numbers of animals the Cimbri still had with them, not to mention the food requirements of the people themselves, and by the following summer it was obvious that they were going to have to make a move.

By July of 101 BC the Cimbri were headed along the banks of the Padus, moving towards Placentia. Unfortunately for them, at Placentia now lay the Roman army, consisting of 54,000 men under Gaius Marius. With him also by then in Italian Gaul were Quintus Lutatius Catulus Caesar, and Lucius Cornelius Sulla.

The opposing sides met on the Raudine Plain, near to the settlement of Vercellae, not far from the Po. It was 30 July and the Cimbri were now ready for a battle, being only too aware that they were at bay. According to their custom, their King Boiorix sent word to Gaius Marius to ask him to settle a time and place. Marius did so, naming the following day, and the Plain itself, ideal battle conditions for the Roman army. Marius fought an infantry engagement, as at Aquae Sextiae, with his men split up into two lots of 15,000 each. Catulus Caesar and 24,000 of the less experienced troops were to form the centre. Marius took the left wing, with Sulla in charge of the cavalry on the right.

The battle is said to have been started by Marius taking the Cimbri by surprise. Trying to recover itself, the Cimbric cavalry moved towards the right, perhaps hoping to draw the Romans with them, exposing them to the infantry, who were to attack from behind.[28]

Marius managed to deflect this movement by halting his own troops and taking the first full brunt of the cavalry charge. Fortunately, as it was still early morning, and Marius had sensibly formed up his lines facing west, it was the Cimbri who had to fight with the sun in their eyes. It was another occasion where the far superior training of the Roman troops, both infantry and cavalry, were to tell only too plainly. The Cimbrian cavalry, though impressive to look at, found themselves completely out of their depth against the Roman cavalry, led by Sulla. In the dense morning mist, they were soon in hand to hand combat with a stronger and more highly trained force and were thrown back onto their own infantry. Once again also, the heat of the battlefield worked against the barbarians, as the mist began to clear and the full strength of the sun bore down on them. By noon the warriors of the Cimbri were defeated. The Roman losses were comparatively few, being estimated at less than 1,000 killed, but the Cimbri were annihilated, with approximately 100,000 warriors killed. King Boiorix fell fighting bravely with his men.[29]

The thousands of wagons, cattle and horses, could not be mustered quickly, and those who were closest to the alpine passes managed to get away, while the others did not. Again, many women, rejecting the idea of a life of captivity, committed suicide after killing their children, but even so around 60,000 women, together with another 20,000 surviving warriors, were sold to the slavers.

The Tigurini, who had remained in the passes of the Alps waiting for word, then fled taking the news of the defeat. Those who managed to escape up the Vale of the Salassi through the Lugdunum Pass, including the surviving free Cimbri, then had to face the Celts, being attacked by the Allobroges and the Sequani. Perhaps only as many as 2,000 Cimbri finally managed to reach what was left of the Atuatuci and finally joined them, to settle eventually where the Mosa River reached the Sabis. It was a truly pitiful number of survivors, from a terrifying host which had once been 750,000 strong.

It was reported that Gaius Marius, after the battle, immediately granted Roman citizenship to his Italian Allied troops, without consulting with the Senate first. When he was later questioned about the action, his reply was that in the heat of battle he could not distinguish the voices of true Romans from the voices of their Italian Allies! From that time onwards all Italian legions would be classed as Roman legions automatically.[30]

The wonderful news of the decisive success at Vercellae was taken to Rome by Gaius Julius Caesar, the husband of Aurelia Cotta, who in the following year would become the mother of their only son, another Gaius Julius Caesar who would in his turn briefly rule the known world.

However, despite the general rejoicing at the good news, many of the Senate were very unhappy at the idea of Gaius Marius yet again being voted in for the Consulship – his fifth and again in absentia. It was beginning to look far more like a dictatorship than a consulship! Some people began to applaud the role of Catulus during the engagement, at Marius' expense, claiming the victory as his, especially as Marius had generously allowed Catulus Caesar to keep the captured Cimbric standards.

It was then suggested that there should be two Triumphs for the successful commanders, one for Gaius Marius in celebration of his success at Aquae Sextiae, and another for Catulus for his supposed success at Vercellae. This would, of course, give Catulus the appearance of having had the greater success as Vercellae had been the more decisive battle.

Lucius Appuleius Saturninus did speak out in defence of Marius' greater achievement, but still the proposed two Triumphs were voted in. When Gaius Marius was given the news he was naturally displeased at the idea of taking the lesser share of the glory which he had achieved for them all. He dealt with the situation by informing the Senate that he was prepared to share just one Triumph between himself and Catulus. This, of course, would mean that Marius' Triumphing would completely extinguish that of Catulus Caesar. All the ordinary Romans would be only too well aware who the true victor was.

Catulus took his revenge by accusing Gaius Marius of usurping the prerogative of the Senate by awarding the citizenship to the Allies after Vercallae, without even allowing the Senate the chance of discussing the matter, let alone granting permission for the action. In retaliation Marius then announced that he intended to found a new colony of his Roman veteran troops at Eporedia in Italian Gaul. It was then claimed, ridiculously, that the only reason Marius had for wanting the colony there was so that he could get his hands on the local gold, which was commonly mined from the riverbed at Eporedia!

This childish quarrelling between the two commanders may well have caused amusement in the Senate, but it was to pinpoint a problem that Gaius Marius would have to face for the rest of his career. He was an inspired soldier, a brilliant general, but a soldier pure and simple. He was not naturally a politician. However, it was in the political arena that he would in future be obliged to spend the majority of his time.

It must have been very frustrating indeed for such a straightforward man to have to learn to deal with the twists and turns of the political elite in Rome, many of whom still believed him to be of a lower social caste, despite his obvious achievements. Ironically, it would be Sulla who would eventually prove to be more fitted to a political role, into which he would step with confidence. This acknowledgement of having to struggle against those who did not wish to see him succeed as well in Rome as he had done with the armies was to alter Marius' temperament. It was coupled with another fact that he would soon have to face, which was that he was a man who was beginning to age, and that despite all that he had done it was obvious that his great career had now peaked.

There would soon begin to grow between Gaius Marius and his young protégée Sulla a strong resentment, which would sour their relationship and end their friendship for good. Also, at around this time, Sulla was to become a widower with the death of his first wife. Whatever the actual legal relationship between himself and Marius, due to their marriages, it too was now severed.

It is not unusual for a master to enjoy helping a protégée to make his start in life, especially when for some reason a promising young man had been held back, as Sulla had been, initially, by his lack of money. At first, Marius would doubtless have seen similarities between Sulla and himself. They could both achieve great success if only they were not prevented from doing so by others – in Marius' case by a lack of social standing, which he had had to ameliorate by the 'purchase' of an acceptable wife.

However, when there is a substantial difference in age, as with Marius and Sulla, it is inevitable that the older man should begin to see his own career, however successful it may have been, reach its peak and then decline. He must then watch his younger colleague advance, perhaps even beyond him. This is often far harder for anyone to accept, especially in Marius' case as he was then facing strong opposition in the Senate. There were many people there who, while glad enough to enjoy the safety from invasion that he had achieved for them, would be still only too happy to snap at his heels once he had to live and work in their closed and claustrophobic environment, rather than his own.

Sulla's efforts at Vercellae were also slightly harder for the Senate to ignore than his other work on Rome's behalf, and it was becoming obvious that he would soon have to have some kind of political career.[31] It must have been very difficult for Marius, with his own strong sense of self-worth, together with his belief that he still had a great deal to offer, being expected to begin to take a back seat, and perhaps even admit that his best days were behind him. It was, in my opinion, the accumulation of such dissatisfaction and frustration which was to sour and destroy their friendship after Vercellae.

Chapter Six

By this time, Sulla had remarried, presumably due to the death of his first wife, as there is no record of a divorce at this point. Marriage was an accepted necessity, particularly to a man whose ambitions and energies would have to be directed elsewhere. Sulla needed to concentrate on his career, now both military and political. Any paterfamilias would require that his children were brought up correctly, and, although any child at that level of society would be well attended to, and educated by servants of various kinds, mere physical attention was simply not enough.

His second wife was named Aelia. She may have been a relative of Lucius Aelius Stilo, (150–75 BC) who was known as a writer and a Stoic and who was a member of the Equestrian Order. Or, alternatively, she may have been of the family of Lucius Aelius Tubero, who was a friend and relative by marriage of Marcus Tullius Cicero. Lucius Aelius Tubero was to be appointed Governor of Africa Province in 48 BC but was later to be excluded by the Senate.

These were decent and respectable family connections, but it was hardly a wonderful match. At this time of his life Sulla was concentrating on trying to make a start on the political side of his career, and he would have to have a wife to attend to his household and bring up his children in the correct way. Despite the number of servants/slaves in any patrician household, no man would wish to leave the upbringing and education of his children entirely in servants' hands. Such an arrangement would certainly bring with it the risk that the children would grow up into little Greeks, or little Gauls, being influenced by the social and religious ideas of whatever origins the servants may have stemmed from.

A wife of suitable position and excellent reputation would ensure that the children were brought up properly, as little Romans, and imbued with proper Roman thinking. It did not, of course, mean that it was necessary for him to have any particular attachment to the lady, provided that she was appropriate for the role assigned to her.

However, affection between husband and wife was quite often achieved, and Sulla was to find in his future third wife, Caecilia Metella Dalmatica, a woman of not only exalted ancestry but also someone to whom he openly showed partiality, deference and respect. Regarding this second marriage, however, we are told little, and do not get to know his wife. We can only assume that she was for him something of a stopgap, someone to supervise his household and attend to his children competently, while his attentions were engaged elsewhere.

It might be useful to note at this point that most histories claim that Sulla had two other wives between his first one, Julia, and his eventual marriage to Caecilia Metella. I do not, however, agree with this reading of the situation.[1]

Plutarch states that Sulla was married to the woman named Aelia, (whose suggested relatives have been given above), but also a little later to another woman, named Cloelia, about whom nothing at all is recorded. Likewise, whatever is supposed to have happened to Aelia is glossed over. General opinion usually seems to follow this line, although I consider it to be a mistake.

I firmly believe that these two women are one and the same. I do not accept that Sulla, as his career advanced, would marry into two such relatively insignificant families, who would be able to do very little for him, and whose members would not be able to advance his children in the future. That he did do so once is a matter of record, and the family connections of Aelia suggest that she was a perfectly reasonable choice, in the circumstances in which he found himself at that time. However, I cannot accept that he would enter into such an unprofitable union a second time.

He would eventually take the opportunity of divorcing this second wife Aelia, allegedly for barrenness, just after Caecilia Metella became available, after the death of her elderly husband, Marcus Aemilius Scaurus, the Princeps Senatus, in 89 BC. This merely shows that he was awaiting a more favourable match, with perhaps a more equal spouse.

That this misinformation seems to stem from Plutarch also needs a little explanation. Firstly, the names Aelia and Cloelia seem to me to be rather similar, and the fact that no family information at all is given about either of the ladies is strange. There was certainly an extended family of Aelius, to one of whose branches a wife named Aelia may well have belonged. There is no trace of a family connection for the supposed Cloelia, which in the somewhat claustrophobic atmosphere of patrician Roman society makes the existence of the lady rather suspect. Also, Plutarch had already given the name of Sulla's first wife as Ilia, which is generally considered to be an error. Historians commonly read this as referring to a Julia. If he is capable of making such a mistake once, I see no reason why a second such problem with the lady's name cannot have arisen. Plutarch is, unfortunately, not as reliable a chronicler as is often suggested.[2]

Though he is still sometimes represented as being a great authority on Roman affairs, a man of consular rank, a tutor to Trajan and a one-time governor of Greece, these qualifications are not based on recorded fact.

He was, in actual fact, a Theban provincial whose visits to Rome were generally quite short. He says of the matter, 'while there I had no leisure to study or exercise the Latin tongue.' He was born in Chaeronea in 46 BC which he describes as, 'my poor little town, where I remained willingly and was loath to leave.' It would seem, therefore, that a good deal of his writing is not only hearsay, which is understandable, but also rather confused hearsay at that. Perhaps that is the reason why there seems to be some difficulty over the proper names and family connections, and even the number, of Sulla's wives.

Therefore, at risk of labouring the point, I contend that after the death of Sulla's first wife, who was a Julia, he was then married to a woman named Aelia, of a perfectly respectable, though not particularly outstanding, patrician Roman family. This lady was later to be divorced, rather suddenly, but not altogether surprisingly, when a later opportunity for the more desirable and advantageous match with Caecilia Metella Dalmatica became available. It was reported, again by Plutarch, that the unwanted wife was sent off 'honourably and with expressions of respect and with gifts' from Sulla.[3]

Whether their divorce was amicable or otherwise, this manoeuvring does, however, serve to show that Sulla's ambitions were still very strong and very active, and that he was prepared to grasp whatever opportunity presented itself to improve his situation and that of his immediate family. An impressive marriage has always been evidence of one's rise in the world and Sulla was to show that he would eventually be quite prepared to jettison the lesser match when the greater one presented itself. This action was, however, something that many other men of his class would probably well understand and perhaps even sympathize with. There were few people who, in such a situation, would not take advantage of the better arrangement, if it offered itself.

This is shown clearly by Gaius Marius, in a similar situation, having divorced his first wife when the opportunity arose to marry a Julia. Also by Gnaeus Pompeius Magnus, who also divorced his first wife when he was offered the chance to marry an Aemilia Scaura, the second union being a far better match for him socially.[4] Therefore, Sulla's divorce of Aelia in such circumstances, while appearing self-serving or even unkind to modern opinion was quite understandable to his peers. It was, in fact, perfectly in tune with the attitudes of his time.

However, after Vercellae, Sulla was still married to this lady, Aelia, and was planning his rise up the political ladder in Rome itself. Normally, one's political career would begin with an aedileship. Aediles were responsible, among other things, for public games, which was always an opportunity to put oneself forward by lavish expenditure in an attempt to have the public's gratitude when higher office was sought.[5] It was also unfortunately often a short road to bankruptcy, but spending money was one of the ways in which a politician made his name and kept his face before the public – then as now. Four aediles would be elected, two plebian aediles and two curule aediles. The plebian aediles were elected by the Plebian Assembly, and did not have imperium, while the curule aediles were elected by the Assembly of the People and did possess the much sought after imperium.[6] They were generally responsible for the care of Rome's streets, water supplies, drains, general traffic, markets, weights and measures and the grain supplies, but of course the games were the way in which they put themselves in the public eye and hopefully gained popularity for the future.

Sulla, though, was in a hurry, probably only too aware that he had started on his course rather late compared with other men, and he wished to skip the aedileship altogether, which in any case did not lead up the Cursus Honorum in itself. He was aiming instead at going straight for one of the praetorships of 98 BC. A praetorship was the second most senior rung on the senatorial ladder, and the position carried with it imperium, which gave a man a particular authority and power, providing he was acting within the rules of his office. The outward sign of this authority was the presence of his lictors, carrying the fasces, or thin birch rods bound with strips of leather, and these lictors would attend the magistrate as he went about his daily business. A curule aedile would normally be attended by two of these bodyguards, a praetor by six and a consul by twelve. A dictator, when there was one, would be attended by no less than twenty-four![7]

Of course, any attempt at political office involves canvassing for public support. Sulla was able to recommend himself on the strength of his military record, which was the usual way to attract attention. However, Gaius Marius, and also Catulus, (along with their friends), were active in extolling their own virtues, and it must be remembered that, despite Sulla's undoubted achievements in the field, he had been only a junior officer, whose superiors were officially given credit for any accomplishments. Therefore, his vigorous attempt to interest the voters in his cause failed. Many people were by then in favour of Sulla's campaign for political office generally, it was only to be expected, but there was still a feeling that he ought to have gone for the aedileship first.

However, refusing to be put off, the following year he applied again and once again aimed straight for the praetorship. On this second occasion, he did not use his military record as an attempt at inducement, but decided to appeal to the baser instincts of the voters – he let it be known that if he were elected as praetor he would give them wonderful games![8] Perhaps many of them remembered – or were subtly reminded – that he still had a firm friendship with King Bocchus, who might be favourably inclined to provide beasts from Africa for those games. This seemed to do the trick, and he was elected as Urban Praetor for 97 BC.[9]

There were apparently two incidents which marked Sulla's year of office as Urban Praetor. One of these was a quarrel with Caesar Strabo, (who was a relative through his first wife), during which Sulla was accused of using bribery in the acquisition of his office.[10] This was a not unusual accusation and Caesar Strabo was considered, and certainly considered himself, to be something of a wit, therefore a clever aside was always valuable ammunition. Also unfortunately slander and other such behaviour was far from uncommon in Roman politics. It did, however, cause Sulla to lose his temper with him, which did little for any future relationship between them.

More important was the holding of the games, which Sulla had promised to his supporters. These games were the Ludi Appolinaris (which had originally been established by an ancestor of Sulla's). They were initially celebrated on 13 July each year, but by the end of the Republic they extended from 6 July to 13 July.[11] (The regular public games were the responsibility of the aediles, the Ludi Plebei being in the hands of the plebian aediles and the two curule aediles being in charge of the others.) This excluded the Ludi Appolinares and would also, after 81 BC, exclude the Ludi Victoriae Sullae, Sulla's own victory games, which remained under the supervision of the urban praetor.[12] The Ludi Appolinaris was, of course, held in honour of the God Apollo.

Sulla, like many of his contemporaries, was a follower of this god, and it is one instance in which his strong religious feeling comes to the fore. Sulla was later to regularly carry on his person a small image of Apollo, although he was not exclusively devoted to this deity. Later in his life he was to show far more devotion to Venus, after whom he named his Pompeiian colony, and especially to Fortuna, who he believed stood with him and protected him throughout his life.[13]

After Sulla's year as urban praetor was finished, he was sent to Cilicia. There was a serious problem with pirates in the area, and it is commonly assumed that he was sent there to deal with this. However, he was not in Cilicia for long when he received different instructions from Rome. King Mithradates of Pontus had expelled King Ariobarzanes from the throne of Cappodocia. Sulla's task was to restore Ariobarzanes.[14]

Mithradates was the traditional name of the Kings of Pontus, and there were six kings who used the name, the last of whom was the most famous. The royal house of the Mithradatae claimed its descent from Darius the Great of Persia. Pontus itself was a large state, which stood at the south eastern end of the Euxine Sea (the present Black Sea).[15]

It is necessary at this point to regress a little in order to explain the problem to Rome posed by King Mithradates of Pontus. While Gaius Marius and Sulla were still engaged in Gaul with Catulus Caesar, Mithradates had begun to cause dissention in the east.

Rome had had for almost fifty years a treaty with Bithynia, which was a fertile and prosperous kingdom, ruled by a series of kings of Thracian origin. It stood on the north eastern side of the Aegean Sea, extending east to Paphlagonia and south towards Phrygia. For generations this kingdom had enjoyed the status of Friend and Ally of the Roman People, and its traditional enemy was Pontus. It was, of course, a very tempting prize for someone with territorial ambitions, such as Mithradates VI.

He decided to attempt to gain for himself the enviable treaty with Rome. As Rome could not, of course, make treaties with two kings who were at odds with each other, the idea would not normally be considered. However, Mithradates had sent an embassage to Rome with the intention of bribing Senators to support his request. If successful, that would naturally mean that the treaty with Bithynia would have to be abandoned, leaving the area without Roman protection, a situation ideal for his purposes. That some of the Senators were actually considering making this move and wavering in their traditional loyalties, in the face of the offered substantial bribes, incensed one Lucius Appuleius Saturninus. He then accused Marcus Aemilius Scaurus, by name, of accepting bribes from Mithradates, and condemned in the Senate all those others who were also preparing to abandon King Nicomedes of Bithynia in favour of his enemy.

This animosity between Saturninus and Scaurus was due to an old quarrel dating back to 104 BC, when Saturninus had been Quaestor in charge of grain supplies at Ostia. He had been dismissed from that post in order to be replaced by Scaurus. Saturninus was a man who seemed to invite controversy, as in 103 BC he was the Tribune who passed a law granting Gaius Marius' land allotments for his African army. In 101 BC he had been responsible for organizing a mob to break up a meeting of the Assembly where he had been accused of insulting earlier ambassadors sent by Mithradates of Pontus. Before he was re-elected as Tribune in 100 BC he had united with one Gaius Servilius Glaucia in order to again stir up the mobs.[16]

Therefore it could be said that he was already well-known for rabble rousing, though in this instance he may have been in the right, as Mithradates VI was to prove a thorn in the side of Rome for some considerable time to come. While Rome had been deeply occupied in Gaul, Mithradates had made a temporary alliance with Nicomedes IV of Bithynia and together they had divided Paphlagonia. Though the Senate had remonstrated with the kings, it was given various excuses and, desperate to deal with the far greater and more pressing problem of Gaul, it was obliged to accept those excuses and leave the matter as it was for the time being.

However, getting away with his division of Paphlagonia had obviously encouraged Mithradates to go further, and he turned his attention next towards Cappodocia. The alliance between himself and Nicomedes did not last, as Nicomedes of Bithynia had tried to establish himself in Cappodocia by marrying the queen. However, around 100 BC Mithradates had driven him out and installed one of his own sons, Ariarathes, on the throne, together with a regent named Gordius. Both sides of the case were put to Rome, (in 98 BC), and the area was declared to be free of the authority of kings from either side. The Cappadocians then asked for the privilege of choosing their own king, and in 97 BC had decided to install one Ariobarzanes as their ruler. No sooner was this arranged, than Mithradates of Pontus promptly chased out the new king. After news of this action was known in Rome, Sulla received his instructions to deal with Mithradates, by expelling the Pontic regent from the area and restoring Ariobarzanes to the throne of Cappadocia. By force, if necessary.[17]

This was, of course, easier said than done, as Sulla had not gone into the area to wage a war against such an opponent. He had insufficient troops with him for one thing and was obliged to call upon Asian allies to make good the deficiency, in accordance with their treaties of friendship with Rome. Therefore, with troops eventually raised in this manner, he was able to make an attempt against Mithradates' regent in Cappadocia.

He then came up for the first time against a man named Archelaus, who was a Greek mercenary general in the pay of Mithradates, sent to support Gordius. He was a very accomplished soldier and Mithradates was said to have the utmost confidence in him. Sulla, unfortunately, was still without enough men to take on the full might of Pontus in his hastily assembled campaign. He was obliged to ask for an armistice on that occasion, with the intention of signing a proper peace treaty, rather than suffer a defeat at the hands of an opponent who had had the time to become far better prepared.[18]

This was not, however, the end of the matter, for during the remainder of the campaign Sulla was successful in driving Gordius out of the area and replacing the new King Ariobarzanes on his throne. He also disposed of many of the Cappodocians who had approved of the pro-Pontic takeover, settling the country down peaceably.

This whole matter is hugely to Sulla's credit. He was, at short notice, instructed to move to an area of conflict, after gathering together troops in sufficient numbers to make some sort of a show against the armies of Pontus. The details of the engagements are very few, but what is known is that he then succeeded in restoring Ariobarzanes to his throne, which was the will of the majority of the Cappodocians. He had, with scant forces, advanced against an army which was not only numerically far superior to his own, but was also far more familiar with the very difficult terrain, and had skilfully routed them.

The Romans amongst his troops were sufficiently impressed with his daring and ability to have hailed him as Imperator on the field, which was an honour reserved for commanders who had distinguished themselves in a great victory. (In order to gain the permission of the senate to celebrate a Triumph, it was necessary for a general to be able to claim that his troops had indeed at some point after the campaign hailed him Imperator on the field.)[19]

The success actually had far reaching effects, for Sulla's movements had brought him to the banks of the Euphrates, where he was attended by ambassadors from Parthia. This was a country on the east of the Caspian Sea, which had grown into a large and influential empire. However, the Parthians were unused to Romans at that time. They were merely intent on establishing friendly relations with any other empire which looked as if it might one day be able to attack them, and Sulla's achievements must have given them the idea that Rome was about to move towards them in a menacing way. They were particularly concerned about Armenia, where they had a protégé in Tigranes II, the new ruler.

This man, the son of Tigranes I, had been a prisoner of the Parthians for some time, and they had only given him back his father's throne in return for a good slice of his territory. They also, to cement the enforced alliance, married him to a daughter of Mithradates VI, which made him very much the puppet of Pontus.[20] They had worked together over the Cappadocian takeover bid, which had caused Sulla to intervene in the area initially, although how much Tigranes wanted to be involved was debatable. No doubt being a released prisoner and son-in-law of Mithradates gave him little choice in the matter. However, he was to go on to rule over Armenia until 56 BC, attacking Parthia in 83 BC. He founded Tigranocerta as his new capitol in south-western Armenia and filled it with the displaced people he had defeated in Soli and Mazaca. However, his alliance with Mithradates of Pontus would eventually lead him into conflict with Rome in 69 BC when firstly Lucullus and then Pompeius Magnus defeated him and split him from his father-in-law clutches, eventually leaving him only with the Armenia he had started with.

However, for the moment Sulla was in the ascendant in the area. He was requested to attend an interview with the ambassadors, to which he agreed, but he staged the meeting carefully and with an unerring eye for show. He had arranged three chairs, placing King Ariobarzanes on one side and the Parthian ambassador on the other, keeping the centre and most important one for himself. This is often interpreted as being a calculated insult to the other two men, in demonstrating that Sulla ranked above them, although this is a ridiculous assumption. Sulla had already shown that he was a diplomat of no mean order and in any case had nothing to prove. He would simply have been, as always, keen to impress the power of Rome on people as yet unfamiliar with it. In such circumstances it would be most important for the Roman emissary to show power and prestige to foreigners. That a psychological advantage would have been gained by the arrangement is undoubted and that also would be a requirement. It did, in fact, have one unfortunate outcome, in that the Parthian ambassador was executed on his return home, for the fault of allowing the Roman general to put him at a disadvantage. But that could hardly be attributed to any fault of Sulla's, rather that a despot was behaving despotically. Despite this action of petty cruelty, the Parthian king had nothing to complain about regarding the result of the talks, as it was decided that the Euphrates should become the boundary between the two countries, which is just what Parthia had hoped for in the first instance.

However, there was another outcome of the meeting, which was to affect Sulla's own life. In the entourage of the Parthian ambassador there was a Chaldean seer. These were a priestly caste of diviners and were greatly respected for their abilities and the accuracy of their predictions. One of these men did a 'reading' for Sulla, during which he expressed great astonishment that Sulla had not yet attained the position of being one of the world's greatest men. He also made the pronouncement that Sulla would indeed achieve the highest position and would die while at the pinnacle of his fame. Sulla, with his belief in such prophecies, would no doubt have been delighted at the idea that he would reach the highest honours and would furthermore have the blessings of the gods in his endeavours.[21]

Sulla, from this time onwards, believed implicitly in the protection and divine assistance he would derive from Fortuna. Not only for the tangible benefits he could receive if he had the goddess' approval, but also because the Romans believed that to have such assistance and regard implied that a man must actually deserve such honours. It implied that he was therefore a good and decent man, whose actions were not at fault. Later historians did, of course, argue against this, when they accused Sulla of all kinds of evil and cruelty. But, in his own day, the matter was considered quite differently and Sulla would certainly not have imagined himself to be a bad man, even if he was sometimes forced into actions which might be unfortunate in their results.

Certainly it was accepted that if the gods thought that any of a man's actions were unworthy, they could easily withdraw their approval and assistance, and for Sulla it appeared that they never did.

This must have given him a wonderful boost of confidence. It was probably at this time that he considered the title 'Felix' for himself, and may actually have used it almost like a lucky charm, although it was not officially confirmed as a cognomen until a decree of the Senate in 82 BC.[22] It may seem that to assume such a cognomen as 'Fortunate' was arrogant in the extreme, although Gnaeus Pompeius was later to call himself Magnus or 'Great' at a very young age when he had hardly done anything to justify it. However, although Sulla's good luck was not to be either continuous or unbroken, yet it was to endure, usually coming to the fore when he behaved with daring and even impetuous courage.[23] Plutarch tells us that Sulla stated that no planned military enterprise of his ever succeeded so well as those he undertook when he was relying on the impulse of the moment. For a man of his exemplary military record it is an astonishing remark, but one which clearly shows that Sulla leaned heavily on the idea that his good fortune rested on the goodwill and support of the gods, and of Fortuna herself in particular. It was an idea which was always to give him great strength of purpose and particularly a degree of certainty in the rightness of his actions which sustained him throughout his future career.

It is not clear how long Sulla spent in the east after he received the prophecy which was to have such an effect on his life. It was probably not until some time in 93 BC that he was able to return to Rome.[24] However, he would have had good reason to feel pleased with the outcome of his governorship in Cilicia. Not only had he stepped in and performed efficiently when conflict presented itself, but he was the first Roman governor to meet with an embassy from Parthia, which had brought with it a treaty of friendship.

However, once back in Rome the usual criticisms began to present themselves, with one Gaius Marcius Censorinus attempting to bring an action against him alleging that he had taken money from Ariobarzanes. On the day appointed for the matter to be dealt with by trial the accuser declined to appear, and the matter was dropped, making it seem rather odd that it was brought in the first place – perhaps Censorinus simply had no real evidence to present. On the other hand, merely bringing such an action into the public domain left a blemish, and such a stain tended to stick to the person accused. Perhaps that was the true reason behind it. It was obvious that Sulla would make an attempt at the Consulship before long and any mud thrown in advance might be useful in making the electors think twice. Later Censorinus would show himself to be a foe of Sulla's and Sulla would eventually be obliged to deal with him accordingly, but it was from this abortive attempt to cause him embarrassment that the enmity stemmed. However, there could also be another reason.

Gaius Marius had for some time been estranged from Sulla. The old comfortable working relationship had fractured and broken. It is a reasonable assumption that Marius had developed an obsessive jealousy over Sulla's successes, all the more annoying at a time when he was growing older and might have to expect slightly less from his own future. Surely, when he had achieved the Consulship more times than any other man in history, he could have been content with his own undoubted achievements? However, human nature is often not so pragmatic. That Sulla seemed to be going onward and ever upward must have been an irritant to a man who certainly knew that only his own fortuitous marriage to a woman of impeccable lineage had allowed him to progress at all. He had always been something of an outsider in Rome's political circles and always would be.

Certainly, whatever Sulla's problems, his birth would not hold him back as Marius' own background had done. That he still had ambitions with regard to the east was unfortunate, bearing in mind his increasing age and the obvious fact that younger men were rising fast through the ranks and that many of them would soon be able to take over.

It is a sad fact of human nature that it can be very galling to see another man begin to emulate one's success and to know that one will be expected to step aside. When any young man no longer needs his mentor it is unfortunate but it happens far too regularly to be remarkable. Throughout history the examples are numerous. In our own country we have two very well-known instances, in Warwick the Kingmaker who became the deadly enemy of Edward IV, when that King chose his own wife (albeit a lady who was highly unsuitable in many ways), without reference to the man who had done everything for him. Also in the case of Thomas, Cardinal Wolsey, being set aside by Henry VIII when the King decided that the man who had shaped him was no longer prepared to agree with him completely and he therefore had become surplus to requirements.

We have no real idea whether or not Sulla felt any regret at the ending of his friendship with Gaius Marius. That Sulla was an unusually loyal man to his friends may well give us a clue, and perhaps he did feel some sense of loss. However, he was also a man who looked to the future and had great confidence in his own abilities, so he would have been able to shake off any sense of blame in the matter.

Unfortunately, Gaius Marius was, at this time, becoming generally rather erratic in his relationships. He had earlier formed an uneasy friendship with Lucius Appuleius Saturninus over the provision of the land allocations for the veterans, but by the year 100 BC the actions of Saturninus and his friend and associate Gaius Servilius Glaucia had become unsavoury to say the least. Saturninus' propensity for violence had apparently increased by the time he was elected Tribune (for the third time) in 99 BC and he had supported Glaucia's candidacy for the Consulship for that year. Gaius Marius then suddenly turned against his old associates and declared that Glaucia's candidacy was illegal.[25]

Saturninus used the often-recurring problem of a shortage of grain to incite the mobs and was then to organize the murder of an opponent of Glaucia's, one Gaius Memmius, immediately after which he pushed a law through the Plebian Assembly declaring Glaucia's candidacy legal again. Riots began in Rome and Marcus Aemilius Scaurus was forced to issue the Senatus Consultum de Republica Defendenda, or the Ultimate Decree, in effect martial law, to settle the situation.[26] This decree enabled the authorities to use all and any means to put an end to the deepening crisis.

Gaius Marius, with an improvised force, rounded up the rioters in the Forum and managed to pen their leaders on the Capitol where they had retreated. From there they were transferred to the Curia, or Senate House, for safety until they could be dealt with properly. This was at a time when there was no real prison in Rome in which to keep prisoners secure, and must have been considered the best option available. However, during the night mobs climbed onto the roof of the Curia, and loosened and threw down the large and heavy terracotta tiles, into the space below in which the men were confined. They were unable to defend themselves against the rain of tiles and were all killed.

Their deaths enabled the Senate to declare that all the legislation that Saturninus had pushed through was then null and void as it had been carried out by the use of violence. Only too ironic, as he and his followers had just been murdered – but by whose order?

Did Gaius Marius send the men who had carried out the deed? It is unlikely that we will ever know, but the final action did solve the problem of what to do with those men. They were of decent birth, not rabble, despite their propensity for causing trouble. It would have been very awkward to have to bring them all to trial and prosecute them officially – and then what should be done with them? Could they all have been executed openly? It would have been a situation fraught with problems. As it was, the problems had been solved by a mysterious act of murder, whose instigator remains anonymous. That they had not actually been tried and condemned meant that their families could at least retrieve their bodies and give them decent burial and the matter was ended.

All in all, it may have been a satisfactory outcome, but perhaps it began to show Gaius Marius in a rather worrying light. Previously he had been a very straightforward type of man, who had never needed to descend to this kind of subterfuge. Now, it appeared that he was prepared to do whatever was necessary, and his obdurate attitude was to show itself again, even more worryingly, when Sulla would later be appointed to go to the east. This had always been Marius' own pet project and Marius would work furiously against Sulla behind his back in an attempt to replace him, to the great detriment of them both.

Certainly, by the time Sulla returned to Rome Gaius Marius had started a campaign of slander against him.[27] His meeting with the Parthian ambassador was now declared to be nothing more than an example of Sulla's vainglory and arrogance, rather than an attempt to impress the power of Rome on foreign nationals. Then another incident added fuel to the fire. In 91 BC Sulla's old friend King Bocchus innocently sent some statues to Rome for erection in the Forum. One of these was of Sulla.

No doubt Bocchus only wished to show respect in sending them, and the one of Sulla was merely intended to do honour to the man who had saved him from his domineering son-in-law Jugurtha. However Marius became furious and made it clear that he thought it showed only too clearly that Sulla was using it to try to claim all the credit for the Jugurthine war. He was determined to have the offending statue removed, even though it and the others had been erected with the permission of the Senate, while supporters of Sulla's did their best to prevent its removal. Open warfare was threatening to break out yet again in

Rome, when the problem of the Italian Allies came to the fore, taking attention away from the petty squabbling.

It almost makes one wonder whether Gaius Marius was beginning to suffer from some kind of mental problem, with his previous friendship for Sulla now turning to open hatred to such a degree. That political allies often separate and become rivals is commonplace, but for a man who had been celebrated for his integrity and common sense to descend to almost childish petulance in his efforts to cause embarrassment is a great pity.

Moreover, to attempt to put obstacles in the way of another man who, despite everything, always spoke of him with the greatest respect is not only a great pity but also a sad reflection of the degeneration sometimes caused by advancing age. Gaius Marius believed that he still had a great deal to offer to Rome. Perhaps in his own way he did – if he could have become the revered elder statesman he certainly could have been a great support and encouragement to the young men who would come after him.

Instead, by choosing to start a slanderous campaign against another soldier who had done well, as if he were consumed by envy of that man to the extent that he could no longer employ good judgement, he showed that he might not be quite so useful after all. That he had always worked very hard and had been under a tremendous amount of pressure was well known. Certainly since he had been in Rome, facing all the opposition that was really only to be expected from the patrician elite, his stress levels must have soared to a terrifying degree. This would surely have had some effect on him, and the obvious impatience and irritation he displayed is a dangerous symptom for any middle-aged man. His increasingly peremptory behaviour may well be evidence of this.

It is important to remember that after his sixth Consulship, Gaius Marius did not stand for election again for some considerable time. Was he ill during those intervening years? We do know of many of his movements at that period of his life, but he still appeared to keep a relatively low profile for a man who had for so long been at the forefront of affairs. He was to emerge again later as Sulla's implacable opponent, with his venom undiluted, when he tried to replace the younger man who had been sent on a campaign to deal with Mithradates. In the process he turned Rome itself into a battleground and was responsible for the deaths of many Roman citizens. A very unfortunate ending to what had certainly been a spectacular and most impressive career, unprecedented in its scale, which was still enough to make his name live on as one of the greatest of the Roman leaders.

Also, it was a sad ending to a relationship that had started with such promise and which had endured for several years with great success.

Chapter Seven

The social wars were to engage the attention of Rome from 91 to 88 BC but it would be truthful to say that the situation which led to them had already been simmering for some considerable time.

There had been sporadic trouble with the Italian Allies from as far back as 321 BC when the Samnites, with whom Rome had had difficulties for almost seventy years, had quite easily defeated a Roman army by trapping them in a gulch near Benuventum.[1] This went down in history as the Battle of the Caudine Forks. It was a humiliating disgrace for Rome, not only due to the defeat itself which was hard enough to take, but because the leader of the triumphant Samnites, Gavius Pontius, made the Romans pass under the yoke in exchange for their lives. For a Roman, suffering this degradation was almost worse than being killed in battle.

More recently, in 125 BC the Latin Rights community of Fregellae had revolted against Rome, which was an even greater pity, since up to that time Fregellae had had an unblemished record of loyalty to Rome.[2] In that instance perhaps recollections of the Caudine Forks prevailed, as there was a determination that a repeat of the outcome at Benuventum was not going to be allowed to happen. Therefore, the uprising at Fregellae was dealt with quickly and crushed by the praetor Lucius Opimius with extreme cruelty. Once the insurrection was over he reduced the town completely, from which it never recovered. However, the problem had not gone away. On the contrary, it had festered.

It all stemmed from the traditional Roman viewpoint of who was and was not considered to be a citizen. A Roman man free born in Rome, however humble, was a citizen, although a man born elsewhere, however worthy, was generally not. In some cases a man could be granted citizenship, as a special concession and it was also often done for people who had been of great value to Rome, Gaius Marius being a perfect example of this. Born in 157 BC into a substantial family in Arpinum, he rose to be considered one of the founders of Rome, due to his wonderful career in the army. However, as we have seen, even he faced opposition from the Roman purists, and even his attainment of the Consulship for more years than any other man had ever achieved, or would ever achieve, was still not sufficient to give him a smooth ride in the Senate. The old guard of Senators never fully accepted him and never would, while some of them actually hated him.

There were several men like him in Rome, and even in the Senate itself, men whose worthiness had earned them the privilege of becoming a full citizen or whose families had been honoured in the past. There were among them Lucius Calpurnius Piso, the two branches of the Pompeius family, Rufus and Strabo, (whose son Gnaeus Pompeius Magnus would soon be a force in his own right), along with Titus Labienus and the Saufeius and Apuleius families. However, these remained exceptions. The vast majority of the men born in the towns from which their families originally came were not considered Roman citizens, and were granted none of the associated rights.

Some towns achieved the status of Latin Rights. This meant that they were considered somewhere between the two extremes, second class citizens instead of third. For a town to hold the Latin Rights gave the residents the prerogative of being able to legally marry a full Roman citizen, or of being able to engage in a legal contract with one. Also of being able to claim legal protection for any such contract, preventing it being declared void. The Latin Rights also gave the right of appeal against criminal convictions, but did not provide the right to vote in any Roman election, nor the right to sit on a Roman jury. In short, it was a typical Roman ploy to soothe ruffled feelings in certain areas, without actually having to concede the full citizenship.[3]

After the destruction of Fregellae, a Tribune of the Plebs had initiated a law which allowed the magistrates of Latin Rights communities to assume the full citizenship for themselves and also for their direct descendants. Although that benefited the magisterial families themselves, it did nothing at all for the wider community, who remained what they had always been – second class citizens.

Better, though, than being third class, which was exactly what most of the rest of Italy remained. It was a manifestly unfair arrangement. The Italian Allies, as the rest of the country was referred to, consisted of nations who lived on the Italian peninsula without having either the Roman citizenship or the Latin Rights. These large numbers of people were required by Rome to provide soldiers, properly armed at their own expense, for the armies of Rome and they also bore the brunt of the general taxation. Much of their land would have, at one time or another, been taken to become part of the *ager publicus*, or land vested in Roman public ownership. This would then be leased out by the State, which tended to favour the larger estates, and from the leasing and administration of which many of the Senators became very rich.

So, although the Italian Allies were very far from being barbarians, they were treated almost as badly as though they were. They lived in much the same way Romans did, they ate the same foods and wore the same clothes, kept the same holidays and worshipped the same gods, yet they were not Romans. It was a situation which simply could not be allowed to continue.

In 91 BC the Consuls for the year were Sextus Julius Caesar and Lucius Marcius Philippus. One of the Tribunes of the Plebs at that time was one Marcus Livius Drusus, who was a young man who already had every advantage. He was of substantial family, rich and aristocratic, married to the sister of Quintus Servilius Caepio and with a very suitable career ahead of him. He was also courageous and sensible and had something of a social conscience, which was exacerbated by his friendship with Quintus Poppaedius Silo.[4] This was considered by many to be a dangerously unsuitable friendship because Silo was a Marsian leader and therefore not true Roman at all.

This must have produced a confusing and embarrassing problem for Drusus. How could his friend, another able and intelligent man, be considered the inferior of any other man? Certainly his brother-in-law did not consider that Silo should be welcomed into the home as an equal, but Drusus persisted in the friendship and began to see the point of the idea of a general enfranchisement of all the Italian Allies. It was a proposal which certainly found no favour with the majority of the Senators, and in particular with Drusus' brother-in-law Caepio, who developed a fierce hatred for Silo. Lucius Marcius Philippus, one of the Consuls, also thoroughly disliked the thought of any enfranchisement, and he was only one of many powerful men who felt the same. Drusus had made great efforts to try to make the House realize that the Allies would not wait forever for enfranchisement and that, if it were not granted, a war would be the most likely result. This declaration was greeted with derision, as very few people believed that the Italians were actually in any position to start a war against Rome. Therefore, it was a problem which they believed could comfortably be shelved indefinitely.

Indeed, Drusus as a reformer generally, was beginning to make himself unpopular with the House. He had pushed through various measures to reform the courts and then proposed that the poor could be assisted by a general distribution of land. He was active in attempts to strengthen the Senate, particularly to restore its control over the extortion court, since the activities of the equites who controlled it were considered detrimental to senatorial authority. In this he certainly had the full support of Sulla, who was also very eager to see the Senate strengthened. In fact, he would later make it a matter of prime consideration in his own policies when he came to power. Sulla was also a close friend of Drusus' other brother-in-law Marcus Porcius Cato, so he would probably be a central figure in those early attempts to shore up the senatorial power. However, now Drusus had a bee in his bonnet about the Italian Allies, which was a proposal with which Sulla certainly did not agree.[5]

Drusus claimed he had done everything during his term of office with careful attention to the correct procedure as he was very aware of the opposition to his strategies and he had no intention of seeing measures he intended for the general good wiped off the tablets through some technicality. However, despite his care, that is what happened.

During this time of argument Lucius Licinius Crassus, who had been a very good friend and supporter of Drusus suddenly died. This proved to be a great blow to the reformers, though it put new heart into their opponents. Philippus was particularly encouraged by it. He began to claim that at the time that Drusus had passed his grain laws, (to give cheap grain to all citizens in lieu of there being sufficient land allotments to go around), there had been various unfortunate omens recorded throughout the area. One of these was of a chasm, suddenly opening in the ground and shooting forth a flash of flames. Any such signs and portents could serve to negate a bill being brought forward at the time of their appearance, as it supposedly showed that the gods were not in agreement. Therefore the auspices were considered to be very unfavourable and the project unlucky.[6]

The then Pontifex Maximus, Gnaeus Domitius Ahenobarbus, was a superstitious and very nervous man. Not only did he oppose a general enfranchisement in principle but also the idea of offending the gods terrified him. He declared himself convinced by the auspices, which nullified the bills Drusus had passed. Sextus Julius Caesar then ordered the new laws removed from the tablets and convoked the Assembly of the People to ratify their removal. Drusus, though he no doubt felt disgusted and dismayed at the way they had maneouvred the failure of his work, declared that he was still intent on acting in a proper and correct way, and therefore did not choose to invoke his power of veto.[7]

Unfortunately, even this defeat was not enough, and before very long Drusus was assassinated by an unknown assailant. It was often said that Caepio, his unfriendly brother-in-law, was suspected of having had a hand in it, but there was no proof. However, Drusus' death meant for a time the failure of his policies, and in Sulla's own agenda the failure of the senatorial reforms was certainly the most important of these. No doubt it was at that point that he determined that when − not if, but when − he had sufficient power, he would deal with those matters himself. Not for his own good, but for what he believed would be the good of Rome.[8]

When the devastating news of the murder of Drusus reached the Marsi, they must have realized that any hopes they may have had of achieving citizenship by peaceful negotiation were at an end, at least in the short term. They then decided on a show of force and began to march against Rome, led by Drusus' friend, Poppaedius Silo.

The Pontifex Maximus, the nervous Ahenobarbus, was given the task of approaching the Marsi, accompanied only by bodyguards, in an attempt to persuade them to disperse without the risk of provoking an incident. However, when he met with Silo he appeared to experience something of a change of heart. Was it the appearance of Silo himself, probably still grieving for his murdered friend and obviously determined to carry on the fight to the end? Was it the knowledge that despite all objections, common sense would eventually have to prevail, and that all these people could not be kept in a state of subjection forever? Or was it merely the sight of the men who accompanied Silo – a great number of men, fully armed and obviously ready and eager to march against Rome? It must have come as something of a shock to Ahenobarbus, when so many men in the Senate were still comfortably convinced that the Italians would never rouse themselves enough to actually arm and march. Now they had done so, and Rome was unready.

Ahenobarbus was no longer quite so sure of his ground. Various promises were made at the meeting, in an effort to defuse the situation, but it was made clear to him that something would have to be done, and quickly, or else Rome would be facing that worst of all wars, a civil war. He was obliged to return to Rome hastily to spread the bad news.

By this time Sulla no doubt wished to try again for the Consulship. He was already past the age considered suitable for a man to do so and now could expect a fair amount of support, for surely the champions of the murdered Drusus would rally behind him this time? Even more, there were by now quite enough people in Rome who had conceived a strong dislike of Gaius Marius, and it would be natural for them to consider that backing Sulla would be rather better than voting for Marius. Perhaps he could even unite the divided opinions and bring the House together again, in the face of this new threat from the Allies?

However, it was still not to be, for the outbreak of hostilities with the Italians took attention away from such simple domestic issues. What Rome needed now was a decent General to deal with the escalating problem. For another couple of years Sulla would have to put his political ambitions aside again and deal with the war beginning on Rome's doorstep.[9]

There was a nasty incident in 90 BC when a Praetor Peregrinus named Quintus Servilius (the branch he came from was not recorded) was travelling around the country, after being delegated to look into the situation within the Italian states.[10] He had reached Asculum Picentum, where he was honourably entertained by the wealthy merchant class of Romans who lived there. Details of the matter are confused, but it would appear that the party attended the theatre, sitting as was normal in the best rows of seats at the front, which were by tradition reserved for officials. During the performance some insulting or inflammatory statement may have been made which incensed the crowd of Picentines, or perhaps it was only the sight of a Praetor in all his importance, being feted in the town, when the political situation was so delicate. Whatever it was that inflamed the people, suddenly a mob attacked the Romans, killing all of them. If it did nothing else, it showed Rome that feelings were running high and the situation was quickly becoming perilous.

Also at around this time, King Mithradates VI of Pontus, taking full advantage of the fact that Rome was facing a civil war and was otherwise occupied, took the opportunity to invade and take over both Cappadocia and Bithynia.[11] He was, of course, someone else who would have to be dealt with firmly, as soon as time allowed, but that was not yet.

It was by then 90 BC and the elections in Rome had already taken place. The new Consuls for the year were Lucius Julius Caesar and Publius Rutilius Lupus. The Quaestors included a young man of great promise, Quintus Sertorius, who had already won the Corona Graminea, or Grass Crown, for his courage in Spain.[12]

The first real engagement in the Social War came when Gnaeus Pompeius Strabo was moving south through Picentum with four legions. As they were crossing the river near Falernum, they were suddenly attacked by a large force of Picentes. While they were defending themselves from this attack, more troops appeared, men from the Vestini and the Marsi tribes. It was clear that the Italian Allies had banded together well enough to make a move. The battle which then ensued did not favour either side, although Pompeius Strabo was heavily outnumbered. The Allies had not yet got the full measure of their opponents, and Pompeius managed to get his troops away to the Latin Rights colony at Firmum Picenum, which was considered loyal to Rome and where they took shelter, but where he was then besieged.

However, on the news reaching Rome, it was decided that Lucius Julius Caesar should march into Campania, as the Samnites were also beginning to make a move. Fortunately, Campania had as residents a large number of veterans of the legions, who had retired in the area. These men were keen to rejoin the legions on the side of Rome. Sulla was with Lucius Julius at that time, and the old warhorse Gaius Marius was serving with Publius Rutilius Lupus.

The towns of southern Campania now feverishly declared their allegiance, many of them coming out in favour of the new Italia and against Rome and the area was quickly in ferment. Nola was already holding as prisoners 2,000 Roman soldiers, who had been inside the town when the trouble started, including the Praetor Lucius Postumius. At the same time Publius Crassus and his sons were driven inside Grumentum by a force of Lucani. It was said that the Apuli and the Venusini were also about to declare for Italia.

Lucius Julius Caesar decided to move his two veteran legions towards Aesernia, but a force of the Marsi, fresh from besieging Pompeius Strabo in

Firmum Picentum, was also headed there. The two sides met and an engagement commenced, made more difficult for all concerned by the terrain in which they found themselves. Lucius Caesar was obliged to retreat back towards Teanum Sidinicum, but he left behind on the field 2,000 valuable veteran soldiers, which was a terrible loss for such a small and relatively unimportant skirmish. The Italians were jubilant at their unexpected success and were able to claim that they had already won a substantial victory against Rome.

However, the other consul, Publius Rutilius Lupus, was also having difficulties. Gaius Marius, rather humiliatingly serving as his second in command on this occasion, had begun to enlist and arm men and Quintus Servilius Caepio, also serving with Lupus, was doing the same. They were encamped on the Via Valeria outside Carseoli, but the atmosphere between the commanders was already acrimonious. Unfortunately, the military experience of the commander Lupus was only minimal, and he already despised the Italians, refusing to give them any credit for military acumen. He seemed to be of the opinion that the mere sight of armed Romans should cause them to flee. Marius, grimly knowing better, was unwilling to move hastily, aware of the lack of training the new recruits had had and it was spring before Lupus finally instructed two legions to advance into the lands of the Marsi, heading for Alba Fucentia, under the command of Gaius Perperna.

They were obliged to travel over rocky tracks high in the mountains on their journey and their lack of training and determination soon began to show. There they were attacked by Publius Praesentius of the Paeligni, and were completely routed. Four thousand of Perperna's troops were lost and the remainder ran off, leaving behind their arms and equipment. Their leader, Gaius Perperna, fled with them, back to Carseoli, where Lupus furiously stripped him of his rank and sent him back to Rome in disgrace.[13]

Lupus was then determined to approach the lands of the Marsi from the north, deputing Gaius Marius to take another column of men and cross the Velinus River separately, reuniting beyond Nersae. However, by the time Gaius Marius, moving carefully, had reached the river, there was evidence that the column of men with Lupus had already been attacked. It would seem that two legions of the Marsi, under the command of Publius Vettius Scato, had been moving towards Alba Fucentia to meet with Quintus Poppaedius Silo, when they realized that Lupus and his men were crossing the river.

It is possible that the inexperienced commander, not expecting trouble there and overly concerned about getting all his men and baggage wagons across the river, had not posted sufficient lookouts to warn the troops of danger. Whatever the lack may have been, the surprised but delighted Marsi fell upon them, leaving 8,000 Roman legionaries dead upon the field, including the Consul

Publius Rutilius Lupus himself, together with his legate, Marcus Valerius Messala. It was a surprising and devastating loss for Rome.

However, it was soon Scato's turn to be attacked. Gaius Marius arrived at the meeting place to find the Marsic troops busy stripping the corpses of the Romans and dealt with them accordingly. It was a rout. Scato escaped in the confusion, but he too left behind him the bulk of his troops, with over 2,000 of his own men dead on the field.

Gaius Marius sent the bodies of the Consul Lupus and the legate Messala back to Rome with all honour and with an escort of cavalry. At the very least, the arrival of their corpses would serve to make the people of Rome realize that a real war was now going on and that it was one very close to home. It would hopefully also make them realize that this was not merely another conflict so far away that it need not concern them. Such shock tactics were disturbing but may have been exactly what the old soldier intended.

It worked only too well, with morale in Rome suddenly plummeting and the Romans actually going into mourning. Probably less for their deceased consul, than for the idea that they were indeed capable of being beaten by a force of Italian Allies. People towards whom they had for so long considered themselves vastly superior.

To make things worse, instead of installing a suffect consul to take the place of the deceased Lupus, as was customary when a consul died or became unable to perform his duties during his term of office, the Senate decided to award a joint command, to Marius and Caepio together. Marius may well have been expecting the appointment of a new commander to be his chance of becoming Consul again, by allowing him to take Lupus' place. It must have been a great disappointment to him, not to mention a humiliation, to have to share command with a much younger and less experienced man, especially a man like Quintus Servilius Caepio.

Was this added humiliation for Gaius Marius merely another example of the dislike for him, which was being evinced by many members of the Senate? It hardly seems likely, as such personal feelings towards him had never previously prevented them from making full use of their most successful and experienced general. Furthermore, he was still popular with the knights, or Ordo Equestor. These were the men who held the purse strings in Rome, having developed into the merchants and financiers. They at least were still able to appreciate Marius' good qualities, and that he had brought a new prosperity to Rome with his provision of greater security for the empire.

Or did the Senate know for certain something that we do not? Was this relegation of Gaius Marius to a secondary post, rather than the Consulship that he might reasonably have expected given his exemplary record, evidence of another problem? Was it due to him not only ageing, as all men do, (he was already 67 years old, a great age at that time for a man still being subjected to the stress and physical exertion of battle), but evidence that he had indeed been ill? Did it show that his health was no longer to be completely relied upon? That the Senate, in fact, was gently but firmly making him step aside. However, the joint command, then decided upon by a distracted and increasingly concerned Senate, was in any case not to last.

Caepio had accepted his elevation with great confidence. He had dealt with a raiding legion of the Marsi at Varia, while Gaius Marius was bringing retribution to Scato after the death of Lupus the Consul and his troops. Caepio then declared to the Senate that he had won the first victory of the Marsic War, and it was just as good a victory as that of Marius. Furthermore, as it had happened on 10 June, while Marius' own victory was not until a day or two later, it gave Caepio the honour of the first success.[14]

Then Caepio attempted to give Marius instructions to return to Caseoli, where he was headed, but this Marius ignored. He stated that he had retrieved the remains of the scattered legions, and until they were again readied for action to his own satisfaction, he would remain where he was. Caepio was then obliged to move his legions back towards Caeoli alone. Once they reached the Arno at Sublaqueum they were attacked by a force of Marsi, led by Quintus Poppaedius Silo. Caepio's column perished to the last man, though it is said that he was killed by Silo personally.[15] Silo probably still believed that Caepio had had something to do with the assassination of his good friend Drusus and he may have taken some grim pleasure in the performance of such an act of vengeance.

In the meantime, Lucius Julius Caesar had successfully defeated Gaius Papius Mutilus of the Samnites at Acerrae. When this news reached Rome it was met with joy and a cessation of mourning. Unfortunately, it was soon followed by further bad news, this time that Lucius Caesar had been repulsed in the Melfa Gorge, a second defeat there, with terrible casualty figures almost equalling the enemy losses at Acerrae. The Senate must have been in despair at the conflicting reports reaching Rome about their progress.

When news finally arrived of the success of Gaius Marius against the Marrucini with the loss of several thousand of the enemy, including their leader Herius Asinius, it was closely followed by further news of success against the Marsi, this time leaving 15,000 Marsic soldiers dead. However, Rome may well have been reluctant to celebrate. The strenuous fight being put up by the Allies was still something of a surprise and a final defeat of the rebellion that Rome had never truly expected to have to deal with still seemed to be a long way off.

Publius Sulpicius Rufus, serving as legate to Pompeius Strabo, did well in taking an army from Italian Gaul and inflicting a defeat on a combined force of Picentine and Paeligni in Picenum. Their leader Titus Lafrenius died with his men. However, Pompeius Strabo claimed the credit for the engagement, as was usual for the commanding officer.

Publius Sulpicius Rufus may, in fact, have had some sympathy with the rebels he was fighting so well. He would eventually become a Tribune in 88 BC when he attempted to pursue the enfranchisement which Drusus had been unable to finish. Being opposed in this by the nobles, he would be obliged to turn to Marius for support, and was later instrumental in pushing through the bill for Marius to replace Sulla as commander against Mithradates. This action would eventually lead to his death when Marius and his followers were expelled from Rome.[16]

However, other leaders would by this time be thinking along the same lines. Lucius Julius Caesar was to promulgate a new law at the end of that year, before his term of office ended, in which he called for enfranchisement of the Italian Allies, provided that they had not been actively fighting against Rome.[17] He had already been awarded a Triumph by the Senate, supposedly for his victory over Mutilus at Acerrae, and it was claimed that this honour was given because he had been hailed as Imperator on the field by his men. When Pompeius Strabo heard of the honour awarded to Lucius Caesar, he also claimed that his men had hailed him Imperator, so the Senate was obliged to award him a Triumph also.

The beginning of winter, the winding up of the campaigning season, saw Acerrae with the armies still camped outside its walls.

Sulla, meanwhile, had been sent to Capua to reorganize the legions which had been decimated by the second action at the Melfa Gorge, although he was shortly to return to Rome, accompanying his commander Lucius Julius Caesar for his Triumph. During his stay in Rome he arranged the marriage of his daughter Cornelia to young Quintus Pompeius Rufus. This was doubtless a part of the deal arranged between Sulla and Pompeius Rufus senior, in which they had also agreed to run in tandem as candidates for the Consulship for the elections two years ahead.

Shortly afterwards, Rome received the news that Aesernia had surrendered to the Samnites. After almost reaching starvation point, eating anything remotely edible in the vicinity, including all the cats and dogs, Marcus Claudius Marcellus had been obliged to hand over the city.

Lucius Julius Caesar would not be returning to his command, as his term as Consul was ending. He had hopes of being elected a Censor (which he eventually managed), and did not want to get bogged down again on a campaign. Because of the enfranchisement law he was about to introduce, details of which were now known, a general feeling of favour towards the Italian Allies was beginning to spread, especially amongst the young Tribunes. However, the President of the College, one Lucius Calpurnius Piso, was still very firmly conservative in his opinions. He stated that he would oppose the two most radical Tribunes of the Plebs, Gaius Papirius Carbo and Marcus Plautius Silvanus, if the strict limitations of the new Lex Julia were ignored, and a general enfranchisement was to be allowed.[18]

The new Consuls had also been elected for the coming year (89 BC) and were to be Gnaeus Pompeius Strabo as senior, with Lucius Porcius Cato Licinianus as the junior.

However, while Rome was still occupied with the Social War (even though some opinions there were beginning to turn to a slightly more reasonable attitude towards the Allies), trouble was brewing again in the East. A commission under the leadership of one Marcus Aquilius was sent to Mithradates of Pontus, to order him to withdraw from Cappodocia and Bithynia, into which he had recently sent his occupying forces.

Mithradates did appear willing to cooperate at first, by removing the offending troops from those areas, but the intervention did little good in the long term. Aquilius then persuaded Nicomedes IV of Bithynia, whose country had so lately been occupied, to attack Pontus itself. Aquilius' forces were divided in three units and completely routed, with Marcus Aquilius himself being killed.

Mithradates, though an ogre to the Romans, actually had the support of the local people, who hated the Roman tax-gatherers. Their support convinced him that he was invincible and that with Rome otherwise engaged, coupled with the successes he had recently had against Nicomedes of Bithynia and Marcus Aquilius, he could do largely as he pleased in the East. For a little while longer, he would do precisely that.

Sulla, however, was just about to embark on not only the busiest but also by far the most successful period of his work during the Social War. He was also about to do the hardest work of the whole campaign, during which he not only succeeded in winning over the Marsi, but also in conquering the Samnites who had led the initial revolt against Rome.[19]

In that same year, he was to besiege the delightful port of Pompeii, both by attacking it on land and bombarding it from the sea. The admiral in command of the fleet outside the port of Pompeii was none other than that Aulus Postumius Albinus who had previously caused trouble in Africa, by provoking King Jugurtha of Numidia into war by his ill-advised excursion into his territory. Apparently, he had learned nothing in the intervening twenty years, for his attitude towards his men was still one of haughty superiority. He had with him a legion of Hirpini who had stayed loyal to Rome, but they obviously did not intend to put up with such a commander as Albinus as the engagement outside Pompeii dragged on.[20] He was to annoy them beyond endurance and be stoned to death by them!

When news of his death reached Sulla he declined to punish the murderers, which surprised the other officers with him. Sulla was only too aware that this was not the time to offend any more of the Allies, neither could he afford to lose any decent fighting men by executing those on his own side. The matter had to be left as it was, particularly as it was clear that Albinus had brought the situation on himself. Sulla had more important things to do, with his thoughts engaged on what he had to achieve with Pompeii.

It was not, in fact, the first time a Cornelius had attacked Pompeii. After the Samnites had taken over the area around the Bay of Naples, the Romans had considered it expedient to push back their enemies. In 310 BC a Roman squadron had appeared, making for the mouth of the Sarno, it was led by an Admiral named Publius Cornelius who landed his soldiers and devastated the countryside. Pompeii had fought off the Romans on that occasion, though in another twenty years the Samnite domination was ended and Pompeii became an ally of Rome.

Since that time, Pompeiians had done well under Roman rule, but they enrolled under the banner of Poppaedius Silo when the Social War began. Stabiae had then been completely razed to the ground, which did not encourage Pompeii to open its gates to Sulla. It reinforced its garrison with Oscan tribesmen and stood its ground. (Some of the walls are still inscribed in Oscan, indicating the sections of the town which were given over to the mercenaries in the emergency.)

A long siege ensued, both at Pompeii and at the neighbouring town of Herculaneum, which had also been foolish enough to kill all its Roman inhabitants. Sulla had approached Pompeii from the north and seen that the defences were formidable, being made of two parallel walls separated by about twenty feet, with the space in between filled with tufa blocks and stones. They also boasted buttresses, around 25 to 30 ft high, to strengthen the walls, topped by crenels giving cover to archers and slingers. At intervals towers further reinforced the walls, and we know that in Sulla's day there were twelve of these.

One tower is still standing at the northern end of the Via Mercurio and has been fully restored. This restoration enables us to peep back in time and shows very well what a defensive structure of Sulla's day looked like.

Very fortunately, original graffiti had been scratched onto the stonework by a soldier, probably idling at his post, stating the name of his officer and the date of 89 BC.[22] History rarely comes so close to us as this! The impressive defences surrounding Pompeii give a fine sturdy appearance, although around the Herculaneum Gate the walls still bear the marks of the missiles from Sulla's siege engines, designed to reduce them.

The city was saved from its bombardment, although indirectly, by a man named Lucius Cluentius who arrived with an army of reinforcements. Not that they were able to drive off Sulla, but he was obliged to turn his attention to them on their arrival and he pursued Cluentius and his men up to the walls of Nola, the town to the north east of Pompeii.

Unfortunately for Cluentius, when he reached Nola he found that the townspeople had closed the gates, and apart from a very small entrance, which was opened only to let in the officers, the Nola residents refused to allow the full forces of Cluentius inside. Proudly refusing to avail himself of the offered sanctuary as it was not also possible to save his men, he turned at bay to fight Sulla and his forces, who had come upon them after determinedly following them, not more than a mile behind.

A terrible battle ensued, under the walls of Nola, with the townspeople watching avidly. The troops of Lucius Cluentius were desperate and fought savagely, but Sulla eventually defeated them there, almost to the death of the last man. It is said that he killed Cluentius with his own hand.[23]

Sulla was now 51 years old and had just won his first battle as commander in chief, having taken over command after the death of Lucius Porcius Cato, the Consul, who had recently died while fighting the Marsi. This time there was nobody who could claim to be his superior, or be able to take the credit for its success away from him. Little is often made of this battle outside Nola, but it must have been touch and go for a time. Cluentius and his men were desperately aware that they were trapped, and must have fought with great ferocity. Sulla was also desperate, in a different way, for he was eager to prove that his previous successes were not merely due to the advice and help of other men. That had already been claimed far too often and now he had the opportunity to show that he was perfectly capable of dealing with, and winning a battle, on his own terms.

The men who fought with him also thought that it was an important and memorable engagement, not just a skirmish. This was proved by the fact that after the battle he was not only hailed as Imperator on the field on that day, but also awarded the Grass Crown, or Corona Graminea.

This award, which was literally made up of the grass, hay, or even corn crops taken that day from the field of battle itself, was a purely private award, given by the men of the legions to a commander whom they considered had saved the legion. It was awarded very rarely and subsequently meant a very great deal to the commander to whom it was given. For Sulla it would have meant not only a mark of honour and not only recognition from his men that he was a good leader and that felt they could rely on him, but far more.

It must have been a very emotional moment, as it showed beyond all doubt that to the actual fighting men of the legions, the people who were in the best position to judge such matters, Sulla was considered a good general and a trustworthy man. That they prized, admired and respected him. It must, in that moment of acceptance, have made up a very great deal for the suspicion and indifference with which he had always been treated while in Rome. It also changed the way in which those people would be obliged to regard him in the future, showing that now he had the full support and loyalty of his troops, which he was never to lose.[24]

He then returned to the siege of Pompeii, but although the town was finally obliged to surrender to him, he did not stoop to resort to the harsh reprisals inflicted on the cities which had been given to Marius. These had been razed to the ground, as had happened with Stabiae, but it appears that Sulla had a fondness for the area around the Bay, and had no desire to destroy it. It had always been considered a beautiful place and many rich Roman families had their holiday villas there. Its prosperity was to be protected.

It was also where Sulla would later build a magnificent villa at Puteoli, to which he would eventually retire towards the end of his life. When he had achieved all that he considered he reasonably could, his health was failing and the life of battle, and the even harder battle of politics, had finally palled for him.

He would also make the area around Pompeii into a haven for his veteran soldiers, giving them land allocations and renaming the town Colonia Cornelia Veneria Pompeianorum.

Sulla, as always, had an interest in religions, and encouraged the worship of Isis in the town. Such foreign gods and goddesses had sometimes been frowned upon and the followers of Dionysus and Isis were in particular often obliged to hold their ceremonies clandestinely. However, Sulla encouraged tolerance, and the Temple of Isis in Pompeii became firmly established and very popular, while her worship continued openly.[25]

As for Nola, that particular city would have to wait a little while longer. Sulla would eventually take it, but not until 80 BC would it fall, having held out for almost a decade, unlike the other cities of the Allies. By the time Nola was in Sulla's hands, the rest of Samnium would be also, and the Social War would be just a memory. Interestingly, it would face another siege, though not so long lasting, when it was stormed by the slave Spartacus, in the revolt he led across the area seven years after Sulla had subjected it.[26]

Sulla now turned to deal with the Hirpini and attacked Aeclanum. When they tried to buy time by negotiating, Sulla arranged for the wooden breastworks, which surrounded the town, to be fired. Such defences must have seemed rather pathetic after the formidable stone walls of Pompeii. The townspeople, seeing that Sulla did not intend to enter into negotiations with them and that reinforcements were unlikely to arrive, sensibly decided that, rather than risk being burned to death, they should surrender.[27]

A soldier named Gaius Cosconius had been sent by Sulla to attack Salapia, burning it to the ground to prevent any word of his presence in the area from reaching the other Samnites. From there he marched to Cannae, taking it easily without a fight, and moved on towards Canusium, fording the Aufidius River.

Shortly after crossing the river he was met by a large force of Samnites, led by Gaius Trebatius.

The two forces were quite evenly matched and the engagement was without any definite result, until Cosconius fell back towards Cannae, with a delighted Trebatius and his troops following. As Trebatius was fording the Aufidius, Cosconius turned his men back and fell on them while they were in some disarray. The result was another substantial victory for Rome, for approximately 15,000 Samnites died at the Aufidius crossing. A few survivors fled with Trebatius towards Canusium, to which Cosconius then proceeded to lay siege, with the town eventually capitulating.

Gaius Papius Mutilus was still alive and still the leader of the Samnites when Sulla decided on a march towards Aesernia, as Mutilus was still at large in the area. He would need to be contained to prevent him from attacking Cosconius. However, Mutilus had already sent one Marius Egnatius to engage with Cosconius and the two forces had met just outside Larinum. The Samnites were to find that Cosconius and his men were still full of great confidence after their success against Trebatius at the Aufidius crossing, and they proceeded to do well again against Egnatius. After a determined fight he too was to die on the field, along with most of his men. Mutilus, however, still survived.

The old Samnite capitol, Bovianum, was now ahead of Sulla. It was a formidably fortified town at the junction of three major roads. Sulla was to attack it strenuously, deciding to use it as a base of operations once it capitulated. It was quite obvious by this time that the Italian Allies were fighting only a defensive war and that the conflict would soon be over, with the victory going to Rome. The engagements from this time onwards were in the nature of cleaning up operations, moving from place to place, putting down hotspots of insurrection as quickly as possible. As examples, Servius Sulpicius Galba cleared up the Marrucini, the Marsi and the Vestini, while Cinna and Cornutus occupied the Marsic lands. Gnaeus Pompeius Strabo had reduced the Picentines, but Aesculum Picentum still held out, while Publius Sulpicius Rufus and Gaius Baebius besieged it.

Sulla met with Catulus Caesar in October of that year, to make arrangements for over-wintering the armies. Meanwhile, Pompeius Strabo joined Sulpicius Rufus in surrounding Aesculum Picentum, finally bringing it to its knees by severing the city's water supplies, which ran down from the surrounding hillsides. By November the city magistrates were obliged to submit to Pompeius Strabo, hoping for reasonable terms of surrender, but Pompeius was by then in no mood to be generous. The siege had lasted two years already and he considered that the city should be punished for its intransigence. He calmly proceeded to execute almost 5,000 of the city's men, who had held out so firmly against the Roman armies, and cast out the women and children to starve in the barren winter countryside, which had already been stripped of any means of survival.

It is interesting to note at this point the huge difference in the behaviour of Gnaeus Pompeius Strabo at the surrender of Aesculum Picentum, compared with the sensible and tolerant behaviour of Sulla after he had similarly taken Pompeii. It is usual for accounts of the period to consider Pompeius Strabo to have been something of a butcher, and doubtless there will always be commanders who prefer to take the line of exacting extreme reprisals when an enemy is defeated. However, Sulla certainly emerges from the Social War with the appearance of being a very different sort of man. Not only did he seem to be far more reasonable and approachable than his colleagues, but also appeared to be the kind of man who did not need to bolster his status or abuse his position by behaving like a savage, particularly towards defeated and helpless captives.

By December Sulla was back in Rome and although he had not officially been appointed Commander in Chief after the death of Lucius Porcius Cato the Consul, he had stepped in and done the job anyway, and with a great deal of success. He was also informed that he had been appointed an auger (in absentia, by the Senate), which was an honour he had not sought and perhaps did not expect to receive, but it certainly showed which way the wind was suddenly blowing for him.[28]

He found that he had now become very popular in Rome among the people and there was no longer any doubt that he would be elected Consul for 88 BC. This was done smoothly with no opposition at all and, as they had originally planned, Quintus Pompeius Rufus became the Junior Consul. It had all worked out very well. Sulla was now where he had always intended to be, even if it had taken rather more time than he would have expected or wanted, he was now the Senior Consul.

Finally, the Senate in Rome would no longer be able to ignore him.

Chapter Eight

In 88 BC Sulla had finally achieved his rise into the genuine ruling class in Rome. He had good reason to feel pleased with himself, but he was to find that ruling in Rome was no easier for him than anyone else and that it was to be no easy ride for him from then onwards.

However, he was to start with a new marriage which presumably brought him some happiness. Since the death of Scaurus, the Princeps Senatus, the previous year, his young widow Caecilia Metella, had been living through her required months of mourning. These were now at an end, and Sulla decided to offer for her and was accepted. That meant, of course, that he would have to divorce his second wife Aelia, which he did with gifts and expressions of gratitude.[1] After all, the lady had brought up his children for him over the intervening years. His change of spouse did bring some ribald verses to the fore, with some people in Rome finding amusement in him having spoken for Caecilia Metalla as soon as she was officially available.[2] It certainly seemed that he had had her in mind for some time and was waiting for the opportunity to speak. However, in his new popularity in Rome, and probably in a cheerful frame of mind, he did not resent the amusement of the wits. He had made many verses himself and may have found some humour in those, even though they were directed at his private life.

Less easy to find amusement in, however, was the reaction of one or two of the nobles, who made it clear that they thought the divorce of Aelia and her replacement with Metella was merely evidence of Sulla overreaching himself.[3] They pretended to think that he ought not to have reached so high, by grasping at a marriage which might do him more service. This was simply hypocrisy, as not one of those men would consider marriage with a woman of no money or family status. Nor had they anything to be high and mighty about, as Sulla's birth was as good or nearly as good as any of theirs. As first consul, and now married to the woman he wanted, he could afford to ignore their spiteful comments.

There had been another irritation, which was that when the elections for the consulship were being arranged, one of the men who hoped he had a chance of being elected was an old adversary of Sulla's, Gaius Julius Caesar Strabo, who was the stepbrother of Catulus Caesar. He put himself forward for the elections, although he did not really have any serious chance of success, his attempt was officially invalid due to him not having served as a praetor first.[4] He intended to call for the return of the friends of the murdered Drusus, who had been blamed for inflaming the Allies into starting the Social War and had been subsequently exiled. However, Marius and Sulpicius strenuously opposed any chance of election for him, resulting in some rioting in the streets which caused the Senate to refuse to allow Caesar Strabo to stand. This must have been something of a relief to Sulla, although in his new sense of security he did not need to fear that Caesar Strabo would be able to take his place. But if he had been obliged to work with Caesar Strabo as a partner he would have found his year of consulship very awkward indeed, being saddled with a man with whom he was already at odds. But things worked out for the best with Sulla's partner being a man he could get on with, in Pompeius Rufus.

Sulpicius may have been hoping that in appearing to help Sulla, he would receive in return his support for further concessions for the Italian Allies, but he had misjudged the situation completely. Sulla had quite different opinions on the matter and did not consider that anything more should be done for the Allies.[5] In fact, in the case of men like Mutilus, who had led the Samnites against Rome for so long, and managed to survive the war, there was resentment. He was now likely to be awarded full citizenship along with the others and it might seem to many people that the concessions had gone too far already.

Disappointed with Sulla's reaction, Sulpicius looked about for a new supporter, and found him in Gaius Marius. Marius now had his own resentments, not only with his dislike and jealousy of Sulla himself but also of the fact that he had definitely been sidelined in the Social War, and had actually retired from the conflict, spending some further time in Rome. Was he ill during this period, or merely sulking? He had certainly not been given the sole command that a man of his calibre might have expected, and although he had performed well while he was in the field, Sulla had done better. There was another thing on Marius' mind too. Back in 100 BC he had made a visit to the East, supposedly to deal with the pirates in the area, but also to take a look at Mithradates and if possible warn him off. This he had done, but as he carried no real authority for that mission he could take it no further. Since then the matter, which had always been a pet project for him, had grown in his mind. He now seemed to consider himself something of an expert on eastern politics, and wanted desperately to be able to command the armies that would soon be sent against Mithradates of Pontus. Unfortunately, it was traditional for the senior consul to get the pick of the assignments, at least if he were still young and fit enough. So it seemed to be a certainty that Sulla would opt for it, and take over for himself the command that Marius still craved and considered his own speciality.

Firstly though, there were concerns in Rome to deal with. No man wished to leave his consulship without putting his name on the tablets as a lawmaker, and Sulla had ideas of his own in that direction too. Sulla started by passing two laws designed to regulate Rome's finances, which were in a very sorry state after all the years of continual war. The first of his Leges Corneliae concerned the interest rates, and stipulated that all debtors were to pay simple interest only, rather than the common compound interest which so easily bankrupted the debtors. Also that the rates of interest were to be agreed between both parties, at the time the loan was made, and should stand for the whole term of the debt, without further increase.

The second was concerned with the *sponsio*, which was the sum in dispute in cases of debts and usually had to be lodged with the praetor before the case was heard. This, of course, meant that many cases were never heard at all, as poorer clients did not have the *sponsio* to hand in the first place, to enable them to bring the case. Sulla's law now waived the lodgement of the *sponsio*, allowing such cases to be heard without it. Another sensible adjustment, with an eye to the difficulties experienced by poorer citizens.[6]

Gaius Marius, meanwhile, had been arranging a betrothal for his son, and had chosen the daughter of Quintus Mucius Scaevola. This young lady, sometimes referred to as Mucia Tertia, to differentiate from two other Mucias who were her cousins, was also half-sister to the two Metelli, Celer and Nepos.[7] Unfortunately, events were to later prevent her marriage to young Gaius Marius, and she would eventually become the bride of Gnaeus Pompeius Magnus instead and mother of his sons Gnaeus and Sextus.

However, Gaius Marius was plotting more than just marriages at this time. He was by then in consultation with Sulpicius, two unsatisfied men, who came to an understanding how they could assist each other. Marius wanted the command of the coming campaign against Mithradates for himself, while Sulpicius wanted not only the return of the exiles, but to distribute them amongst all the tribes. This was obviously intended to make things difficult for Sulla and his supporters, who would then find themselves facing the return of all their enemies.

There was another bill on Sulpicius' mind, which was one to deny a place in the senate to any man who had debts exceeding 2,000 denarii. It has been said that this was also aimed at Sulla, though it is quite unlikely that he was completely without money at this point in his life. In fact, shortly after the Jugurthan War, Sulla had been accosted in the Forum by an unknown man and had been accused of getting rich too quickly.[8] Although such a law, if passed, might make life uncomfortable for many of the Senators, as borrowing money was a way of life in Rome, and most of them were to a greater or lesser extent in debt most of the time. Particularly so at that point, as many of them drew revenues from their estates in various parts of Italia, and since the onset of the Social War their money would not have been reaching them as it should.

Probably they were his true targets after all, as his plans for the Italian Allies caused fury in the senate, culminating in days of rioting in the city.

Sulla, meanwhile, had temporarily left Rome in order to attend to the final cleaning-up of the Allies, especially with regard to Nola. He was besieging Nola again when he received what he took to be a sign of divine approval. While conducting a sacrifice, a snake crawled out from under the altar. His haruspex, Postumius, declared it to be a sign of success to come, and they did go on to capture a fortified camp, although Nola still stubbornly held out.[9] It was while they were working in this way some distance from Rome that Sulla heard details of the trouble then taking place in the city, and he was obliged to return.

When he did so, it was to find that Sulpicius was about to pass his programme of reforms, pushing them through by a mixture of violence and by general intimidation.[10] To avert this, Sulla and Pompeius Rufus immediately declared several days of public holiday (*feriae*), during which no legal business could take place. This was to prevent the matter going any further and in the hope that a break from argument might help to defuse the dangerous situation.

Sulpicius, however, refusing to accept this, led his rioters into the Forum while the two Consuls were holding a meeting at the Temple of Castor and Pollux. Another violent riot broke out, during which the son of Pompeius Rufus attempted to calm the mob, but only succeeding in inflaming them the more as his appearance suggested to them that he was merely another haughty aristocrat, after which he was attacked and killed. Horrified and grieved, Pompeius Rufus was extricated by his friends and managed to get away to safety, and even Sulla, seeing the state of fury the mob had reached, also decided that retreat was safer for the time being. He left the Temple and took refuge at the house of Gaius Marius, which was nearby.

We cannot, of course, know what was said between the two men while Sulla was inside the house with Marius, and speculation on the subject is useless. What we do know is that Sulla, obviously realizing that the rioting had to be stopped, cancelled the *feriae*. He was then able to leave Marius' house safely. With Rome a little quieter, he was then able to rejoin his troops outside Nola. However, it left Sulpicius triumphant in Rome, at least for the time being. There must have been a certain amount of loss of face for Sulla, but if Sulpicius had exercised any common sense, he would have realized that pushing Sulla into a corner in that way might be a stupid thing to do and one he would be obliged to pay for.

Still, there was the eastern campaign to be organized, and Sulla would be obliged to leave Nola still holding out grimly and turn his attention towards other matters. The rioting and general unrest in Rome would leave a stain on his year of Consulship, unless he could produce some definite result in the east. He no doubt started making his preparations, with the firm intent that he would give Rome something to be proud of, something that would make Sulpicius' demands seem merely an unpleasant incident. He surely cannot have known that Gaius Marius and Sulpicius were plotting to give command of that campaign to Marius, instead of himself. That Marius had always wanted it was probably common knowledge, but since his visit there some years previously he had aged considerably, and had had a less than spectacular campaign against the Allies. Surely he had the sense to give up that idea, in the face of increasing age and quite likely some ill-health? But it seemed not.

Sulpicius, meanwhile, proceeded to bring forward his bill regarding the redistribution of the Allies. No doubt this was done in his usual way, by using rioting and public disturbance to intimidate the voters, but however he achieved it, he did manage to get the vote of the people to remove both Sulla and Pompeius Rufus from their provinces. He then actually handed over the command of the Mithradatic campaign, now in the offing, to Gaius Marius! Plutarch tells us that Marius 'through a mad affectation of glory and thirst for distinction' still coveted the command 'though he were now unwieldy in body and had given up service, on account of his age, during the late campaigns'.

When Sulla heard the news he must have been stunned at the presumption of Sulpicius and disgusted at the stupidity of giving such an important command to Marius, a man now obviously past his best. Worse than all those things, he would certainly have been furious at the idea that anyone, in his year as senior consul, should arrogantly dare to remove him from his command. Sulpicius had certainly overstepped the mark this time, and would have to pay for it. If Sulla did not act, and act quickly, he would find himself reduced to nothing. Unfortunately for Sulpicius, he had reckoned without the utter determination of Sulla, a determination bred in a hard school, and which was to serve him well again. Sulla, taken by surprise, now only had his army to rely on but he had always treated them very well and had proved himself to them before. In this extremity they were loyal to him. Once they knew what had been done behind his back they were angry for his sake and eager to march with him to Rome.

This was not a decision for any man to take lightly. In fact, it had not been taken before. Never before had a general been obliged to take his army to the gates of Rome, and Sulla cannot be accused of having planned to take such an action.[11] He had been preparing to take his men abroad, as any consul might be expected to do. That he found that he was being figuratively stabbed in the back, having his hard-won authority destroyed and his command taken from him, was certainly not a situation that he had maneouvred. It had been done against him in his absence, but even so his options were now limited. If he allowed the situation to continue as it was his consulship would become a sham and his political career ruined, together with all that he had worked for and achieved so far. He would not, could not, allow it to happen, and if Marius and

Sulpicius had ever imagined that he would calmly accept it, they must have been deranged, or so blinded by their own egos that they could not clearly see the sort of man they had chosen to reduce.

However, even then, Sulla hesitated a little. This was such a huge thing that he must do, he must be sure that the gods approved of it. He was reassured by his haruspex Postumius, who told him that various omens were favourable, but still Sulla had doubts. He then had his answer in one of the prophetic dreams, of which he wrote later in his life. He said that in his dream he had seen the goddess Bellona, and she had put into his hands both thunder and lightning, naming his enemies and giving him leave to strike them.[12] He told his colleague Postumius of the dream, and that he was finally convinced by it. The following day Sulla began to lead his army back towards Rome.[13]

When Marius and Sulpicius heard that Sulla, at the head of an army, was making his way to Rome, they behaved as if amazed, just as though they had genuinely expected him to give way to their stupendous demands. It says much for the decline of Marius' mental processes at this point, that he should have so far mistaken the man he had once known well, as to expect him to humbly submit. Marius had actually had the audacity to send some officers to meet with Sulla's troops, with instructions to administer a new oath of loyalty to the men and then to take over the command from Sulla. These men were stoned by Sulla's troops, who understandably became furious at the insult offered to their commander. In revenge, Marius put some of Sulla's friends to death in Rome, while Pompeius Rufus, along with others, fled for their lives to sanctuary with Sulla.[14]

However, in the Senate another kind of panic began. It seemed that Sulla was about to dare to do what no other man had ever dared – he was about to enter the sacred pomerium with armed men, and without the authority of using the Ultimate Decree. Although they knew perfectly well what had been done to him in his absence, they still considered this action beyond the pale. In this, they too had mistaken their man. Not knowing what to do to control Marius, they attempted instead to control Sulla, by sending an embassy to order him to desist in his attempt to march to Rome. When asked why he was marching, he answered simply that he intended to deliver his country from tyrants. Unfortunately, Sulla's soldiers took exception to the haughty tone in which they addressed the Consul, and they handled them roughly, breaking their rods of office and beating them, before sending them back towards Rome. Other embassies were sent, no doubt becoming more desperate the closer Sulla came to the city, but they met with the same answer.

The fourth set of officials who arrived behaved in a more conciliatory manner towards him – no doubt because he was now so dangerously close to Rome. Sulla had stopped and appeared to be about to make a camp, but when the officials had returned to the city, he sent after them a force, led by Lucius Basilus and Gaius Mummius. They seized the city gate and walls on the Esquiline, but as they attempted to enter the city itself, they were met with a shower of tiles and bricks thrown down on them from the buildings alongside. At this point Sulla himself arrived, and gave the order for the hail of tiles and other missiles to cease, or he would fire the buildings. Rioting was something of a local sport in Rome, and anyone might have the amusement of throwing things down on the heads of people passing by, but fire was another matter entirely. The high-rise insulae in the poorer areas were only too susceptible to being burned down, so the rain of tiles and other assorted missiles immediately stopped. By this, he was able to clear a path through, which allowed him entry into Rome. Meanwhile, Pompeius Rufus and one legion had occupied the Colline Gate, another had taken possession of the Wooden Bridge, and a third legion was already in control of the Esquiline Gate.[15]

Sulla was met just inside the city itself by a force led by Marius and Sulpicius, who had some of the experienced war veterans fighting amongst their number. The opposition was fierce for some time, and neither side had the advantage. Sulla was eventually obliged to take a silver standard from a soldier standing close to him and, carrying it as a banner, push to the front of the battle line in order to stiffen and rally his forces. Few consuls had ever had to fight for their consulship the way Sulla was being obliged to do, but he responded to the situation that had been forced upon him valiantly and in the way that Marius, at least, should have been aware that he would. When the fight was at its height, Sulla sensibly sent a force of men around by the Suburra, in order to take Marius and Sulpicius from the rear. When they arrived in place it was clear that the forces fighting with Marius and Sulpicius were becoming unsteady and that their line was unlikely to hold. Marius was obliged to call out for slaves to join them and help them defend Rome, promising them their freedom if they were successful.[16] It is hardly surprising that this brought no sudden influx of slaves to his aid. Why should those poor things risk their lives by getting involved in the personal arguments of their masters?

When it was obvious even to Marius that there was not going to be any help forthcoming, he suddenly stopped fighting, abandoned his men, and turned and ran, concentrating instead on getting himself safely out of the city.

Sulla was then able to march without opposition along the Via Sacra and into the Forum, where he found various people taking the opportunity the civil unrest gave them to do a little looting on their own behalf. Sulla had them dealt with firmly. Then when he reached the Capitol he found that a small group of Marius' sympathizers were still occupying it. It did not take him long, however, to deal with them too, and then Rome was completely in his hands. He must have looked around at the city in dismay when it was all over, angry at the position that had been forced upon him and saddened that such an action had been necessary. Few consuls had ever been faced with such a ridiculous situation or been driven to defend their authority in such a way.

To prevent any further unrest, he and his fellow consul, Pompeius Rufus, spent the night moving from place to place throughout the city with a small force, to make sure that all was kept peaceful and in order. They had achieved what no men had ever before attempted to do, and now they would have to explain the reasons for their actions to the Senate and spend the following days trying to contain the unrest and restore peaceful conditions in Rome.

Sulla and Pompeius Rufus had to meet the following day with such members of the Senate as were in the city. The Princeps Senatus, Lucius Valerius Flaccus and the Pontifex Maximus, Quintus Mucius Scaevola, were still there and obviously uneasy. Both these men were affiliated with Gaius Marius, which made their position delicate. Scaevola had recently betrothed his daughter Mucia to Gaius Marius' son and Flaccus had relied upon Marius' influence with the polls to achieve his position. However, Flaccus at least, would come to change his allegiance. (He eventually became Sulla's Master of Horse, but that was for the future.) In the meantime, they must have faced Sulla with some resentment and a good deal of wariness.

However, Sulla was in a magnanimous mood. He made it clear that since entering Rome he had done no harm to anyone, nor had he attempted to restrain or restrict any magistrate, even though his colleague's son, young Pompeius Rufus (who was also his own son-in-law), had been murdered by the mob! He also pointed out that he had taken refuge at that time in the house of Gaius Marius, in an amicable way, and that surely that proved that he wished no man any harm – yet both Gaius Marius and Sulpicius, who had started the trouble, had now literally run away. He reminded the Senate and People that he was not only Senior Consul, but also the legally appointed commander of the proposed campaign to the east. That command had been taken away from him while he was out of the city, again working for Rome, in attempting yet again to reduce the town of Nola. The action was particularly ridiculous when that same command was then given to a man who, despite his previously wonderful record as a general, was now obviously old and sick and not well enough to perform such onerous duties.

It would also have been sensible to remind them that if he, Sulla, had not marched back to the city, and yet still refused to give up his legally appointed command, there would have been a real civil war in Rome. Not just against the Italian Allies, but between the forces of Sulla and Marius and their respective supporters. By taking the action he had, reprehensible as it might seem, he had nipped the situation in the bud. That Rome was now safe and quiet again showed plainly that he intended only peace and furthermore, in Roman eyes, the success showed that the gods were with him.

He had entered Rome on the Ides of November, which was very late in the year for bringing in new laws, but somehow it would have to be managed. He could not leave the city again without attempting to regularize the situation. Unfortunately, there were rules already in place which dictated the length of time required to elapse between the promulgation of new laws and their implementation.[17] (The Leges Caecilia Didia.) By the time any such bills were passed, Sulla would find that his term of office was already over.

Therefore, it was first necessary for him to make a new law, which would waive the restrictions imposed by the Leges Caecilia Didia to allow him to pass his own bills quickly. This could be done, but it was already the end of November and time was running out for his consulship. Sulla then arranged for his own bills to be passed, a series of six laws firmly attempted to control the situation, yet presented in such a way that nobody could take exception to them.[18] One of those laws was to bring charges of treason against the men who opposed him. However, despite that charge he made no attempt to confiscate the property of those opponents and their wives and families remained safe.

He was fully aware that the continued presence of his soldiers in the city made for unease with the people, but it was necessary for a time. However, moving carefully, Sulla expected no opposition from the Senate, or indeed the people, with regard to these new bills, and there was none.

Sulla's laws showed that apart from dealing with the constitutional crisis, he was also attempting to deal with the economic problems. The Social War had disrupted trade and production of all kinds, and prosperity had particularly suffered with Mithradates of Pontus taking over Asia Province. Sulla was still concerned about finding sufficient land for allotments to the veterans, which now included veterans of the Social War.

Though Sulla's new laws were pushed through quite quickly, there is no indication that they were thought out hurriedly.[19] In fact, it certainly appears that he had had these ideas in mind for some considerable time, so well detailed were they. Only the press of other business and being obliged to deal with the ongoing conflict had prevented him from bringing them forward previously. However, the one thing he did not do, perhaps could not do, was to deal with the ongoing problem of the Tribunes of the Plebs, whose all-powerful veto still remained a problem. There is, however, absolutely no evidence that any of his laws were passed by force, in fact it seems that a large part of the people actually welcomed the new measures. However, he had certainly done all he could, and it would have to suffice. His consulship was soon to end and he would need to be away.

First, though, the elections for the new magistrates for the coming year would have to take place. He had already sensibly sent his troops back to Capua, knowing that he had to tread carefully to ensure that they caused no friction with the people in Rome, but their presence had apparently caused no undue problems.

Naturally, Sulla had his own preferred candidate for the consulship for the following year (87 BC), as he would rather leave behind him a man who would continue his policies after he left. His choice was Publius Servilius Vatia, but this man's attempt at election failed and Sulla had to put up with the election of Lucius Cornelius Cinna and Gnaeus Octavius Ruso, men he knew would certainly not be sympathetic towards him. In fact, it was immediately apparent that Cinna was firmly opposed to Sulla and was boasting that as soon as he was in power he would prosecute him for marching on Rome. Octavius then declared that he too was angry at the intrusion into Rome of Sulla's troops and that furthermore he wanted the return of Gaius Marius and the other exiles.

This is another moment when it is possible to take a look at Sulla's character. It would have been quite easy for a ruthless man, such as Sulla is often supposed to have been, to use his troops against those two new consuls–elect, men who had already declared their antipathy towards him. Such things had happened before and casual killing was a facet of Roman society which cropped up from time to time. However, Sulla did not make any such attempt against them, even though he knew perfectly well that they would both work against him indefatigably once he had left Rome. Again, we have to face the fact that Sulla was a far more reasonable man than he is generally given credit for, and moreover he definitely did not see himself as being a ruthless or lawless person. He was still acting within the rules of law and if these men chose to oppose him, dislike it though he may, he would simply have to put up with it. Sulla did not believe that he had done anything wrong, having marched to defend himself against the actions of Marius and Sulpicius, not Rome herself, and even then for what he honestly believed was Rome's eventual good. At no point until then had he overstepped the limits of the official position which he held. Even when obliged to do so it was only under extreme provocation and after his success he quickly made every effort to restore calm to the city.

He would certainly take up arms against Gaius Marius and Sulpicius, who had initiated the dangerous situation and worked against him when he was simply doing his appointed duty. But at that time he obviously saw no justification for harming Cinna, who was also acting within the limits of his office. In this, again, Sulla showed his keen regard for proper law and order.[20]

There was, however, one more thing that he could do to protect himself from another attack once his back was turned. While he still had the authority, he could require both the consuls–elect to take an oath, in which they would swear to respect the new laws he had put in place. This they did, but only because Sulla still held the power and if they had refused to do so, he could simply have refused to step down. If he did not officially renounce his consulship on the appointed date, they could not assume their new positions.

It later became apparent that while Octavius did consider his oath binding, Cinna certainly did not. Unfortunately, there was little more Sulla could legally do. He needed to go east and strengthen his position by making a good job of the Mithradatic War, in order to improve his overall popularity and wipe out the stain of his march on Rome.

However, before he did so he had one last worry to deal with. He was concerned about the safety of his consular partner, Quintus Pompeius Rufus. He would be left behind in Rome and his support of Sulla might well make him a target when Sulla had left. (Another indication that Sulla was not the selfish, self-centred man often portrayed.)

He decided that if he could send Pompeius Rufus to Gnaeus Pompeius Strabo's army, those troops could serve as his bodyguards, protecting him from attack by Cinna.

He obtained the Senatus Consultum in order to replace Pompeius Strabo with Pompeius Rufus, and then laid the whole matter before the assembly in the correct manner. The move was initially granted, which must have been a relief, but then a Tribune named Gaius Herennius (who was possibly in the pay of Strabo), vetoed it, so that Pompeius Rufus would be obliged to take over his command with only the authority of the Senatus Consultum behind him. However, things rapidly went from bad to worse, for when Pompeius Rufus arrived to take over the command that Sulla had arranged for his safety, his reception was not what he might have wished, and within a few days the troops had actually killed him! This action too might well have been on the orders of Pompeius Strabo. Sulla was horrified when the news reached him. He had honestly tried to ensure his partner's safety and found it hard to come to terms with people who were so at odds with what he considered to be decent and correct behaviour.

Cinna then made a direct attack on Sulla himself, taking steps to repeal his laws by using a Tribune to bring a prosecution against him. However, the authority of a Tribune did not extend beyond the city of Rome itself, and once a general had assumed his military cloak, or paludamentum, signifying the start of a campaign, his imperium then protected him.

It is perfectly possible that Cinna was trying a last ditch attempt to remove Sulla from the command once again, but in this he received very little, if any, support.

The Senate was now only too aware that Sulla was desperately needed. Rome was poverty stricken, largely because the huge revenues from Asia Province were not coming in. The situation had to be rectified and they had to have a reliable man who could deal with Mithradates. That important, indeed vital, piece of work would now certainly have to take precedence over any merely personal animosity.

Sulla assigned Appius Claudius Pulcher to command the still ongoing siege of Nola and prepared to leave for the East. He was going with a very thin purse, for the treasuries in Rome were almost empty due to the years of continuing wars. To raise a little money for the campaign some of the land around the Capitol, which had been intended for the use of the priestly colleges, was sold and the sum raised, a mere 9,000 librae of gold, was given to Sulla as a campaign fund.[21] It was a pitiful amount of money on which to be expected to wage a war against such an adversary. Never had a campaign so important been sent off with less. Sulla would be obliged to raise more along the way however he could, a practice which would leave him open to accusations of everything from robbery to sacrilege and would only succeed in bringing more odium onto his name.

He was also leaving behind him as Consuls two men who would very quickly begin to work against each other and who would once again plunge Rome into disorder.

Chapter Nine

Sulla had left for the East knowing that he was facing a very difficult job. Not only from his chronic lack of funds but also the fact that Mithradates had for a long time been building up his power in the East, while Rome did not have either the men or the money available to turn aside from the Social War to deal with him. However, it was not merely the annoyance of having an arrogant eastern potentate busily extending his authority over lands which Rome considered her own. By the time the Romans had the leisure to move against him, all of Asia Province was in his hands, and that meant in real terms that all the abundance from that supremely wealthy Province was also lost to them.[1]

There was not only the problem of trying to do the good job, indeed the spectacular job that was needed, with no funds or men available, but also the knowledge that Rome itself, left behind him, was still unstable. He had had to leave things in the hands of men who would immediately move against him and destroy his work. It must have been a depressing thought. Rome was to prove even less stable than he feared, and was very quickly to slide into revolution. Although Sulla was not present at the upheavals at home (the revolution was at least one thing they could not blame him for), they would affect him and his family. Even his wife Caecilia Metella would be obliged to flee Rome the following winter, leaving all their possessions, including their luxurious new home, in burning ruins behind her. Ironically, when she did flee to her husband in Greece for protection, she was accompanied by many other distinguished refugees, who were now forced to try to find safety with Sulla, despite him having been the object of their spite while he was at home.

Rome was, of course, on its knees financially, Sicily and Africa were suffering from droughts and very little grain was reaching the city. The gold from Asia Province, which should have paid for grain to be bought for distribution to the people, was no longer available due to the depredations of Mithradates, so Rome was ripe for trouble.

However, by the time of the Ludi Romani, the main games of the year, people were travelling in from all over Italy, eager to be in Rome for what they hoped would be the best games for years. Always a good way of taking the collective mind of the populace away from their more pressing troubles, the games could not be cancelled, despite the dangers. The aediles of that year were rumoured to be rich, so great things were expected. Unfortunately, not only were the Romans looking forward to the games, but also far too many of the newly enfranchised citizens were planning on making the journey. They may also have been eager to watch the games, but they were not happy in other respects, particularly with the way their citizenships had been distributed among the tribes, making their long-awaited powers of voting practically useless.

Cinna, however, had announced a *contio* in the Centuriate Assembly for the Ides of September, during the performance of the games. This might, on reflection, have seemed a foolish thing to do, as the games that year ran between 5 and 19 September, placing the *contio* while the games were still running.²

Cinna had announced that he intended to demand a proper distribution of citizens in the tribes, together with the recall of the exiled Gaius Marius and his friends, plus the good old standby of a general cancellation of debts. Surely the games-hungry crowds were easily inflamed enough, with their many resentments already close to the surface, without promising reforms that would be difficult, if not impossible, to implement?

His colleague, Octavius Ruso, now strongly disagreed with his aims. He had been in favour of some of Sulla's senatorial reforms, and in any case he had sworn to uphold them, a vow which he took seriously, even if his colleague obviously did not. Cinna tried to push through the *contio*, where his new measures could be discussed. The Senate made it clear that such matters as the distribution of citizens throughout the tribes and the cancellation of debts had been discussed enough already, and that they did not intend to debate them again. Cinna however, was determined. He not only wanted a *contio* to discuss the measures he proposed, but he also wished to push them through quickly, which by law he could not do in *contio*. Unless, of course, he intended to try to waive the Lex Didia, as Sulla had done, which might allow voting within the three-market-days interval. He may also have hoped that the presence in Rome of so many outsiders, with the ever-present threat of riots, would force the Senate to agree with him.

However, there was some fighting in the Forum, as might have been expected, and the Flamen Dialis, Lucius Cornelius Merula, reported bad omens in the Temple of Jupiter Optimus Maximus on the Capitol. Octavius Ruso, using this opportunity, declared that this showed that Cinna should be removed from his office as Consul. It was not generally considered possible to remove a consul during his term of office, but Octavius appointed a suffect consul to take his place, none other than the Flamen Dialis, Merula. Octavius must have been pleased with his ploy, and quickly had Cinna declared a public enemy, to be driven out of Rome.³ He no doubt expected that Cinna would merely flee to join Gaius Marius and the other exiles.

Cinna, however, had no intention whatever of becoming just another exile. He met with Quintus Sertorius and together they intended to drum up enough support to enable them, in their turn, to march on Rome. Sertorius, at least, had a splendid war record and was popular with the soldiers, so by October Cinna had 20,000 men behind him. At this point the news came that Gaius Marius had returned to Italy, therefore Cinna and Sertorius started their move towards Rome with sufficient men to make a difference.

To many of the people in Italy the name Gaius Marius still exerted a special spell. When news of his return spread there were popular demonstrations of affection, particularly in Ostia, where he was welcomed joyfully, with the city opening its gates to him. However, the Gaius Marius who entered Ostia was not the man they remembered so fondly. This man was now aged, far from well, carrying too much weight for his own good, and in a mean temper.[4] Whatever had ailed him when he retired from the Social War had not improved and he was obviously a sick, as well as a resentful, man. He was unimpressed by Ostia's welcome and gave orders for the sacking of the town. Ignoring the sufferings of the people, which became acute while the assorted collection of troops he had brought with him committed atrocities, he concentrated on putting a barrage across the mouth of the Tiber, to prevent grain barges from reaching Rome and relieving the food shortage.

It had been dry in the area that year, and Pompeius Strabo's camp outside the Colline Gate had become notorious for contaminating the water supplies, although he still made no real attempt to repulse Cinna, whose own camps, now also outside the city, added to the problem. It was quite likely that Pompeius Strabo was waiting on events, before he decided which men to side with.[5] When the Senate heard that Gaius Marius was preventing the grain barges from reaching the city they began to panic, and decided to call for volunteers to defend Rome, promising that all those who fought would be rewarded with full citizen status whatever their degree. However, it did not succeed in persuading many volunteers to offer themselves.

Marius, who was now approaching Rome, had the Tribune Gaius Flavius Fimbria with him. He had been with the legion outside Nola, and transferred himself to support Marius as soon as he heard of his arrival. Octavius Ruso and Merula, with the Senate still in Rome, must have been dismayed at the reports coming in, realizing that their position was worsening by the hour. Gaius Marius stopped his troops south of the Janiculum Garrison and was only prevented from penetrating the fortresses's defences by Pompeius Strabo. Deciding finally to make a stand, he engaged Sertorius, taking Cinna's attention away from Gaius Marius. Octavius Ruso and the censor Publius Crassus then led a force across the Wooden Bridge (the Pons Sulblicius) and managed to relieve the fortress just in time.

However, Pompeius Strabo, perhaps in a divine punishment for keeping an unhygienic camp, caught dysentery himself and died a few days later, still in his camp outside the Colline Gate. When the people heard of his death they dragged his body from its bier and abused it, blaming him for the spread of disease throughout the area, due to the contamination of their water supplies.[6] There was already a huge death toll in the city due to the spread of the infection, and the grain supplies were gone. The populace was by then in desperate straits.

Once Pompeius Strabo was finally buried, his men offered their services to Gaius Marius.

Marius had already been in touch with Mutilus of the Samnites, through his Tribune Fimbria, and the Samnites had also gone over to support Marius. His position was already gaining strength daily.

By the end of November it was obvious to everyone that the government in Rome was doomed and early in December a treating party, led by Quintus Caecilius Metellus Pius, met with Marius and Cinna. Cinna's demand was that he immediately be reinstated as consul, but he also wanted his original proposals too. That the citizens be distributed properly in the tribes (always a good sop to public opinion), and that their slave army, which consisted of men who had deserted their lawful masters to fight with Gaius Marius, should then be manumitted. However, he not only wanted these slaves to be given their freedom, but also to be granted the full citizenship! This might be expected to be a step too far, even given the situation Rome was in, but it was not wise to object. Gaius Marius, in his turn, demanded that the convictions against him and his fellow exiles should be quashed, and that he be appointed as senior consul, with Cinna as his junior. In return, he granted that there would be no proscriptions, banishments, confiscation of property or executions – a promise he obviously did not intend to keep!

Cinna then entered Rome again in some state, having been restored to his position of consul, and was accompanied formally by twelve lictors as evidence of his new position. Appian tells us that both Cinna and Marius had promised the Senate that they would spare the life of Gnaeus Octavius Ruso, who had taken refuge in the fortress of the Janiculum. But it was not to be. He was brutally murdered by Gaius Marcius Censorinus, even though he was still officially consul. He was actually wearing his robes and sitting in his official chair, while awaiting his death.[7] His head was taken to Cinna as a trophy.

Within a very few days all of Sulla's laws were rescinded. The Plebian Assembly was restored to full power and Gaius Marius was granted a proconsular imperium and formal command of the war in the East against Mithradates, against whom Sulla had already been sent but without the funds to perform his work properly! A whole new collection of magistrates were then appointed, with the Censors probably thinking it far wiser for the sake of their own lives to make no protest at all the worrying irregularities.

When Cinna and Gaius Marius were formally elected as consuls for the following year (which would give Cinna consecutive appointments) it went through with the intention that Cinna be the senior consul with Marius as the junior. At that point it did not seem to matter. Gaius Marius was openly jubilant, delighted that he had achieved the consulship for the absolutely unprecedented seven times, in accordance with the prophecy of Martha the Syrian all those years before. However, when the two consuls were officially inaugurated a couple of weeks later, Marius had by then transformed himself into the senior partner, with Cinna relegated to junior consul. He, too, probably thought it wiser in the circumstances not to protest.

Since Sulla had left Rome the city had suffered a year of such upheavals that it could hardly be believed. However, there was far worse to come, as Gaius Marius, now completely in control of the city, set about ousting Cinna's power. He then permitted his army, which had been transformed into a personal bodyguard, completely free rein to rampage about Rome, doing exactly as they pleased. It rapidly became a bloodbath. Nobody was safe, as the slaves and ex-slaves abused the ordinary people with atrocity after atrocity. Gaius Marius made no move at all to prevent them from desecrating the city and killing whoever was unfortunate enough to stand in their way. On the contrary, he had murders of his own in mind.

The proscriptions of Gaius Marius after his return to Rome are often glossed over, as if they were no more than an unfortunate incident at the end of the life of a brilliant man. They certainly were unfortunate, but should not be either ignored or made light of. Gaius Marius had certainly been a brilliant man, and a general of no mean order. His record speaks for itself and nobody can take away from him the successes he achieved, let alone the reorganization of the Roman army into a fighting force which was capable of carrying all before it. He was indeed a very special man and a very gifted one. However, by this time, he was not only old by Roman standards, but also ill, both physically and mentally. He had put on weight, was probably suffering from the high blood pressure which often goes with increasing weight and age, and he had become extremely erratic in his behaviour, as was shown by the sacking of Ostia, while it attempted to welcome him. Beesley gives the opinion that by this time Gaius Marius was insane and it is saddening but very tempting to go down that road.[8] The most charitable description of his behaviour is that he had become senile. He had certainly changed completely from the bluff and easy-going man who had been so popular. He had always been a man who found it impossible to delegate, believing that nobody could do anything so well as he could. Hence his later behaviour and jealousies towards Sulla, when the Senate decided that Marius was too old to command. Since then, his belief that he was all-important, all-powerful, had reached dangerous levels, and was about to be unleashed on Rome.

His Tribune, Fimbria, had Lucius, the son of Publius Licinius Crassus, killed and the young man's father, a supporter of Sulla who knew he would be next, then committed suicide.

Gaius Atilius Serranus; Marcus Antonius Orator; Lucius Julius Caesar and his brother Caesar Strabo were murdered, along with Quintus Mucius Scaevola the Auger; Publius Cornelius Lentulus; Gaius Nemotorius; Gaius Baebius and of course Octavius Ruso. Their heads were displayed on the rostra for all the people to see, if indeed anyone wanted to stand and stare. Most people were too busy trying to avoid being killed themselves by Marius' out-of-control slave legions, who were thoroughly enjoying their licence to rape, loot, burn and rampage through Rome, destroying anyone who happened to be in the wrong place at the wrong time.

Quintus Lutatius Catulus Caesar and Lucius Cornelius Merula (the Flamen Dialis) were indicted for treason, Merula for no other reason than he had been elected suffect consul.

Both men committed suicide rather than face the shame of being hounded and killed.

Mamercus Aemilius Lepidus Livianus (the brother of the murdered reformer Drusus), who was Cornelia Sulla's second husband, managed to arrange for Sulla's wife Metella and his daughter and grandchildren to be hurriedly taken out of Rome, in fear of their lives. With them went whatever other exiles could manage the journey in time. Behind them, when their absence was noted, all their properties were destroyed.

It says much for the mental degeneration of Gaius Marius at this time that he would think nothing of persecuting the women and children of his opponents. It was something that Sulla would never stoop to do. Nor would he, even when in possession of absolute power, allow the poorer people of Rome to suffer as Gaius Marius was now doing. In fact, it now seemed that Marius, as completely without restraint as his followers, gloated in the carnage he had created.[9] Cinna did try to remonstrate with him, but Marius said that he would allow no selection of victims for death, or life, but simply intended to massacre all the people who in any way opposed him. Sertorius also begged Cinna to try to contain Marius and stop the slaughter and although he did attempt to curb the worst outrages of the slave bands roaming the streets, he could not afford, for his own sake, to have any open break with Marius. However, it was not to last for much longer.

After the two consuls had been inaugurated the violence in the city reached a crescendo, but Gaius Marius, delighting in his consulship, had only actually been consul for a couple of weeks at most, when he suffered a collapse. This should only have been expected, as he had shown signs of ill-health previously. Whether it was a heart-attack or a stroke we may never know, but the balance of probability is that it was a stroke. Had he been suffering from heart trouble there would probably have been some sign of it previously, and the angina-type pains which would be likely to affect a sufferer could not have received any effective medical help at that time. The discomfort of the condition would also quite likely have prevented him from taking such a major part in a revolution. Considering his increasing weight and his appalling stress levels over a considerable period, it is far more likely that he finally suffered a stroke.[10] He was then reported to have been ill for only a short time before he died.

It was a most unfortunate end to the life and career of a man who had given so much to Rome and whose memory should have been only of the greatness of his achievements. Had he been prepared to retire from active participation in affairs, he could have continued to be revered by the population who still loved him, and may well have lived longer. As it was, his behaviour in the last months of his life became an ignominious ending to that life, which should have been filled only with distinction.

However, it is not reasonable or just to those hundreds, perhaps thousands, of innocent people who suffered during the horrors of his final consulship, to attempt to ignore or whitewash what he did to Rome at that time.[11] In releasing an army of assorted riff-raff to do as they pleased in the city and in perpetrating a massacre, he certainly marred the memory of the splendid earlier achievements.

As soon as he was dead, Sertorius and Cinna, freed from the stranglehold he exerted over them, rounded up his slave army from their evil work, and killed them to the last man.

Lucius Valerius Flaccus succeeded Marius as consul.

It was now Cinna's turn to be the most powerful man in Rome. He was consul for four successive years from 87 to 84 BC but he was not a man who used such supreme power wisely.[12] He removed the restrictions on grain, proclaimed Sulla and Metellus to be outlaws and, with Flaccus, passed a law making one quarter of a debt full payment for it. This was probably in response to the appalling results of the compound interest commonly charged, which Sulla himself had tried to end. He then, however, tried to send Flaccus and Fimbria to the east, to take Sulla. A futile venture, when Sulla, despite his poor start and lack of assistance from Rome, had already been enjoying some successes.

It is now necessary to retrace our steps a little, to clarify the situation in the east, as the events in Rome had been taking place concurrently with Sulla's experiences there.

Earlier, Mithradates of Pontus and his son-in-law Tigranes of Armenia had dethroned Nicomedes of Bithynia and Ariobarzanes of Cappodocia. One of the last things done by Marcus Aemilius Scaurus, the Princeps Senatus, before he died in 89 BC was to send a commission to Mithradates and Tigranes, requiring them to remain behind their own borders.

In April of 88 BC while Sulla and Pompeius Rufus were consuls, a Roman invasion of Galatia and Pontus had begun. Manius Aquilius, who had been legate to Gaius Marius at Aquae Sextiae was sent, along with Titus Manlius Mancinus and Gaius Mallius Maltinus, to reinstate the original sovereigns of Bithynia and Cappodocia. At that time the governor of Asia Province was Gaius Cassius Longinus.

Gaius Cassius and Manius Aquilius had planned together to invade Pontus with the help of Nicomedes of Bithynia and his ally Pylaemenes of Paphlagonia. The governor of Cilicia at that time, one Quintus Oppius, was also in conference with Gaius Cassius, as it was obvious that war was now inevitable. Manius Aquilius had led the one legion of Roman auxiliaries then available in Asia Province, while Quintus Oppius sailed from Tarsus to Attaleia and marched with two legions into Pisidia.

Marcus Aquilius saw 100,000 of the Pontic infantry waiting for him at Lake Tatta and decided that it would be wise to retreat across the mountains. King Mithradates went after Gaius Cassius Longinus personally, who had retreated in his turn into the fortified town of Apameia.

Quintus Oppius went to ground at Laodiceia but the Pontic army caught up with him and he was dismayed to see the townspeople open their gates to them, after which he was handed over to Mithradates. However, rather surprisingly, after some humiliating treatment he was released under escort to Tarsus.

Gaius Cassius Longinus fled to the coast, finding sanctuary with the ruler of Nysa, before going on to Rhodes. By the summer, all of Bithynia and Asia Province were in the hands of Mithradates and approximately 250,000 of his soldiers. One of the great assets to Mithradates in his programme of expansion had been forty years or so of Roman mismanagement during Rome's occupation of the Province. Mithradates played cunningly on this by announcing that for the following five years he would require no taxes or duties from the area now under his occupation. This had very nicely aided anti-Roman feeling to grow.

Meanwhile, Manius Aquilius, who had escaped across the mountains, had finally been captured at Mytilene and sent back to King Mithradates, who had him killed. Shortly after, Mithradates gave his famous order to kill every Roman or Italian citizen in Asia Province. This resulted in the deaths of 80,000 citizens in one day, along with 70,000 slaves.[13] By forcing the local Greek communities to actually perform the murderous work, he ensured that they would be implicated by their action in the blame. Very few Romans had survived that holocaust, some of them being those who were exiled from Rome, thereby not officially citizens at all, including Publius Rutilius Rufus, who had been living in Smyrna. King Mithradates then took up residence for a time at Ephesus and announced that any detachments of militia surrendering to him would be freed. He later made an attempt on Rhodes, but was stoutly fought off by the Rhodian navy, still one of the best in the world and far superior to that of Mithradates.

While Mithradates was trying unsuccessfully to subdue Rhodes, his favourite general Archelaus was determined to bring an assault against Europe. He had travelled west to the Cyclades and the Isle of Delos and successfully slaughtered the helpless but rather large and very prosperous Italian trading community then living there.

Athens was, of course, the main target and the main entry point for Greece itself. However, Athens was yet another great city which had been suffering from considerable turmoil for several years past. There had been friction between the ruling aristocracy and the tyrant Medeius since 91 BC which had resulted in an appeal to Rome for intervention. Rome, of course, had then been occupied with the Social Wars and was obliged to decline to intervene. By 88 BC Medeius had disappeared and the Athenians, angry at Rome's refusal to mediate in any way, had turned gladly enough towards Mithradates and his promises. An ambassador named Athenion was sent to treat with him and appeared to get on well with him, finally returning home to convince his own people that Rome was now finished, both politically and militarily, and that they should turn to Mithradates, relying on him instead. Athenion then became just another tyrant, ruling in the place of the previous one, working against his former aristocratic supporters and finally killing them. When he considered he had amassed enough power on his own account he turned away from Mithradates and back towards Rome, hoping for their support. Mithradates, in retaliation at his betrayal cut the grain supplies to Athens, which had been formerly coming from the Euxine Sea, and finally Delos, a dependency of Athens, revolted against Athenion, disliking his connection to Mithradates.

He was forced to attack Delos but the Romans scattered his forces, after which he disappeared from the records, to be replaced by a man named Aristion, who had once been an ambassador of Mithradates. He was obviously well connected to the Pontic king as he was able to keep a personal bodyguard of 2,000 Pontic troops with him, and soon had enough power to murder all the aristocracy who had favoured Rome. The Pontic General Archelaus was able to secure Athens, and with Aristion's connivance advanced against the town of Thespiae which still held out for Rome.[14] It was obviously becoming increasingly necessary for the Romans to show that they were still able to defend their Grecian allies.

Gaius Braetius Sura fought the Pontic forces at Chaeronea and defeated them there, although Archelaus got his troops away by sea. Sura was able to hurry towards Athens and take control of what had been until then the Pontic centre, although Archelaus soon arrived with his fleet and Sura was obliged to retreat northwards. Further skirmishing was held up by the onset of winter weather, and by the spring of 87 BC a large Roman force landed at Epirus and was reportedly marching on Athens. Sulla had finally arrived in Greece with his quaestor Lucius Lucullus.

Lucullus, commanding an advance force, met with Sura and ordered him to withdraw, as the sole command had been given to Sulla, an order which he had no choice but to obey.

Archelaus, seeing the size of the Roman army and realizing that his forces would be no match for it, decided to remain in the Piraeus, where he could defend himself. His intention, no doubt, was to await further reinforcements from Pontus before tackling Sulla in open battle.

Sulla, of course, did not wish to see the Piraeus left in the hands of Archelaus and decided that Athens was, at all costs, to be taken. If any further force was sent from Macedonia, he would be better able to deal with it if he held Athens under his control.

As he marched, he received several delegations from Greek cities, trying to convince him that their recent allegiance with Mithradates had been mistaken and that they could now be trusted to side with him. Whatever his opinions of their loyalty, he did find some solace in another one of his prophetic dreams. He reported that he had dreamed that he saw Venus, in full armour, leading his army. Confused by this, he asked the Oracle at Delphi to explain it, and he was told that Venus herself would in future champion his cause. He was told that although he had neglected her previously, he must from then onwards show her special devotion. It was probably from this time that Sulla began to use the name 'Epiphradatos'[15] as it gave him a particular connection with the goddess, particularly while he was in Greece.[16] The instructions he received from the oracle were that he should sacrifice annually to all of the Gods, that he should bring gifts to Delphi itself, and that he should dedicate an axe to the shrine of Aphrodite at Aphrodisias in Caria. For a man as superstitious as Sulla was there was no possibility of ignoring such a decree. The gifts were duly sent, and Sulla began an exciting new phase during which he felt strongly that he now had the support of Aphrodite for his work in Greece. Not necessarily for him personally, but as her representative and the general who would restore Roman power in her name.[17]

After this, probably given extra confidence at the idea of her support, he made an attempt to attack the Piraeus. However, it was an ill-considered action, based on attacking the walls without siege engines. Unfortunately, but unsurprisingly, the Romans were repelled. Sulla retired to Eleusis, but only to plan, for shortly afterwards he reappeared with the same venture in mind, but far more carefully thought out. No doubt Venus intended to support her favoured general, but she also wanted him to think for himself!

This time the construction of proper siege towers was begun. To do this, Sulla was obliged to cut down the olive groves which had been considered sacred. Thousands of mules had to be used to carry the wood to the place where it would be transformed into siege towers. Thebes also, very wisely, sent supplies of all kinds, desperate to show Sulla that their rejection of Mithradates was now complete. Sulla intended to use the siege towers to protect the mound he was constructing from the remains of the ruined Long Wall, which had once connected Athens and its port.[18] While this work was continuing, a message was passed through to Sulla, from a spy inside the town, to the effect that on the following day Archelaus intended to make a sally. Sulla prepared an ambush and when the Pontic forces came out, convinced that they would take him by surprise, they met an ambuscade.

Still determined to find a way to win, Archelaus built his own towers, opposite to those of Sulla, and equipped them with engines also, initiating a fight between the towers as they rose. There was damage to both sides, including the burning of one of Sulla's towers due to a nighttime foray by Archelaus' men. However, it was soon replaced, and the race for each side to build more and bigger and better towers continued.

Eventually, though, reinforcements arrived by sea and, heartened by this, Archelaus decided on a pitched battle at last. The battle was more or less equal, and neither side appeared to have the advantage, until a foraging party of Sulla's returned from the surrounding area where they had been searching for wood and added their weight to the Romans. This caused the Pontic troops to flee back inside, in their panic unfortunately leaving Archelaus locked outside. He actually found himself shut out of his own town and was obliged to be hauled humiliatingly back in by ropes![19]

Despite the approaching winter, the siege could not be called off. Sulla sent his quaestor Lucullus to try to raise what ships he could manage from the eastern Mediterranean, as their lack was by then beginning to prove a serious problem for the Roman war effort.

It was also at around this time that Sulla's wife, Caecilia Metella, arrived in Greece, along with his daughter Cornelia and her husband Mamercus. They brought with them bad news from Rome, of the revolution which had taken place there and the fact that they had had to flee as refugees, leaving the majority of their belongings behind. They also had with them other refugees, which must have been a grim sort of triumph for Sulla, as many of them were the very men who had opposed him not long before. They were now fleeing to him along with his wife and family, and were just as desperate for sanctuary. However, apart from personal losses, which must have been considerable, the news brought other worries too. It was now obvious that there would be no help from Rome since the upheavals there and also that there would be no further sums of money, with which to continue the war. The necessary funds would have to be found elsewhere.

The solution Sulla found has often been misconstrued. He certainly did have the idea of finding the money from the Greek temples and shrines. Several treasures were indeed carried away and melted down to make the necessary coinage to pay for the essentials for the ongoing war. But it is also often said that he desecrated these shrines and important temples, and that the Greeks were incensed at the pillage he instigated there. However, this is rather far from the truth.

Sulla was a superstitious man, certainly. He would not have liked the idea of sacrilege any more than any other man, even though he knew the desperate need of the army. What he actually did was borrow the money from the temples, of which fact there is plenty of evidence.[20] Not only that, he made definite arrangements for the loans to be paid back and indeed made sure that they were paid back, as soon as the money was found. Sulla's close and confident relationship with the gods who supported him so firmly was not only important, it was sacrosanct! He could not allow it to be jeopardized by any foolish or ill-considered action. Borrow he must, and did, but he could not and would not risk the wrath of the gods by breaking his agreement with them. In fact, his confidence in their approval was such that he declared that his cause could not now fail, as the gods had so far supported him as to invest in his cause. It seemed, once again, that he was right.

However, there were other troubles first. (The gods may well have loved and supported Sulla, but that certainly did not prevent them from putting problems his way.)

While he was hanging on grimly to his siege at Athens, another Pontic army was advancing through Macedonia and Greece to take the Romans in the rear. Caught between this new threat and Archelaus, still holed up inside the city, it appeared that he would have very little chance of any real success.

However, the gods stayed with him yet again. What happened next can only be described as crazy miscalculation on the part of Pontus. A swift advance on Greece would have crushed Sulla's forces and stopped any further chances of success for Rome. However, a Pontic commander named Archatias, who had recently overwhelmed a Roman garrison in Macedonia, stopped to involve himself in administrative details, parcelling out captured land and generally wasting precious time instead of advancing to help Archelaus. In fact, this behaviour was in step with the ideas of Mithradates himself, who seemed to be of the opinion that the Romans would be beaten easily without any great attempts against them being necessary. In fact, he seems to have been quite unworthy of his commander Archelaus, who was a resourceful and courageous man, being unable to appreciate his undoubted abilities as he should. There had already been considerable conflict between them concerning how the war against Rome should be conducted, with Archelaus no doubt becoming very frustrated at not being able to make the king see sense.[21]

Sulla now had more time to prepare and he used it well. He had managed to put in place a blockade of the city and then there was a severe famine within the walls, causing the inhabitants to eat whatever they could find, including weeds, boiled shoe leather and, occasionally, each other.[22] The Romans determinedly tightened the blockade by adding more towers around the walls, and finally a ditch. Stone balls continued to be hurled into the city, landing just short of the Acropolis. Modern excavations of the area of the Agora have revealed signs of the damage done by them, and several large catapult balls have also been found preserved on the site. Sulla's main artillery position appears to have been on the northwest, outside the Sacred Gate. To prevent Sulla's men from acquiring any further timber for siege towers, the Athenians themselves burned down the largely wooden Odeion of Pericles on the south slope, which seems to have been a rather unnecessary sacrifice, on the line of cutting off one's nose to spite one's face. The situation for Athens was already beyond help, and Sulla's triumph there now seemed inevitable.

Archelaus, still on the Piraeus, had done his best to get provisions into suffering Athens, but food convoys sent into the city were betrayed and intercepted by the Romans, so that all attempts to relieve the city's distress finally had to be abandoned.

Aristion, who had been living in comfort while his people starved, quite indifferent to their plight, had also been approached for help, but their suffering was made light of. He still refused to see that the position was desperate and he amused himself with nightly drinking parties, dancing in his armour and mocking the Romans from the walls.[23] This behaviour disgusted Sulla, who developed a hatred for the effete and useless man, who he considered was not fit to be a ruler. When the city fell he would be executed, but it would not be any grief for the city and its inhabitants, who had already realized that a man like Aristion was worthless and not the kind of leader they or anyone else could respect.

Sulla finally broke through the city walls on 1 March 86 BC. The siege had lasted since the previous autumn and even then the Acropolis held out for several more weeks, before it too finally fell to the Romans.

Sulla specifically spared the city from fire, but had to allow a few hours of looting by his soldiers. This, again, has been reported as some kind of fault in him, in that he either could not, or did not wish to, control his troops. It has been forgotten that every army, having taken a city which held out, then looted and pillaged. It was a quite necessary part of taking a city, after it had refused a sensible surrender on reasonable terms, as it served as a warning to others. It was certainly not done by Sulla in a fury, nor in a spirit of revenge against Athens, but simply because it was customary, and was to remain so for many centuries to come, as standard practice. Soldiers who had been besieging a city or town for months, suffering their own hardships outside the walls, could only be kept disciplined if their commander allowed them a slack rein now and then, particularly with regard to loot and pillaging after the city fell. It is right to say that people in Athens suffered at that time, as people in every city in a similar predicament did. It is not right to say that Sulla was in any way at fault in allowing a few hours of licence for his men. On the contrary, it prevented maddened men from attempting a mutiny and allowed the commander to regain control of them relatively quickly. It certainly did not equate to Marius allowing his slave army to rampage through Rome as had happened the previous year. Sulla was not a cruel man, nor was he a foolish one. It would have been very foolish for any commander to deny his men their release in the usual way. Sulla, like any experienced commander, knew when to allow his men their heads for a short time. That he is accused of extreme cruelty and cold-blooded, callous behaviour in this instance is merely ridiculous.

Sulla, on the contrary, was a man of natural warmth, one who easily made, and kept, friendships. His relationship with his troops shows that he was able to deal with them in a sensible way, performing his task of leader not only conscientiously but also very effectively. The men revered him, trusted him and knew that he did not need to indulge in wanton cruelty. That was simply the way things were after a battle – not only in ancient times, but often in our own, despite our preferred belief that we are different.[24]

During this time, the attack on the Piraeus was continuing. Sulla had been revitalized by the taking of Athens and assaults were renewed. His troops operated in relays while he worked tirelessly alongside them, encouraging them. Archelaus, seeing that he could not hold out much longer, retreated to the most strongly fortified part of the Piraeus, the Munychia. Sulla then fired the dockyards. Archelaus, realizing that the area was too small to hold him and his troops, took to his fleet. He then had word that the Pontic army in Macedonia was finally on the move, and no doubt hoped that reinforcements would arrive, knowing that the Romans could expect no help at all from Rome. However, he was also sent word that he was to immediately join the Pontic forces at Thermopylae. There was no possibility of refusing an order from Mithradates, however ridiculous it might seem, so he had no choice but to obey, sailing off as instructed. However, an ideal opportunity to take Sulla had been lost and Archelaus, far better at warfare than his master, must have known and resented it. However, the war was not over. Despite taking Athens, Sulla still faced the problem of the Pontic army to the north, which had been menacing him from the rear for the past several months. He now had to move his troops into Boeotia.

It is perhaps sensible at this point to consider Sulla's motives in continuing as he did. He knew then that Rome had abandoned him and that any effort he made against Mithradates, indeed any success he achieved, would not be rewarded. He had already been removed from his command officially and had supposedly been replaced by a lesser man, sent out from Rome to take over from him. He could expect no reinforcements and no further money or supplies of any sort. Why, then, did he continue?

Many men might have thought at this point that they were wasting their time. Nothing they did would be appreciated. Indeed, in this, he was actually more in concert with Archelaus himself, who was another able general working for a master who was unworthy of his talents. Why did Sulla not decide to cut his losses, stop risking his life, take his wife and children and simply disappear? Find somewhere to live where he would not be constantly harried from Rome, as well as from whatever enemies he was fighting?

I believe that the answer to that lies in Sulla's character, that he would not give in despite the odds against him. Even more importantly, he was convinced that he was the right man for the job, not just in the theatre of war, but in Rome itself. If he could manage to make even a decent treaty, possibly a lasting one, he could then return home to restore order in Rome. That is the key, Rome itself. Sulla was not fighting for the Senate, that bunch of self-seekers and time-servers who came and went like the weather, and were often his enemies, but for Rome, the entity in which he believed implicitly and for which he would continue to struggle on.

Chapter Ten

Sulla still had a great deal of work ahead of him, including battles against Mithradates' General Archelaus, the winning of which would add to his already impressive record. First, however, there was to be for him a pleasure of a more domestic kind.

Sulla's wife, Caecilia Metella Dalmatica, who had joined him in Greece early in the previous winter, now produced twins for him, a boy and a girl. Delighted, and also aware of his new responsibilities towards the gods, he decided to break away from the usual familial names for these children. Instead of the fashionable Roman names then in use, he initiated a new fashion of his own. He called them Faustus and Fausta.[1] This break from tradition seemed at first remarkable and was considered very strange. But for Sulla, who was also bearing the name 'Epiphradatos', it was a logical step. He was dedicating these two children to the gods who supported him, particularly to his favourite Fortuna.

He had also at around this time begun to use another cognomen himself. Apart from the purely Greek name that he found useful at that time, he was now also using the name 'Felix'. Though the significance of 'Faustus' in Latin and 'Felix' itself is not identical, the two words were certainly associated. Therefore, in naming his children in this way, Sulla must have intended that they represent this new beginning, this new felicitas. His obsession with this 'luck' had been with him for some time already, but since the new and strangely prophetic dreams had become such a part of his life, he wanted this knowledge of his remarkable fortune to be conveyed openly to all. He did not, officially, take the title of 'Felix' at this time; although there is evidence that he was already addressed in that way. Certainly his friends and his soldiers used the name for him. However, later, in November of 82 BC he would be officially allowed to bear this name in addition to his own, by a confirmation of the Senate.[2]

The reason for this emphasis on his 'luck', 'fortune', and good standing with the gods is obvious. There were other Romans in Greece at that time, who intended to snatch away from him the eastern command to which he had already given so much. To confirm, not only to his own troops, but the troops of his opponents, that he was an especial favourite of the gods, both Grecian and Roman, was a powerful affirmation. It showed that he was the one to follow, that in supporting him they could also assume some of that good fortune, and that he could not be vanquished while the gods gave him their approval.

So, both in himself for the present, and the naming of these children for the future, there would be a connection to the gods which would ensure their support and guarantee success.[3]

Sulla, however, now had to make that success a reality. The responsibility was his, despite the fact that he knew that he had been virtually outlawed back in Rome and that at the first opportunity attempts would be made to take his command from him. Already the main part of the army was travelling towards him, led by Lucius Valerius Flaccus, (the consul for 86 BC).[4] Sulla was firmly contemptuous of the idea that Flaccus could replace him. Not only did he have a poor opinion of his abilities, but he believed equally firmly that the Cinna-led government had no rights whatever to make such a decision, being nothing but usurpers themselves. However, Flaccus was unwittingly and certainly unintentionally about to do Sulla a service. An advance guard, led by the legate Lucius Hortensius, found itself cut off when they had landed and the Pontic fleet had burned their ships. They had advanced into Thessaly, where they soon realized the danger they were in. Their legate, Lucius Hortensius, decided that it would be far better for them simply to desert to Sulla. After sending a message to him to that effect, Sulla sent guides to help them unite with his army and this they did, usefully strengthening Sulla's forces.

He could then afford to turn his attention back towards Archelaus, and with his men occupied Philoboeotus, which was a fertile and well-watered hilltop in the plain of Elatea. In the plain was Archelaus, along with another Pontic general Taxiles. Archelaus was not particularly keen on the idea of fighting the Romans at this point, even though he had a vast numerical superiority over Sulla, plus a very useful cavalry, including the terrible and damaging scythe-wheeled chariots. He also easily controlled both the northern and eastern sides of the plain, knowing that the open area was ideal for his troop movements, which required the optimum amount of space. Sulla only had with him 15,000 foot soldiers and around 1,500 horse, which was a pathetically small force indeed compared to the over 120,000 men commanded by Archelaus.[5] Nevertheless, despite the odds against the Romans, the attempt had to be made.

Overruled by his more eager colleagues and finally forced to make a start, Archelaus then began by trying to force the Romans off their hilltop, to give battle on the plain where the Pontic troops had the advantage, but Sulla had, very wisely, refused to co-operate.[6] Sulla was instead busily digging an entrenched palisade, within which he had placed the field artillery he had brought with him from the siege of Athens.

Archelaus' idea was, of course, to follow the usual Pontic tactic of throwing vast numbers of men into the fray, in the belief that superiority of numbers would automatically mean success. However, the next attempt was against the Roman lines of communication and trying to seize the heights of Parapotamii which dominated the pass, hoping thereby to cut off any possibility of Sulla's army making a retreat that way. Sulla, however, was quickly aware of the activities of the Pontic army and a Roman detachment was sent to prevent them seizing the pass and cutting Sulla off.

Archelaus, still confident that he could cut Sulla's communications, then marched over Mt. Hedylium and took up a position on the north bank of the River Cephisus, which flows through the plain. Another Pontic detachment was sent to take Chaeronea but again Sulla was quick to realize their intentions and they were turned back by a legion led by Gabinius. This force then took up a waiting position just to the west of Chaeronea, at Thurium.

By this time, Archelaus, pressed by his fellow-commanders who were eager for real action against the Romans, allowed them to fill the plain with horses, men and chariots.

Plutarch said that the various nations under their overall command filled the air with noise and shouting, and that their armour, blades and shields, glittering blindingly in the sunlight, along with the bright and varied colours of their coats, made a brave show.

This was not only for ostentation's sake, but to try give an intimidating impression to the relatively soberly dressed and certainly undermanned Roman forces opposing them.

The Romans, however, were safe enough for the moment, having dug the impressively deep trenches around their encampment, but the shouts and catcalls from the enemy managed to unnerve many of them, and they appeared unwilling to make a stand. Sulla was obliged to wait with them, reluctant to have to force the issue with his own men. However, the period of apparent quiet on the Roman side had a similarly unnerving effect on the Pontic army, who were unused to inactive and apparently coolly indifferent enemies. Sulla's decision to wait had given him a slight advantage. The Pontic troops then became very unruly, particularly as they had never been very well disciplined in the first place. They soon fell into disorder, with contrary commands issuing from too many leaders.[7] Sulla, meanwhile, still apparently ignoring the shouts and gesticulations of the enemy, kept his men engaged in throwing up more ditches, allowing no idleness in them and keeping discipline by the simple expedient of keeping them busy. Shortly after this, the men were in a better humour to fight and actually asked if they could make a foray against the forces of Pontus.

Sulla could see a division of the enemy troops, known as the Brazen Shields, making their way up a rocky hillside nearby, which had once led to a citadel of the Parapotamians. Their city on its summit had since been laid waste, but the promontory itself was still a useful position for the soldiers to occupy.

He immediately sent troops to intercept the Brazen Shields, which they did successfully. Archelaus' men, driven off from there, set off instead to take Chaeronea itself. Becoming aware of this, the Chaeroneans among Sulla's troops begged him to do something to prevent it and not to abandon their city to the enemy. He then sent the tribune Gabinius, with one legion, plus the furious Chaeroneans from among his men, and they easily saved the city from the Pontic troops. This division then took up a strong position on the south side of the plain.

Sulla went to sacrifice on the banks of the Cephisus, always aware that the gods needed to be propitiated. He then set off towards Chaeronea to meet the forces there and take a look at Mount Thurium, upon which a good many of the enemy had stationed themselves. As Sulla approached Chaeronea, the tribune led out his men in arms, meeting him joyfully with a garland of laurel in his hand, which Sulla graciously accepted. Some Chaeroneans, pleased at the saving of their city and led by a man named Ericius, then offered to dislodge those men who were on Mount Thurium. Pleased with their initiative, Sulla allowed them to proceed.

In the meantime, he drew up his army, posting cavalry on both wings, with himself in command of the right, and Murena in charge of the left wing. His lieutenants, Galba and Hortensius, placed themselves on the upper ground with the reserves, to keep an eye on the enemy. These enemy troops had also formed their wing, and it appeared that they intended to carry it so far out to the sides that they could entirely close the Romans in.

The Chaeroneans, meanwhile, had crept stealthily up Mt. Thurium and taken the Pontic troops stationed there completely by surprise. There was a rout amongst the barbarians and a great slaughter, which caused further confusion. About 3,000 of the Pontic troops escaped by running down the mountain, but were met lower down by Murena, and there destroyed by him. The few who managed to return to their own ranks very successfully caused further consternation among their fellows by recounting what had happened to them on the mountain and how easily they had been dislodged.

Seeing this confusion, Sulla decided to take full advantage of it by moving his own men forward, lessening the distance between the two sides. By shortening the distance between the two armies, he prevented the enemy from making full use of their most dangerous weapon, the scythe-wheeled chariots, which needed a good deal of space in which to gather speed. Without that, they were far less effective. So much so, that the Romans were able to mock them, catcalling in their turn and shouting out that it was like watching the games, daring further chariots to make the attempt.[8] However, when the furious Archelaus finally ordered his chariots to charge the Roman centre, it was only to see them destroyed on the palisades. Next after them went the phalanxes, but they too found the palisades to be impassable. Not only that, but while engaged in trying to force their way through, they came under withering fire from the Roman field artillery.

By this time the mass of both armies met, the barbarians using their long pikes and the Romans discharging their javelins, before rushing swiftly forward with their swords drawn. They struggled past the pikemen and suddenly realized that they were facing 15,000 slaves, whom the Pontic commanders had recently freed, and set among the men at arms. A Roman centurion was reported by Plutarch to have said that he had never seen such a sight in his life, with servants being allowed to take their masters' part, except at the Saturnalia.[9]

Murena, who had been acting as a rearguard, had unfortunately allowed his men to swing round, exposing his left wing on the plain, leaving a gap between it and the Roman camp. Sulla was therefore also obliged to turn his troops to the left, in order to face Archelaus. Sulla then put himself in command of the centre, and the left and centre began to engage the enemy at close quarters, leaving the right wing temporarily unengaged.

Archelaus continued to extend his own right wing, intending to curve around and overlap Murena, who was still stationed on the Roman left. Hortensius, seeing what was happening on the plain, went in to enforce Murena's rescue, but he was in his turn beaten back, towards the foothills, by Archelaus wheeling around suddenly along with 2,000 of his horsemen. Sulla, becoming aware of the extent of the battle then taking place at the far side, raced over with his cavalry to assist. He managed to stabilize the situation, but Archelaus responded by flinging in even more troops from his right flank, intending to try to overwhelm Sulla, but the action had the effect of destabilizing his own lines. This merely caused more confusion among his own men and Archelaus, in order to regain some control, was forced to temporarily withdraw.

Leaving a detachment of troops to continue to harry Murena, Archelaus then moved around to attack the weakened Roman right flank. Sulla, leaving four cohorts to reinforce Hortensius, had to race back again with the fifth to help to protect his right wing. He found his men there were resisting well, but they were greatly encouraged by his arrival, and made a final great effort. He was further gratified to find that Murena had also managed to gain the upper hand against the troops Archelaus had left to harry him, so he was then able to order a general advance. The legions, supported by the cavalry, dashed forward and managed to burst through the enemy ranks. Archelaus' army, deprived of central support, folded in upon itself, suffering subsequently a terrible slaughter. As the Romans advanced in formation the rout of the forces of Pontus was absolute. Archelaus himself, with the remnant of what had been his huge army, escaped towards Chalcis. After that, the relatively few stragglers remaining from Archelaus' original vast horde were quite easily chased off by the Romans.

When the battle was finally over, Sulla gathered together all the useless parts of the spoils, and sacrificed them to the gods by burning, as was customary. A great many of the enemy forces had been killed on the battlefield itself, and many more were cut down as they tried to escape.

Out of the vast multitude, which had initially faced the Romans so confidently, a mere 10,000 men arrived safely in Chalcis, leaving behind in excess of 100,000 casualties. Sulla later wrote that he had only fourteen of his soldiers missing, and that two of those men returned to their camp later that night. Whatever the exact final total, it was a stunning victory for the Romans, and a great credit to their commander, not only because it was the first recorded time that such battlefield entrenchments were used, but also given the appalling inequality in numbers that the Romans began with.

Two permanent trophies were erected to mark the battlefield. One on the plain was inscribed in Latin, commemorating the victory and dedicating it to Mars, Victory and Venus. It stood in the place where Archelaus first gave way to Sulla. The second one was placed on the top of Mount Thurium, where the barbarians were stationed, and it bore an inscription in Greek. This one recorded that the day's victory in that place belonged to Homoloichus and Anaxidamus, who were Sulla's Chaeronean allies.[10] It also bore his title 'Epiphradatos' and a dedication to Ares, Nike and Aphrodite.[11] In the 1990s the remains of this memorial were found, with some of the engraved names still readable.[12]

Sulla then held victory games at Thebes, during which plays were performed, special stages being erected for the occasion. Singing and musical concerts also took place, with prizes given for the best performers. Sulla, with his great love of the theatre and of music must have thoroughly enjoyed these, especially as a release from the strains of battle only recently ended. It might seem unusual that a general, fresh from the battlefield, would institute such games, as opposed to the purely physical ones then customary. However, Sulla was a very cultured man for whom a more cerebral entertainment was also very important, and Greek culture was still considered the best in the world. He had chosen Greek judges to give their opinions of the talent on offer and to award the prizes.

When this period of relaxation and commemoration was over, he then returned to Athens to hear that Aristion had finally surrendered to Curio, whom Sulla had left in charge of the siege. It was said that the final surrender was due more to lack of water than lack of food, with the besieged town suffering greatly from thirst. In this regard, another incident which happened at this time, caused amazement, confirming the general opinion that Sulla was the beloved of the gods. As the still-thirsting prisoners left the Acropolis a sudden heavy rainstorm drenched the place, immediately filling the surrounding area with abundant water!

Aristion was killed, unsurprisingly enough and he must have had very few mourners. There had been slaves sold after the first attempt on the city, and Sulla now realized that he had a small bonus also. When the Acropolis finally fell, 40 librae of gold and 600 librae of silver were found. It was certainly not a fortune, but to Sulla, who was chronically short of money as usual, it must have been a welcome addition to his purse.[13]

There was not, however, very much time in which to rest or enjoy the victory, for Sulla soon heard that the main Roman army, from which Hortensius had recently defected, had then arrived in Thessaly, under the command of Flaccus. Sulla once again had to face the bad news that he was expected to give way to this man, but it was an idea that he treated with absolute contempt, particularly after his marvellous victories at Athens and Chaeronea. It was now even more ridiculous that he should hand over his command to Flaccus. Determined to meet the problem head on, he decided to set off towards Thessaly to deal with it. Unfortunately, his intention to prove the point was again thwarted, as he had only reached as far as Melitea when he heard that yet another Pontic army had landed in Greece.[14]

This was still the most important and urgent matter to be dealt with. In his own mind it was perfectly clear that he was still the properly constituted proconsul, who had been sent to Greece to deal with the armies of Mithradates.[15] Once again he would rise to the challenge of whatever work was presented to him, doing his best to deal with it.

After having fled from Chaeronea, Archelaus had gone to Chalcis. Sulla had made some attempt at having him pursued, but as he had no ships available to him he had no choice but to order his men to stop at the Euripus channel. Archelaus, knowing that Sulla had no fleet he could use was then able to sail, tauntingly, back and forth along the coast, doing largely as he pleased, which included laying siege to the town of Zacynthus. This time, however, he had taken his licence too far, forgetting that he was safer on the sea than on land. He was attacked by another party of Roman soldiers, who involved him in a fight which unnerved him and forced him to flee back towards Chalcis. Being the sort of man he was he was also, unfortunately, soon back out again. A great number of Pontic reinforcements, under the command of a man named Darylaus, had arrived to assist him.[16]

Together the commanders moved their men into Boeotia, where they were then joined by further reinforcements, as the men of the town of Thebes, along with one or two other towns, decided to abandon any loyalty to Rome and defect to the side of Mithradates.

Unfortunately, as was only too common amongst the commanders employed by Mithradates, Archelaus and his new colleague Darylaus quickly began to disagree. There was probably a definite policy in the Pontic military of keeping the commanders at odds with each other, in order to prevent them from gathering together in opposition to their master. But it not only made for a very difficult working relationship for the commanders concerned, it was also an extremely inefficient way to run an army.

Darylaus, in his turn, newly arrived but presumptuously over-confident, seemed to think that he knew the opinions of Mithradates far better than Archelaus did. He subsequently demanded that they arrange a pitched battle against Sulla's troops, still believing in the old idea that superiority of numbers must automatically win the day. Archelaus, now wearily knowing the capabilities of the Romans far better than his colleague did, argued instead that a war of attrition was a far better option against such a well disciplined and successful army.

Darylaus was openly contemptuous of this suggestion, believing that Archelaus' new respect for his opponent showed only that he was lukewarm in his attempts against Sulla. He firmly expressed his opinion that there must have been some treachery involved in the defeat of Archelaus at Chaeronea, since he started with a vastly superior army to Sulla, yet his defeat was total. In his mind such an outcome was impossible, unless the commander of the superior force had simply not tried hard enough.

Archelaus suddenly realized the danger he was in. He was only too aware that his master, Mithradates, was a man of an extremely suspicious and mistrustful nature, who would very quickly turn against him if he was led to believe that he was not exerting himself to the utmost against the Romans. Bearing this in mind, and fearful now of giving the wrong impression to his unstable master, he was obliged to submit to the suggestions of Darylaus. He would have to go along with the strategy he deplored, even though he knew, of his own experiences so far, that it was almost certain to end in failure.

Darylaus, in his turn, was soon to find out that Archelaus did indeed know what he was talking about, and was correct in his estimation of Sulla's ability, despite him having far fewer troops. He was quickly involved in skirmishes with Sulla himself, from which he emerged with worryingly substantial losses. He was finally forced to admit that pressing for an open battle with such a foe was a poor idea, even though the troops he had brought with him were supposed to be the best that Mithradates could offer.

Eventually, they found themselves encamped near to Orchemenus. This city was on the edge of another very beautiful plain, wide and useful for cavalry manoeuvres. The plain itself spread out from the city, towards the edge of a series of fens, near to the Melas, which was the only Greek river considered to be deep and navigable, and from which a small branch joined the Cephisus. No doubt the sight of such a wide-reaching flat plain gave Archelaus some faint hope that this time the outcome of a pitched battle might have a different ending to what he had experienced so far in his attempts against Sulla.

Meanwhile, the army commanded by Flaccus had moved into the area and found itself camped not very far away from Sulla's own. Sulla was able to encourage his men to infiltrate the newly arrived troops under Flaccus, spreading dissention among them. Hearing of Sulla's great successes so far, many of the men supposedly fighting under Flaccus were impressed and decided to desert to fight with Sulla, preferring to help intercept the Pontic army under a known and now greatly respected leader. Flaccus meanwhile, probably aware that he was outmanoeuvred, decided to move north to try to threaten Mithradates' more northern dominions, although his move did appear merely to show that he preferred to keep out of the way. Sulla, with the resulting welcome additions to his own troops, then moved away to deal with the Pontic army.

After Chaeronea, Sulla had received a messenger, one Quintus Titius, who told him that the oracle of Trophonius, a son of Apollo, at Lebadea, had prophesied that there would be yet another great battle, like the one he had just won, from which he would again be victorious.[17] To a man like Sulla, whose more down-to-earth accomplishments were always combined with strong spiritual belief in divine assistance, such news must have been a great encouragement, especially as he had so easily deprived the departed Flaccus of a good number of his troops. He must also have been very pleased to find that the terrain around Orchemenus was ideal for his innovative use of entrenchments. Soon he set his men to digging not only wide ditches, but also dykes, with the intention of forcing the opposing side towards, or preferably into, the surrounding fens.

The Pontic army was camped on the plain, facing the now very busy Roman forces, and close to a large lake. Archelaus was probably dismayed to realize what Sulla was up to, when he began to find his army being surrounded by a web of dykes and ditches successfully hemming them in and preventing them, yet again, from using their men and equipment in their traditional way. Once again he was to be deprived of any opportunity to use his damaging scythe-wheeled chariots, or to use the wide plain to deploy his men advantageously.

However, he was unlikely to be able to sit idly by and watch Sulla hemming his men in. He had to try to prevent the Romans from completing their net of ditches. He ordered an advance and his move was so sudden that the soldiers protecting the working parties were taken by surprise and fell back. The left wing appeared about to flee in disorder, when Sulla, quickly realizing what was happening, leapt from his horse and, accompanied only by a bodyguard, he snatched at an ensign, and rushed through the press of men, to station himself before them, shouting aloud, 'To me, Oh Romans! It would be glorious to fall here! When they ask where you betrayed your commander, remember to say it was at Orchomenus!'[18] The men, taken again by surprise, swiftly rallied behind

Sulla. Two cohorts of reinforcements then arrived from the right wing, where Archelaus' stepson had attacked and had been repulsed, allowed the Romans to once again go onto the offensive and regain their trenches, continuing their work.

While these actions were taking place on the wings, Archelaus made an attempt to use his scythe–chariots in the centre. Putting them in the first line, with his phalanx in the second, he used his auxiliaries in the third. Amongst these auxiliaries was a troop of Italian deserters, fighting for Mithradates against their own people. Archelaus considered that these people could be relied upon to fight hard, knowing only too well what their fate was likely to be, if they were caught alive by the Roman army.

Sulla also drew up his centre into three ranks, with extremely wide spaces in between each section. When the scythe–chariots charged head on, the first rank simply moved aside, leaving the rushing chariots to become entangled in a mass of stakes which the second rank had put there for that purpose.[19] They were then easily attacked by the second rank as they struggled to get free and turn away from the carnage. This caused great panic, as it threw the chariots back onto the next rank of their own men, who were still approaching them from behind. Archelaus tried to help them by withdrawing his cavalry from the wings where they were engaged in harrying Sulla's men, but they too were immediately attacked by Sulla's own cavalry, preventing them from being of any assistance to their own men. The whole Pontic army had no option but to retire from the field, leaving large numbers of casualties behind them.

The following day Archelaus was to find that his own camp was under siege. He was astonished to see that Sulla had been busily engaging his men in digging further ditches all around it, at about 600 yards distance, trapping them in and preventing yet again any use of the chariots.

It might well have amused Sulla, with his every-ready sense of humour, to picture the expression on Archelaus' face, at that point. Perhaps leaving his quarters to plan his day, deciding on his method of attack, then realizing that there would be no attack at all, that while he slept he had been trapped inside his camp by a wide ditch. It begs the question of what exactly his sentries were doing overnight? If they did see Sulla's men frantically working around their camp in the dark, why did they not think to raise an alarm at the sight of the digging activity surrounding them? It says very little for the training of the Pontic soldiery that they were oblivious to it and apparently allowed it to happen without any form of protest or response.

However, it does say a very great deal more on Sulla's behalf, that he was able to instigate it. Not only by his innovative use of the encircling ditch, but equally importantly in the other battlefield entrenchments, then most unusual in current warfare. It needs to be remembered that these were the very first recorded uses of such battlefield entrenchments and Sulla should be given full credit for his original use of them.

It is true that Gaius Marius is rightly famous for his brilliant work in turning the average Roman legionary into a far more mobile and effective fighting machine. However, it is a pity that Sulla is so rarely praised for his equally brilliant work in finding a way to defend his relatively small army against an enemy with far superior numbers of fighting men.

By the use of the ditches he not only prevented his army from being totally overwhelmed in those battles, but he created a defensive strategy which was used extensively from then on. It became the commonest form of defence in medieval warfare, when a ditch filled with stakes or branches had to be negotiated by most armies at some time or other. Caesar used a similar method at Alesia, and recognizably similar entrenchments were used as long afterwards as the debacle of the First World War. A full 2,000 years of effective use of an innovation started by Sulla in 86 BC! It is, in my opinion, a stunning epitaph for him and an unprecedented move which affected the way troops were defended from his own day, right up to very nearly our own.

Archelaus, typically, decided on a desperate attempt to escape from this humiliating encirclement by hurling the entire Pontic army at the Romans. However, the Romans were equally determined on success, and in the confusion of the struggle some of them, led by the tribune Basilus, succeeded in demolishing a section of the camp defence wall and the whole of the Roman army poured through. The Pontic army put up a brave fight, in trying to push their way through the advancing Romans and fighting with desperation. However, Sulla's men were so closely packed together that their short swords became an impenetrable and devastating barrier, against which it was impossible for the enemy to properly defend themselves or force their way through in the confined space.

The battle turned into a rout, with a terrible destruction of life on the Pontic side. Those of Archelaus' men who did manage to escape met their end in the surrounding fens. However, Archelaus managed to find a hiding place there, from where he made his way in a small boat to Chalcis, yet again and where he eventually managed to gather around himself the remnants of his army.

Plutarch tells us that over 200 years after the battle, armour and weapons were still to be found there, abandoned by the soldiers as they fled to whatever safety they could find.[20] It was certainly one of the most decisive battles of the era, determining as it did that Asia Minor would return to the Roman fold for a long time to come. It also showed the great superiority of Roman troops and their methods of training, particularly when led by a commander they respected and trusted to get the work done.

Sulla decorated Basilus after the battle, in appreciation of the courage he had shown in leading his men during the storming of Archelaus' camp. He then went on to punish Boeotia for its treachery. Also Thebes, which had openly sided with Archelaus, needed to be punished. It was this necessary retribution against the town which gave Sulla the opportunity to raise the money he still needed, with which to repay what he had been obliged to borrow from the Temples. A very satisfactory conclusion and probably also a considerable relief to him to know that he was finally able to pay his debts to the gods.

However, he still had heard nothing from Lucullus, and there were still no ships available, without which he would find it impossible to deal with Chalcis itself, where Archelaus usually fled and from where he could easily assemble yet another army.

Faced with this problem, Sulla could wait no longer for Lucullus to provide any ships he could use, so he then made the decision that he would initiate the building of his own. He made a start on this work of building a fleet, which was so necessary to enable him to attack Archelaus directly at his base at Chalcis, but his work was stopped by the onset of winter weather, forcing the Romans into making a winter camp at Thessaly.[21] However, his efforts towards the making of a fleet of ships would not be needed, although at that point he could not be aware of it.

Mithradates had, in fact, decided to withdraw from the conflict. He had lost an unbelievable number of men already fighting in Greece, and was by then also facing serious problems in Asia itself. There had already been some talk among his nobles of the possibility of ending the war, even before the catastrophic defeats he had suffered. To his ever-suspicious mind it began to seem that his so-called friends were disloyal to him, and likely to turn their coats on behalf of the Romans. He decided to deal with this threat in his usual way, by massacring any nobles and their families who might have given the impression of not being firmly enough on his side.

However, many of these nobles, aware that their deaths were planned, managed to rouse their towns into defiance of Mithradates, and rose against him. He fought several of them, but then decided it was wiser to cut his losses. However, before he did so, he proclaimed freedom for all the Greek cities, freed all the slaves, and announced a general cancellation of all debts. By this he comfortably assumed that he would leave behind him a nice mess for the Romans to have to sort out. People who now stood to benefit from the new laws changed sides again, deciding it might be better for them to support him after all, but they had little power in themselves, and the changes made on their behalf merely infuriated the nobles and turned them even more against Mithradates. Plots against him became rife and he decided on a purge, which resulted in the deaths of well over 1,000 of the most prominent men together with their families.[22]

With these problems troubling him at home, and devastating defeat after defeat on the battlefield, it is not surprising that Mithradates decided a withdrawal from his current conflict with Rome would be sensible. Particularly so as Flaccus had by then also reappeared, still intent on making good his claim to the command against Pontus and making his own name against King Mithradates.

Chapter Eleven

Sulla was by this time feeling the pressure, with Flaccus behind him, and Rome still beckoning. He needed to make a satisfactory treaty with Mithradates, in order to be free to deal with the other matters occupying his mind. He must also have been aware that back in Rome, where he was still officially outlawed, whatever he managed to do in Asia would be likely to be misrepresented. He must have been desperate to get back, but there were still many things pressing him where he was, to prevent him from returning.

One of these was his health, which was not as good as might have appeared. Plutarch tells us that at this time he began having problems with his feet, which were causing him some pain.[1] Gout is quite likely, and an imbalance of uric acid is sometimes a side-effect of unsuitable diet, which in a campaign situation is something of an occupational hazard. Sulla was later to visit the healing waters at Aedepsus for this complaint, when he also took the opportunity to consort with actors.[2] Needless to say, this proclivity for what was considered 'low' company was always likely to bring criticism. But it is good to see that Sulla's more cerebral interests had not waned. Or that he had not stopped enjoying the theatre when opportunity arose, let alone lost that taste for meeting 'ordinary' people with whom he generally got on very well. However, particularly at that time, he did not allow the ailment to get in the way of the work he still had to do. On the contrary, he appears to have been as busy as ever, especially in his attempts to arrange a suitable treaty.

Sulla might not have realized it at that point, but the presence of Flaccus in the Province, still intent on making a success of his own mission against Mithradates, was already a worry to that king. Enough to actually be of assistance to Sulla, who was still concerned about the making of his treaty, rather than the hindrance it might otherwise have been.

After Sulla had left Melitea, Flaccus had not, surprisingly enough, made any attempt to follow him. He had moved further eastwards, looking for an opportunity to deal with the King of Pontus personally. However, his time in Asia Province was about to come to an end in a sudden and, for him, very unpleasant manner. Flaccus and his second-in-command, Fimbria, had been quarrelling for some time, unable to agree on the best way to conduct their part of the war. Flaccus had crossed from Byzantium to Chalcedon and, in his absence, Fimbria made every effort to induce the troops to mutiny against their commander. As Flaccus' troops already hated their general, this was probably not too difficult an object for Fimbria to achieve.[3] Flaccus, hearing of this, returned as quickly as he could to attend to the matter, but on nearing his army he was informed of the success of the mutiny. Realizing the danger he was now in from Fimbria, he fled immediately back towards Chalcedon and then onwards to Nicomedia. He was, however, pursued by Fimbria, who caught up with him in Nicomedia. Some say he was actually hiding in a well at this point, but he was dragged out, then summarily executed on the orders of his treacherous lieutenant.[4] Fimbria immediately took Flaccus' command and, confident in his new position, proceeded to defeat the son of Mithradates and pursue the King himself. He followed him to Pitane, where he would have very likely have captured him, except for the King swiftly being able to take a ship to Mitylene. Fimbria had no ships in which to follow him, so he was baulked of his prey.

However, at this point he encountered Lucullus, who had some time previously been entrusted by Sulla with the task of acquiring ships. It was the delay of Lucullus in returning with the necessary fleet, which had obliged Sulla to attempt to produce some on his own account. But Lucullus had, in fact, been very busy. He had travelled to Egypt, had failed to find the required ships available there, but was eventually able to procure some from Syria and from Rhodes. He had also taken some time to deal with a side issue, in inducing Cos and Cnidos to revolt against Mithradates, and he had also managed to drive out the Pontic sympathizers from those cities. It was at this point that Lucullus received a request from Fimbria, of all people, actually asking for his help. Could Lucullus let Fimbria use those ships to follow and hopefully capture Mithradates?

It is greatly to Lucullus' credit that he refused absolutely. It might be argued that the capture of Mithradates was the prime concern in the matter, and that he should probably have agreed to allow Fimbria to use the fleet to achieve this object. However, Lucullus was a faithful adherent of Sulla. To Lucullus, as to Sulla himself, Fimbria was nothing more than a usurper with no proper authority whatever. The ships had been assembled after great difficulty to help Sulla, not his enemies from Rome, who were merely there to take his command away from him and negate all the excellent work he had already done in Asia. Lucullus considered Fimbria to be no more or less than a renegade; therefore he would make no allowances for him at all. His contemptuous refusal to help by loaning the ships intended for Sulla then allowed Mithradates to sail away unopposed. Infuriated by his inability to follow the King, Fimbria then began to tour the Province, attacking all those who had taken the side of Pontus and ravaging the lands of those cities who would not give in to him.[5] However, it must be admitted that he would hardly have been able to make such headway with his task of destruction, if Sulla had not been so hugely successful in his own campaign against King Mithradates.

It was entirely due to Sulla's excellent generalship that the Romans had so effectively produced their truly spectacular achievement of greatly reducing the immense numbers of Pontus' original forces. Particularly when it is considered that he had so few men to work with and such an underhand and unhelpful base back in Rome.

However, Lucullus had not forgotten his original purpose, and he went on to defeat one of Mithradates' admirals, Neoptolemus. When this was accomplished (at least the fleet he'd acquired was finally being used successfully on Sulla's behalf), he set off to meet with Sulla in the Thracian Chaeronese. By this time, both Sulla and Mithradates might well have been wondering if the other were likely to side with Fimbria and come to terms with him, to their own detriment. Sulla's own men were extremely eager to move deeper into Mithradates' territory, as they were very keen to avenge the massacre of the Romans that had been ordered by Mithradates. Sulla had to make a special effort to keep them under control and prevent any such incursion without his authority. It was becoming all the more obvious that Sulla needed to make a reasonable treaty with Mithradates, if only to negate his influence and allow him to turn his full attention to dealing with Fimbria.

Mithradates also, now harried enough, was pushed to make some kind of agreement with Sulla. He must have recognized by then that Sulla was easily the more capable and therefore the more dangerous of the two Romans on his tail, even though Fimbria was often considered to be a reasonable soldier in his own right.[6] Therefore, at bay, though still reluctant, he finally instructed Archelaus to open negotiations with Sulla.

His first move was to send a merchant of Delos, also named Archelaus, with a message for Sulla. When this emissary received a friendly reception, Archelaus was then confident enough to suggest that they meet in person. The meeting, once agreed, was eventually arranged to take place at Delium, on the coast of Boeotia.

It must have been a very strange meeting. These two men had been trying to kill each other for the better part of a year and Sulla, at least, had had great successes on the battlefield. Archelaus had suffered terrible losses, for which he would no doubt have to make some explanations to his erratic and terrifying master but it seems certain that, although they may have met warily, they also had a fair measure of respect for each other. Each one was a good general in their own right and eventually they would be able to see that they had a good deal in common.

However, to start with, bluster was the order of the day, with Archelaus immediately going in to the attack. He asked Sulla why he did not abandon his pretensions to Asia and to his master's kingdom of Pontus. If he agreed to leave Asia, Archelaus told him, he could be provided with ample money and ships and also with whatever men he would need. Mithradates would be happy to equip him with all that was required to deal with matters in Rome successfully. He could go back to Rome in style and take over easily, becoming the master there, with Mithradates' willing support. Naturally enough, it was implied, Mithradates would pay almost anything to see Sulla leave Asia Province and become busily occupied elsewhere.

Sulla may well have been amused at the idea of returning to Rome at the head of a colourful, jangling, noisy force of Pontic soldiers, but he was not tempted. Instead, he rounded on Archelaus, asking him why he did not overthrow Mithradates and become King of Pontus himself. He could then let Sulla have his ships anyway and become a Friend and Ally of Rome into the bargain. When Archelaus refused indignantly, Sulla reminded him coldly that Mithradates was no friend to him, as he believed he was, but that Archelaus was only his servant. 'You Archelaus, a Cappodocian, a slave, a friend – if it please you – to a barbarian king, you would not be guilty of what is dishonourable. Yet you dare to talk to me, a Roman general, of treason?' he said cuttingly.[7] Then he demanded insultingly to know whether he was not the same man who had fled so ignominiously from Chaeronea. 'Are you not the same Archelaus who ran away from Chaeronea?' Sulla challenged him. 'The man who left few remaining out of 120,000 men? Who lay for two days in the fens after Orchemenus and left Boeotia impassable for heaps of dead carcasses?'[8] At his angry tone, together with the obvious truth of the statements, Archelaus saw himself beaten. He altered his demeanor and begged Sulla to lay aside any further thoughts of war and to make a peaceful settlement with Mithradates.

Sulla was quite prepared to do so and had already drawn up a list of articles, which he thought needed to be agreed.[9] The discussions may have taken some time, as Archelaus must have been conscious of his master's lack of real enthusiasm for any concessions, but he eventually agreed the terms of Sulla's treaty on behalf of Pontus.

Archelaus was to hand over all the ships in his possession and withdraw from Greece. Mithradates was to give up Asia and Paphlagonia, restoring Cappodocia and Bithynia to their rightful kings. All captives, deserters and runaway slaves were to be returned. (Those Italians deserters in Archelaus' army would not have been happy with that!) All the Roman generals who had been captured by Mithradates were to be handed over.

Sulla at this point made a special mention of Manius Aquilius, requesting that he be handed over along with the other captured commanders. He was evidently not aware that Aquilius was already dead. The other commanders were apparently still alive and able to be returned in accordance with the treaty.[10]

In addition to the fleet which Archelaus was to hand over, Mithradates was also to supply a further seventy warships to Sulla, together with all that was necessary to crew them. Finally, he would also have to pay a war indemnity of 2,000 talents. In return for all these concessions, Sulla was to guarantee Mithradates full possession of all his own dominions, and allow him to be made a Friend and Ally of the Roman people.

Messengers were sent off with the treaty, to be inspected and approved by Mithradates himself, while Sulla and Archelaus journeyed by way of Thessaly to the Hellespont, intending to eventually cross over into Asia. Sulla and Archelaus had time during this journey to get to know one another properly, and it is recorded that Sulla treated the admiral well. So well, in fact, that when Archelaus fell ill, Sulla ordered the journey halted while he had time to recover fully. He was not only very attentive to him, but also gave him a present of land in Euboea and styled him personally, separately from his master, as a Friend and Ally of the Roman people. Archelaus may well have been gratified at these signs of friendship and attention from Sulla, but there was to be a downside. Their growing friendship also gave the impression that the two of them had been in collusion all along, and added fuel to the fire of suspicion that Archelaus had deliberately thrown away the battles that he had recently lost to Sulla.[11] It was then easy to forget that Archelaus had done his best to give sensible advice to Mithradates on the course the war should take, but that his attempted contribution had been ignored.

It was even suggested that Sulla had killed Aristion on Archelaus' behalf, as he had been his enemy at court. It was said that Sulla had had the man poisoned. There is, of course, no evidence whatever that any such thing ever took place. Indeed, it is not in Sulla's nature to have dealt with an enemy in that way. Leopards do not change their spots, whatever people might wish, and people tend to stay true to their own characters. It was not characteristic of Sulla to use poison to dispose of anyone. He was a far more straightforward type of man, while poison is an underhand method of killing. However, such rumours were well circulated and Sulla still thought it worthwhile to give a very detailed refutation of them in later years, when he wrote his memoirs.[12]

At the time, however, they may well also have caused some uneasiness in Rome, where there were several people who had good reason to fear that Sulla would soon return and then would begin to deal similarly with them. They certainly had very good reason to feel guilty and uneasy about such a return, considering that they had sent Sulla out of Rome, with no money and precious few men, to fight the war in the east. Particularly against such an enemy as Pontus, which had such immense resources at its disposal together with a casual disregard about the lives of the hundreds of thousands of men it could throw onto the battlefield. Then when Sulla was, almost miraculously, managing to do well against that enemy, they attempted to take his command away from him. They caused his wife and children to flee from Rome in fear of their lives, while they destroyed his property behind them and outlawed him into the bargain – what on earth did they expect? What sort of people must they have been in themselves that they could honestly expect any man worth his salt to tamely submit to such treatment? They were probably judging him by their own standards of behaviour. If they feared Sulla's eventual return home, they had indeed very good reason to regret their stupid and ill-considered actions against a man who was, quite rightly, likely to bring retribution for them.

For Archelaus, however, the rumours then circulating freely had a far more serious and dangerous outcome for him in Pontus. King Mithradates effected to place no faith in them at that time, but Archelaus knew his master only too well and was to be proved correct in his assessment of him. After he had had time to ponder over the accusations and morbidly meditate on the subject, Mithradates changed his mind completely. He then decided that he did, after all, believe that Archelaus had had some criminal association with Sulla and had committed treason to his master's detriment. Archelaus was some time later obliged to flee Pontus in order to save his life.[13]

On Sulla's part, now that he was making terms with Mithradates, he would have considered it only wise to make a friend of Archelaus at the same time, particularly as he knew that he still had Fimbria to deal with. It would be necessary to turn his back on these people before long, and far wiser to leave them with feelings of amity and gratitude.

However, things did not all go smoothly with the treaty. When Mithradates became aware of the full details, he did not approve of them. He did not, in particular, want to part with Paphlagonia and wished to discuss with Sulla the possibility of retaining it. However, the question of the ships was simply not to be under discussion at all. He had no intention of surrendering any of them. The ambassadors who brought his comments to Sulla also mentioned that Mithradates now felt rather aggrieved with Sulla's terms and further considered that he might have received better terms if he had negotiated with Fimbria, rather than Sulla.

This mention of that man, who was no better than an outlaw to Sulla, threw him into a fury. He told them very firmly that he would deal competently with Fimbria when he had time to turn his attention to him, therefore he was not to be considered. As for the King of Pontus, he should consider himself very fortunate that Sulla had been so generous.

Mithradates should be grateful to be allowed to live, let alone be free to quibble about the terms of a treaty, in Sulla's opinion. Sulla reminded the ambassadors that their king had done nothing in person regarding the war just ended, not having been present at it.

'I thought to have seen him prostrate at my feet to thank me for leaving him so much as that right hand of his, which has cut off so many Romans!' said Sulla furiously. 'He will shortly, at my coming into Asia, speak another language. In the meantime, let him at his ease in Pergamum, sit managing a war which he never saw!'[14] In other words, if he wished to be obdurate, Sulla would move into Asia and give him first-hand knowledge of the war. If he wanted to continue the conflict, Sulla would oblige. The ambassadors were astounded by Sulla's angry outburst and quite frightened by it, fearing to offend him. Archelaus was obliged to try to calm him down. He made Sulla a firm promise that he would go in person to persuade Mithradates to agree to all the terms of the treaty, taking all the responsibility and if he failed in that task, he would then kill himself.[15]

Whatever Sulla may have thought about this rather melodramatic declaration, Archelaus was allowed to go back with the ambassadors, to try to talk some sense into Mithradates.

In the meantime, Sulla kept busy by reaffirming Rome's rule over Macedonia, which had been evacuated by Archelaus. The area had for some time been troubled by raids of barbarians from Thrace, many of whom had been in collusion with Mithradates. A campaign against them was to prove useful at that time, by occupying Sulla's troops in the interval of Archelaus travelling to meet, and hopefully reason with, his king. It kept the troops busy and disciplined and also gave them an interest, as they all hoped to find some loot for themselves, the lack of which had spoilt their time in Greece.

Sulla had already sent Hortensius ahead to make a start on dealing with those barbarians, while he was still in negotiation with Archelaus. Hortensius had found two tribes in particular, the Maedi and the Dardani, who were causing most of the trouble in the area and he had managed to put them to flight. Sulla then took the opportunity to cross into Thrace personally and ravaged the territory previously controlled by those nuisances. No doubt there was an amount of plunder to be divided between Sulla's troops, to satisfy them. More importantly, it had the effect of taking to the pirates a firm warning about the advisability of obeying the rule of Rome.[16]

Sulla eventually set off to meet again with Archelaus, at Philippi, and this time there was good news. Archelaus told Sulla that Mithradates had been made to see sense and that the treaty could now be approved as had been originally set out. Moreover, King Mithradates now wanted to meet with Sulla, in person. Archelaus had done very well to bring around his difficult ruler, but the fact that Fimbria was still at large also had something to do with it. If Mithradates did not want to fall into the greedy hands of Fimbria, it would be sensible of him to make what terms he could with Sulla, who had already proved himself to be a far more honourable sort of man. Mithradates certainly could not afford to be in opposition to them both. He knew that in actuality he could get better and fairer terms from Sulla, than from the other man, still something of an unknown quantity.

The arrangement was made, and the two antagonists finally met face to face at Dardanus. Mithradates had come in from his hiding place at Mitylene, while Sulla had been taken over by Lucullus to the meeting place in Asia, in the ships he had brought for Sulla's use.[17]

Mithradates, true to the usual form of an eastern potentate, intended to use the opportunity to try to impress the Romans and was determined to show that his power was still vast. He probably would have been dressed most magnificently but, far more importantly, when he arrived he was attended by a large army. He had with him 200 ships, with 20,000 men at arms. He had also brought with him 6,000 horse and a large train of his famous scythe-wheeled chariots! Sulla went to meet him far more modestly attended by only four cohorts of his men and 200 horse.[18] He was quite unimpressed by the barbaric magnificence and the unnecessary scale of Mithradates' retinue and showed it plainly.

Mithradates began by striding towards Sulla, holding out his hand in greeting. Sulla, unsmilingly, ignored the outstretched hand completely. He instead started off by speaking angrily, demanding that Mithradates should openly agree to the terms of the treaty, as laid down, and that he should do so without further argument. Mithradates, perhaps taken aback by Sulla's unfriendly stance, at first said nothing. He may have been unprepared for a verbal attack and at a disadvantage, but he was not happy with the terms, and was still reluctant to agree to them. Despite the acceptance he had seemed to give to Archelaus, his real opinion had not changed. He still refused to answer Sulla, and certainly made no attempt to agree to the treaty.

This angered Sulla anew, and he spoke sharply to Mithradates again. He told him that he, Mithradates, was the man who was defeated and therefore the one who should have to beg. Sulla, as the victor, did not have to beg and would not. 'Ought not the petitioner to speak first and the conqueror to listen in silence?' he asked.[19] Seeing that Sulla was so obdurate, Mithradates then tried to explain away his actions to Sulla, giving many and varied excuses for them, blaming everyone but himself, even the actions of the gods. Sulla cut him short, not wishing to listen to his evasions and then proceeded to demolish his arguments one by one. Sulla said to the assembled people that he 'had long heard that Mithradates was a powerful speaker, and now knew it for himself as a truth. A man who in defence of the most foul and unjust proceedings had not wanted for specious pretences'.[20] Finally, he impatiently demanded that Mithradates agree to the terms of the treaty with no further excuses and Mithradates, seeing no other way out of the impasse, and that there was no further leeway, finally did agree to Sulla's terms.[21]

Once he had given in, Sulla could then afford to show that he was pleased. He went forward to embrace Mithradates openly and made a scene of public reconciliation, which must have been something of a relief to the anxious ambassadors from Pontus. In this touching scene of friendship Sulla then included Archelaus and Nicomedes.

However, despite the signs of acceptance and amity, Mithradates was still obliged to provide the seventy ships he had disputed, officially handing them over to Sulla before being allowed to sail back to Pontus.[22] Whatever the two antagonists still actually thought of each other, the first war between Rome and Mithradates of Pontus was officially over.

Sulla could now turn his attention to Fimbria, leading his men towards Thyatira in Lydia, where Fimbria then was. On his arrival in the area, Sulla sent a message to Fimbria, to the effect that he should hand over his men to Sulla's command. Fimbria, as might have been expected simply refused outright, indignantly reminding Sulla that it was he who was still the public enemy so far as Rome was concerned. He still had some hopes of defeating Sulla, but the army with him was becoming restless and Fimbria was having difficulty controlling the men. Perhaps that too was only to be expected, as he had used them to mutiny against and finally help to murder their original commander. However, he had second thoughts when Sulla began to make a line of circumvallation around his camp.

To his horror, Fimbria realized that many of his own troops, realizing that they were no match for Sulla, simply joined in with his men and helped them to dig! Sensing that he was likely to lose them all completely, Fimbria attempted to make them swear an oath of allegiance to him personally, in the hope of preventing a mass desertion. He was then obliged to go so far as to kill the first man who flatly refused to do so.[23] It may have seemed to him to be the action of a firm leader, but men held by force are never reliable and it only caused further resentment.

His next action was equally ill-advised. He then attempted to have Sulla assassinated, by sending a slave to kill him. Whether or not that individual was a volunteer, or just some unfortunate under duress, we cannot know. The man who was sent to do Fimbria's bidding was, of course, easily captured before he could do any harm, and dealt with firmly. Fimbria was now losing control completely, panicking in his desperation to rid himself of Sulla, who was on his trail and whom he knew would not be put off until he had captured Fimbria and had his army under his own command. That he should have acted so clumsily as to send an assassin to try attack Sulla, with a highly unlikely possibility of success, was only evidence of his despair at that point.

Sulla then sent a message to Fimbria, in which he offered him a safe-conduct to enable him to surrender himself to Sulla, but Fimbria knew that his life was by then worth nothing and that his own army was full of men who despised him. They were already busy deserting in droves to Sulla, knowing him to be the better commander. Fimbria, despite the promised safe-conduct dare not face Sulla; neither did he dare to return to Rome, as he had already been responsible for the death of his own commander Flaccus.

With no way to turn, he finally took the only honourable way out, and slipped away to Pergamum, where he killed himself in the Temple of Aesculapius. Sulla then took command of all of Fimbria's troops, making them a part of his own army.

Sulla then gave orders that all runaway slaves in the Province were to return to their original owners, under threat of being slain when caught. The towns which had resisted Sulla and had given in to the blandishments of Mithradates were punished by being fined, plus having to pay the five years' worth of taxes from which Mithradates had exempted them. There were certainly no murders of ordinary people and the innocent citizens were not harmed, (as was usual with Sulla, with his ready sympathy for the underdogs). The ringleaders who had been responsible for the massacre of the 80,000 Romans and their 70,000 slaves naturally had to pay for what they had done. They alone were killed. Otherwise, apart from the fines and the arrears of tax (which Lucullus was instructed to collect), the towns' only other formal punishment was the complete removal of their defensive walls.

Sulla had done all the work in the East that he reasonably could and had to think about returning to do what he could again in Rome. Before he did so, he allowed dedications to himself and his wife Caecilia Metella to be erected at various sites in Greece, intending them to be a memoir of his work there.[24] These used his Greek cognomen of Epiphradatos, which acknowledgment of the support of the gods he no doubt considered had been a great help to him.

There was, however, still one matter which was to delay his return home and that was his health. He had already had some problems in that direction, having had to take a course of treatment at the hot waters at Aedepsus in an attempt to get relief. Now, though, he had a more difficult of treatment, and very much more distressing, complaint to worry about.

He may have had some trouble with the skin of his face for some time. There are certainly references to him being in pain and having a patchy complexion before this date.[25] However, it was at this point in his life that he began to suffer seriously with a very debilitating ailment, which was destined to change his famous good looks completely and actually alter the course of his life. Many writers claim that he suffered from scabies at this time of his life, but this is certainly not the case and can be quite easily refuted.

Scabies was perhaps a difficult (skin ailments are quite often difficult to deal with), but certainly not an impossible condition to treat in those early days. It is caused by a tiny mite, which burrows under the skin, in any part of the body, but often into the hands and feet, where the insect can actually be seen moving about under the thinner skin of those areas. The mite deposits its faeces under the skin, and the patient, irritated by the intense itching, tends to scratch the inflamed area, causing rashes and damaged skin. However, this also, eventually, has the effect of destroying the burrows in which the mite lives, thus depriving it of a habitat. Therefore, unpleasant as the condition can be when at its height, it is not generally considered to be a lifelong problem.[26] The intense irritation can also be alleviated by lotions, or by infusions.

The pretty, blue-flowered, scabious plant, which has been used with some success for centuries (properly known as succisa pratensis), is known to ease the skin in such cases. Also useful would have been Hamamelis (common witch hazel) which is a sovereign remedy for cooling and healing inflamed skin. Both these plants are native to Europe.

Many people have no faith in natural remedies for general ailments. However, while often slower in their effects, natural remedies can be just as useful and effective as more modern medicines. A medieval remedy known as St. Bartholomew's plaster, long used as a wound treatment, was often very effective indeed. It consisted of parsley (Vitamin D to promote healing), plantain (very effective for killing infection, especially in dirty wounds), and honey (also useful for general infections and promoting healing), with cornflour to make a paste to hold it all together. This was commonly used for battlefield injuries and was a very useful aid in fighting infection, which was the main worry after receiving wounds and a great curse before the advent of antibiotics. Many people did manage to survive even terrible injuries, without any sign of infection. Firm evidence of this is given in the book *Blood Red Roses*.[27] This is the stunning archaeological record of the bodies found in one of the grave pits at Towton in Yorkshire, buried after the battle there in 1461. Full detail is given of previously inflicted horrendous wounds, which have fully healed with no infection present, and which were *not* the wounds from which the victims died during or after the battle.

Even the simple and innocent little Yarrow (Achillea millefolium), is supposedly named after the Greek hero Achilles, who is reputed to have used this plant to stem bleeding in wounds after the Trojan War.[28] Also, during the First World War in Europe, huge supplies of garlic were gathered in order to deal with the infections present in the battlefield wounds, used before the days of penicillin. Garlic is still the best remedy for infections.[29]

The point being made is that there is a wealth of evidence relating to the efficacy of some common herbal preparations. If Sulla had merely had scabies, there were in his own time remedies available to give him reasonable relief from the condition, until it ended of its own accord.

However, I am quite convinced that what Sulla was actually suffering from was shingles, (post herpatic neuralgia). This is a very painful and very debilitating condition, caused by the chickenpox virus, (otherwise known as the Herpes Virus Type 3). Shingles attacks the nerve endings and is even now very difficult to treat, often causing pain to a patient for several years, in the worst cases.

In Sulla's case, we know that he was only subject to pain and itching in his face, and that is common when the shingles is concentrated in the nerve endings of the face itself. There would have been no pain or irritation anywhere else on the body, but to have this ailment in the face is, even now, a terrible condition and almost impossible to treat. In a middle-aged patient (Sulla was already in his mid-fifties at this time), the prognosis is, even now, very poor indeed, with no real likelihood of the patient being able to receive any long-term relief.[30] In Sulla's time, when the condition was not even recognized, he would have had to suffer it with no hope at all of there being any medicine of help to him.

The condition, once established, causes intense and uncontrollable itching and tingling of the skin, which leads to the patient being obliged to scratch, tearing at the skin and causing serious pain and the possibility of infections. We know that Sulla is reported to have taken to over-indulgence in drinking at this point in his life, and this is very likely to have been the only remedy he could think of to offer him any relief from the constant and unbearable irritation. The poor man may well have tried every lotion and potion offered to him, but none of them would have done the slightest good, as the condition was not actually a problem of the skin itself, therefore no topical application could have reached it. Even with modern painkillers, unavailable to Sulla, relief is still highly unreliable.

Not only is the irritation itself a problem, but the constant scratching which the patient is forced to perform in an effort to ease the torment leads to the characteristic scarring caused by this involuntary self-harming. To a man like Sulla, whose famous good looks were by then quite ruined, it must have caused some psychological damage also. It is quite true to say that 'the face is the person' and Sulla must have felt that his persona was destroyed as well as his health.[31] Fortunately, it did not seem to have any effect on the affection which was shown to him by his wife (and even his subsequent wife) and family, or his true friends and soldiers, who were fortunately still able to see the man behind the by then permanently damaged face.

However, that must have been of very little consolation to him, knowing that he now appeared outwardly very different to the way he had previously been. For him, certainly, there could have been some loss of confidence and probably also some resentment at those who thought it amusing to make mock of his misfortune. Even in Greece verses were made which referred to his scarred and reddened facial skin, and he must have known that his enemies in Rome would be delighted to be able to pounce on this new and humiliating problem in order to make a point.[32]

It has long been considered that facial attractiveness – or otherwise – was a sign of the inner man, an indication of whether or not a person was 'good'. Assuming of course that an ugly face indicated the presence of some kind of evil. It must have been particularly galling for Sulla, who had until recently been so handsome that it was remarked upon (and swooned over by many), that he should have lost those very pleasing facial features. That they were then replaced by an uglier visage, one which left him only too easily open to the mockery that could be turned against him, suggested to some that his altered appearance proved that he was a person of wicked, sinful and debauched habits.

Unfortunately, many writers still seem to subscribe to this view, as if the physiognomy was transparent and showed the character beneath the skin. There is precious little real evidence for any other kind of 'evil' or 'debauchery' though he is usually, almost automatically, accused of it. He did not rape, murder or torture victims for his personal amusement, though doubtless many did. Considering that he spent all his adult life chasing about on Rome's business, it makes one wonder where he would have found the time! On the contrary, what evidence there is shows plainly that he was a man who had always tried to do his best and attempted to be fair, particularly to innocent people of the lower classes, who had his understanding and sympathy and were usually fair game. Also, the approval of the gods, in which he still believed implicitly, was dependent upon his correct behaviour as a Patrician, yet he still brilliantly performed his function as the archetypal Roman general. That his friends (of all social levels) were loyal and devoted to him throughout his life, speaks far more in his favour than the vituperation of people who have generally had a vested interest in making him appear to be overly venal. Evil and debauched people do not possess real friends, who stay faithful through good times and bad. They only have cronies, sidekicks, henchmen and sycophants. Sulla had the gift of real friendship, which was his one great blessing, even if the gods had chosen to take away his previously attractive appearance. That it was such an altered face that he now had to show to the world for the rest of his life, makes it hardly surprising that he hesitated before returning to Rome, even though he knew that he needed to be there without much more delay.

It must have been pleasurable to know that one city Helicarnassus, erected a statue to Sulla while he was still in Greece. Many others would probably have still been resentful under the exactions ordered against them, in making them pay the arrears of their lapsed taxes together with the fines imposed for their support of Mithradates. However resentful they may have been, they can hardly have been surprised. They ought, indeed, to have been grateful to be placed once more under the mantle of Rome. Had they remained under the unreliable and erratic rule of Mithradates they might well have found themselves far worse off in the long run.

It is true, though, to say that Sulla's own dire financial situation made him all the more determined to make sure that they all paid their dues in full. He had from the very beginning of the campaign been starved of funds and any kind of support from Rome.

He saw himself only as the one designated to exact a just punishment from those who had stood out against Rome, and to him, as a Roman, there was nothing at all wrong with the rule of Rome. That others might see it differently was not his problem. If people entered into a treaty with Rome, and then broke that treaty, they could and should expect some form of retaliation. That was what being a militaristic society was all about.

Moreover, there had been that great massacre of innocent Roman people, which was to stay in the Roman mind for a long time to come. Indeed, many of those among his army still did not consider that he had been anything like firm enough, with regard to the Asiatics, in relation to what they had done. Even when Sulla had made the peace of Dardanus with Mithradates, there were still rumbles of discontent. Many still believed that Mithradates himself had escaped far too lightly. After all, the order for that appalling massacre had been given by him personally. In the light of all this, Sulla was justified in claiming that he had acted with considerable leniency.[33]

However, Sulla's thoughts were by this time no longer with Asia Province. He had been absent from Rome since 87 BC and the quarrel between him and the Cinna-led government had had to take a back seat. It could do so no longer. The power which Cinna held was still shaky and now provinces were being lost, though Sicily and Sardinia were still loyal. The rather small force which had been led by Flaccus showed how poorly things were going back in Rome, though there was still a solid nucleus of rich 'money-men' sitting firmly upon their millions. They were the sort of people whose first thought was, and always would be, of their own security and wealth, rather than that of Rome, despite all the benefits that such a capital city could give them. Their selfishness would not change, but might have to be nullified. Sulla, who had frequently done wonders with hardly anything, can be forgiven for considering these people to be nothing more than traitors themselves.

Ignoring the fact that he had been declared a public enemy, Sulla then sent to Rome a full account of his dealings in Asia, as any proconsul was expected to do at the end of a campaign. It was nothing more or less than a declaration of intent to Cinna. It made it clear that he did not acknowledge the validity of the decree against him, and therefore by implication, did not acknowledge the validity of Cinna's rule either.[34] Cinna now knew that the day he had feared had finally arrived. Sulla would not be abroad much longer and soon he would have to deal with him face to face. He ignored the letter Sulla had sent as proconsul and, with his colleague Carbo, began to gather together an army. They intended to cross over to Greece and deal with Sulla there, rather than in Italy.

Sulla wrote to Rome again, quite rightly in the circumstances, as he had received no official reply. He itemized all the services he had rendered to Rome, and made a particular point of his recent successes against Mithradates of Pontus. He also mentioned that he had taken under his protection those members of the Senate who had fled to him for sanctuary, away from Cinna. He also did not fail to mention that he had received no acknowledgment for any of those services, except to have his property destroyed and his wife and children made homeless! He said that he intended to shortly return, when he would exact recompense for all that had happened, not only to his own family, but to those others in the city who had suffered.

However threatening this second letter may have seemed, it ended on the most personally threatening note of all. He made it perfectly clear that he did not intend any harm to any ordinary citizens of Rome, as he considered them all to be quite innocent. His quarrel was with Cinna and his faction alone. He held them entirely responsible for all that had happened in his absence, and the situation in which Rome now found itself. The warning was obvious, that they would soon be expected to pay for all that they had done.

It was at this point that he confirmed his claims and emphasized his belief in his own imperium by minting and circulating coins, one of which showed Venus accompanied by a cupid with a palm branch. On its reverse were war trophies and the symbols IMPER and ITERU(M). The second coin showed a helmeted head of Rome, with on its reverse a triumphant victor in a chariot, being crowned by a figure of flying victory.[35] The trophies, of course, commemorated not only his battles at Chaeronea and Orchemenus, but also his victory over Mithradates personally. They also, very usefully, showed that the gods could be said to be still with Sulla, still supporting him and blessing his actions. Still, in effect, approving of him and protecting him. Bearing in mind the superstitious nature of the average Roman, for whom the support of the gods in any enterprise was vital, it also was a very strong warning indeed, and one that his enemies in Rome would do well to heed.

Chapter Twelve

Despite Sulla's successes abroad and the validity of his claims as itemized in the letter he had sent to Rome, he still had opposition to face at home. While fighting in Asia Province he had been hailed as Imperator by his troops, this for the second time in his life. It was, in fact, also the second time that he had been hailed as Imperator while fighting against the same enemy, as the first occasion had taken place while in Cilicia.[1] He now certainly deserved and was fully entitled to a Triumph on his return to Rome, another thing that Cinna and his friends and associates could not possibly allow. They preferred to make sure that Sulla never returned home at all, and with this intention at the forefront of their minds they determined to raise an army to fight him in Greece. They certainly could not risk the possibility of a popular rising in Rome in his favour, if the hero of the hour should return and demand recompense for all he and his supporters had suffered at the hands of the Cinnans.

Sulla's letter to them had not only the intention of establishing his rightful claims, but also the intention of separating Cinna and his faction from the more moderate and possibly more amenable members of the Senate. There were also the newly enfranchised Italians to take into consideration. The Senate at this point found themselves in a cleft stick. They did not and officially could not accept Sulla's earlier march into Rome. It had been an unprecedented move, which had left a very sour taste behind it and they could not countenance it. However, even worse in retrospect was the appallingly violent and destructive action of Gaius Marius, who had so casually and callously turned Rome into a bloodbath. He was by then deceased, but his supporters, Cinna and his favoured sidekick Gnaeus Papirius Carbo, were very much alive and well and unfortunately still in power.

Some of the members of the Senate, having learned the lessons of the recent conflicts only too well, and desiring to achieve some kind of internal peace for Rome, made an attempt to bring conciliation between the two parties. It had been with this in mind that they had allowed Flaccus and Fimbria to move into Asia Province, with the hope (or perhaps merely wishful thinking), that they and Sulla could work together against the common enemy. It had not proved feasible. Now the situation had hardened still further and various members of the Senate were actually with Sulla, having fled to him for sanctuary and protection against Cinna.

The ones who had remained in Rome still walked a tightrope of indecision and possible censure. They were certainly under Cinna's control where they were, and genuine anxiety for their own safety and that of their families must have been a factor in their deliberations.

However, it was also becoming obvious that Sulla, still officially the public enemy, had actually shown far greater concern and consideration for the eminent refugees and far more respect for the authority of the Senate. He had taken pains to address the Senators and behave towards them in the appropriate manner, as a triumphant general should. The resentment, which was then inherent in any Roman of position who felt himself to be under duress, was rising against Cinna's faction who were presently still holding Rome, but without either real authority or enough support, which was already beginning to drain away. The members of the Senate must have been aware, as Sulla doubtless intended they should be reminded, that he was still, despite everything, the legally appointed proconsul. Not only that, but he was also the only person who was likely to be capable of freeing them from the grip of the tyrants.[2]

The newly enfranchised Italians were another concern. Sulla had originally made it clear that he did not agree with them receiving full citizenship, particularly if they had taken up arms against Rome. Cinna, once he had taken over, had gradually eroded that idea, giving not only citizenship to all innocent parties in the Italian ranks, but eventually even to those who had fought against Rome in the recent wars. Indeed, many among the Samnites and others still bore arms, and they were still effectively independent. Dangerously so, if they could be used as a private army on Cinna's behalf, as Cinna may well have hoped. However, Cinna had also made many promises to the new citizens about re-distribution over the entire thirty-five tribes, which he had not actually implemented. This meant that the support, which on the face of it should have been gladly given to him by all the Italian armies, might not have been as freely available as he had expected. There was, because of his dilatoriness in keeping his promises, a distinct lack of enthusiasm for his cause and this growing indignation allowed Sulla to step in.

He made it clear that he was prepared to abandon his previous opposition to their full emancipation, and would respect the concessions they had recently acquired. This of course meant that the Italians were then being openly wooed by both sides in efforts to gain their support, and they were in the enviable position of being able to decide which leader they liked best. It wasn't much of a contest. Sulla had already proved, time and time again that he, at least, was a man of his word. Even though he had been obliged to change his stance with regard to their rights, he had done so openly and apparently willingly and had made it clear that he would now respect that decision. What is more, they believed him.

He was also by far the best general and certainly the most capable and reliable man to side with. He was likely to be the victor in any open conflict with Cinna and his cronies, and not only the battle-hardened veterans thought so. There were plenty of ordinary people who by then disliked Cinna and his crowd. Those remaining Senators who were still moderate and sensible refused to see that the situation was quite so cut and dried as Cinna suggested it was. Many had already come to the conclusion that it was time to heal the rift with Sulla, which had been largely imposed upon them. Lucius Valerius Flaccus, the Princeps Senatus, was concerned and immediately recommended that they negotiate with Sulla, almost as soon as his letter arrived in Rome.[3] This haste is indicative of the impatience to come to some agreement even though it certainly cannot have pleased Cinna. However, the Senate agreed to officially reopen communication with Sulla.

Sulla naturally refused to accept any conciliatory move which would have brought him into any kind of partnership with Cinnans. But it also showed that he was aware of the element of disunity within the Senate, which gave those who had already fled from Rome a new importance. That men such as Catulus and Marcus Antonius had been obliged to flee to his side to escape from Cinna had already caused a good deal of indignation from the other moderates who were still trapped in Rome and therefore largely still subject to Cinna. Sulla's avowed intent to take firm action against Cinna and his adherents encouraged them to reconsider their own loyalties. To that end they could bear in mind that Sulla was actually exactly what he claimed to be. Legal proconsul, victorious general, devoted to Rome, and a man resolved to be fair and just and restore the *mos maiorum*, or established order. If they turned to him, he could at least free them from the oppressive rule of the usurpers.

Cinna and Carbo became aware that they were losing support and that their troops were unsettled and unwilling. When they prepared to embark for Greece they must have been horrified to realize that many of their troops were prepared to mutiny, rather than fight against Sulla.[4] The Senate had chosen that time to request Cinna and Carbo to make no further attempts to embark, until they had had an opportunity of arranging terms with Sulla. They made it clear that they at least wished to hear what his demands might be. This seemed to be agreed, but as soon as the ambassadors had left Rome on the start of their journey to meet with Sulla, Cinna and Carbo broke their word again. They immediately proclaimed themselves consuls for 83 BC so that, as they claimed, they would not have the bother of returning to Rome for the elections![5] The Senators implored them to wait, at least for the return of the ambassadors, but their pleas were ignored. They made preparations again for immediate embarkation to Greece.

Cinna had travelled to Ancona, in an effort to enlist more men for the attempt against Sulla, being only too aware of the deficiencies in determination and willingness of the troops he already had. Unfortunately, his further efforts were still in vain, as the response he met with was much the same as the one he had already faced with his original manpower. Not only were they unwilling, but some actually refused outright to enlist with him. They did not wish to fight with him against Sulla and made it perfectly clear that they would not. They stated firmly that they saw no reason to do so.[6]

What happened next is still, unfortunately, shrouded in mystery. Some records state that a scuffle ensued, due to a lictor of Cinna's pushing a soldier out of his way. The soldier who had been pushed retaliated by pushing back, much to the surprise of the lictor, and other soldiers became involved. The pushing and shoving escalated into a fight, during the course of which Cinna was slain with a sword.[7]

Other records claim that Cinna, foolishly trying to enforce enlistment, became involved in an altercation with the reluctant soldiers, and after some heated exchanges between them, he was stoned to death by them.[8]

What is certain is that Cinna was killed by the very men he had attempted to gather together to tackle Sulla. There is one account, possibly apocryphal, in which Cinna had tried to bribe a centurion during the brawl, in an effort to save his life. The centurion, on being shown the heavy gold signet ring, which Cinna offered to him, is said to have replied that he did not want the ring. He declared that he had not come to that place in order to seal a bargain, but to kill a tyrant![9]

Gnaeus Papirius Carbo, hearing of the death of Cinna at Ancona, immediately took over Rome and the control of the Senate. He decided that it was impossible to get troops over to Greece to attempt to attack Sulla there, and that it would be better for him to bring back the troops already waiting to embark. He would have to allow Sulla to return to Italy, and trust to providence that the men, realizing that Sulla was moving towards Rome, would consent to stop him. He began to lay plans for Sulla's reception.

Again records are divided as to whether he secured the election of two consuls whom he believed would be easily controllable, Scipio Asiagenus and Gaius Norbanus,[10] or whether he kept sole consulship for himself.[11] However, Carbo himself left Rome and went off to govern Italian Gaul. He possibly considered he would be able to keep an eye on developments from there without actually being in the front line facing Sulla. He settled himself and his portion of the army in the port city of Ariminum to await events.

Meanwhile, Sulla's reply to the embassy had been received in Rome and they must have been relieved to see that it was reasonable. He made it clear that he could not work with the Cinna-led faction. (He had presumably not then heard of the death of Cinna himself.)

However, if the Senate did not wish these people to be punished by him, he would obey any instructions they gave him and desist from doing so. He expressed, as always, great respect for the Senate, but also made it perfectly clear that he was the only person who had sufficient power to protect that Senate, as was then necessary. He was quite prepared to do that, so long as his basic demands were met. These were the same as they had previously been, namely that he and all of the exiles from Cinna's regime should be reinstated in their properties and honours and that his triumphs in Asia Province should be fully acknowledged and respected also.

These were not only perfectly reasonable demands in the circumstances but the Senate was aware that they were being made from a very strong position. Sulla was also very aware that he was in a position to dictate far stronger terms than those. He and the Senate had come very close to a civil war already, and he had done his part in behaving with restraint and perfect courtesy towards them, making no moves that might be considered inflammatory or immoderate. On the contrary, he asked for no more than his rights. He was clearly putting the ball very firmly in their court. If they chose to refuse his terms, then the blame for any future conflict would fall squarely on them, rather than on him. It seemed that he could not lose.

However, the talks were doomed. The Princeps Senatus wielded power, but he and his friends did not and could not control the Cinnans. The Senate had already decreed that all further recruiting in Italy should cease, pending the outcome of the talks, but that sensible directive had been ignored. Even though a majority in the Senate considered that Sulla's terms were reasonable and should be accepted, Carbo, now head of the Cinnans, thought otherwise, and they were rejected.[12]

Sulla was still in no hurry. The talks so far had gone on until the early summer of 84 BC and while negotiations were still in progress he had sailed with his army from Ephesus and arrived after a short journey of three days in Piraeus. He decided to stay there for a further period of rest. This was probably not only for the sake of his troops, who would undoubtedly appreciate the recreations on offer, but also because of his own health, which had caused him such problems already. He too would need rest to recover himself and the situation in Rome, while still needing attention, was beginning to fall favourably towards him. It would not spoil for a little more waiting time.

It was therefore not until much later in the year that he made a move, at which time he found that he had acquired some new allies. When Cinna had taken over in Rome, the people who fled to Sulla with his family group were not the only refugees from the hated regime. Quintus Caecilius Metellus Pius and Marcus Licinius Crassus had also left Rome and had gone to Africa and to Spain respectively.[13] Now they considered that the time had come when they could join Sulla. They may have opposed Cinna's power while it lasted (even now that it had been transferred to Carbo), but they were not powerful enough on their own to make any headway against it. However, if they now combined with Sulla, they could not only oppose the current regime, but also, due to having their own armies with them, could retain some measure of independence. They now considered that they could approach Sulla, and join forces with him, from a greater position of strength.

Sulla was now in a position to attempt to unite all the exiles behind him. He even made an effort to include Publius Rutilius Rufus, although that was unsuccessful. That man, closely connected to the highest families and much respected, was still very eminent and influential, but had been exiled for some time due to the machinations of members of the Ordo Equestor, whose unreasonable powers, often arbitrarily wielded, Sulla was also determined to curb. However, there was unity amongst the exiles eager to return with him, and their support made a firm base from which to work.

By the autumn of 84 BC they were ready, but there was first a curious apparition to investigate. Near to Apollonia a strange creature had been found, which was described as a 'satyr' of some kind. It was dragged before Sulla but when questioned it could not speak, making a noise something between the neighing of a horse and the bleating of a goat. The poor creature was much feared and considered an omen of bad luck, but Sulla, instead of ordering it killed, merely had it sent away.[14] Before embarkation, Sulla had a happier incident with his soldiers, who decided on their own account to take an oath to stand by him in Italy, in order to show their devotion to him. Not only that but, being aware that he was, as always, short of funds, they actually offered to donate some of their own money to him, as a 'free-will offering, each man according to his ability'.[15] Sulla, greatly touched by their generosity and affection, thanked them but refused to accept their offerings of money. Nonetheless, the unprecedented offer had been made, showing yet again the devotion that Sulla's men had towards him and the confidence they had in his ability to bring them safely to success.

Their first landfall was at or near to Tarentum, where Sulla sacrificed as was usual. To add to his pleasure and confirm the faith that the gods still had in him, he found that the victim's liver showed him 'the figure of a crown of laurel with two fillets hanging from it'.[16] This was considered to be a very fortunate occurrence and a sign of great success to come. Furthermore, a little later, a short while before he arrived in Campania, 'two stately goats' were seen fighting together, 'performing all the motions of men in battle.'[17]

This apparition was then seen to rise into the air and disperse like the clouds. It was at the place where Sulla was later to meet the armies of Marius the Younger and Norbanus, and was to be remembered at that time as having been a prophecy. Sulla believed that these visions were excellent reasons why his men did not desert him, as they also believed that they showed he would be successful in his future endeavours. As it was usual for troops to disperse once their campaign was over, returning to their homes, it was clear that this time things were very different. There was still a good deal to be done to re-establish peace and security at home, but it was a good and very encouraging beginning.

Sulla's first division had landed at Tarentum, where he had sacrificed, but the second landed at Brundisium. The Brundisians welcomed Sulla's troops eagerly, as they had heard and now believed that he would respect their rights and claims to citizenship. Carbo had already feared such a reaction from the area when Sulla's men arrived and had already tried to counter it by attempting to secure hostages from amongst the people of the leading towns, as pledges of their good faith and loyalty to him. Sulla, on the other hand, showed gratitude for the welcome received by himself and his troops on their arrival and made sure of its continuance by giving the people exemption from the portorium, or harbour tax.[18] By this generosity, he gave them more than mere gratitude for their pleasing welcome, he also gave them his own pledge that he would deal with them fairly and keep his promises to them, as his opponents patently did not do.

Armed by their goodwill, as well as the good omens from the sacrifice he had made, Sulla began to move inland. He was heading for Campania, where he knew that the armies were being gathered to prevent him from reaching Rome. While on the march he was very careful indeed to give instructions to all his followers that no persons were to be accosted in any way, that no farms or towns were to be pillaged, that no livestock or crops were to be destroyed or damaged. He made sure that all foodstuffs were paid for in coin (which his men were easily able to do, with their income from the Asian campaign they were probably financially better off than he was), and that their passing gave no offence of any kind to the locals. It may seem to be simple common sense not to antagonize the local people while travelling with large numbers of troops through their territory, but it was not the usual way of dealing with ordinary people. Armies were (and remained) notorious for their destructive powers, not only with enemies, but also with any unfortunates who came across their path. Living off the land was the norm, along with rape and pillage for entertainment along the way. The local people were relieved to see that Sulla kept his men in check, and were delighted that his moderate and reasonable behaviour showed them clearly that he was not their enemy. This moderation was reassuring and they began to say that he had come home to Italy to bring peace, not war.

At this point, Metellus Pius and Crassus finally joined him. Metellus, particularly, was valuable as an ally. He was a relative of Sulla's by marriage, being connected to his wife, Caecilia Metella Dalmatica.[19] Metellus was still a proconsul in his own right and still commanded a considerable amount of personal prestige. He was not only a great boon to have on Sulla's side, but by his presence he was a powerful incentive for others to join.

Their welcome arrival in Sulla's camp was soon followed by that of the Princeps Senatus, Lucius Valerius Flaccus, along with the others who had recently done their best to arrange a reconciliation between the opposing parties. Even they could now see that no such thing would be forthcoming and they could only join with Sulla, considering him to be the best option they had in their attempt to free Rome.

At around that time, another arrival made his appearance. This was a young man of very different stamp from the others who had decided to stand alongside Sulla. He had for some time been in retirement on his family estates at Picenum, having been originally a part of Cinna's ill-fated attempt against Sulla, acting as Cinna's legate in 84 BC.[20] He was actually a part of the army whose mutiny had ended in Cinna's death. But if he had not stepped forward sooner, it was not from fear or guilt, rather that he was waiting to see which way the cat would jump. By 83 BC he had decided that Fortune was favouring Sulla and that by joining him he would succeed and also rise higher along with him.

This was not a young man who feared anyone, not even Sulla; he was far too much convinced of his own greatness. He was the son of the Consul Pompeius Strabo who had died from dysentery during the Social War and whose body had been abused by the local people, in retaliation for his contamination of their water supplies. However, the cognomen 'Strabo' probably comes from strabismus, from which some unfortunate ancestor had suffered, and this young man, who was proud of his blonde beauty and his clear blue eyes, did not wish to be burdened with such a name. He had already chosen one he preferred for himself. He called himself Magnus.

Gnaeus Pompeius Magnus had decided to join Sulla on his own terms, leading his own men, because he was certain that the cause was one which could not lose, especially with his assistance. His belief in his capabilities and future greatness was boundless. He joined Sulla with an air of doing him a favour, but nevertheless he joined, taking with him many useful men in the process. He arrived leading an impressive private army of three legions, composed entirely of his Picentine clients.[21]

Sulla might have been amused by the posturings of Gnaeus Pompeius Magnus, rather than being repelled by his conceit and pretensions. He must have known what it felt like to be full of confidence and courage, wanting to have the opportunity to show his mettle. The young man claimed greatness but had not, as yet, done much to demonstrate it. But Sulla was not a fool. He probably could see that despite the young man's immense ego and his desire for glory there was some real ability there and that it might yet prove very beneficial. It was the start of a connection lasting many years, which was to eventually be advantageous to them both, when a marital connection was formed.

The Cinnan faction seemed to have had the same opinion of him. Once Pompeius Magnus had declared openly for Sulla, they sent a force against him, to prevent him from joining his new leader. Sulla had heard that the young man was on his way to meet him and had attempted to speed his men forward, in case Pompeius needed help in getting through. But no help was required. Pompeius Magnus had dealt with the Cinnan force sent to intercept him with almost casual ease, and Sulla was pleased to receive him, safe and very proud of himself. He treated him with courtesy and addressed him as Imperator. There may have been some semblance of a smile to accompany the use of the title, but if so Magnus would not have noticed it. He was oblivious to slights or sarcasm, delighted with his reception in Sulla's camp and convinced that he had chosen well and wisely.

The Cinnans now faced another problem. Up until that time, the men they had lost to Sulla's forces had been only men whose allegiance was doubtful and whose loyalty was shaky. This time it was very different. This man, Publius Cornelius Cethegus, had been a firm supporter of Gaius Marius, and had been instrumental in having Sulla declared an outlaw.[22] His loss to their cause was far more serious and his defection caused several others to reconsider their position. The feeling that Sulla now stood a very good chance of winning any war was growing daily. After Cethegus' arrival, there was yet another of the 'omens' for which Sulla's campaigns were becoming famous. This time it involved the slave of a Samnite named Pontius. This man accosted Sulla at a place named Silvium, and promised him that Bellona, goddess of war, would give him great victory. However, there was a problem. If Sulla did not make haste to reach Rome, he would find when he arrived there that the Capitol would be burned down! This hillside, overlooking the Forum, was crowned by the Temple of Jupiter Optimus Maximus, the best and greatest of all the gods who protected Rome, along with other gods who shared its site, looking down over Rome's Forum, the heart of the city. Its destruction or even damage was too horrible to contemplate.

This tragedy did, in fact, happen at the end of summer that year. All the temples there were destroyed, leaving the Capitol Hill a shambles of debris. Not only was the Temple of Jupiter Optimus Maximus burned to the ground, being largely built of wood but also the statue of the great god inside it was totally ruined.[23] That, too, had been of wood with a face of terracotta. (Triumphing generals painted their faces red with minim to imitate the god's terracotta face.) The temple had stood on the hill for almost 500 years and the fire, which so easily consumed it, had burned for almost a week. The other temples alongside, which shared its prominence on the Capitol Hill were destroyed with it. These included the ancient numinae, or faceless, formless gods, such as Ops Consiva, who was the guardian of Rome's public wealth and plenty; Fides Publica, who held in her hand the republic's faith and loyalty. The Temple of Honour and Virtue had been only recently rebuilt by Gaius Marius in marble rather than wood so, although damaged, it was not totally destroyed, but Fortuna Primagenia was also gone.[24] Not only the buildings themselves, but the treasures inside them were lost. Ivory and bronze statues; law tablets and ancient records; the Sibyllene Books, which were usually consulted in times of emergency; and a gold statue of Victory donated by Hiero of Syracuse after the battle of Trasimene. Works of art from the most revered sculptors, Praxiteles and Myron, Strongylion and Polyclitus, Scopas and Lysippus, all were ruined and so ancient and valuable were they that they could not possibly be replaced, a truly irreparable loss.

It was a disaster for Rome, and caused the Romans to fear that the gods must have turned their faces away from them all at once. However, for the Senate still in Rome there was one benefit to be found in the situation. The shapeless lumps of melted gold and silver which represented the fortunes of Rome, either from the statues or that which had been stored away as coin in the chambers under the temples, gave them the idea of melting down all the precious metals, to make new coins. Carbo therefore was able to 'borrow' Rome's treasure, leaving behind only a promissory note, never to be honoured, regarding the amount he had taken. It was something that Sulla had never contemplated doing. Even when leaving Rome to begin the war in the east against Mithradates, he had taken only the price of a small piece of land, 9,000 librae, with him. Now Carbo found himself in possession of all the wealth that had been denied to Sulla, leaving Rome's treasuries completely empty.

Not only the temples damaged by the fire were emptied of whatever treasure they had left. The opportunity was taken to strip the others too. There was a vast amount of treasure hidden, in the interests of Rome's security, under the temples to the gods. Each citizen gave a coin regularly, both at public festivals and to commemorate private celebrations. A coin would be given to Juno Lucina at the birth of a child, a coin to Juventas when a male child became an adult. A small donation to Mercury by a travelling businessman, or a coin to Venus Libitina at the death of any citizen, even the coins given by successful prostitutes to Venus Erucina![25] The many temples all had their share and the flood of small coins, given regularly, had made a vast fortune in total. Carbo took the lot.

However, there was nothing Sulla could do about it. The only comfort to be gained from it was that at least Carbo and his men would also be in a position to pay for their food and comforts, without the local populace having to suffer. The consuls were still waiting in Campania to prevent Sulla access to the city, and they had managed to enlist Italians into the armies led by Scipio and Norbanus. These people had been very unwilling to embark to fight Sulla abroad, but now that he was on Italian soil the situation was different, as they could now be persuaded that they would be defending their homeland. The senatus consultum ultimum had already been passed.[26]

Sulla had sensibly begun to treat Metellus as a co-commander of his forces, in recognition of his position as a proconsul, but also in awareness of his political importance in Rome. Together they moved towards Capua, to find Norbanus blocking the crossroads of the Via Appia and the Via Latina. Sulla, eager as ever to prevent bloodshed if it were possible, and not yet convinced that a full-scale war should be necessary, decided to attempt to persuade the enemy to come over to his side. He must have been confident of his ability to do so, probably due to the numbers of eminent men who had already decided to join him, so he sent an ambassador to Norbanus, with the suggestion that they might join forces and prevent a conflict. Unfortunately, the only reply was that Norbanus, who was to show himself to be a vicious and implacable foe of Sulla's, grossly mistreated the envoys and by doing so brought the matter to a head.

A battle ensued, which Plutarch tells us was not conducted in the usual way, with men being put into formation. Sulla is said to have allowed his men, on this occasion, to fight as they wished. Plutarch states that their natural enthusiasm swept them over the enemy, and their victory was total.[27] Several thousands of Norbanus' men were killed and he was obliged to retreat to Capua. This town was in fact the obvious place for Norbanus to go. Earlier that year, the tribune of the plebs, Marcus Junius Brutus, had brought in a law giving Capua the status of a Roman city. After centuries of being punished by Rome for various insurrections, this new status pleased Capua greatly and so the town was predisposed to favour the government at that time in power in Rome.

Plutarch also states that Sulla may have had doubts at this point about whether his troops, despite their protestations of loyalty would, when faced with yet another battle, have opted to flee to their homes. If that were so, then Sulla was doubtful only of what appeared to be his amazing and continual good fortune at the hands of the gods. It must have been only a momentary blip in his confidence, such as any man may be subject to when things seem to be going almost too well for comfort. In any case, the behaviour of his men, once allowed to show their courage and eagerness, was enough to convince anyone. Again, with fewer numbers than their opponents, they had secured a victory, with almost embarrassing ease. When it was over, Sulla attributed the success to the local goddess, one Diana Tifata, to whom the region was sacred. He dedicated certain lands in the vicinity to her as an act of gratitude.[28] However, despite their success over Norbanus, it did show them that the conflict was unlikely to be settled by any form of negotiation, as they may have hoped. A fight it would have to be.

Sulla now pushed on towards Scipio, who was advancing to meet him from Teanum. Somewhere between there and Cales the two sides met. Sulla, still determined to avoid all-out war, was hopeful of one last try at negotiation, so envoys were sent forward to attempt to arrange talks, and this time there was some success. Scipio might have been a more pragmatic man than Norbanus, or it may simply have been that he was aware that his men were unreliable. Perhaps his troops were more willing to listen to Sulla's arguments, or perhaps Scipio realized that forcing them into battle with Sulla's very experienced and very eager troops was foolish in the extreme. Whatever the cause, Scipio decided it was worth his while to agree to talks. If he could obtain some concessions from Sulla, then it might be possible to avoid further conflict, without appearing to have cravenly given in.

There were differences in ideology as well as personal differences between Sulla and his enemies in Rome. Sulla had naturally been anxious about the laws he had recently brought in, fearing that Cinna and his faction would immediately repeal them, thereby destroying the work he was trying to do for Rome. This, of course, is exactly what happened. But Cinna's faction had gone further, they had also brought in Sulpicius' proposals for the redistribution of the new Italian citizens, which was the point Sulla had so strongly objected to. These were still issues causing dissention.[29] However, Sulla had been obliged to quite drastically change his position on the matter and had already declared that he was now prepared to agree to such redistribution, along with respecting the recently given rights of the new Italian citizens. He had, in fact, done all that he could do to show that he was genuine in his desire to behave reasonably.

Senatorial authority was another point which needed to be discussed between Sulla and Scipio. One of the issues there was the question of who was to be able to vote on laws, as Sulla had already decreed that the Centuriate Committee should be pre-eminent in this.

However, some sort of agreement was certainly reached. As there was no personal quarrel between Sulla and Scipio, there was no barrier to reaching some middle ground, no old antagonisms to prevent sensible accord. Therefore, the end result of those useful talks was that a truce was declared. This was intended to allow Scipio time to inform Norbanus of the result of the talks. He obviously did not feel comfortable in making any final assent without the authority of Norbanus, and did not feel empowered to take such decisions alone. He wished for Norbanus' approval before the talks could be finalized.

That was reasonable enough. However, while Scipio had no axe to grind regarding his personal relationship with Sulla, there were still people within his camp who did, people who still feared and hated Sulla and had no desire to see any kind of a reconciliation.

One of these people was the Praetor, Quintus Sertorius, who had fought in Gaul with Sulla years before. He was the man who had spent time with the Germans as a spy, and was a very good, courageous and determined soldier. One who had been awarded the Corona Graminea by his men, as Sulla had, and also one of the very few who were considered (also like Sulla) to be beloved of the gods. He had been a firm follower of Marius, who had thought highly of him. However, it seemed odd that such a man should now be an adherent of Carbo and his crew, until it is remembered that Sulla had opposed Sertorius' attempt to stand for election to the tribuneship back in 88 BC. He had neither forgotten nor forgiven this and had formed a dislike against Sulla which at that time outweighed any distrust he may have felt for the Cinna/Carbo regime.[30]

Quintus Sertorius then told Scipio that the talks with Sulla were pointless and that he was not to be trusted, despite all the evidence to the contrary. Having heard this and seen that Sertorius was so opposed to any truce between the two sides, it seems curious that Scipio should then entrust this man with the task of taking the details of the talks to Norbanus. It seems a most unlikely thing for Scipio to have done. However, to be fair to Scipio, who must have felt that at that time that he was being ground between two powerful forces, he may have had no choice but to choose Sertorius as his messenger. It might have been that he was the highest ranking officer then available to Scipio, making the choice an obvious one. However, it was to prove a very damaging choice.

Sertorius set out with the communication to Norbanus, but he made a detour to the town of Suessa, which had only recently gone over to Sulla's side. He attacked the town and captured it, thereby deliberately breaking the truce that had been agreed between Sulla and Scipio. Whatever regret Scipio felt about that, he appeared to have had no real power to control Sertorius, and was then obliged to declare that the truce was at an end and return Sulla's hostages to him. Sulla may also have been disgusted by Sertorius' deliberate provocation, but as usual he was keeping his options open. Sulla had already, during the short time of truce, encouraged his men to fraternize with Scipio's troops. He was, of course, fully aware that Scipio's hold over them was not firm, and that they were wavering in their loyalties. By the time the truce was regretfully called off by Scipio, his men were very friendly with Sulla's and eager to listen to their flattery and promises.

Once it was obvious that the conflict would resume, Sulla had made such inroads into the loyalty and confidence of Scipio's men that he had more control over them than their own commander had. Sulla then advanced towards Scipio's troops with his whole army, but when they neared them, at a prearranged signal, a greeting was called out. This was answered in friendly fashion from Scipio's camp, and to Scipio's dismay, the whole of his army moved out of his camp, and went across to join with Sulla![31] Scipio and his son were therefore easily captured while still helpless in their camp. Sulla, exerting his famous charm and behaving in a courteous and chivalrous manner, offered them his protection and asked them to join him. Scipio, perhaps fearing reactions in Rome, and perhaps also simply being an honourable man who did not think it the right thing to do, refused to join Sulla. Despite this, Sulla was determined to treat Scipio decently, and he and his son were released without harm, and allowed to go on their way.

This show of courteous magnanimity has sometimes been used as an example of Sulla playing a part, but I consider it to be only his genuine reaction to a foe whom he did not despise and had no wish to harm. He was still determined to show everyone that he was prepared to deal fairly and honourably with those who were reasonable in their turn. He considered that he had been forced into the struggle on which he was then engaged, but he wished to find a solution to it without any unnecessary bloodshed. No doubt it was also his intention that Scipio, on being reunited with his friends, could and would inform them of Sulla's reasonable behaviour. This obviously is what happened, as Carbo, hearing of Scipio's release together with his son, declared that Sulla was in part a lion and in part a fox, and that of the two, the fox was infinitely the most dangerous![32]

Sulla, still determined to find a peaceable solution if it were at all possible, made a final attempt to deal with Norbanus. He must have realized that it was highly unlikely that his foe would agree to any accommodation with him, but still considered it worth a try. However, the result was as might have been expected. Norbanus refused even to reply.

Sulla, therefore, had no option but to move forward, taking all hostile territory which lay on his route. Norbanus naturally enough did the same, devastating land around him as he withdrew towards the Cinnan stronghold of Praeneste.

It was at this point that Sulla heard that the prophecy about the burning of the Capitol Hill and the destruction of Rome's famous temples had come true. It must have been a devastating blow to someone as superstitious as he was known to be. It could be taken as an omen that the gods were displeased, but with which side? At the same time, he also heard that Carbo, who was in turn becoming alarmed by the desertions of troops which he was continually suffering, had declared that all Sulla's supporters, whoever and wherever they might be, were now all officially public enemies.[33]

There was then a lull in the fighting. Carbo appeared, at least at that point, to be in a far stronger position than Sulla, as a large part of Italy still believed, as he had intended they should, that they were fighting for the freedom of their homeland. He also still had substantial support in Umbria and Etruria, where the magic of the name of Gaius Marius was still alive and well. Carbo's intention was to use that name as a battle flag, and in order to keep it at the forefront of people's minds he deliberately arranged the election of Marius' son, Gaius Marius Junior, to the consulship for the year 82 BC.

This was another unprecedented move and was completely at odds with correct procedure. It was customary for a man to attain the consulship at a later age, preferably around 42. Young Marius was only 27 and was a completely inexperienced young man, who had done nothing at all to make anyone feel any confidence in his abilities as a general. However, that did not matter, while the magic name did. Carbo had every intention of using him as a puppet and a figurehead. At the end of the year the voters had the pleasure of seeing Young Marius elected not only as a consul but as the senior consul, with Gnaeus Papirius Carbo as his junior. Carbo might have been forgiven a smile at the idea that the young man would be able to hold things together as his father would have done. His election, heartily canvassed for, showed only that the people of Rome were getting desperate and were voting for the name rather than the man. However, it was to prove a very useful move, at least for a time, as recruitment increased, with the sons and grandsons of Marius' old veterans joining eagerly.

Rome would be prepared to turn out in the freezing cold of the following January to see the consuls inaugurated. But the usual festivities would be dampened not only by the weather but also by the fact that the temples, outside of which the new consuls usually swore their oaths of office, had completely gone. This year they would be able to do no more than stand under an awning, rather than the shelter of Jupiter Optimus Maximus himself. It all seemed to be a bad omen for any stability in the future, although the new young senior consul, uplifted at finding himself in such a position at such an age, and quite oblivious to what would be required of him, managed a show of confidence.

Sulla, meanwhile, could still count on forces from Calabria, Apulia and Picenum, where Pompeius Magnus was sent to raise further troops. This he did with his usual ease, for he too had a great name to live up to. Despite the deficiencies of his father's character and his reputation for being something of a butcher, Pompeius Strabo had been a clever and capable general. His son, Pompeius Magnus, had inherited his father's military ability, a legacy which was unfortunately passed on only too rarely, but he was to show himself to be far more capable than his opposite number, the son of Marius. He quickly returned to Sulla bringing with him a further two legions.

He also brought with him further news of Scipio, who had during the autumn attempted to rejoin the fight for the other side, when he had yet again suffered the humiliation of seeing his men desert en masse to the enemy. He must have been a very poor general indeed who gave his men no confidence so that they were prepared to change sides at the first opportunity if a better man hove into view. His failure at his career was a very sad recommendation for his generalship and for his apparent lack of character as a man.

Sulla had also sent Crassus to recruit among the Marsi, even though he did not appear to like the man personally and probably had little faith in him or his loyalty. Crassus had actually asked Sulla for an escort on his mission, as he presumably considered it hazardous. Sulla refused the request, and made several cutting remarks about the deaths of his father and brother during the Social War. Crassus was obliged to set off without the desired escort, but still he managed well enough, returning after completing his task.

Sulla, as it turned out, could now well afford to spend what was left of that year in winning over to his side those Italians who were not actually committed one way or the other. He reiterated that he would respect their citizenship rights, and it seems that only the Samnites and the Lucanians were unimpressed and remained with the enemy. Sulla now had good reason for having considerable confidence, as it seemed that Carbo was beginning to lose support all around, with only his backers in Rome still firmly with him. Even Carbo's own troops were by then lukewarm and there was a good deal of trouble within the ranks, while groups supposedly acting for both sides clashed with each other and towns were rent with dissension.

But when the true winter came on, it was to prove to be an unusually severe one, with any further attempts at military action being obliged to wait for the better weather of Spring.

Chapter Thirteen

It was early March of 82 BC before the weather allowed either side to consider any reopening of the campaign. One army, under the command of Metellus, headed up through Picenum and Umbria towards Cisalpine Gaul, to confront Carbo at the old Cinnan stronghold there. With Metellus was Gnaeus Pompeius Magnus, who had lately joined him, and together they faced a commander of Carbo's, one Carrinas, at the River Aesis.[1] Pompeius was able to show his abilities in this confrontation by routing the cavalry reinforcements, which had been sent by Carbo. Metellus was equally successful in capturing the camp, after first engaging in a determined battle with Carrinas, which lasted several hours. The whole district then considered it sensible to go over to the Sullan side.

Carbo then managed to put Metellus under siege, blocking any further progress for a time, until he received bad news from the other front, where Sulla was still single-mindedly marching towards Rome. Carbo decided the wisest course would be for him to retreat to Ariminum, which he did, but was harassed all the way there by the troops led by Pompeius Magnus, who succeeded in depriving them of a good deal of their armour together with their horses.[2]

Sulla was marching along the Via Latina while his Lieutenant, Dolabella, travelled along the Via Appia Velarae, stopping only to capture Setia on his journey. On both of those roads all opposition melted away as their troops approached. Gaius Norbanus had already left Capua with six of his eight legions, with the intention of re-joining Carbo at Ariminum. This arrival brought Carbo's numbers up to around thirty legions, which was a vast amount of people to find supplies for. It was fortunate for him that he had already had the foresight to 'borrow' Rome's money and melt down its treasures to fill his war chest.

It needs to be remembered, as the two leaders of the conflict were certainly aware, that this war was not one in which the ordinary people could be too much involved. For many people, this was not in any way a 'real' war at all, not in the way the Gallic or Jugurthan campaigns had been, or the recent Mithradatic campaign was. This must have seemed to many ordinary people to be merely a quarrel between two leading men, both wishing to rule Rome for themselves. Even the Social War, so recently ended, had many reasons for ordinary people to become involved on one side or the other in the conflict. In this struggle, however, whichever side won, it might seem that little advantage either way would be gained by most people. Therefore it was essential that the population should be inconvenienced as little as possible, with the minimum of suffering caused to them, else their support, which might be vital later, would be lost before the campaigning ended. Hence the need for the opposing commanders to make sure that all supplies be paid for, and therefore the need for large sums of money to be available, which had always been something of a problem for Sulla. He had already proved that he was a little more particular where the money came from in the first place, than Carbo had shown himself to be. He had also confirmed that he had some scruples about stealing from the temples in Rome, as well as being concerned that at some point in the future all the borrowings that had been unavoidable should be paid back in full, as had been done in Greece.[3]

Carbo, also, had enough to cause him anxiety with the handling and advising of young Marius, a headstrong but rather less capable young man than Pompeius Magnus, whom Carbo needed as his figurehead. He could not allow himself to become too much of an object of hatred for the people. Young Marius, unfortunately, bore many of the faults to which the sons of famous fathers are prone. He had been brought up as an indulged young man, one who now considered that the mantle of his eminent father's ability and authority would automatically fall on him, as if out of the sky, endowing him with ability and inspiration once he decided to lead his men into battle. Certainly his youthful freshness of appearance and his great name had caused many people to flock to his cause, but also far too many of these soldiers were themselves young and idealistic, rather than being the experienced and hardened troops which he and Carbo really needed.

In that he was so very different from Gnaeus Pompeius Magnus, who while he might be equally young and perhaps just as idealistic, also had a fundamental ability and clear-sightedness which would always stand him in good stead. Furthermore, while many of his men might have appeared to be as youthful and eager as he was himself, they were in actual fact not only young and strong, but also capable and very well trained. Pompeius Magnus had been brought up by his father, which meant that he had learned in a very hard school. His father, Pompeius Strabo, while being hated by the populace, had been nevertheless a very good fighter and a determined man. Magnus had inherited all of his father's abilities for warfare, but in his case without losing his charm and pleasing naturalness, which drew people to him. His troops found, on being accepted by him, that he was just as capable, just as well trained, just as determined to succeed as his father had been and with a 'bold and warlike spirit' of his own.[4]

He also demanded similar qualities from the men he worked with, which made for an extremely useful and efficient army.

Alongside Marius, at that time, was Gnaeus Domitius Ahenobarbus, who may well have wished himself elsewhere. He was already a slightly reluctant follower of young Marius' because he belonged to a worthy family which was essentially Sullan in sympathy. However, he was married to one of Cinna's daughters, and that had brought him into close contact with the opposing side, which by then might have begun to feel like the wrong side, leaving him out on a limb. He was still bound by his marriage to Cinna's daughter and therefore on Carbo's side of the struggle, but it must have been a rather uncomfortable place to be, when most of his friends and relatives were actually with, or at least in sympathy with, Sulla's army.

By early April of that year, young Marius had decided that he would head south-east into Campania. He had no doubt heard that Sulla and Dolabella would wish to link together the two sections of their army, and had also probably heard that the bulk of Sulla's manpower was already with Metellus and Pompeius, detached in order to deal with Carbo at Ariminum. To Marius, the time was therefore ideal for him to make his stand, with Sulla's forces presently somewhat under strength due to the amount of men with Metellus. If he could prevent Sulla from joining Dolabella that was the time to do it and it would probably best be done at Sacriportus, which was an area surrounded by wide plains and ideally suited for the deployment of large numbers of men. This place is now gone, and its precise location is still a matter for dispute, but it was probably situated somewhere around Segni (the modern Signia).[5]

Sulla may well have been willing enough to confront the young leader, as he had recently had yet another of his prophetic dreams. In this dream he said that he had seen the deceased Gaius Marius who warned young Marius, his son, telling him that the following day's fight would only bring him fatal consequences if attempted. However, when Sulla came into contact with Marius' forces he was to receive something of a surprise. They maintained their hold on the roadway with unexpected determination and Sulla's men were unable to make any progress at all in managing to break through.

The weather then took a terrible turn for the worse, with a cloudburst of very heavy rain, which sapped the strength of the men fighting valiantly to make some headway. Sulla's officers had then become very concerned at the level of exhaustion being shown by their troops. They were by then 'stretched on the ground, where they had thrown themselves in their weariness, with their heads on their shields attempting to gain some repose'.[6] These officers prevailed upon Sulla to allow them give the order to pitch a camp, deferring any further struggle that day in order to allow their men to find some rest.

This they were preparing to do, when young Marius decided to move onto the offensive. They were still preparing a ditch and throwing up defensive ramparts when Marius rode up to them furiously, at the head of his troops, hoping to take them by surprise and beat them while they were still in confusion and disorder. But here again, it might be said that the gods stepped in, bringing Sulla's dream into reality. His men, certainly taken by surprise while working to make a camp, reacted not so much with confusion or fear as with extreme anger! They stuck their javelins into the muddy bank, drew their swords, and set upon the army of young Marius with furious shouts.[7] They fought with such vigour and ferocity that it was Marius' turn to be taken by surprise, being attacked at close quarters by fierce and resentful men, who had apparently been provoked out of their tiredness. Marius' troops were then put on the defensive and obliged to try to protect themselves, instead of moving easily into the attack, as they had so confidently expected to do. Marius' left wing then began to waver and five cohorts of foot soldiers, along with two of horse, promptly decided to desert to Sulla, leaving their own side in total disarray. The collapse of Marius' force followed quickly, and what was left of his men fled in the direction of Praeneste, young Marius riding with them. They were so closely pursued by Sulla, Quintus Lucretius Afella and their troops that, for the few miles of that race towards Praeneste, they were able to determinedly harry them and pick off stragglers. Young Marius, on that occasion, did what he could to protect what was left of his men, but he had only around 7,000 with him when he finally arrived at Praeneste. On their arrival at the town the gates of the city were so rapidly and firmly shut behind the earliest arrivals that they prevented even young Marius himself from getting inside.[8] He was unfortunately forced to climb up onto the walls by means of a rope, which had been thrown down for him. But despite the indignity of his arrival he was far luckier than the remainder of his army, which was trapped outside the city and defeated alongside the walls, which prevented their admission to the place where they had hoped to find safety.

Domitius Ahenobarbus had been with Marius' right wing, and more of his men had survived than had been saved from the battle's centre. Led by Ahenobarbus, they managed to break away, and made a run for Norba. This had been the stronghold of the Volsci from ancient times and was still considered to be loyal to Carbo. However, Ahenobarbus was not. He had possibly by this time decided that he could no longer cope with such divided loyalties, or at least that he stood a better chance of survival elsewhere. Once he had managed to get his troops safely to Norba, he left them there. He then made his own way to the coast, and took ship for Africa Province.

Meanwhile, back at Praeneste, a large number of prisoners were taken, and Sulla, seeing that many of those prisoners were Samnites, separated them from the others and had them executed. This was on the grounds that they were incorrigible rebels who, due to their intransigence against Rome, could never be trusted. Sulla, according to his own accounts, had lost only twenty three men in the battle, but had killed 20,000 of the enemy and captured upwards of another 8,000.[9] Similar successes had attended his lieutenants, Pompeius Magnus, Crassus, Metellus Pius, and Servilius in their own battles. With comparatively few losses of their own, they too had managed to cut off vast numbers of the enemy. So much so, that Carbo, now finding that he was apparently fighting in an ailing cause decided, at least for the time being, to cut his considerable losses and save his skin by fleeing to whatever sanctuary he could find.

Praeneste, appearing defensible and showing no sign of wishing to yield, had then to be put under siege. However, Sulla had no intention at all of sitting outside Praeneste indefinitely; waiting for something to happen that might cause young Marius to surrender. He knew the young man was unlikely to give himself up, seemingly being safely enough entrenched in the city, which had appeared at first to welcome him. No doubt the inhabitants thought that they could easily sit out a siege, as the city was well supplied with all that was necessary, both in food and water, to enable them to hold out for a considerable length of time. Initially at least Marius was welcome and comfortable enough, until Sulla made his next move.

Wishing to get on towards Rome, he gave orders to circumvallate Praeneste completely putting Lucretius Afella in charge of the operation. He was another of those men who had deserted young Marius' rather shaky cause and had gone to serve under Sulla.[10] The theory, simple enough in itself, was that if Marius wished to be ensconced there in Praeneste, he could stay there. On the other hand, he would find it difficult if not impossible to get out, as would the other inhabitants. This was calculated to make Marius a rather less than welcome guest after a period of time, during which it could be remembered by the inhabitants that his presence had brought serious troubles upon them.

It was a relatively simple matter for a wall to be built around the city over the following few weeks. The stone in that area, like that in many parts of the Mediterranean, is easy to quarry, being very easy to cut and able to be sawn into blocks speedily. Once these blocks are exposed to the air they harden, making a very useful building material. It must have been a very worrying sight indeed for the people of Praeneste, who had at first been so calmly confident that Sulla would move on, to then see his men busily engaged in building a wall around them, which grew day by day, until they were entirely enclosed. For Marius too, hiding in the town that had seemed like a haven, it must have been obvious that in those new circumstances he would soon wear out his welcome.

Unfortunately, the fraught situation in which he then found himself caused young Marius to develop some of that paranoia which had characterized his father in his last days. Seeing clearly the destruction of all he thought he had been fighting for, and realizing that his abilities had been found wanting on the battlefield, he began to believe that those around him were all spies, traitors or agents working against him. He sent orders that his Praetor, Brutus Damasippus in Rome, should proceed to kill all those people who might be suspect in their loyalty. The merest suspicion of lack of enthusiasm for his doomed cause was all that was needed for many people to lose their lives due to his savage order. It sadly went to prove that he had inherited, not his father's great ability, but only the dangerous suspicion and inhumanity that had so marked Gaius Marius in his later life.

Four important public figures were killed even while they sat in the Senate House. Publius Antistius (who was the father-in-law of Pompeius Magnus), Lucius Domitius Ahenobarbus, Gaius Papirius Carbo Arvina, (who was a relative of the Carbo who had recently fled to Libya), and Quintus Mucius Scaevola, the Pontifex Maximus, who was the greatest legal writer and teacher of Republican times.[11] A great pity that such a man had to be openly murdered to suit the whim of a frightened and foolish boy. Both Antistius and Ahenobarbus obviously had relatives who were prominent in fighting for Sulla, so they had to be removed. Carbo Arvina also had relatives in both camps, so became distrusted for that alone and Scaevola had long been suspected. He had, in fact, already been assaulted by Fimbria some years previously, during the murders ordered by Gaius Marius Senior, for no good reason that any sensible person could see. From that attack he had been lucky to escape with his life. That life was now forfeit.

These were not, however, the only sufferers of the purge ordered by the imprisoned young Marius. By the time Damasippus had finished his work, there were around thirty heads adorning the rostra in the lower Forum. Most of them had belonged to men who would have been proud to have called themselves neutral in the present political difficulties, but that distinction did not save them from the killing impulse of young Marius, who showed himself to be his father's son in that if nothing else. Men such as Catulus, Lepidus and Hortensius also died at that time, taking Rome's honour with them.

These were the men who had mainly been instrumental in attempting to persuade the government, then in power in Rome, to reach some sort of agreement with Sulla. They believed that by such a move they might be able to not only shore up the authority of the Senate but also prevent the start of the civil war. These were the moderates with whom Sulla had tried to negotiate and their attempts to make a peace had cost them their lives, while in the hands of men to whom real peace meant little. Ironically, if the order from Marius to Damasippus had come just a little later their lives could have been saved – their saviour, Sulla, was by then approaching Rome.[12] Unfortunately, having to deal with Marius holed up in Praeneste had cost him precious time, and that loss of the irreplaceable time he had available made the difference between life and death for those decent men.

When he considered that he had fulfilled the task set for him, Brutus Damasippus fled from Rome, taking with him his fellow Praetor Gaius Albius Carrinas. Both of them set off to join Carbo. Rome, shaken and uneasy with all the upheavals of the last months, went about its business as well as it could, while even more anxiously waiting to see what would happen next.

Sulla, along with his officers and men, approached Rome in three separate detachments. As Sulla was still invested with proconsular imperium it was not possible for him to enter the city, without giving up that imperium. As the fact that he was a properly instituted and officially appointed proconsular was one of the things he had insisted upon in his letters to the Senate, he would certainly not wish to lay down that authority. So he and his force waited outside. However, he was not idle there. If the Cinna–led government could declare him and his followers to be outlaws (hostis) then it was necessary for him to return the compliment. The sympathizers of Sulla who were already within the city then arranged for the all followers of the Cinna/Carbo faction to be declared outlaws in their turn. As confirmation of their newly decreased status, all their properties were seized and confiscated and were then put up for auction to the public.

However, there could not be too much delay wasted in general congratulations regarding the capture of the city, even with such apparent ease, as the matter was still not completed. After camping outside for a short while, Sulla moved off. His intention was to travel to Etruria to deal with the enemy stronghold there, but what he found was that Carbo was there also. Carbo had decided to use it as his centre of defence against those Sullan sympathizers who were moving up towards him from the South. Carbo, probably equally surprised at Sulla's appearance, then found that he would have to fight him without the support of his lieutenants, who were still held down at Ariminum by Metellus and Pompeius Magnus, who were continuing their advance.[13] Metellus had routed one of Carbo's armies when yet another desertion, this time depleting his forces of five cohorts, took place. These men had left Carbo's army and gone over to that of Metellus actually during the battle, an ignominious as well as a damaging loss to be sustained.

Magnus, meanwhile, had gone further along the coast and been successful in first capturing and then plundering Sena Gallica. Not only had Carbo these constant reverses to worry about, but he then heard that his forces in Etruria would have to be even further divided. Information arrived that not only was Sulla advancing from the south towards him, but that Crassus was in the East, also headed his way.

Sulla divided his troops into two, leading one group himself, heading for Clusium by way of the Via Cassia. The second headed for Saturnia along the Via Clodia. On the way there, Sulla came across a large cavalry force belonging to the enemy near to the River Clanis. Yet again there were the desertions from Carbo's army, which were happening with depressing regularity. This time a group of Celtiberian cavalry decided to side with Sulla and went over to him in a body. The rest of the cavalry, still ostensibly fighting for Carbo, were then soundly defeated, while their erstwhile colleagues sat and watched. Carbo must have been in despair at the sight of so many of his men going over to the other side, but there was absolutely nothing he could do about it. He began to blame the Celtiberians for starting the movement towards his triumphant enemy, infecting the rest of his forces with their dissatisfaction and disloyalty. In his fury against them he decided to punish them all by slaughtering every one of them that he could get his hands on.[14]

Sulla, however, then came face to face with Carbo in person not far from Clusium, where battle was immediately joined. It proved to be a very hard fight between the two sides, neither of whom was prepared to yield. The battle lasted all day and there was still no clear winner when night fell, which necessarily stopped the fighting for the time being. The other Sullan force had in the meantime been completely successful, defeating its opponents near to Saturnia. Good news of other victories also began to arrive. Metellus had managed to sail around the heavily fortified town of Ariminum in an effort to deal with it from the other side, and although he had so far not been able to subdue it, he was established firmly near to Ravenna and confidently preparing an advance. Further south, Marcus Philippus was enjoying another success on Sardinia. It seemed that all was going very well for the Sullan forces, with their enemies losing ground all around them and particularly with the numbers of men from the enemy deserting to them with impunity.

However, instead of engaging again on the following day and making an end of the action against Carbo as might have been expected, Sulla was forced to make a retreat from Clusium, leaving Carbo behind. He had heard that Afella's situation outside of Praeneste was becoming difficult, as he was then being threatened by a force of Samnites and Lucanians, who had decided to throw in their lot with the Cinnan cause. Carbo had already made one attempt to relieve the town in young Marius' favour, by sending Gaius Marcius Censorinus to lift the siege. However, he had come unstuck before he ever reached Praeneste, due to being ambushed on the way by a surprised but delighted Pompeius Magnus who had been marching to the aid of Crassus in the east. Magnus was perfectly happy to have an interesting diversion on the way in the form of a skirmish with Censorinus, which he was able to win quite easily.

However, the attack by the Samnites was a far more serious concern, and Sulla was obliged to make the decision to put Magnus in overall command. Despite his youth, Pompeius was doing very well indeed and Sulla must have felt that he could put some trust in the capable and willing young man. Certainly, at that point he needed him, while he prepared to move south to try to prevent Afella and his siege outside Praeneste from being destroyed and resulting in young Marius being set free again.

On the way, he was met by yet another enemy force on the road, sent by Carbo to give assistance to one of his lieutenants, the Praetor Gaius Carrinas, who had recently been defeated by Crassus and Pompeius Magnus and had finally found himself shut into the town of Spoletium. Sulla managed an ambush of his own at that point, with Carbo's men being forced to give way to Sulla, with another unfortunate loss of around 2,000 of them.[15]

When Sulla finally arrived at Praeneste, he took up a good position on the hills overlooking the town from where the many springs, which fed the town's water supplies, began. When the enemy, intent on relieving Marius, arrived nearby they were unable to dislodge him and get into the town at all. Marius had already been equally unsuccessful in finding any way to break out of the cage, which Sulla had skilfully built all around him. Afella's siege works were made at some little distance from the town itself, which allowed movement in between them and Praeneste. Young Marius had even made a small fort in the space between Afella's walls and the town. From this he made several attempts, on different days, to force his way through Sulla's encirclement. However, the circumvallation Sulla had ordered was done efficiently and was guarded equally well. When Marius and the men he had with him were repeatedly defeated, they eventually had to abandon their attempts and retire back inside Praeneste.

Marius must by this time have been desperate to escape from the net that Praeneste had become, just as Sulla had intended that it should. It was becoming obvious that the young man was beginning to outstay his welcome. Food and water supplies were sufficient, but could not be guaranteed forever, particularly when Sulla had already shown the ease with which he could take a stand on the surrounding hillsides from which the essential water supplies sprang. The hills also had many tracks, paths snaking around the hills, sufficient for pack animals and which had been used for resupplying the town in the past. That, also, had stopped. The surrounding wall, together with the efficient guarding of Sulla's troops, was by then proving to be a tightening noose around Praeneste's neck.

Carbo and Norbanus, meanwhile, had decided to attempt to stop the relentless advance of Metellus, by attacking him near to Faventia. They had decided to take Metellus by surprise by organizing a nighttime attack. This, unfortunately for them, went disastrously wrong, as so many things had gone wrong for them in that war. Many of their soldiers, more accustomed to ending their fighting when darkness fell, got totally lost in the unfamiliar surroundings and floundered around uselessly in a vineyard. Their struggles alerted Metellus to their presence and their difficulties also made them a very easy target for his troops, who were able to dispatch a great many of them without much trouble at all. On hearing of this disastrous attempt, and its unfortunate result, a legion of Lucanians went over to Metellus in disgust at so inefficient a plan, so Carbo had to suffer the mortification of seeing yet another mass desertion.[16] The chief of these Lucanians, a man named Albinovanus, on seeing what was happening with his own men, and realizing that they were no longer prepared to fight for Carbo, decided that it would be wise of him to follow their example and go over to Metellus. He sent him a message to this effect, making the suggestion of his change of allegiance, in order to open the way for his own defection. He received the reply that if he could give some definite pledge of his good faith, then he would be welcome. Metellus was already in possession of a fair number of his men and might have been concerned that Albinovanus was merely playing the spy. However, Albinovanus was only too happy to give proof to Metellus that his intention to change sides completely was genuine. He sent a reply that he would quite happily give some firm sign of his good intentions towards the Sullans.

He did this by inviting Norbanus' lieutenants to a feast, sending out invitations to them all. During this feast, which most of them attended, he had arranged to have them killed. During the evening's feasting he calmly carried out his intention and then went over to Metellus, leaving the carnage behind him. As a direct result of those murders, which had been arranged so casually, Ariminum and several other fortified camps decided to finally surrender to Metellus. Gaius Norbanus himself, who had been invited to join the fatal feast, but had fortunately for him declined, realized after that catastrophe that the cause for which he was fighting was as good as lost. In despair he left his post, took ship and sailed away to find refuge in Rhodes.[17]

Carbo, after so many losses and humiliations, knew that it was essential for him to break the siege at Praeneste and rescue young Marius. He still had sufficient troops with him, and sent two legions with Brutus Damasippus to make a determined attempt to lift the siege. However, despite every effort, Damasippus was quite unable to make any headway at all. Then came news that one of Carbo's worst fears had actually come about. Cisalpine Gaul had surrendered to the Sullan forces. Carbo's army there had been soundly defeated near to Placentia, by Metellus' legate, Marcus Lucullus.

Carbo was actually at that point still in possession of a substantial number of men, but the continual reverses and disappointments, despite every effort that he had made, were taking their toll on his confidence and his ability to keep shrugging off defeats. He could now see that there was no real improvement in the general situation whatever he did, and if he continued to fight in that way then the ultimate ending must be that he would lose. It was then he decided that there was little point in him continuing to struggle on as he was doing, with the strong likelihood that he would be overcome and lose his life. If he withdrew from the conflict, at least for a time, there might be another chance to continue later, but he would need to be elsewhere, with a new army, and with some new plans in view. He must have given the matter much thought before deciding that he would have to abandon his army, flee to his friends in Africa Province, and do his best to make that Province the new centre of any opposition to Sulla. This decision he then put into action, and left his army behind, which was later to fall into the hands of Pompeius Magnus.

A fourth and final attempt was made to raise the siege of Praeneste, which shows just how vital it was considered to be. The remaining Cinnan loyalists, Carrinas, Damasippus and Censorinus moved south to join their Italian allies. They must have had considerable confidence that this time, considering the power of their combined forces, they must be able to succeed, free Marius and finally beat Sulla. To their astonishment and dismay, they still failed completely to move Sulla from his commanding position.

They then came up with the new idea that if they appeared to be marching to attack Rome, which was at that time undefended, it should draw Sulla from his position of prominence on the hills, and force him to leave Praeneste to make an attempt to defend the city. They had to move quickly though, as they had heard that Pompeius Magnus, who had already dealt most efficiently with all resistance in Etruria, was then on his way towards Sulla, travelling with substantial numbers of his own men to join forces with him. He was apparently approaching them from the rear of their present position, which would effectively trap them between Pompeius and Sulla if they were still there when he arrived. Also, once young Pompeius arrived, any advantage they might have thought they had, as a combined force, would be irretrievably lost. It was already becoming obvious that Pompeius was just another man like Sulla himself. A younger version and probably still idealistic, but equally capable and determined and just as well loved a leader to his men. Combined in amity, as they now seemed to be, they would be unbreakable. The Cinnan faction then decided that they would have to make a last throw, in trying to entice Sulla from his safe hillside and persuade him into chasing them towards Rome.

On 30 and 31 October, the Samnites, probably congratulating themselves on the clever idea they had come up with, advanced with other Italians along the Via Appia. By the following night they were all encamped outside of Rome.[18] It might be imagined that the sight of a great number of armed men, already battle-stained and ferocious, suddenly arriving outside the city and apparently determined to stay there, would have caused great consternation to the Roman people. They had suffered considerably over a long period of time, first with one leader and then another apparently taking over and forcing his preferences upon them. They had witnessed a bloodbath and then the sight of armed men gathering and preparing for further battles. They must by then have been desperate for stability and peace, though they might have been forgiven for thinking that it was unlikely to arrive in the short term. Even Gaius Marius, once so loved and respected, had betrayed them by performing his murders and leaving his carnage within the city before his death. Now they probably did not know whom to trust, or whether any of the leaders were worthy of any trust, while the sight of more armies drawing up outside the walls of their city must have been terrifying. It encouraged their fear by giving them the idea that they were about to suffer persecutions all over again. Whichever leader became the victor, they might expect the sacking and looting of their city, let alone personal dangers.

On the morning of 1 November the city was in uproar. Eventually a brave and dedicated band of young Roman nobles managed to gather together a small force of cavalry, with which they intended to ride outside the city and attempt to defend it from the hated Samnites and other Italians waiting outside. Unfortunately, daring and resourceful though those young men certainly were, they were actually no equals at all for the enemy camped and waiting outside the gates, who must have dispatched those eager youngsters almost contemptuously. Their courageous attempt was wasted, as were their lives, as they were all defeated.

Fortunately, then, the first of Sulla's cavalry appeared. It was an advance guard led by Gaius Octavius Balbus. He paused only a little while before attacking the enemy outside of Rome's gates. This kept them occupied until, before long, Sulla himself also arrived. He had marched his men at full speed along the Via Praenestina towards Rome, and arrived at around midday, immediately setting up camp near to the Temple of Venus Erucina, outside the walls of Rome, but not far from the Colline Gate.[19]

Once Sulla had set up camp his officers, Cornelius Dolabella and Manlius Torquatus, attempted to prevent him from ordering any immediate action. They said that the troops were overtired due to the forced march from Praeneste, and would need to rest before they could fight. Sulla, however, was aware that the situation could only deteriorate with time. The Samnites, triumphantly outside the gates of the city, were known to be the most determined and ferocious of fighters, people whom Sulla already had occasion to distrust and dislike. He knew that they hated Rome thoroughly and contemptuously and that while ever they were on the loose, armed and dangerous, they would continue to present an appalling threat, which would have to be dealt with before any more innocent Roman people lost their lives. Sulla knew that there could be no compromise with the Samnites.

Due to the time of the year, the days were short and it was already late afternoon with darkness beginning to gather, before any final decision could be taken.[20] Sulla ordered the shortest of rests for his men, with the opportunity to refresh themselves a little with food and drink, but he was aware that the fight could not be left for another day. The matter, for all their sakes, especially that of Rome itself, had to be settled, it simply could not be left to drag on any longer. Sulla was not the sort of man who would wish to allow the other side to disappear into the dark overnight, although at that time they appeared to be eager for a fight and in no mood to leave their positions. Neither, though, would he want to find himself at a disadvantage if they should attempt to attack him while his tired men were trying to find some rest. It was imperative that battle be offered just as soon as his men were able to put up a reasonable fight, and that the matter be finally concluded.

Once they had rested for a short while, he lined them up in order of battle and had the trumpets sounded. Battle was immediately joined. The right wing, led by Crassus, was immediately successful against the enemy it faced, although the left wing was foundering when Sulla rode over to it, to personally bolster the courage of the men by his presence and encouragement.[21] During this effort, he was almost killed when two members of the enemy forces saw and recognized him, then threw their spears at him in a determined attempt to kill. Sulla, concentrating on the job in hand, had not seen the spearmen, but fortunately his life was saved due to the quick thinking and conspicuous bravery of his groom, who was alongside him at the time, and who realized what was happening. This man, acting quickly, lashed out at Sulla's horse, which caused the animal to bolt forward. Sulla may have been surprised, but the possibility of being unseated was nothing to the greater danger he was in and he soon realized that his servant had saved him. The spears aimed at Sulla had then fallen short and harmlessly struck the ground.

However, despite all his efforts being concentrated on keeping the left wing together, the soldiers there were already showing exhaustion and were unable to maintain the fight. Sulla turned, as always, to the gods, calling out in desperation to Apollo, after pulling from his tunic the little statuette of the god, which he was accustomed to carry with him into his battles.[22] He prayed fervently for a few moments, reminding the god who he was and asking for aid, but it seemed that the gods would not assist him, as nothing happened. There appeared to be a general panic starting, which swept the men away towards the Gate, at first bearing Sulla with them. Sulla managed to extricate himself and retire to his camp, but in the melee he had lost contact with the victorious right wing under Crassus. This confusion and lack of knowledge of the other side's movements then caused some of the men, apparently giving in to their uncontrollable panic, to run off towards Praeneste, to tell Afella that they were vanquished and that the siege must be raised.

If this story is not apocryphal, it makes one wonder where they suddenly found the energy to run all the way along the Via Praenestina again, a distance of upwards of ten miles, when they had not the energy to stand and fight where they were. However, it is never possible to guess reasons for anyone's reactions in the muddle and confusion of a battlefield. If they did indeed set off towards Praeneste, they were merely wasting further time. Afella, still at Praeneste, would be hardly likely to raise the siege on the word of a few fleeing deserters, even if they did reach him with their story of supposed defeat.

Other soldiers of Sulla's left wing had been forced towards the city walls, unfortunately running over and killing several Romans, who had come out filled with a doomed and tragic curiosity to watch the battle. Seeing them approaching, and fearing that they might be chased right into the city by the enemy soldiers, that feared Samnite force which was presumably following them, the soldiers whose duty it was to guard the city gate slammed it shut. That prevented them from entering and taking refuge within the city.

Not entirely surprisingly, this had the effect of forcing the fleeing soldiers to turn again when they could run no further, and they then found enough courage to face the enemy. They began again to fight fiercely, and by about 5.30 pm when darkness was falling, the enemy right wing, which had been in close pursuit of them, was finally beaten back.[23] Eventually, the enemy camp was also taken and their leader, Pontius Telesinus, was killed. The knowledge of his death seemed to take the fight out of what remained of his men, and most of the Samnites perished in the area of the camp.

Later in the evening, when the fighting was ended, messengers to Sulla from Crassus arrived. He was asking for supplies for his now very tired but victorious men. It was in this way that Sulla first had the confirmed news that Crassus had done well. He was then informed that the right wing led by Crassus had finally broken the enemy opposing them, who had then fled before night fell. Crassus had followed them, not only having beaten them outside the gate, but also being determined to pursue all the remnants of the army. They had chased them as far as Antemnae, where another desperate struggle took place but where Crassus was again successful. This had lasted until darkness fell.[24] His exhausted but ecstatic troops now needed refreshment and rest, but all was well. Sulla, who had heard no word of Crassus and his men when his own battle ended, must have been enormously relieved, especially when he also heard that Brutus Damasippus himself, along with Carrinas and Censorinus, were among the prisoners.

There would naturally still be a few areas of resistance, some tribes who would never be entirely happy with the situation as it was, but they had been defeated again and again and much open opposition would now be not only wasteful of lives and property but completely futile. With the battle at the Colline Gate, the civil war was effectively over and Sulla was the victor.

Shortly afterwards Sulla sent a messenger who summoned the members of the Senate to a meeting at the Temple of Bellona on the Campus Martius.[25] There were around 6,000 prisoners still alive and he had them sent to the open area not far from Bellona, known as the Villa Publica. When Sulla arrived at the Temple of Bellona it was to find the members of the Senate waiting for him. He began to address the senators, telling them what had been done by him during the recent Mithradatic War and also what needed to be done to put Rome back on her feet. His speech was disturbed by the sounds of people being killed not far away, and when the senators expressed alarm at the sounds and asked the reason for them, Sulla merely replied that a number of criminals were being punished.[26]

This action is commonly used to show the extent of Sulla's cruelty, but there is another explanation. Cruelty does not simply descend upon a man for no apparent reason when he had not been in the habit of cruelty before. On the contrary, Sulla had always made a special effort to show that he was prepared to be reasonable, particularly with regard to the common people, whom he considered were not responsible for the faults of their leaders. In this case, it must be remembered that he had been kept out of his own city by the Cinna/Carbo faction for no good reason, after suffering a great deal at their hands. Not only had he quite rightly refused to stand down in the face of their arrogant insolence, neither would he give in to threats nor disorder from the people he had been obliged to fight in the recent civil war, it was simply not the Roman way. Most of the people killed at the Villa Publica were the remnants of the Samnite forces, and were people he had already found many a good cause to dislike and distrust, as he had shown outside Praeneste, when he had separated the Samnites from the other captives. These people hated Rome's ascendency and eagerly grasped the opportunity to fight against her.

Sulla had already made his opinions perfectly clear, when he had refused to agree to the emancipation of the people who had fought against Rome during the Social War. He had good reason for opposing their grant of citizenship, as it would seem to be far too much like rewarding them for defying Rome openly and taking the lives of Romans, something he simply could not condone. However, he had been overruled, and was eventually obliged to agree to the citizenship being given, without regard to whether or not the recipient was an open enemy of the state he still faithfully served. Then the Samnites and their allies had gone against Rome's interests again, supporting his enemies openly and creating further death and disorder, when all Sulla had wanted to do was return home from his eastern campaign and attempt to regain his properties, destroyed in his absence. Now that they were defeated, or apparently defeated, what was he to do with them?

He certainly could not imprison all those men in any way. Rome had no prisons to support them, no concept of prisoner-of-war camps. Was he supposed to simply let them all go back to their homes, where they could spend the coming months in formulating new plans aimed at Rome's destruction? What kind of fool would he be to leave alive behind him an army of people who were not only openly avowed enemies but also an independent people, with a firm hatred of Rome and all that it stood for? They were armed and dangerous and still totally intransigent, despite their recent defeats. It would merely lead to more wars against them in the future, causing the waste of further lives and resources when he and Rome had so pathetically little left. It would also prevent him from doing what he genuinely saw as his duty, which was to try to set Rome back on her feet by making the necessary reforms. Or was it necessary to end it, once and for all?

It is a dilemma of terrible proportions, but not without parallels in our own times, when despite every effort there are still people who will happily accept concessions with one hand, while preparing to kill with the other. That, unfortunately, was the situation with the Samnites. Sulla dealt with it in the only way possible for it to be dealt with at that time, which was in the Roman way. If those people could not live contentedly under the protection of Rome, enjoying all the benefits that their newly granted citizenship gave them, then no further time could be wasted on them. For Rome's sake they would have to be eliminated, to prevent further trouble from them in the future.

It seems harsh to us in our modern world, but they were harsh times and we must always remember to judge people in accordance with the standards of the world in which they lived, not by our own.

Sulla lived in a world in which Rome held pre-eminence over other nations and it cannot be reiterated too often that this is what a militaristic society is all about. He was certainly not a cruel man by the standards of his own time, as he had frequently proved. But he was a soldier and a good one, war was his business and sometimes any real peace can only be achieved on the other side of a battlefield. Once those people had stood out against the best interests of Rome it was no more than his duty to punish them. Once defeated, but still alive, they presented yet another problem for him to deal with. He dealt with that problem in the only way there was in the time in which he lived, in order to clear his country of future dangers from known enemies and allow Rome to move on.

He could do no other, but that Sulla is too often judged by a different set of rules to any which would have made sense to military men in his own time, is his personal tragedy.

Chapter Fourteen

O nce that matter had been dealt with, as a matter of necessity due to Sulla's presence being required elsewhere, he had to move on. He needed to go back to Praeneste to finalize the situation with regard to young Marius, and whatever few of his supporters were still holed up in the town.

The heads of the executed Samnites had already been sent on ahead, as a warning to those who might still harbour ideas of holding out.[1] Lucretius Afella exhibited them outside the town, which naturally enough caused consternation among the townspeople.

After some discussion, the town leaders then decided to surrender Cornelius Cathegus to Sulla's forces, waiting outside the walls. Young Marius, still in hiding within the town, must have realized even earlier than this that his position was hopeless. But hope is a part of youth and he probably still found it hard to accept that his career, and his life, were to come to an end so soon and in such an ignominious fashion. He made a final attempt to escape his prison, by crawling through the town's drains, in the hope of finding a way through the outer walls. Eventually, however, he found his way blocked, and knew also that every other possible avenue of escape was too well guarded for him to force a way through and there was nothing else that could be attempted. Then he was forced to accept that there was no escape to be had and he took the only way out that was possible for him; he committed suicide.[2]

Afella then collected together the ranking men of the town, some were executed immediately, but others were kept aside for Sulla to deal with when he arrived. This again seems harsh, but was customary right up to our own medieval period. If any besieged town agreed to surrender on reasonable terms once a breach was made, then the inhabitants could usually be released without further harm. However, if surrender was refused, even after the besiegers had shown that they could conquer the town and had offered terms, then the town and its people could expect to be besieged to the end. Once that end came, any inhabitants left alive could also expect to be either killed or enslaved.

The most perfect example of this system in action is that of the Knights of St. John, the Hospitallers who were besieged, by the Turks, on their island of Rhodes in December of 1522.[3] They surrendered their city and were allowed to leave by their enemies, not only unmolested further, but also with honour. However, in 1565, they were again besieged by the Turks, this time on the island of Malta, which they had made their new home. This time they absolutely refused to surrender and the siege was therefore fought to the bitter end, with terrible loss of life. They finally managed to fight off their attackers and were able to achieve a victory at St. Angelo, but there is no doubt at all that if they had fought and lost then the Turks would have killed every last man, as they had already killed without mercy all the valiant defenders.

Therefore, what happened at Praeneste was only what commonly took place in such cases, and did not show any particular cruelty or depravity on the part of the successful besiegers. Even then, when Sulla arrived after the fall of the town and the execution of the Samnites and those Praenestian troops who had held out, he merely lectured the Romans who were found within the town walls. He told them that they deserved to die as the others had done, due to their holding out against Romans like themselves and causing further loss of Roman lives. However, he went on, he would not order their deaths. He would pardon them. The wives and children of the Praenestian troops and the Samnites were likewise unharmed, and allowed to go on their way in freedom.

Sulla, yet again, was showing that he did not intend to punish any innocent parties for the crimes or faults of others. The men who had fought and killed his troops must naturally be punished, but their families were blameless and he would not stoop to reproach or condemn them, or cause them to be harmed or enslaved. That many of the important men of that town were still living there many years later has been shown by recent research, which proves that any punishments meted out on Sulla's orders were not indiscriminate.[4]

However, many of Sulla's followers began to see themselves as harbingers of justice, and considered that their erstwhile opponents were all now public enemies. Many of them began to hunt down those people they then saw as criminals because they had fought against Rome. This behaviour, without benefit of trial, often means that innocent are killed alongside guilty, which is precisely the situation which Sulla had always striven to avoid. Sulla had already been asked to curb the more over enthusiastic members of his forces, or at least to make sure that the ones punished were actually deserving of their punishments. This request was likely to have been put to him by Quintus Catulus.[5] Sulla's reply to that request was to say that it would soon be clear who was to be punished officially for their actions during the civil war, and a day or two later a list was put up in Rome, in the Forum. This was the first of the proscription lists. It gave the names of the first men who were to be considered as public enemies. Again, it has been suggested that the idea of using these lists was not actually Sulla's but that of his centurion Publius Fursidius, who might possibly have had the original idea and passed it on.[6]

The fact remained that many of those men whose names went on the list had been personally instrumental in preventing Sulla and his family, together with the other refugees who had been obliged to flee from Rome to save their lives, from returning to their homes. Many of those homes, along with other family possessions and property had by then been totally destroyed, and there had been attempts to attack Sulla while he was abroad on Rome's business, together with the open murders of friends and supporters of his who had been still in Rome. They had then also continued to oppose him on his return from his successes abroad, causing the loss of further Roman lives in the recent civil war. Those men who had organized and perpetrated those crimes were now to be executed in their turn. It would seem that it was no more than they deserved and their fates were no more than should have been expected in the circumstances.

Sulla agreed that the lists of criminals to be found and executed should be finalized and closed by 1 June 81 BC at the latest, and that no further names could be added after that date. He also took pains to make it perfectly clear what manner of people should be executed, and as was usual with him, he declared that all of the rank and file should be spared. He had no intention of punishing any persons simply for obeying the orders of their superiors. However, those commanders who had fought against him, and therefore against a properly appointed proconsul of Rome, would have to die. That included all men who had helped to ferment the conflict, which had cost Rome so dear. It made no difference whether those men were of consular rank, proconsuls, praetors or whatever they might be, their exalted position would not save them. Only innocence could do that, and they could not be considered innocent.

Anyone of rank who had given their support to the Cinnan uprising could then expect to find their names on a proscription list, and a good many of these people were of the rich Equites. Men like Sextus Alfenius, and Gnaeus Titinius who had given financial help to both Cinna and Carbo. In must have been a particularly heinous offence in Sulla's eyes, that when he had been sent into the east, to do battle with the forces of Mithradates, no money could be found with which to equip his troops. Nor was there any available to support him and his men once they were there. He had been obliged to leave with no more than that very meagre 9,000 librae and had been told to find the rest where he could. Yet these immensely rich Equites would find it possible to open their purse strings for Cinna and his follower Carbo, lavishing money on people who were not fighting for Rome's security, as he had been, but set on just the opposite, their own aggrandizement. The Equites were once a fighting force and in a few cases were still capable of performing that useful function (as with young Pompeius Magnus, who was from a family of the Ordo Equestor and one which held the right to a Public Horse).[7] Though most of them had of latter years given up that more active role to become the bankers and wealthy businessmen of Rome.

These were people who could well afford to support their city through its times of trial, but had for their own reasons chosen not to do so.

The injustice of their choice of action must have been a particular sting to a man of Sulla's extreme patriotism. He had always attempted to do his best for his city, usually with very little to work with, as he was not a personally wealthy man at that time, and had on occasion even been offered hard cash by his own soldiers, who knew his financial limitations while on campaign. In cruel contrast to his efforts and the devotion and support of his working troops, these other 'knights' had merely sat back in comfort at home and nursed their gold, while better men had risked their lives to maintain their security. It must have been very quickly decided that it was now high time for these men to pay the price for the ease and comfort they had enjoyed at the cost of other men's safety. Let alone for the treachery in which they had indulged, by giving their financial support to men of Cinna's stamp, while Sulla had been risking himself and his men in battles abroad for Rome's benefit. These men would now pay, but not only with their own lives, as so many of his brave soldiers had already done, but with their estates as well. The money from those estates, once confiscated, could provide for Rome's good in restoring the empty treasuries, which Carbo had denuded of cash and valuables in order to pursue his own egoistic goals.

Sulla, on his eventual return to the city, must have been not only dismayed but also disgusted at the state to which Rome had been reduced in his absence. He intended that not only those people responsible for the city's debasement, but also those who had sat back and allowed it to happen, would now be obliged to pay the full price for its restoration. Rome, as the centre of the world, needed to look the part, and at that time she was not much more than a ruin, with her largest temples burned down and neglect evident everywhere. It must have been a very sad and daunting task to add to all the others for which he would be obliged to find answers and take appropriate action.

Commissions of enquiry were to be set up, in an effort to find out the people who had for so long resisted his forces, and one of these commissions was to be headed by Marcus Licinius Crassus and another by Gaius Verres.[8] Now was the time for those who had opposed Sulla (and therefore, in his eyes, the properly appointed authorities of Rome itself), in the civil war to find themselves condemned. All those who had supported Cinna would be included, except of course the rank and file soldiers who had been merely doing their duty by obeying orders.

Naturally, such situations can only too easily degenerate into mere revenge killings, which was never what Sulla intended. He was far too busy concentrating on his political enemies, who were still present and still active enough to be able to prevent him from doing the restoration work on the Roman state that he knew was necessary. Various forces had rampaged through Rome in recent years, from Gaius Marius himself, to Cinna, then Carbo, then the puppet leader Gaius Marius Junior. These depredations had cost far more in money than Rome could possibly afford (bearing in mind also the other recent conflicts in which she had been active, the German, the Jugurthan and then the Mithradatic Wars). But worse than that, these continual wars, even the just-ended civil war itself, had cost far too many Roman lives. Rome, as an entity, was bankrupt, of available men as well as of financial resources. Sulla needed to find a way to peace, even if peace still seemed in some ways a distant dream. He could not afford to have, continually at his back, those people who would oppose the very real improvements and alterations he would need to make to the way Rome worked. It might even be fairly said that his mind at that crucial time was on things higher and more essential than overseeing every action of any vengeful or grasping chancer. Any such man might well use the situation in order to improve his own position by accusing some innocent party in order to acquire his goods. That such things did happen is undoubted. Such abuses always will. In such times as theirs, when brutality was always a little closer to the surface of life, they are to be expected, though regrettable. Sulla did not intend that another bloodbath should descend on Rome, as in the savagery of Gaius Marius' return from Africa, he wished only to save Rome from those people who had used and abused it, brought it into disrepute and would do so again, given the opportunity. But he was not personally interested in petty persecutions and was not even present in the city at that time. It would have been impossible for him to oversee every action even if he had been. Unfortunately, therefore, he has been held responsible not only for the executions which he did order, considering the removal of certain people necessary and with the best of intentions for the city's future security, but also those which he did not order.

There were many, unfortunately, who grasped their opportunities while they could and added names to the lists because of their own inclinations, rather than that those victims had done anything for which they should be punished. However, it has to be pointed out, that when Sulla did become aware of such abuses, he moved quickly in his attempts to prevent them. As always, he tried to keep to the moral high ground and was unwilling to allow any of his officers to denigrate what he was attempting to do by any foolish exploits.[9]

Even Crassus himself was to find out that Sulla intended to keep his given word, that only guilty people should suffer punishment. When Sulla was informed that Crassus, during his commission in Bruttium, had ordered the execution of a certain man merely to take possession of his estates, Sulla rapidly repudiated Crassus. He made it perfectly clear that he was not proscribing Rome's enemies as private or personal enemies in any way, and that nobody was free to use the present emergency as an opportunity for them to wreak vengeance of any of their own personal enemies. Nor would they be allowed to make money out of making false accusations against innocent parties. He also made it perfectly clear that he would never employ Crassus again, in any capacity, on any public business, as he considered that he could not be trusted.[10]

Sulla was obliged to reiterate that the task in hand was one of punishing only Rome's public enemies, whose continued presence would not allow Rome to regain her prosperity. In his opinion, that public role did not allow any man, like Crassus or any others of the same persuasion, to take the opportunity to enrich themselves at Rome's expense.

Later, it was discovered that Sulla's own steward had made himself a tidy fortune by buying up at auction cheaply the estates of people whose names had been put on the proscription lists. He and his personal friends had set their sights on acquiring particular estates; therefore the original owners were being falsely accused. When the crimes were discovered, that steward was executed on Sulla's personal order, sharing the fate he had intended for others. Sulla must have been disgusted by such shabby attempts at fraud when he was engaged on work that he considered essential and right. It went completely against the spirit of what he was trying to do in punishing wrongdoers, but it is always very difficult to control others who do not share the same ideal or inspiration, or who continue to believe that the idealist is merely showing weakness rather than mercy. Once such a system swings into operation it becomes self-perpetuating and there are always plenty of people who wish to use it for their own advancement. I cannot believe that any of that was what Sulla had intended. Not all the people who suffered at that time were known to Sulla, nor ever would be, nor could he watch (or would wish to witness) every execution which did take place. It is true that for a time Rome again became a very dangerous place to be, although the executions were still confined to those people of a certain standing. Nobody would wish to proscribe, or would gain anything from proscribing, the people of the more humble elements of society, therefore their very poverty gave them security.

Sulla's concentration was, as always, on those who had supported his enemies against him. Censorinus was executed, along with Gnaeus Pomponius who had supported Caesar Strabo against Sulla. But particularly virulent were his feelings towards those members of the Ordo Equestor who had profited so much from Cinna's rule over Rome. These people were to become known as the 'saccularii' or carpetbaggers, by their Sullan opponents and they were, perhaps rightly, to be shown no mercy.[11] There were also teams of professional accusers to be dealt with. They had in their turn become very wealthy by denouncing Sulla's supporters to Cinna, thereby causing their deaths, and these people also were to pay the price for their treachery and cruelty. Sulla seems to have developed a feeling of absolute hatred towards many members of the Ordo Equestor. That is perhaps not really so surprising, considering their wealth and that paltry 9,000 librae he had been furnished with, which must have continued to be a fermenting resentment. His disgust towards them would be particularly also with regard to their reluctance to assist Rome when their help had been so necessary, which in itself would have been something to which Sulla could never relate. In actual fact, their open selfishness seems to have worked against them generally. There seems to have been no sense of outrage in Rome at the fate of these people and certainly no protest or complaint from the ordinary people at the fall of those who had put their own prosperity well ahead of that of their Republic.[12]

During the proscriptions, one of the worst perpetrators of avarice and cruelty was Catiline. (Lucius Sergius Catalina).[13] This man had served under Pompeius Strabo during the social war, then under Sulla himself during the march on Rome. He was to develop a complete career as a disaffected and ambitious man, one who would fall easily enough into murder and conspiracy. That proclivity started early, when the proscriptions were taking place in Rome under Sulla and Catilina took the opportunity which offered itself to use the disorder to rid himself of his brother-in-law. This was one Quintus Caecilius, who though a member of the Ordo Equestor was personally a decent and peace loving man who was not in any way involved in politics. Catilina added his brother-in-law's name to the proscription lists retrospectively, to give himself the apparent legality of arranging the man's death in order to profit from the confiscation of his estates. He then went on to do the same with the names of several other members of the Ordo Equestor.

Once he had achieved these murders for the improvement of his own finances, he went on to arrange the murder of his sister's husband, Marius Gratidianus, who was a nephew of the late Gaius Marius Senior. This man had apparently been in his turn responsible for the death of the elder Catulus, during the earlier proscriptions instituted by Cinna. Catulus' son now asked for his revenge for the death of his father, but, being unwilling to undertake the act himself, he gave the task to Catilina. He actually took Gratidianus to the tomb of the murdered Catulus and killed him there.[14] No doubt several similar episodes took place, when vengeful people grasped their chance to settle scores dating back to the time of Gaius Marius' return from Africa. Plutarch declares that after killing Gratidianus, Catilina then washed his bloodied hands in the water of a nearby fountain, which was sacred to Apollo.[15] If this action ever took place, then Sulla could not have known of it. With his tender sensibilities towards the gods, and Apollo in particular, he would certainly not have allowed such a blatant sacrilege.

One of the people who would certainly have been on Sulla's list of political opponents to be eliminated was none other than Papius Mutilus. He had been the rebel commander at Nola and therefore the object of Sulla's fixed dislike, along with all of the Samnites who had fought so long and determinedly against

Rome. He had by then actually been cast out of his home by his wife. That lady, probably considering that Sulla's revenge would deal with him sooner or later, and that it would be foolish on her part to be in too close a proximity to him when it did, had decided that any further attachment to the hated Samnite cause was undesirable. Mutilus must also have been aware of the unenviable fate awaiting him if he fell into Sulla's hands, but his subsequent death is not one which can be laid at Sulla's door. Mutilus, realizing that the Samnite cause for which he had so long fought was now totally lost, along with any attachment his family or friends may have once felt for him, took his own life.

Another young man in Rome, who was destined to make his mark after Sulla's death, was Gaius Julius Caesar. He was at that time of no political importance, being a member of a junior branch of the Caesaris clan, one which like Sulla's own could claim noble, indeed patrician, birth but was unfortunately always short of ready money. What made him noticeable during the present proscriptions was that he had been recently married to a daughter of Cinna. During the sixth consulship of Gaius Marius this young man had also been made Flamen Dialis.[16] This would have been sufficient to prevent him from ever achieving a military career, as the extreme prohibitions which formed so large a part of that office did not allow a Flamen to be involved in any military action. However, Sulla's concern was for his marital connections. It was Sulla's new policy in these cases (where the previous leaders had arranged marriages with socially acceptable families), to permit the person concerned to merely divorce the partner to whom they were tied in the newly formed and now suddenly undesirable connection. This was again in line with Sulla's extreme reluctance to kill out of hand any party who might be considered innocent of wrong doing, as in this case. Several other people had already taken advantage of similar offers, including Marcus Pupius Piso who had been an opponent of Sulla's originally, but had sensibly changed his coat in time to join the new regime. He was actually married to no less than Cinna's own widow, but was content (perhaps even eager?) to divorce her in order to safeguard his new alliance with Sulla.

However, young Gaius Julius was to prove less accommodating. When he was offered the opportunity to dissolve his marriage to Cinna's youngest daughter, Cornelia, the suggestion was refused. Consequently, he would have to leave Rome, quite likely with a price on his head. Such a refusal to agree to divorce his Cinnilla would give the appearance of his having some remaining allegiance to that lost cause, which would mean he would probably prove difficult to fit into the new order which Sulla intended to introduce.

However, his reputation, perhaps even his life, was saved by other Sullan sympathizers. They may have agreed that the youth was foolish in his insistence on clinging to the now obsolete marriage, but decided to try to persuade Sulla of his lack of malice. These included Mamercus Aemilius Lepidus and Gaius Aurelius Cotta, who was one of his mother's brothers and a pontifex, together with Lucius Cotta, who was an auger.[17] These men, with other important people including the Chief Vestal, Fonteia, went to plead with Sulla personally, in order to save the young man. Sulla, perhaps amused by the deputation, decided to pardon him, despite the apparent insolence shown in his refusal to cooperate. Sulla was later to allow Gaius Julius to lay down his Flaminiate, which was to eventually allow him to pave the way for his future spectacular military career.

Frightening as this time must have been for anyone with any reason to fear an avaricious relative or the genuine retribution of Sulla himself, it must be reiterated that it did not actually affect people of humble status. Sulla, in accordance with his often repeated intention to prevent any ordinary people from suffering unnecessarily during Rome's times of turmoil, kept his eyes away from them. He certainly had no reason to persecute humble people, and did not allow anyone else to do so. All those who did suffer during those times were people of substance, and most of those were people who had given reason for mistrust. The whole nasty business did not last long, and Sulla, once again true to his given word, stopped the official proscriptions completely by 1 June 81 BC.

Many histories have dwelled on this time almost with relish and have then gone on to give fanciful, if not absolutely wild, estimates of how many people are likely to have died during that period. Some have claimed that as many as 10,000 or even 12,000 people were destroyed, either officially or by someone who had reason to cast acquisitive eyes on their property. Fortunately, modern scholars now entirely disagree with these estimates and consider that it is a mistake to be influenced by such sweeping statements.

It is now generally considered that the true figures of the people affected throughout the whole time of the proscriptions in Rome were somewhere between one and two thousand, with the general consensus of opinion leaning strongly towards the lower figure.[18] This is a vastly different conclusion to reach than the earlier ones, and paints a rather more reasonable picture of what was happening at that time than the previous, often deliberate and certainly suspiciously inflammatory, estimates.

It also presents a very different picture of Sulla himself than the one which has until lately been widely accepted. It is far more on a par with the other recent proscriptions in Rome, for example those of Gaius Marius himself. His memory tends not to be so permanently stained by his actions (although it is as well to remember his entry into and destruction of Ostia, even as it prepared to welcome him), however erratic they may have been, and despite the paranoid and homicidal excesses of his final days.

It certainly goes a long way towards rehabilitating Sulla's reputation, which has for far too long been exaggerated in its supposed evil, debauchery and mindless cruelty. This contention is not, however, intended in any way to dismiss the fact that people did become victims in Rome at that time. On the other hand, there were certainly not the indiscriminate bloodbaths perpetrated on his orders that we have previously been led to believe. On the contrary, Sulla always intended only to rid the city of those people who had done real harm, firstly to the Republic, then to his own family, friends and political supporters. It was the only sensible way, at that time, to deal with such people. It would be impossible to make the changes he needed to make with enemies constantly plotting and waiting for another opportunity to attack, and Rome itself certainly could not afford to be involved in any further wars. But at the same time he had, in accordance with his usual practice, done everything he could to ensure that innocent parties should not be involved.

When other people, owning rather less tender consciences than his own about indiscriminate killing, took the law into their own hands, he made every effort to punish such actions, wherever he found them. Furthermore, he did not intend that his city, the Rome for which he had always worked so hard, should permanently become a centre for insurrection and general disturbance. He intended, always, to clear the decks only in order that he could then begin the work he considered totally essential. That of regenerating the city and restoring it to a firm prosperity, which could not be found during times of civil unrest, and which had been damaged both physically and spiritually during too many years of debilitating war.

Lastly, when he considered that the criminals who had endangered Rome had been punished, he stopped the proscriptions as he had already promised he would, keeping his word to his people as he had so often done before.

Scipio was allowed to stay unmolested in Massilia, where he had gone into voluntary exile, without suffering further persecution. However, one other man was destined to die, though not on Sulla's orders. This was Gaius Norbanus himself, who was still in Rhodes. The Rhodians, naturally hearing of the punishment of traitors which was taking place in Rome, debated whether or not to hand him over to the authorities for execution. Their decision, if it was ever finalized either way, was to prove unnecessary. Norbanus was another man who must have realized that he had fought for the wrong side and that there was by then little future for him. He committed suicide in the market place in Rhodes.

Sulla then needed to turn his attention towards the future, but there was still one person he could not forgive, one man whose actions he could never forget. That man was already out of the reach of any retribution on Sulla's part, but the memory still rankled. That man was Gaius Marius himself. The great old soldier who had once been Sulla's friend and mentor and who had allowed his jealousy of a rising young man to destroy that intimacy they had once known. Sulla did not seem to be able to bear the idea that Gaius Marius' trophies should still be displayed in Rome (perhaps he still had painful memories of Marius' almost childish resentment of his own). There must have been other painful memories too, such as Marius' persecution of Sulla's family on his return from Africa. In the good old days of their first association it would have seemed incredible that the friendship could be so completely destroyed.

Sulla then ordered that Marius' trophies should be torn down.[20] Further even than that, he gave instructions that Marius' ashes should be scattered, to prevent any possibility of a central point from where Marius' memory could be idolized. It is still very doubtful whether such actions eased Sulla's pain at his rejection by Marius, and the remembrance of a great friend who had become an implacable enemy.

Sulla still had other friends, who had proved themselves more reliable. Not only the time-servers and turncoats who can always find it in themselves to smile on whoever manages to hold on to power. Sulla, in all his ups and downs, had never forgotten his old friends. Now came the time when he would at last be able to give some reward to those who had stood by him when he had nothing and was nothing. There were the confiscated estates to be auctioned off, and the profits from such estates had to be given to the right quarter. The temples were, of course, his first concern. Throughout everything, Sulla was a man who never lost sight of the gods.[21] They had supported him in battle, brought him success after tribulation, and placed him in a position where he could begin to pay back some of that which had been stolen from them by others. That this should come from the auctioned estates of those who thought nothing of the gods would have been only proper in his eyes. Rome was desperate and it was now in Sulla's gift to put right some of the depredations of years of wars.

The lands, which had recently been confiscated from conquered Italian cities, were given to his veterans, to be divided between them, which was normal procedure. Some, of course, went to the friends and supporters who had been faithful to him. That, too, was only to be expected. People were not surprised at the idea of any man finally being able to make awards to those who had proved themselves reliable. However, their feelings underwent something of a change when they realized what sort of people Sulla still counted as real friends, and reserved a good deal of his affection for.

Not just people of status, though he had friends in those quarters too, but people who were counted as less than nothing by the majority of Romans. They were astonished at the idea that Sulla, now so important, should still be concerned about the feelings of people from the theatres, and other low caste professions.[22] That he should now hand out property and wealth, apparently on impulse, to show his appreciation of these people who had always loved him, has often been debited against his good name, which seems very unjust. Surely it is far more to his credit that he did not easily forget, or casually cast off, those very people who had been his only friends in the days of his poverty? It can only be social prejudices of the worst sort that prevent anyone from understanding how much pleasure he must have felt in finally being able to give back something to those lowly people, for whom he had always had understanding and compassion. These were the very people who had befriended him when members of his own class would not, a rare gift for which he had been grateful and felt gratitude still.

For someone who has never had anything to spare, there is an especial delight in being able to give largesse to those who expect nothing. There must already have been far too many of the other sort gathering, men whose smiles were suspect and whose friendship was unreliable. Sulla's more 'disreputable' friends were his real friends, they had proved their loyalty to him and he was fully able to appreciate it.

However, most of the confiscated property was simply auctioned and this, again, is given as an example of Sulla somehow behaving wrongly. It is correct to say that much of it went cheaply, and that many people were able to benefit from the low prices, buying estates or properties which would otherwise have been beyond their reach. This is far from being a sign of Sulla's corruption, it is merely market forces working in the normal way. When there is suddenly a glut in the market, as there was when so many estates were sold off in a short time, it is understandable that the finest of those should be sold first and that they should still fetch the highest prices. However, when the very best have gone and the novelty of seeing such estates on the open market begins to wear off, while there are still likely to be many very good estates available, these can be snapped up at a discount. Because of the number still on the open market, the price naturally drops. Therefore, many people are able to take advantage of the situation and acquire property relatively cheaply. To ignore normal market forces at work and instead use even that phenomenon as a stick to beat Sulla with is patently ridiculous. The great majority of the money thus raised went back to the temples, as he had always intended, to refill Rome's treasuries and help to restore Rome's security.

However, when all this was done, Sulla is then supposed to have become, suddenly and overnight, and without any apparent reason, a veritable monster of cruelty. This, it has been claimed, was due to the fact that he was always a vicious and vindictive man, who had simply been able to successfully hide his true nature in all those years when he had appeared to be reasonable and just. Now that he was master in Rome, he could afford to release all his pent-up tendencies towards evil and allow himself to do as he wished. It seems to be another ridiculous accusation made against him, when every scrap of evidence is to the contrary. In fact, he had always proved exactly the opposite. He had actually worked against his own interests on many occasions, when he had made every effort to display his tolerance and a natural desire for justice. He had always shown himself to be perfectly reconcilable and reasonable. He had strained every nerve to act in accordance with accepted procedure. Even when kept out of Rome by the government of the time, he had written to them in the most reasonable and just terms, merely explaining his complaints and asking for no more than his rights. At no time had he ever made an aggressive move or taken an inflammatory or vindictive stance against those who had wronged him so blatantly. He had merely given his opinion of the situation clearly and waited for others to come over to his way of thinking.

That known criminals were eventually executed, and retribution asked from those who had done so much damage, was no more than could be expected when Rome had been on a war footing for so long a time. Civil unrest must be curbed and people who would not fit in with society as it then was could not be understood. Sulla had never harmed those who were not at fault, and had never attempted to. He was, on the contrary, one of the most long-suffering of men, compared to others, always aware that his dignitas was at stake, and eager to show that he knew how a man of his standing should behave.

Gaius Marius, once Sulla's good friend, had been a general of no mean order, and a competent and resourceful leader of men in the field. He had that desirable and essential knack of making his troops respect and revere him, but when he left the field of battle he realized (and showed to others) that he was no politician.[23] Sulla, on the other hand, could also behave competently and even brilliantly on the battlefield, and was a man who was always indefatigable, persevering towards his goal and not expecting ability and inspiration to fall on him out of the sky. Yet when he left the battlefield he was equally capable of moving easily into his other persona, that of an able politician. In this field he was able to show his extremely strong sense of duty and devotion to Rome. In this sphere also he intended to work to right the wrongs Rome had suffered, and no doubt even looked forward to making the necessary changes, in an effort to prevent similar disruption in the future.

To suggest that throughout all this time, hiding behind this façade of a decent and reasonable, hard working and dutiful man, was another face, that of a predator and a monster, ready to lash out and destroy without compunction, simply does not make sense. That he was capable of losing his temper like any other man must be undeniable, for he was just a man, although he had shown time and time again that he was capable of being patient and sensible. He had suffered a great deal in Rome's interests, losing his own property, spending year after year fighting in Rome's name, risking his life time after time for little or no reward. If he had had any tendency towards cruelty there would have been nothing to stop him from exercising it in all those years, when other generals permitted themselves any excesses. (Even Pompeius Strabo had another nickname by which he was commonly known, that of Carnifex or 'butcher'.) Sulla at no time gave way to such behaviour nor did he show that he had such inclinations. He did not like to allow such behaviour to be exhibited by others, although he could be very firm and exact extreme penalties for crimes when he considered it necessary. He did believe that he was always under the eyes of the gods, and that if his attitude did not please those gods, they would take away his ability to gain and keep success. He would never have risked losing that goodwill he considered so necessary.

Neither a leopard (nor a man) changes its spots, and there is no reason for Sulla to have lived a life of pretence for all of those years. He had always behaved far better than many other Roman generals did, in fact often against his own interests in his efforts to show concern for those he wished to protect from suffering. To blame him for the proscriptions getting out of hand, due to the greed and avarice of self-seekers, is perhaps only to be expected. He had instituted them initially and therefore ultimately must take some responsibility for the situation which later ensued, whether or not the outcome had been his original intention. But that he personally wanted or enjoyed murders, thefts, attacks or cruelties is quite against his character, which he had already had ample opportunity to display. Mob rule is always a danger and often uncontrollable, at least temporarily. Sulla did make every effort to prevent it getting out of hand, and made a point of exacting punishment from those people who took the law into their own hands and dragged his name into the mud with their own.

All this from a man who had never been able to rest or enjoy a normal family life. A man who was getting older and no doubt feeling the strain of it all and furthermore a man who was suffering from a painful and debilitating illness. It seems almost incredible that he should remain as tolerant and reasonable as he still was, in the circumstances. Now that he had achieved the authority he needed, he had more important things to do than to waste his time indulging in a killing spree, which would only lose him the support that he needed in order to do his work.

Sulla was certainly not a wicked man, nor was he generally an unusually vengeful one. By the standards of his time he was amazingly even-tempered and that he was respected and even loved is shown again and again in the manner in which other people responded to him. The evil reputation which follows him around like a bad smell is apparently something which came to him later on, after his death, rather than something with which he lived in his own time. He had opponents, which was only to be expected. No man lives in a bubble, nor can he expect every person he has contact with to admire him or agree with him, but the people who knew him best were fond of him and did not fear him. Neither were there any attempts made to assassinate him, during any part of his political life, which might have been expected if he was really so greatly hated by the people as later writers have often claimed.

Certainly Caesar, in his own time, and despite his achievements and his many admirers, would not have dared to live as Sulla did, in the centre of things and without any excessive protection from bodyguards.[24] Nor was Caesar able to eventually retire from public life, without danger of attack from enemies, as Sulla was later to do when he considered that he had done all that he reasonably could for Rome, in the time left available to him.

Sulla had always been at pains to show humanity at a time when humanity towards others was not only a commodity in short supply, but one which in some quarters was mistaken for weakness. Yet he was never weak. If during the proscriptions the situation in Rome got out of hand, fuelled largely by the greed of others, then it would not have been what he wanted or what he saw as being the best way for Rome to move forward.

This time in his life, through which he tends to be judged, was a very short time indeed compared to all the long years he had spent working without complaint and without reward, and should not forever be held against him. It cannot be used as evidence that he was in reality some sort of an evil and dangerous madman, who had for so long lived a lie in order to explode into an orgy of cruelty during his dictatorship. There was no reason for it and such an accusation makes no sense. He was not being pushed aside, as Gaius Marius had been, nor had he suffered a mental illness, as Gaius Marius appears to have done. He was, in fact, about to bring into being some of Rome's most sensible and reasonable laws, which were not opposed by the people.

This period of time has given many the opportunity to blame him for everything that was wrong with Rome, forgetting that abuses always take place in wartime and that a civil war is the unkindest war of all. By its very nature it is indicative of the treachery of one's own people and feelings run correspondingly high. By the end of it Sulla was ill, ageing, exhausted by work, tired to the bone, stressed to the limit. It is not that it is so surprising that something like the proscriptions actually took place; what should be more alarming is the knowledge that with many other commanders of the period it would have probably happened sooner, been more frequently used, and been even more damaging. It is purely because Sulla had always been more humane, more reasonable and more decorous in every way than others in a similar situation, that this incident shows up so clearly. With other generals it would very likely have been merely a passing incident, hardly worth a mention, in a time when murdering, looting, raping and enslaving were commonplace.

It is often forgotten, or even deliberately brushed aside, that Sulla did his level best to minimize abuses during the proscriptions. If the idea of the lists had indeed been that of his centurion, Sulla must have had time to reflect that what might at first have seemed a good idea had turned out to be a grave mistake. He then called a halt to the whole matter, as he had originally agreed to do, allowing several guilty people to escape unscathed.

Unfortunately, whereas for another military leader it might well have been just another passing event in a life filled with brutality, for Sulla it has been allowed, indeed one might say deliberately used, to define him. To wipe out all the evidence of his true character and courageous achievements in battle, along with all the charm and decency that he was commonly known to have shown in everyday life, and to cast opprobrium on his reputation.

Sulla is one of the few people of his time whose motives were as clear as glass. His personal motto was 'no better friend, no worse enemy' and he proved it repeatedly.[25] He fought tirelessly against his rightful enemies, but he would always support and help his friends, and he was recognized for his kindness and generosity among those who were his closest associates. It is simply not sufficient to admit that a man is kind, decent, honest, hard working and well loved, but then add, 'and he was also cruel and evil!' The characteristics for which he was famous in his own lifetime do not sit happily with the idea of a bloodthirsty tyrant.

It would greatly astonish those people who knew him best to see the image which is usually shown of him and they would not be able to reconcile the Sulla we are presented with as being the same man as the one they knew, loved and respected. That is the real result of what the proscriptions did for him, after his death, when his actions were open to misinterpretation by times which could not understand or appreciate his motives. It is a great pity for his sake, due to the undeserved reputation for evil, which has since been attached to his name.

However, at the time, Sulla had to concentrate on the work in hand. For the first few weeks after his return to the area around Rome he was still proconsul. That position is what had given him the power to do what had been necessary to free Rome from her enemies. It is well worthwhile to note that the Senate had already ratified that position in his name, confirming again that he was a properly constituted Magistrate.[26] The Senate also eagerly confirmed that the decree, which during Cinna's term of office had made him a public enemy, or outlaw, was declared null and void. Therefore, all his acts as proconsul were official, including those laws he had made back in 88 BC as consul, which had later been cancelled by Cinna. The Senate also recognized his title of 'Epiphradatos', with Sulla making clear that from then onwards he wished also to be known by the cognomen of 'Felix'.[27]

The Senate, now falling over themselves to be amenable, also declared that an equestrian statue of Sulla should be erected in Rome in the lower Forum. This, also, would bear the inscription of 'Lucius Cornelius Sulla Felix'. This may well have been the statue originally sent to Sulla by his old friend King Bocchus of

Mauritania, the father-in-law of King Jugurtha, to which Gaius Marius in his jealousy had once objected.[28]

However, Sulla's position as a proconsul could not continue indefinitely. The position still prevented him from entering the city itself, as crossing the pomerium with proconsular imperium was illegal.[29] He would not be able to work to put right Rome's ills from outside the walls. He had returned to Rome not only to punish enemies but also to reform the state that had allowed abuses to happen. He naturally needed to be in office, but not in any position which prevented his access to the city. Therefore, with that concern for the niceties which characterized him, as it did the other magistrates who were anxious about the *mos maiorum*, it was finally decided that it could not be considered correct to hold any consular election while Carbo was still free.[30] Despite the obvious irregularities of how he arrived at the position, he was still strictly speaking able to call himself a consul.

That difficulty did not, in fact, hold matters up for long. Pompeius Magnus had been sent to Sicily by Sulla in order to subdue the island and secure the last grain harvest for Rome. While he was there, he came across no less than Carbo himself, who had recently made his way from Africa Province into Sicily. Whether or not he intended to make an attempt to reach the mainland, or eventually even Rome, cannot be known. Pompeius Magnus gave the fugitive no opportunity to move any further, and Carbo was to be eventually killed by Magnus at Lilybeaum. That meant that, by anyone's reckoning, both the consuls were dead. The Princeps Senatus, Lucius Valerius Flaccus, was therefore appointed as an Interrex to fill the breach until a proper election could be held.

However, Sulla was aware that, in order to do all that was needed to get Rome back on her feet, more time would be required than the usual one year granted to any consul. After some consideration, and doubtless talks with the Interrex, it was suggested that the old title of Dictator should be revived in this instance, although it had last been used over a century previously. Unfortunately, this would present further problems regarding timescale, as the old title of Dictator had been commonly held for only a six month period during a national emergency.[31] During that time the Dictator would also have to appoint a second-in-command, known as the Master of Horse.

The main problem Sulla was faced with was that in this case the Dictator, or whatever title they arrived at, would have to be in power for a far longer period than the obligatory six months for a Dictator, or one year for a consul. Nor could he afford to have to stand for election again at the end of each designated period, with the waste of time involved, together with the concomitant difficulty of needing to justify his actions and position on each occasion.

What was really needed was for Sulla to assume some official position, which would allow him to do the necessary work without outside interference, for whatever time was required for its completion. Therefore, it was finally agreed that Valerius Flaccus, acting as temporary consul, should pass the Lex Valeria, which would allow Sulla to then be awarded the Dictatorship on those unusual terms.

Valerius Flaccus named Sulla '*dictator legibus faciendis et republicae constitudinae*' i.e. 'for the making of the laws and settling of the constitution'.[32] He was awarded full powers, which meant that he could bring in laws and have them confirmed by the people, but it would not actually be strictly necessary for him to do so, as any decree he made could become law automatically. He could, in fact, now alter the laws in any way he thought fit, and he also held 'Lectio Senatus' which was the power to appoint new senators on his own authority, when he chose to do so. He had, in reality, received the power over life and death, to confiscate property, found cities, found new colonies, or bestow kingdoms on client princes. The existing Provinces, the treasuries and all the law courts now came under his direct control and he was furthermore empowered to decide whether or not Rome should enter into any foreign war. This is the main reason why the dictatorship was so little used, and usually for only a very limited time, as it conferred supreme power on the man so appointed. Sulla therefore assumed both judicial and military power over Rome.[33] Because of Rome's recent difficulties and the fact that she was still in a state of national emergency it was also made clear that Sulla would need to retain the powers he had been given for as long as he needed them. That is, without any definite limit of time.

It must have come as a shock to many people to hear that he had been given such all-embracing power for as long as he wished, but it also clearly showed the great trust that Lucius Valerius Flaccus reposed in him. However, Flaccus had good reason to believe that he would be able to work with Sulla.

When the Cinnans had first antagonized, then endangered and forced the exile of other leading men from Rome, they had behaved very foolishly. Most political moderates are not overly concerned which faction is actually in power, so long as good order is maintained. Many of those men exiled under the Cinnans did not actively espouse either cause, preferring to remain sitters-on-the-fence, waiting in the city to see what would happen. A few of them actually opposed Sulla, but they were treated in the same dismissive way and their expulsion forced them to re-evaluate their position. They must have gone into exile, along with Sulla's family, with considerable trepidation, afraid of the reception they would receive when they arrived.

However, Sulla, to their surprise and relief, had greeted them very warmly. He had welcomed them with friendly assurances, guaranteed their personal safety and promised that he would do what he could to deal with their grievances. His kind consideration must have been overwhelming, after the disorder they had left behind. Sulla, for his part, could see that instead of cultivating these people, moderates and undecided in their allegiances as they probably were, the Cinnans had merely played into his hands. These exiles, now firmly on his side, could form the backbone of his power on his return.

Sulla was astute enough to realize that while a general-cum-politician can often be carried into power on a wave of euphoria when battles have recently been won, opinions can quickly suffer a change when reforms need to be put into place. For the continuation of support when the novelty of his rise wore off, he would need Flaccus, who was already renowned as a sensible, tolerant and eminently respectable man.

Flaccus, for his part, must have been hugely relieved to know that the new leader, powerful and charismatic as he was, and with a victorious and devoted army behind him, was also a reasonable man, prepared to put in the work required. He did not need to prove himself by acts of senseless aggression or bouts of vainglory. He must have seemed to Flaccus, and to the other members of the senate who stood with him, to be a far better bet for the city's future security than either Cinna or Carbo or any of their supporters.

There would be, of course, a certain amount of derision to be faced from the detractors who were still alive and well in Rome. (Despite the proscriptions, there were still many people who held their own opinions, and would feel free to express them.) Sulla took pains to emphasize that when the work was done to his satisfaction, he would step down from the position with which he had been entrusted. Even though the total amount of work must have seemed to loom over him, and he could not possibly give any firm date at that stage, he fully intended to keep his word, though there would have been people in Rome who might be forgiven for doubting it.

There had been so many promises given before, by other leaders, most of which had amounted to nothing at all, for his opponents to believe him at that stage. They would have to learn by experience that Sulla was very different and that he did not give his word lightly, nor did he break it, once given.

His first task would be to appoint the important Master of Horse to assist and support him, and for this post he very naturally chose Valerius Flaccus himself. Flaccus was actually a most competent and distinguished man and ideally suited for the position Sulla wished him to occupy. His decency and known moderation would help to shore up Sulla's authority. His presence in the new order would confirm that he approved of Sulla's elevation to the first position, and that he agreed with his aims.

It is particularly interesting to note at this point that Sulla was not actually nominated as Dictator by a consul, although Flaccus was Interrex at that time, he was technically chosen by a vote of the people, under the presidency of the Interrex.[34] Sulla apparently did not wish to be appointed in the usual way, as it would require him to resign the office after the usual six month period. The acceptance of that term of office would be implicit of his agreement to this, if he took the dictatorship under the old form. He certainly could not afford to have people looking over his shoulder the whole time he was in office, demanding accounts of his every action and limiting his freedom of movement. He knew that Rome's obvious problems could be dealt with by one man, if that man were strong enough and dedicated enough to deal with the lengthy process involved, and provided he had the authority to do so.[35]

The republic was, in fact, safe in Sulla's hands and he was at heart firmly a republican in sympathy. Sulla needed the power, not as a tyrant who would wish to make himself into a king in all but name, the very idea of which would be anathema to him, but only to allow him to be the reformer and restorer that was needed. He was not the sort of man who would allow such power to change his basic character or intentions, despite the usual belief that absolute power corrupts absolutely. That really depends on the man himself and whether he allows himself to believe in his own divine right to rule. Sulla did not. He had been in positions of power before without feeling the need to shore up his authority by abusing them. He was not the sort of man who had anything to prove regarding his ability to rule fairly.

He believed in his own strength and in his determination to make changes, knowing that Rome needed a firm hand at the helm and a leader who would put her interests first for as look as it took to restore her to security and prosperity. He knew he was that man. He also knew that he would not wish to live that life for however many years were still left to him. He was already 57 years old, and he was growing tired, he would not wish to spend the remainder of his life in harness. Sulla, during his dictatorship which lasted just as long as he thought it was needed, was to show that he could do the necessary work without having his head turned by his elevation to supreme power.

Everything he was to do while in his position of Dictator was fully sanctioned by Roman law and custom, in continuance of the way in which he had conducted his campaigns in the past. He had not seized power for his own aggrandizement or to acquire riches to which he was not entitled, although as leader of the Roman state he naturally earned a certain amount of wealth, which went with the position. Also he would perfectly fairly require the restoration of the estates which had been taken from his family during their exile.

However, as a successful soldier he was aware of the dangers of conflict and had seen the damage it did, not only on the battlefield itself, but at home too, where Rome was still reeling and desperate for stability. His intention was to use basic common sense to return Rome to a state of normalcy, as well as solvency.

Therefore, with the official confirmation of his new position, Lucius Cornelius Sulla became not only the master of Rome itself, but also for as long as he required it, the Master of the whole Roman world.

Chapter Fifteen

For just a short time, Sulla's intended constitutional reforms could wait; there could be a breathing space. In this time, Sulla was to celebrate his long-deferred Triumph, in relation to his successes in the east against Mithradates, which had been put aside when he initially returned to Rome, due to the civil war. It may actually have seemed a long way away, considering all that had happened since. Had he been able to return home in the normal way after the eastern campaign was concluded, the Triumph would have been dealt with as a matter of course, but the intervening civil war had turned all attention away from mere celebrations. Now, however, it would be a wise move to remind the populace of Sulla's successes in the field, together with the excitement and pleasure of not only the Triumphal procession, but the accompanying feasting, which could be shared by all the people in Rome.

A Triumph was not only considered to be a privilege and reward for the triumphant general, it showed to all the people in the city just what had been achieved abroad. It greatly boosted public confidence and restored general morale. In this case, it might also be expected to paper over the cracks a little, covering the bitterness of the recent civil war and hopefully dousing any lingering resentment due to the hardships suffered. Sulla's Triumph could therefore be expected to serve a dual purpose, not only reminding them that he was a successful military man, willing and able to win wars on Rome's behalf, but also including them personally with him. Confirming that the new future, which he intended to make for Rome, and the new peace and security that he was capable of providing, was for the benefit of them all. This brief time of celebrations should bring all the people together, and help to wipe out the miseries of the recent past, encouraging the Romans to look to Sulla, and to look ahead.

He started, of course, with the procession itself. This normally took the form of a march around the city, with the Triumphator in a ceremonial chariot, his face painted with minim to represent Jupiter's terracotta statue (sadly now defunct, due to the recent fires).[1] Following the Triumphator would be a selection of his army, joining with him in the praise for work successfully completed, and followed in turn by evidence of the victory. This could take the form of goods and valuables from the conquered country, along with representations of the key moments of the battles won, along with slaves, if any. In this case there would not, of course, be a captured king to display, as the campaign had ended with a treaty, but this would not prevent the procession including statues of the defeated king, even if he could not march behind Sulla's chariot in person.

For the majority of the people, however, it was the feast which would draw most of their interest. This could take the form of a purely private affair, for the senators and other important persons, or better still, it could include all of the people too. Sulla did not make the mistake of keeping this feast private. He ordered that tables should be set up at various sites around the city, and that they should be kept filled with food and drink, so that the ordinary people could join in the celebration. This must have appeared to be a huge and unnecessary extravagance, given the perilous state of Rome's finances, and the fact that so much had to be done to repair and restore the city itself. But Sulla was never a fool, nor did his life up to then give him any belief that money was something to be wasted. On the contrary, he was fully aware that the people of Rome needed to be able to feel themselves included, not only for these days of celebration and feasting, but also in the work about to be started.

He was only too aware of the devastation of his beloved city. Temples burned to ashes, valuables destroyed or melted down for coin, which would never be replaced. Treasures carried off that also could never be replaced. Rome was effectively a ruin, due to no fault on his part. But he would be expected to put in train the necessary works to restore it all, and for that he would require the approval and support of the Roman people. The gesture of sharing with them in his triumph was necessary, not only for his own prestige, but also to show that he included everyone else in his vision of how Rome should be, and remind them that they too could look to a new beginning. He may have been forced by circumstances into taking up an unprecedented position, but now that the civil war was over it was time to show the people that here was someone who was prepared to put in the work to draw the factions together.

He could also draw together the shattered city and make it and the republic whole again. Sulla was also at around this time to institute another public occasion even more popular with the masses than merely feasting, and in his case far more lasting. The games!

He gave instructions that the Ludi Victoriae Sullae would be an annual event, and this was in fact to be a popular spectacle for many years, which would develop into one of the most important and greatest of the sets of games.[2] The Victoriae Sullae, started in 81 BC initially ran from 26 October, but they eventually ran for a full seven days, from 26 October until 1 November. This meant that they finished only three days before the even greater games, the Ludi Plebei, started which in their turn ran from 4 November to 17 November.[3]

For the first of these games Sulla received a gift from his old friend King Bocchus of Mauretania. That king, still eager to be considered an intimate of

Sulla's, sent him 100 lions for his initial games. These celebrations, in which all the people could take an interest and feel included, were to become a regular and eagerly anticipated part of the Roman calendar for many years after Sulla's death.

Once these public occasions were completed, Sulla turned his attention briefly to the young man on whose behalf he had been approached a little while before. Gaius Julius Caesar. Sulla had kept the promise he had made to Aurelia, Caesar's mother, in not allowing any prosecution of him despite his obstinate refusal to divorce Cinna's youngest daughter Cornelia, even though the unfortunate match brought back many unpleasant memories of the civil war just gone. When that young man finally returned to Rome, Sulla allowed him to lay down the Flaminiate which had threatened to blight his life and all his future prospects.[4]

However, before allowing the youth to take up the beginnings of his military career, Sulla is reported to have made a very prescient remark. Acceding to the pleadings of the mother, perhaps against his own better judgement, Sulla gave a warning. 'In him I see many Mariuses!'[5] Sulla then sent Gaius Julius to Pergamum, to join the staff of Thermus (Sulla's proquaestor), who was to put down a revolt in Mitylene. Caesar's career in the military therefore started as a junior tribune during Sulla's Dictatorship.

Sulla, watching the youth's bearing and arrogance and his stubborn refusal to give way, may well have reflected that when he grew to full maturity he could easily become a threat to the security and stability of the republic. He had the same pride of birth which Sulla shared, but he did not believe in the sanctity of the republic itself, which was so close to Sulla's own heart. Fortunately for Sulla, all that would be some years in the future, and he would not be there to see it or have to deal with the results of it.

However, also at this time, which should have been exclusively one of satisfying work and hope for the future, Sulla had to face personal tragedy. Plutarch reports that later, when Sulla's own death was approaching, he had one of his prophetic dreams in which he saw his deceased wife and also his elder son, who had died a little time before her.[6]

This elder son would have been the child of Sulla's first wife, Julia, and brother of Cornelia Sulla, who was by that time a young woman. This young man, the other Lucius Cornelius Sulla, is lost to us in detail, and we do not even know the date of his death, his age, or why he died. If Plutarch is correct in placing his death around this time, then he would have been either approaching marriageable age, or in his teen years.[7] It is not fair to underestimate what this death must have done to Sulla. Every man, however humble, wants a son to follow after him, particularly in a patriarchal society such as Rome. That this elder boy, the carrier of Sulla's own name, should be lost on the threshold of hopeful manhood, must have been a truly devastating blow. It may also explain why Sulla, in naming his twins by Caecilia Metella, did not use the name Lucius Cornelius for the boy she produced, as would be usual if that were his only son then living. After a Roman funeral there would be a period of family purification, which lasted for nine days, during which time the family would be excused all public functions. After this time there was generally a public feast held in memory of the deceased, which must have been a painful occasion.

Not only was he to suffer this appalling loss, but also another. Sulla's then wife, Caecilia Metella, had become ill and it was soon obvious that she was dying. It has been suggested that she died of venereal disease (given to her by Sulla himself of course), but there is no evidence for this. Venereal disease does not kill quickly, passing as it does through several different phases over a period of years, with times when it appears to be quiescent. Sulla certainly did not die of it; therefore there is absolutely no reason to suspect that he had passed such a disease onto his wife, who then expired very quickly.

It is far more likely that she died of cancer, which can sometimes move swiftly, and was a killer then as much as now, though a less acknowledged one.[8] Plutarch records that she became 'unclean' which would fit with the problems created by a cancerous growth in all its horrors. The poor woman cannot have been very old, was fairly recently a mother and must have realized that her life was about to be cut short. We know that Sulla had chosen this lady personally and valued her as a wife, having included her name with his own on the memorials erected in Greece to celebrate his victories there.[9]

Sulla had by this time become an auger (occupying the place vacated by Scipio after he became hostis). At the news of Metella's serious illness, his fellow augers quickly pointed out to him that he could not continue to associate with the woman due to her unclean state. It was made clear that Sulla should break off all contact with her and that he could not even be allowed to visit her. She should be removed from his house, which her presence was then polluting.[10] In his unique position, he was reminded, he must be shown to be pure in his daily life and that purity was now being compromised due to his connection with Caecilia Metella. Sulla has been blamed for actually divorcing his wife at this time, but there is no evidence whatever that he did this with any malice. On the contrary, Sulla was never casual in his personal relationships and he must have been under enormous pressure from his fellow priests to make this gesture. With the approval of the gods always in view, he must have acquiesced very reluctantly, but with resignation.

Plutarch remarked that 'thus far, out of religious apprehension, he observed every rule to the letter'.[11] The only criticism made of his behaviour at that time is that he spent too much money on Caecilia Metella's funeral, after her death. This seems a pitiful and even cruel criticism to make. It is correct that Sulla was keen to see a cessation of the extreme extravagance of some of the more notable funerals in Rome, but at this time, in view of his personal involvement, he cannot have been thinking too clearly. He would certainly not have considered it a waste to show his late wife every possible respect.

Despite his reliance on the help of the gods and his own belief in his ability to do the work ahead of him, it still must have seemed to him as if his personal happiness was now destroyed. The two people who were probably closest to him had died within a fairly short time and his future on a personal level was now uncertain. Certainly the gods who had so far supported him in his public career were apparently pitiless in his private life. He would have been unable to spend much time with his family over the past years and it must have been particularly painful to find that now there was some light at the end of the tunnel regarding his work, he had been hit by these devastating losses. It was enough to shake any man's faith in his favourite gods. That for Sulla it did not once again attests to the more mystical side of his character, which would have persuaded him to carry on with fortitude, even though he would now miss the prospect of a loving family life when he was able to retire.

Whatever the bleakness of his lack of close companionship at home, he still had to continue with the task that he had set himself to perform. He could not afford to show weakness, or allow any suggestion that the task might prove too much for him to cope with, as there were still people in Rome who would have been pleased at the prospect of his failure. He would be obliged to find what compensation he could in the work ahead of him.

However, I believe that the work he completed during the following year showed only too clearly that he was not only in a hurry to get everything done that he thought necessary, but that he was actually totally immersing himself in it. It certainly seems to have been a form of escape for him. He had always been a high achiever, but over the coming months he completed such an amount of work that it would certainly have seemed quite impossible for any man who was less driven.

Sulla was still as eager as always to make sure he gave praise where it was due and show appreciation of the efforts of others. One of the most important of these people, who had given him their support, was Gnaeus Pompeius Magnus. A little earlier, Magnus had been sent to Africa in order to deal with the army raised by another Cinnan sympathizer, Gnaeus Domitius Ahenobarbus. Magnus had already proved very useful in Sicily where he had dealt successfully with Carbo and Sulla and the Senate no doubt thought that he could do equally good work in dealing with Ahenobarbus. Magnus certainly proved that their confidence in him was not misplaced, for in a campaign of only forty days he was able to destroy the army of Ahenobarbus and his allies.[12]

After his work in Africa was completed there was a short haitus when Magnus was requested to return his army home, while he remained in the province until he could be replaced by a new governor. However, his soldiers refused to leave without him (or he claimed that they had) and Magnus was obliged to accompany his troops home. He may, in fact, have been flattered by the display of their affection for him. On his return, Magnus made it clear that he now considered that he was eligible for a Triumph. Sulla initially refused his request, on the perfectly reasonable grounds that Magnus had only the imperium of the propraetor and strictly speaking the Triumph was reserved for consuls, praetors and dictators only.

Magnus showed openly that he was very disappointed at the decision and Sulla may by then have realized that the young man's usually sunny temperament could easily be clouded if he did not get his own way. Sulla is reported to have said at this time that he was 'fated in his age to have to fight with mere boys' but he eventually agreed to allow Magnus to have the Triumph he had demanded.[13]

Sulla had other plans for Magnus, and did not see any need to alienate him so soon. He knew now that the youth could be sulky, but he was important for the moment. Sulla decided that it would be wise to bind him more firmly to his side and with this in mind he suggested that Magnus be married to Sulla's own stepdaughter. This young woman was Aemilia Scaura, the daughter of Sulla's late wife Metella and her first husband Marcus Aemilius Scaurus, who had been the Princeps Senatus and had died in 98 BC. She was therefore a woman of high birth and was very marriageable.

Unfortunately, she was married already, to Manius Acilius Glabrio, but that was not an insurmountable obstacle as Magnus was also already married, to his first wife Antistia. None of this presented any real problem to the Roman mind, for marriages could always be quickly and easily dissolved if a more prestigious or profitable one came into view, even if the young woman concerned was actually pregnant by her first husband, as in this case. Even her pregnancy was not considered to be a real impediment to any further marriage, for, once divorced, she would simply go on to bear her child in her new husband's house. Once delivered, it would then be returned to her first husband, the child's father, for its upbringing and it was not necessary for her to see it again. She would be expected to concentrate on whatever children she bore from the current marriage. This was the true situation regarding the servitude of marriage for an upper class Roman woman, despite the apparent privileges of her position. She would be expected to consider first and foremost her family's overall advantage.

As Aemilia Scaura's paterfamilias Sulla certainly had the authority to choose her marriage partner for her and could divorce her from her first husband at will. Pompeius Magnus was of age and free to make his own decisions, so there was considered to be no real impediment to the match between them. It was a perfectly normal arrangement and one to which no sensible person could take exception. The opinions of the bride were not, however, recorded and were probably considered to be of no importance.

There was, however, one major humiliation for Pompeius Magnus to face, though it did not concern his new marriage. It concerned the Triumph that he had been so determined to celebrate. It had been his wish that this great day should eclipse all previous ones and in pursuit of that aim he had decided that he would not have his triumphal chariot pulled by mere horses, which had satisfied everyone else. He wanted elephants! He had in fact brought several of these animals back with him from Africa. He then arranged for four of the elephants to be brought into Rome and they were to be harnessed to the chariot to pull it and him in all his regalia through the streets, to the conclusion of his procession in the Forum. Sulla and the senators and all the other notables would be on the podium on front of the Temple of Castor and Pollux in order to see him go by in all his glory. The common people of Rome would be watching closely to see what booty he had collected and probably even more to enjoy the feasting afterwards. Unfortunately, they were all due to endure a long, cold wait.

Magnus was to find, to his dismay and embarrassment, that not only were elephants rather less tractable than horses, but they were a great deal larger. So large in fact that they would not fit under the archway of the Triumphal Gate, through which his procession had to pass. After several time-wasting attempts, he had to admit defeat and give the order for horses to be brought in to replace the elephants.[14] Word of his transport problems would by that time have reached the centre of the city where the VIPs were waiting for him. It is reasonable to assume that Sulla, with his very ready sense of humour and appreciation of the ridiculous must have found the whole matter immensely amusing, particularly in view of that young man's determination to promote himself and boost appreciation of his apparently glorious achievements.

Unfortunately, that was not the end of the embarrassments he was to suffer on his supposedly special day. When the procession was finally moving slowly through the city, some of Magnus' own soldiers, encouraged by their officers (and forgetting their often declared devotion to him in the heat of the moment), tried to take away some of the booty from the open displays. This was, so they claimed, because they had not received their fair share. It must have all seemed a little sordid to Sulla, and a very far cry from his own far more genuinely devoted troops, who had offered him their own money when he had little, rather than trying to steal his! By the end of this very stressful day, they may have both felt that they were paying a rather high price for the marriage designed to join them together as relatives.

Following Magnus' great day there was to be yet another triumph, which was that of Gaius Valerius Flaccus, who was the brother of Sulla's new Master

of Horse. Gaius Valerius was the governor of Celtiberia and Gaul and may well
have been a moderate, like his brother, and therefore a supporter of Sulla.[15] Sulla
was always willing to show honour and gratitude towards those who supported
him, therefore this particular triumph would be a welcome one. Not so much,
unfortunately, could be said for the one intended to follow it.

A third triumph to take place around that time was Lucius Licinius Murena's.
Sulla had left him in charge of Cilicia back in 84 BC and he had been confirmed
as governor of that province by the Senate. As already mentioned, Mithradates
had only agreed to his treaty with Sulla under pressure and he had always been
disinclined to give up Cappadocia, even holding on to the area after Sulla had
left Asia. Archelaus had of course persuaded him to concede on Sulla's terms,
but later Mithradates had decided that Archelaus had become more Sulla's
friend than his own, and the general had had to flee. He had, in fact, made his
way to Murena's headquarters and eventually had received his estate in Euboea
from Sulla, in recognition of the friendship they had formed.

Archelaus had later warned Murena that Mithradates planned to invade his
province, therefore a pre-emptive attack had been made against Cappadocia in
83 when some of Mithradates' cavalry was defeated. When Mithradates then
invoked his treaty with Sulla in protest at the attack, Murena declared that he
did not accept that it was legal. He claimed that he believed the treaty had never
been properly ratified by the Senate, therefore it was invalid.[16]

Mithradates again decided to try to regularize his position by sending an
embassy to Rome. In reply to this move the Senate sent a man named Calidius
to attempt to stop Murena's depredations, but he was simply ignored. King
Mithradates then turned on Murena personally and defeated him. By 81 BC
Sulla was obliged to intervene and had sent Aulus Gabinius as an envoy to make
Murena stop his personal war against Mithradates. Murena then very wisely
decided that he should not antagonize Sulla any further and returned to Rome
in order to celebrate his triumph as though nothing untoward had happened in
Asia.

Mithradates of Pontus and Ariobarzanes of Cappadocia became reconciled
yet again and the matter appeared to settle down for the time being, though
the rather petty disputes of the leaders hardly deserved the rather grand title
of 'Second Mithradatic War' by which their altercations eventually came to be
known. However, as soon as Murena was out of the way, Mithradates quickly and
cheerfully returned to his old ways, clinging on to Cappadocia in defiance of all
agreements and furthermore repudiating the marriage which had formed a part
of the treaty of 'friendship' with his neighbour Ariobarzanes. He only attempted
to ratify his treaty with him when he had already started another campaign in
the Bosphorus. In the meantime, Ariobarzanes had wasted no time in sending
ambassadors to Rome to make a firm complaint and demand assistance. When

Sulla was informed, he ordered Mithradates out of Cappadocia yet again. This time, realizing that he had gone too far and was facing a dangerous situation, Mithradates was obliged to comply with Sulla's demand.[17]

For Sulla, these arguments regarding Mithradates must have been on the periphery of his mind. He had far more important things to consider with Rome itself to put to rights and a great deal of work to get through in the shortest possible time. The recent bereavements he had suffered must have sapped even his resolve, but he was to work grimly on. As determined as always to try to set Rome on the road to proper stability in the time he had left to him, which he may have realized might not be very long.

His first main object was to reform the tribunate. It had originally been designed to protect individuals from any arbitrary decisions which might be made against them by magistrates. However, over the years the tribunate had moved far from this excellent ideal of public service and of latter days had usurped many far-reaching powers to which it certainly was not entitled. In fact, rather than being a force for good, as was originally intended, the tribunes had almost become the opposite. The powers by then held by the tribunate were actually able to threaten public peace. Sulla was certainly not the kind of man to allow such an anarchic situation to continue to flourish, believing as he always had in the pre-eminence of the Senate. He knew that it only ever took one or two corrupt and bribable tribunes to effectively destabilize the status quo and cause serious problems.

He was also very aware of the great temptations to which these young men were subject, when their main object was to amass a tidy fortune for their futures. That any venal or unscrupulous man was able to 'buy' the veto of a tame tribune who would then act on behalf of the individual who paid him had become almost a Roman sport. It was, however, very far from being a joke for whoever found himself then being vetoed without a chance of having his case heard. Sulla was determined, to start with, to take away their right to pass legislation (by bringing bills before the people) together with their right to summon the Senate, which he considered entirely beyond their remit.

Vitally important, thought, was that dangerous power of veto or *intercessio*. In Sulla's opinion, such a dangerous weapon should only be allowed to be used by the tribunes where the rights of an individual were involved. They should certainly not be able to use it simply to prevent honest justice or any necessary reforms. He intended to cut down the uses to which it could be put drastically, in order to prevent the obvious corruption into which it had fallen. The tribunes would still be allowed to keep the power to hold *contiones* as it was considered that this right was still necessary for the work they were intended to do.[18]

The whole matter was, in fact, merely one of bringing the power back down to its original intention, that of protecting individual Romans from any arbitrary acts made against them. There would be no attempt on Sulla's part to take away their ability to do their work on behalf of the people, he merely intended to prevent any more of the appalling abuses which had grown around it and prevent any person from buying a veto for his own ends. The fact that a tribune, along with his precious veto, had become so eminently saleable was something Sulla particularly detested, and he would no longer allow them to interfere with the proper running of the business of state.

However, that was not the only problem to be addressed regarding the tribunate. The office was generally used as a stepping stone to higher things, hence the great temptation for a young man to take substantial bribes, in order to fund his future political career.

Those very men most likely to be bribable, with their future financial security in mind, were the ones most likely to be tempted into the office in the first place. Sulla decided to cut at the root of the problem, simply by making the tribunate less likely to be attractive to those people who most wanted to abuse it. Sulla cleverly countered this tendency by announcing that the tribunate would no longer be a stepping stone onto the *cursus honorum*, in fact, it would essentially become a dead end. A man could no longer move from that office into a higher one, and this move effectively closed it off from precisely the sort of man who was least likely to use it for the public good.[19] Those men unlikely to do an honest job were deflected away from it. This was typical of Sulla's genius in understanding a problem and being able to find a simple solution to it in order to out-manoeuvre dishonest practices.

Sulla's next move was to enroll among the tribes 10,000 ex-slaves who had once been owned by the people who had been lately proscribed and whose estates had been confiscated and sold. This action has often been shown as a cynically calculated move to alter the voting of the tribes in his favour – after all, those 10,000 newly freed people would have very good reason to be grateful to him. But there was far more to it than just that. It must be remembered that a general, like Sulla, did not receive any form of salary for the work he did on behalf of Rome. He was expected to find his pay from booty, which mainly came from the sale of slaves. Many great generals over the years had become seriously wealthy from the selling of unfortunate captives into slavery alone.

This was not considered culpable, but was a customary and perfectly acceptable practice at the end of a campaign. We know already that Sulla had never had a great deal of money, it might even be said that its lack had certainly blighted his life in his younger days and even latterly he had never been in possession of large amounts of funds. It would have been a perfectly natural move on his part if he had instructed that the slaves from the confiscated estates were to be sold on again. They were, after all, a part of those estates, just as definitely chattels as the furniture or statuary. They would actually have expected to be sold on to new masters, even while they may have feared and dreaded the move. Also, Sulla could certainly have used the money, for Rome, if not personally.

However, he decided to forego that short-term gain in favour of manumitting all those people. They may well have been enormously grateful, but very few Romans would have been concerned with their feelings, and the temptation of so much available money – on the hoof, as it were – would have been too much to ignore and would certainly outweigh any more altruistic motives. But not for Sulla.

These people, newly freed and newly grateful, were given his name, as was also usual in such cases, and became known as the *Cornelii*. It would certainly be a wonderful public relations exercise for any man to make, but it might also be calculated, considering Sulla's more mystical side, to be more intended to impress the gods and convince them anew of his good intentions.

Sulla then turned his attention to the pro-magistracy. For a long time they had used their right to appoint provincial governors. This right had, over time, been taken over by the Senate itself, but again abuses had crept in. Sulpicius had personally used it against Sulla when he had taken away his command in the East, supposedly 'by the vote of the people'. The problem raised by the abuse of that right was then swiftly countered merely by Sulla confirming that only the Senate itself held either the right or the power to appoint or discharge pro-magistrates.

Another problem landed firmly in Sulla's own lap. He had, by his own march on Rome, set a very dangerous precedent. This was, of course, despite the fact that at the time of the march he had been acting for the best of motives. Any such precedent, once set, could and sooner or later certainly would, be copied by others whose own motives might be far less clear cut. This was to be dealt with by a more stringent use of the treason law itself. Sulla's new law, the Lex Cornelia de Maiestate stated that the acts of a provincial governor were far more clearly defined, in order to show just what sort of behaviour on his part might be considered to be treasonable.[20] For instance, if in the future a governor refused to leave his province within thirty days of the arrival of his replacement it could be treasonable. But it most certainly would be if that governor were to lead out an army from the province, either to go into an allied kingdom or to start a war. Obviously, for any such action on the part of a governor, the full permission of the Senate would be essential.

These measures all hinge on the Senate itself, which still held the supreme power and was still perfectly capable of enforcing that power, despite the difficulties of the past years. This was of course due to the fact that Romans could not and would not tolerate the sole rule of any one man, which accorded perfectly with Sulla's own opinions. He was very anxious to shore up the authority of the

Senate and for this his devoted veterans were of great importance, and could be relied upon to defend that authority wherever and whenever necessary.

The pro-magistracy itself also presented another problem. Over the past thirty or forty years it had gradually become customary to allow pro-magistrates to extend their posts for long periods. This also, naturally, extended their imperium. Other men, eager for a quicker turnover of such offices, were not content with these extended tenures, which effectively prevented any other person from having a chance at the job.

More important though was the very real danger that any man, holding a post for a long while, might be able to form alliances with troops who then became loyal to him personally, which might be a temptation for him to use that loyalty for his own ends.[21]

Both Gaius Marius and Sulla himself had been carried along on the loyalty and enthusiasm of their devoted troops. This, again, went against the firm republican ideal that no man should be greater than any other man of his station, which might again threaten the power of the Senate. Sulla was able to counter this by measures intended to ensure that there would always be a sufficiently large number of men willing and able to take on the jobs in the provinces. This would allow a more rapid turnover of governors, and prevent any one man from delusions of grandeur which might encourage him to think of any area as being his own private domain.

Also to be aimed at governors (Sulla had obviously seen all the many vagaries inherent in the position), was the measure to be known as the Lex de Provinciis which allowed a provincial governor on his way home to retain his imperium until he reach Rome. More importantly, it made provision for a suitable civilian to be able to replace a governor, if no other military man was suitable or available to do so. This *privati cum imperio* allowed for the conferring of imperium on a person who did not already hold any magistracy. Therefore, it was another method of discouraging any governor from clinging onto a post indefinitely by claiming that there was nobody of the correct rank to replace him. One extra benefit which led from that was the fact that no private person would be likely to succeed in inciting the troops to back him in any other situation than the one he was assigned to, therefore he would certainly be unable to lead them against Rome.

Still on that subject, Sulla also increased the number of praetors, as a further way of ensuring that there would always be a substantial number of magistrates, sufficient to govern all the provinces. This would, of itself, guarantee a quick change over and also prevent any possibility of shortages being used as an excuse for a man not laying down a comfortable sinecure. By this time Rome already had ten provinces, Nearer Spain, Further Spain, Transalpine Gaul, Italian Gaul, Macedonia/Greece, Asia, Cilicia, Sicily, Sardinia/Corsica and

Africa/Cyrenaica. Therefore the need for sufficient officials to administer to these provinces was acute.[22]

One of Sulla's pet hates was the idea of any man, in defiance of good order, being able to rise too quickly through the ranks of the political elite. He also particularly disliked any man 'collecting' more than one office at once, which again tended to increase the power of that one man beyond his rightful due. Sulla became determined that any movement from one public office to another should be in accordance with proper procedure, and with a proper time scale appropriate for the moves. This was to be enforced by his Lex Cornelia Annalis which stated that no man could become a praetor unless he had first been a quaestor. No man could rise to the consulship unless he had first been a praetor, and so on. This had always been the intended way to rise along the *cursus honorum* but, as always, over time, matters had grown lax.[23] Sulla intended that a man should acquire offices only at the correct time in his life, and that in future minimum ages for the ranks would be enforced. This meant that a man should be 36 years of age before he became an aedile, 39 years old before he could assume a praetorship, and 42 years old before he could expect to be able to stand for the consulship. Also, a period of two years should elapse between the holding of curule offices.[24] This was actually a rule which had first been set down in 180 BC and Sulla had merely revived it.

Sulla's main aim, as is obvious from these improvements, was to leave behind a solid constitution, one which would endure long after he had been obliged to step down. He certainly encouraged the making of new laws where they could be most useful, but he also wished to strengthen the old ones, also reforming them where necessary. He was concerned, as always, to ensure that there was a strong Senate, upon which the strength of Rome itself rested. The census of 86 had filled in some of the empty spaces left behind by the losses in the wars and also by the massacres perpetrated by the Cinnans, but there were still 125 seats empty in 81 BC which it would be necessary to fill. Sulla not only intended to fill those seats, but he also wished to extend the Senate beyond its accepted total of 300 members. It is not really possible to say just what number Sulla would have finally considered sufficient, but his intention was already clear. He raised 300 men of the Equites to fill some of the spaces, but also looked to the future by raising the number of questors from their original eight to a new total of twenty. This was to allow for a regular number of suitable young men rising through the ranks.

A strengthened Senate naturally meant a strengthened Rome, but it also meant that there would be a division of authority within the ranks. Sulla considered this to be the proper way to deal with things. He has often been accused of raising his own patrician class to even more power above that of the plebians, but that was not the reason for his reforms of the Senate. It must be remembered that many of those in the Senate had not proved themselves to be his friends, and in his early days his own class had effectively abandoned him. It was certainly not in order to raise them higher personally that he made the changes, but because he truly believed that the power of the Senate itself, rather than the individual senators in it, should be pre-eminent and unassailable. Increasing the numbers to form a far larger ruling body was likely to be necessary to cope with an increasing and enlarging empire, but it also divided authority and lessened that of any one member. It effectively prevented one man from taking over within it, rather than working with it, as was intended.[25]

In 216 BC a previous Dictator, Marcus Fabius Buteo had been obliged to deal with much the same situation as that in which Sulla found himself, namely that of a much reduced Senate with relatively few surviving magistrates. Sulla was obliged to recreate the solution which Buteo had arrived at, which was that of raising to the magistracy the best and bravest of his troops, in fact men who had already proved themselves by their winning of the Civic Crown. This meant that the new members would certainly be men who had worked for Rome at grass roots level and were already proven soldiers. This influx of 'new' blood might also be expected to produce welcome new ideas.

It was incidentally to also eventually work in favour of the young Gaius Julius Caesar, who quickly achieved the Corona Civica despite his youth and was therefore entitled to become a member of the Senate automatically. Holders of such honours were also required, by Sulla's ruling, to wear their 'crowns' on all public occasions, which must again have been pleasing to young Caesar. He had unfortunately begun to lose his hair early in life, and the wearing of the Corona Civica on public occasions would nicely have covered the lack.[26]

Sulla eventually began to deal with the courts themselves. He wished that in the future they should be comprised of senatorial juries, intending to tidy them up generally and also to simplify the system. With this idea in mind, he formed the criminal courts which have long been associated with his name and with his dictatorship. It is obvious from these courts that he was particularly concerned about fraudulent practices. Money was probably always at the forefront of his mind, as it tends to be for someone who has never been able to be free with it. With Rome's dire financial situation at that time, it would be particularly galling to him to be obliged to allow wastefulness in general and endure embezzlement in particular.

The Quaestio de Sicariis et Veneficiis was intended to deal with cases of murder and poisoning.[27] These matters had originally been split into two courts but under Sulla's administration they were able to be all dealt with under one, which also was to handle cases which involved the possession of any offensive weapon. That this might have become a necessary requirement at that time might have been due to the social upheaval which Rome had suffered for some considerable time. The penalty was basically exile, but was defined as Aquae atque Ignis Interdicto which effectively meant that the perpetrator was denied fire and water for a certain distance from Rome. That meant, of course, that he was exiled from Rome itself as he would be unable to find any sustenance there, nor would anyone be able to offer it to him. To the Roman, exile from the centre of things was a far greater punishment than anything else, even death, could ever be.[28]

The Quaestio de Falsis Testamentaria was one of Sulla's own inventions.[29] He intended it to deal with false coinage, false weights, together with the forging or altering of wills or other legal documents. Penalty – Aquae atque Ignis Interdicto.

There was actually a permanent court or Quaestio already in existence and Sulla appears to have revived this. One clause made it clear that any man found guilty of this fraud should not only lose his office but would not be allowed to stand for election again within ten years of the crime.

Personal injury claims were also to be dealt with, allowing the victim the right to sue for compensation. Sulla brought in a measure which allowed for actual criminal proceedings to be brought, in some cases, against a perpetrator of assault or burglary. These would be tried by a special court, which would be set up for the purpose when necessary, rather than in a court which was permanently available for the purpose.[30]

There was, however, a permanent court for extortion cases, *res repetundae*, which may go some way to show just how much this particular crime figured in Roman society. It had already been the subject of legislation and Sulla confirmed that the capital penalty should be able to be used against anyone convicted of the offence. He did, however, increase the amount of recompense from twice the amount stolen from the victim, to two and a half times the amount, to be paid by the guilty party.

It is also useful to note from these courts that the increase in the numbers of the praetors and other officials would come in very handy. Not only for the necessary work in the ever-expanding provinces but also in the much shorter term for dealing with the courts, which would no doubt keep any number of those young men busily employed for a considerable time.

Once the actual legal system had been revised, Sulla turned his attention to religion. This was always an interest for him. It was not, as in our own time, merely something in which the general populace had little interest, and confined to special occasions, but something closely associated with every aspect of everyday life. Correct observance of all the rituals was considered essential in order to acquire and then retain the favour of the gods, without whose assistance nothing could be done. With this feeling being general, and quite apart from his own strong religious convictions, Sulla was very eager to start on the programme of rebuilding and refurbishing of the temples, and the restoration of the worship of all the gods in the proper way.[31]

It was not an option to neglect the gods and it must have been a definite concern for many people in Rome at that time that this apparent neglect, even contempt for the gods, had crept in, and the valuables from the temples effectively looted during the recent troubles. Nobody was prepared to take responsibility for the burning of the temples on the Capitol Hill, but they still stood in ruins and someone would have to take the responsibility for rebuilding them and attempting to restore them to what should have been their glory.

Sulla appears to have started this work by increasing the number of augers to fifteen. Domitius Ahenobarbus had given the people the privilege of electing members of the colleges, but Sulla rescinded that right, preferring to restore the old way of co-opting the new members. The loss of the Sibyllene books was another matter of huge concern. These ancient books had been consulted in all matters when Rome was in extremis, but they had been destroyed, burned to the ground along with the Temple of Jupiter Optimus Maximus during the civil war. Sulla had no doubt been deeply grieved by their loss, knowing them to be irreplaceable. He now instructed the guardians (whose numbers had also been increased), to attempt to reconstruct these all important prophecies, by sending throughout the known world to search for any surviving copies of them.

Whilst this work was in progress, Sulla also restored the Lusus Troiae which had been an equestrian exercise, very popular with the young nobles of the city.[32] It consisted of an extremely complicated military tattoo, similar in form to a medieval tournament, which involved ceremonial riding and then a mock battle.

When he had done all he reasonably could in the political, judicial and religious spheres, Sulla then attempted to make some sort of reformation of Rome's moral standards. It was not merely from what would now be considered puritanical beliefs on his part, but a general feeling that part of Rome's ills had been caused by laxity of one form or another.

Not merely moral laxity or indulging in sexual freedoms was involved, but all kinds of wastefulness, extravagance and carelessness.

Many of the main problems were concerned with the waste of money. This was not merely a personal thing, but a feeling that general waste was wrong, particularly while Rome was in difficulties. Many people, particularly among the nobles of course, had fallen into extravagant habits. They were fond of spending large sums on clothing, jewellery, food and drink, athletics contests, gambling in all its forms, particularly on the games, and even the wasteful display which was then common in upper-class funerals.[33]

One new law was designed to limit the amount of bets which could be laid on athletic contests, while another attempted to prevent the common waste of money on exotic foods and drink. Sulla actually fixed the prices of such luxuries by law, declaring that no man should be able to spend more than 30 sesterces on a meal, except for festivals, where the limit would be 300 sesterces. Funerals were then regulated, particularly with regard to their cost, and even the price of tombstones was fixed by law, preventing extravagance on ceremonies and the unnecessary elaboration of memorials. This must, however, have come as something of a relief to the poorer people, who usually wished to follow where other fashionable people led, and would have been unable to afford to spend the amounts they might have wanted.

A further set of regulations, the Lex Cornelia Sumptuaria placed a tax on luxury goods such as perfumes, expensive wines, spices, jewellery and dyes like Tyrian purple, which were still available but must be paid for in accordance with their rarity, if one wished to indulge in them. Sumptuary laws have been attempted time and time again over the centuries, usually to prevent people from wearing garments or jewels which were considered to be the preserve of their betters. They have always proved practically impossible to enforce. Perhaps Sulla was well aware of this fact before he brought in his new regulations, on the assumption that if people were determined to waste their money on idle display he could hardly stop them, but that the state may as well benefit from their unnecessary expenditure.

Any person of decent social standing might be expected to have a position to uphold, with the resultant purchase of special clothing and ornaments. Perhaps such regulations were not always intended to be taken fully seriously, as with the rule about banquets, a fault to which Sulla himself was prone. It was probably more a case of having to be seen to make the attempt to regulate the situation, without actually expecting any great change to be made to people's habits. At least the extra taxes thereby created would come in useful.

The 'Lex Cornelia Frumentaria' was the grain law. This, to simplify, abolished the sale of cheap grain by the state. It did not forbid the state from selling grain, but it did prevent the state from undercutting the prices of the private grain merchants.

One set of regulations even attempted to deal with sexual irregularities in marriage. The details of these are unfortunately lost to us, which is a pity as they might have made very entertaining reading.[34] It must be an impossible task to try to regulate people's private moments, either in marriage or out of it. There were, however, several laws already on the books appertaining to homosexuality, known as the Lex Scantinia.[35] There was actually no law which demanded that any man known to be homosexual should be compelled to retire, although such practices were certainly frowned upon and condemned.

The provisions of the Lex Scantinia actually called for the death penalty, but this stemmed from earlier times and it was hardly ever enforced. Most people tended to take a fairly tolerant and reasonable attitude up to a point, but there was still a certain amount of contempt involved in the general opinion of the situation. It was definitely still considered to be a vice, not a normal part of everyday living. Any man in Sulla's position would need to be particularly careful not to bring censure down upon himself by openly behaving in an unsuitable way.

This is no doubt why Sulla had to be so very circumspect with regard to Metrobius, a person of whom he was very fond but had probably not been able to meet for several years. Some men simply moved out of the country, taking up residence in Greece, where such practices were common and caused no concern. Anyone choosing to remain in Rome would have to be rather careful about his general attitude, to ensure that he did not draw too much attention to himself. However, as always, people will privately do as they wish, and most people simply turned a blind eye.

Sulla's legislation was generally sensible, even if some of the laws were a reintroduction or even a rehashing of old ones. That he was genuinely well-intentioned is quite obvious. He was eager to put Rome back onto a solid footing, hence his obsession with monetary waste when Rome had so few funds and had to make them spread so far. He was desperate to repair and rebuild the ravages of the wars, as well as set the Roman people themselves back onto the right path. He particularly hated wastage of funds, especially among the noble families where too much indulgence in extravagance could easily lead to the loss of family estates. It is interesting to speculate whether he had had some personal experience of that kind of family loss, which coloured his attitude towards it.

On the whole his new measures were well received, with certainly no evidence that he was hated or that his attempts to regularize Roman life were greatly resented. On the whole the people of Rome simply got on with things and it is quite likely that very many of his fellow Romans felt that things had gone downhill far enough. Because of the burning of the temples, the ruination of their city, and the losses of the wars, they would have acknowledged that a new start would have to be made.

There was one other concern for him to deal with, and that would have been of special interest to him. It was the distribution of land to his veteran troops. This was tied up with the settlement of Italy in general. He would have to find land enough to give to the men who had served him, as he had promised. This might seem to be easy, as so many of the towns who had stood out against Rome during the civil war had lost their right to their surrounding lands, but things are of course never quite so simple. It was, of course, only to be expected that defeated towns would lose their lands, due to the exigency of war and on the face of it there were certainly large enough areas apparently available, which was just as well. Sulla was looking to having to find enough property with which to satisfy approximately 140,000 men, of different ranks and different expectations.

The nobles from among his followers would expect to receive substantial estates taken from the upper classes among the Italian rebels, while for the rank and file the ideal arrangement was the distribution of decent small farms.[36] Naturally, where opposition to Rome had been greatest, there was the greatest amount of newly available property, therefore a greater concentration of new settlers could be accommodated in that area. Places such as Campania, Etruria and Umbria were an example of the greatest changes, while areas like Apulia, which had not stood out against Sulla, were not required to give up any land at all.

Samnium was, of course, badly hit. During the civil war Sulla had found the very fiercest opposition had come from this area, and he had come to believe that they were essentially a nation of untrustworthy rebels who deserved to be treated in the most extreme way. However, this applied to fighting men while the fighting was going on. Sulla could never tolerate opposition to Rome, and any area behaving in what he considered to be an ungrateful and rebellious manner could expect to receive appropriate treatment from him. This leads many people to believe that he hated the Samnites as a race, which is not strictly true.

Certainly he punished them with severity when he defeated them, knowing as he did that they felt the same way about Rome, despite their defeat, and that they would be highly unlikely to compromise. On the other hand, he certainly never made any attempt at genocide once the matter was settled and done with.[37] There was never an idea of clearing the area of those people completely, particularly of innocent women and children, as some people might have been willing to do in order to deal with the question permanently. Sulla was never so simple a thing as a vicious or cold-blooded murderer. There was no attempt at any time to exterminate the Samnites as a people. Unfortunately for the land settlement requirements, Samnium itself had never been a particularly prosperous area in the first place. Mountainous regions rarely are and thin soil generally makes for a thin population. Despite the amounts of land becoming available in the area, most of it would be found to be entirely unsuitable for purpose and useless for the small farms which were needed.

Sulla's settlements were divided roughly into three types, as some of them were to be made in already existing municipia and coloniae. In the case of coloniae such as Aricia and Puteoli he merely needed to adjust the town's existing charter in order to accommodate the new residents. Some of the municipia were allowed to continue much as they had done previously, but they were required to give up some, or even most, of their territories to provide land sufficient for the veterans. This happened in towns such as Faesulae and Nola. In some other places the very large influx of veterans actually brought about a change in the status of the indigenous population, for in comparison with the incomers their standing fell.[38] Pompeii is a good example of this in action, after the town became a colonia bearing Sulla's name, along with that of the favourite goddess, it was known as Colonia Cornelia Veneria Pompeiiana.

The way the new settlements were intended to work was that the land given to the veterans would still remain the property of Rome. However, they would be free to live and work the farms, and hopefully raise families on them. There was the question of funds, of course. Many of these homesteads would also need a fair amount of money to be spent on them, after the years of wars, therefore a bounty would be granted to each man who took up a farm. This also came in the form of a levy, enforced on those tribes who had been Rome's opponents in the civil war.

Naturally, a man of rank would not wish for a small farm. Even a man who had served in the legions for an extended time would expect more from Sulla, in recompense, than merely a smallholding. The larger estates would be relatively simple to apportion, being already viable, simply a matter of transferring estates from one owner to another.

However, the land for the lesser ranks would require more thought. The land itself, whether some areas were fertile and some not, was obviously an important factor. Any man would require at the very least ten iugera of land in order to make his holding viable, but in some less productive areas in order to achieve the same yield he would require far more, sometimes as much as one hundred iugera.[39]

The farmers who had previously owned or worked the land would necessarily have had to move out. The upper classes here fared far better, as might be expected. They generally left the area completely, often heading for Spain, where Cinna's supporters still held sway. Lower classes, though, had to find alternatives. Some may well have drifted towards Rome, looking for work. Those who failed to find that work would doubtless be obliged to turn to crime. There would have been a small number, probably bewildered by the changes, who simply had no desire to move, knowing there was nothing for them elsewhere, and they might well have found work on the original farms, now working for the new owners who possessed their lands. These people would then live much as they always had.

However, the settlements were not always a great success, which was a pity, given the spirit of gratitude and recompense in which they were given, and the ultimate intention of the exercise. The lands of the small farmers had from time immemorial been the backbone of Roman society, the Roman dream, in fact. They were to provide not only foodstuffs for the cities and towns but also children to replenish the Roman population.

These children represented Rome's future wealth in a very real way and it was the loss of such farms initially, being replaced by large faceless estates owned by speculators, which had so incensed the brothers Gracchi.[40] This had led to the attempt at a social revolution which had taken both their lives. It would certainly have been a part of the original intention, when distributing land to veteran troops, that they should eventually raise families there and replenish the solid and reliable Roman stock.

That this largely failed is due to several factors. Partly it was due to the land itself, some of which was infertile and some simply neglected, but the main problem lay with the new owners themselves. These men, who had often spent many years in the legions, may have had a distant desire to settle down, a dream of a little place in the country, like many another man. However, the reality is often different when it is to be faced in actuality.

The life often proved very different to the one they were accustomed to, and the daily routine of farming can quickly become tedious to those not suited to it. Also the sheer volume of work required in order to make even a small return can be daunting. It is often not at all what was expected. The grind and boredom of it quickly sets in, then the man might decide that he does not like life in the country after all, and he drifts back into the towns, or even re-enters the legions.

There were also the usual difficulties with the administrators given the task of sorting out all the claims and apportioning the land in the first place. The management of such estates must have given many opportunities for plain fraud, involving everything from simply swapping good land allocations for bad ones, to straightforward seizure of land intended for others and misappropriation of funds. Even after Sulla's death there were still officers who were trying to sort out some of the fraudulent practices, which had caused problems and ruined the smooth running of the original allocations.

In some cases, however, the veterans settled in happily enough, at least for a time. Later on there would be another great need for experienced troops, particularly during the 70's when conflicts started up in several places, with wars against Sertorius, Spartacus and Lepidus needing men. There was also the everlastingly troublesome Mithradates who kept things on the boil, so the need for men capable of soldiering became acute again. For every man who settles comfortably on a small farm, there are another dozen for whom the battlefield is his true home, and the sight of the standards being raised also raises their blood. In these cases, the old soldier will quickly abandon the new life he has taken up, to go back willingly to the one he knows best and the companions he is comfortable with.

There were also basic monetary considerations, which affected such decisions. Life on a farm might be regular, but it was hard. Life as a soldier might be dangerous, but it often gave back far more in the gathering of booty and the sharing of spoils. It also offered excitement and the chance to see the world. It might be uncertain in many ways, but it could also be far more interesting and satisfying than the humdrum life of a small farmer, who would forever be trapped in one place.

Therefore, it must be admitted that the larger part of the settlement of land on veteran troops probably, rather regrettably, ended in failure. Not only because of the nature of the land available but also because of the nature of the men involved. It was a pity, as Sulla had tried to provide honestly for them all, in accordance with his promise.

Much of the land itself would gradually be taken over by the magnates again, working the estates as large concerns with gangs of slaves to perform the labour. This was the very situation, blocking the land off from the vigorous and productive peasantry who should have held it, which had already caused great concern to many decently minded men from the days of the Gracchi down to Sulla himself. It is more than likely that the full intention behind this attempt to restore a decent, loyal and entirely Roman workforce on these lands, had indeed also been to restore a prosperous peasant class to the areas, ultimately to provide Rome with the manpower it required. That aim had been defeated by the changing nature of the soldiers themselves. It had been, however, a good and honest aim, genuinely designed to provide a solid foundation for Rome.

Whether most of Sulla's improvements were to prove lasting or not, it was at least apparent that this man had turned from a very able soldier into an equally able politician, and that his ultimate intention was to restore Rome's stability for the benefit of all her people. Many of those reasonable citizens – and most reasonable people simply want to get on with their lives in peace – would have admitted that they would do better to help the process of regeneration than consistently oppose it. That it was necessary to work together in order to make the city of Rome once again what she ought to be.

To make her the glowing and glorious centre of the known world, occupied by a peaceful, healthy and prosperous people, who were secure under the benevolent eyes of the approving gods.

Chapter Sixteen

Sulla's stepdaughter, Aemilia Scaura, recently married to young Pompeius Magnus, did not live long enough to provide the bond between them that her marriage had been intended to secure. She died within the first few months of the marriage, in childbirth, bearing the child she had conceived with her first husband, Glabrio.[1] The child died also. There was no further chance of a child between her and Magnus who could provide that permanent link which Sulla had doubtless hoped for. Pompeius Magnus could be a very charming young man, as well as being very capable on the battlefield, but he shared his rather too ruthless streak with his late father, Pompeius Strabo, known as 'the butcher'. Sulla, however, had already realized that his good opinion of himself totally outweighed everything else, and that he was in many respects a rather slippery character, very difficult to hold onto. He was to prove correct in that surmise, as Pompeius slowly but inexorably began to slide away from Sulla's side in the months ahead.

Whatever the reality of Aemilia Scaura's relationship with her stepfather, she had at least formed part of a family bond, and she was a living link with Caecilia Metella which Sulla may well have valued for its own sake. The twins his late wife had left him were only small children and could not be the companions he needed. It must have seemed as though his personal family was shrinking, leaving him with fewer people he could be close to for any sort of private life. Due to the prominence of his position, let alone the huge workload he had undertaken, he would probably not be able to see much of Metrobius or any of his other friends from the theatres. Even if he had, the pleasure he gained from their company would be too open to criticism again, therefore he must have felt rather bereft. However, that situation was about to change.

Marcus Valerius Messala 'Rufus', a politician and historical writer of no mean order, had returned to Rome to find that his sister, Valeria Messala, had recently been the victim of a divorce by her first husband.[2] The reason for the divorce is not known, so no fault is recorded, nor does it signify at this stage. The woman was apparently considered to be a beauty, was young, healthy and also, fortunately, intelligent and well educated. She was now free again and Marcus Valerius would not, of course, wish her to be on his hands for too long. He was to find a husband for her beyond his wildest expectations.

One of the wealthiest men in Rome had recently died, and his sons had arranged splendid funeral games in his honour, with pairs of gladiators employed to fight.[3] It was an occasion where most of Rome would expect to have a day off and enjoy the show. Even Sulla must have been pleased to attend, not only to do honour to the family concerned, but also to have a little light relief from the cares of state.

There was nothing in the *mos maiorum* which prevented women from attending such games, nor from sitting alongside the men, although they tended to be segregated at the theatres. Funeral games were then considered to be more of a circus performance, rather than a theatrical one, and in the days before the building of purpose-made amphitheatres, specially designed for such games, these shows tended to be held in the Forum, or some other designated space which was large enough.[4]

Valeria Messala had apparently attended the games under the chaperonage of her cousin, Marcus Valerius Messala 'Niger'. Sulla, as guest of honour, would no doubt have been sitting in some elevated and central position, from which he would get an uninterrupted view of the proceedings. It is said that Valeria Messala had to pass behind his seat in order to reach her own, having arrived slightly late. She and her cousin were apparently intending to sit with other family members, and with friends including the retired Chief Vestal Virgin, Caecilia Metella Balearica.[5] This explains why an otherwise relatively unimportant young woman was given a seat in such a position of honour, directly behind the dictator.

Whilst walking behind Sulla's seat, Valeria Messala touched his toga, apparently taking from it a small piece of woollen fluff. Sulla, surprised at the gesture, turned around in his seat to see who was behind him. He would then have seen the girl standing holding a small piece of woollen threadlike material in her hand. Valeria Messala was obliged to excuse herself, explaining that she had picked it from his robe thoughtlessly, and had meant no harm. She told him that she had given in to temptation in the hope that the tiny piece of Sulla's robe would enable her to share in a tiny amount of his proverbial luck, his *felicitas*.[6] The flattering excuse must have amused him and intrigued him. Whatever other words passed between them, he was certainly not untouched by her charm and appearance, or her boldness in approaching him.

It is said that he then spent some time in turning around in his seat, to get a better look at the young woman, and she no doubt smiled and simpered in return. Whilst the games were in progress, he asked who she was and later made further, fuller, enquiries about her, learning that she was not married, but that she had all the required family connections and background. He was told that she was a niece of the orator Quintus Hortalus Hortensius.[7] This man had gone over to Sulla's side after the Social War and was married to a daughter of Quintus Lutatius Catulus Caesar, another of Sulla's most reliable supporters. Therefore all seemed perfectly satisfactory, and no doubt her family was surprised but delighted at Sulla's interest in her, which would have been encouraged. A marriage between them was arranged relatively quickly.

It would certainly have intensified the circle around Sulla. The consul at that time, Quintus Caecilius Metellus Pius, another cousin of hers, was also Pontifex Maximus, and Sulla's partner in the consulship. It is a moot point whether at that time Sulla was still, strictly speaking, dictator or not. He had taken the consulship, along with Metellus Pius, for 80 BC, which suggests that he had already stepped down from the dictatorship, officially, after only one complete year, and was now working as a consul in the normal way. He would, however, still retain fully all the respect and effectively all the power he had previously held, and obviously still considered that he had work to finish for the benefit of the republic. Despite the apparent change of title, he was still master of Rome.

There was, moreover, to be a famous court case recorded around that time which showed Sulla's constitutional reforms working in the just the way he had intended them to when he had formed them.

Sulla's interest had certainly been aroused by the case of one Quintus Roscius of Almeria. This man had been a supporter of Sulla's, but his name had recently been placed on the proscription list by the venal and greedy steward of Sulla's known as Chrysogonus. This was done even though the lists had already been closed.

This man, Roscius, was then murdered in order to allow Chrysogonus and his equally voracious friends, some of whom were already open enemies of the unfortunate victim, to claim his estates.[8] As we already know, Sulla was easily incensed at the damage which could be done to his good name and proper intentions by such machinations as those being committed by his freedman and others of the same ilk, or anyone likely to use the system for their own advantage.

The details of this particular case are actually quite interesting. When the conspirators realized that Sulla did not intend to let the matter rest, and had set enquiries in motion to find out exactly what had happened to his supporter, they actually dared to accuse the son of Quintus Roscius of patricide. In blaming him for the death of his father, they hoped to shift the culpability from themselves. This case was subsequently to be heard by Sulla's new Quaestio de Siccariis et Veneficiis which was the newly formed joint court dealing with murder and poisoning cases.

No less a personage than the young Cicero was then delegated to defend the bereaved son, although Cicero made it clear at the time that he considered that he faced certain dangers in undertaking such a defence of the accused. He did not appear to fear actual physical violence from the accusers, so much as to be concerned that his support and defence of this man might appear to be a form of opposition to Sulla. He took pains to avoid any chance of this idea by making it perfectly clear that the actions of Chrysogonus and his friends did not concern Sulla directly, nor were they in any way his responsibility.

That was most certainly true, but it shows a streak of cowardice in Cicero's character that he was more concerned with his own showing in the case, than with that of the accused.

Sulla had, in any case, already made it clear that he personally would not take any responsibility for criminal actions taken by others, even if they had appeared to be his supporters. His behaviour towards Crassus, when he was found to be acting fraudulently, made it obvious that he would not protect those who acted with criminal intent.[9] In fact, he was delighted to see that his reforms were working properly, without giving any favouritism to those who might have hoped that having some connection with him would protect them from the consequences of their actions. His greatest desire, in ensuring stability and justice, was to see that all men should be treated equally with regard to the law. At the end of the trial the decision went, of course, to Roscius and Sulla's steward Chrysogonus was executed as a result of it. It was exactly the message Sulla had intended to give, to show all the people that he meant what he said and that he would ensure that his reforms were working properly and in the full spirit of justice for all.

When the people had elected Sulla as consul for 80 BC he had attempted to refuse the honour, making it clear that he still intended to step down from public life and become a private citizen. However, there were probably still far too many loose ends to tie up to allow him to do so, even if his new marriage had given him a new incentive to make the attempt to achieve some personal time for himself before it became too late.

However, for a man like Sulla, there could never be any such thing as a true retirement.

Rome had in so many areas to be rebuilt and Sulla had to give orders for the restoration of the temples, burned down a short while before, together with something which must have been equally close to his heart, the rebuilding of the Temple of Fortuna Primagenia at Praeneste. This huge, terraced sanctuary had been built originally a century or so previously, but had sustained severe damage during the Social War. Sulla was known to be particularly annoyed at its spoliation and he gave orders for it to be not only repaired but enlarged, beautifying the building. Remains of it can still be seen and it is a tribute to what could be achieved in the way of buildings intended to impress.[10]

Also still visible (at least the lower part of the building) overlooking the Forum are the imposing remains of Sulla's Tabularium. These now have other, later, buildings above them, but the foundations of the structure remain, together with the lower walls and some passageways inside. Again, there had been a building there previously, which had also burned down, but Sulla rebuilt and enlarged it. It became a home for the state archives and a record office.

The Curia itself was another of his repair projects although this little gem of a building was again lost to Rome a while later. The Curia Hostilia has gone through several incarnations and the building now on the site is a much later replacement. The whole Curia was moved forward slightly from its original position when Gaius Julius Caesar was in power. (This was to make more space behind it for his Forum Julia, which was to hold as its centrepiece the Temple of Venus Genetrix, (Venus the Ancestress), as a tribute to the goddess from whom Caesar believed himself descended.) Sulla's own Curia Hostilia building was to be burned down after his death and was eventually rebuilt yet again by his son, Faustus Cornelius Sulla.

There was also Ostia itself to repair. This was, of course, a vital area for Rome's merchant shipping, though never as large as the imposing Portus, which would be a short distance away. Portus had, of course, to be built specifically for large ships and was eventually to cover a huge area, containing quays and warehouses along with a canal made to allow ships to proceed towards the city without having to take the slower route along the Tiber itself. Ostia was smaller, though a busy town as well as a place for storage of goods, particularly the all-important grain. It had been severely damaged by Gaius Marius and his followers when they had first arrived back in Italy from Africa. The act of betrayal of the killing of the people of Ostia, when they attempted to welcome Marius home, is often skipped over, but that and the depredations of his followers had left scars which Sulla at this time tried to eradicate. He ordered substantial building works to take place at Ostia and the townspeople had good reason to be grateful to him.

There were further settlements outside of Rome to be established around this time, many of which were small towns, or merely even roadside stations along major routes. These formed a particular class of settlement known as a forum. Although they bear the same name as the central square of larger towns or cities, in this context the name was used to denote a place founded purely as an administrative centre with a market, similar to small market towns in Britain. Many of them took their names from the road on which they stood, but some from their founder, among which was Forum Cornelii, and is present day Imola.[11] Many of these new foundations (which continued to be made as late as Hadrian's reign), were very successful indeed. They had started by being merely useful stopping places on a busy road but many eventually became prosperous towns in themselves.

One project, which might also be considered as a part of Sulla's rebuilding work in Rome itself, was the enlargement of the pomerium. This was, of course, the boundary officially enclosing the city of Rome. It was marked out with white stones named *cippi* and had reputedly been inaugurated by King Servius

Tullius. The space within this boundary had remained unchanged until Sulla's dictatorship. The whole of the ancient Palatine city of Romulus was contained within the boundary, whereas the Aventine was outside of it. However, so was the Capitol itself, with its most important temples, which Sulla was so eager to repair and reinstate. Tradition held that the pomerium might only be enlarged by a man who had significantly increased Roman territory, which Sulla could reasonably be said to have done. He therefore extended the pomerium to include the most important areas, being concerned to include them in the officially designated city as, in religious terms, it was considered that Rome herself existed only within that holy boundary.

Any part outside of that official boundary could strictly be considered only as 'Roman territory', rather than an intrinsic part of Rome itself, hence the use of the Campus Martius for generals and troops waiting to enter the city, which despite being close by was not actually within Rome itself.[12] However, being outside of the boundary was not sufficient for the most important temples. Only for ones such as Bellona and her patch of 'enemy territory' where foreign wars were officially proclaimed, or Venus Libitina, where citizen deaths were registered, and whose work with funerals and the dead were obliged to be actually outside the boundaries of Rome due to their context.

It can be seen from this that Sulla was very much the kind of man for whom retirement would always be more of a dream than a reality. He was simply not the type of person who could walk away and sit quietly somewhere, giving up all his work to the care of others. However, he now had a new wife and perhaps even hope of a new family, so preparations had to be made. We know that at this time he owned villas outside Rome, both at Puteoli and at Cumae. This was the favoured playground of all those Romans rich enough to afford to live further south, away from the heat and smells of crowded Rome, in the wonderful bay area. Many of these villas were literally jewels set in the countryside, with extensive sea views. They had every convenience known at the time, together with many beauties we can only envy. The rooms themselves were decorated exquisitely and they enjoyed gardens (in some cases vast ones), with what we would today call extensive water features. Beyond their walls they were surrounded not only by farms, which helped to make them self-sufficient, but also by vineyards. The villas still standing (albeit in ruins) outside of Pompeii today testify to the standard of living available at that time, and the level of luxury which could be achieved for those who could afford to pay for it.

It had always been something of a political joke in Rome, that if a man were banished from the city to the hundredth milestone, he would find himself in the Bay of Naples, where if he were rich he would probably already have a villa anyway. Some wall paintings have come down to us showing what was once believed to be fanciful images of villas of supreme beauty, almost floating over the sea, sometimes actually spreading out along the edge of the water. We now know that these were not merely imaginary, but true representations of some of the homes of the fortunate in this very special place.

We know that a little later, Cicero himself would become addicted to buying villas in this area, and that he owned a large one just outside of Pompeii, in a very privileged position overlooking the sea. He also became an avid collector of statuary, which was an unfortunate hobby, as he was never a truly wealthy man. His wife Tarentia, to whom he was married for over thirty years, seemed to have been in control of the purse strings, but perhaps the money was from her family and she resented its loss through extravagant spending. She certainly seemed less than enthusiastic about his uncontrollable collecting habits. Cicero divorced her during the winter of 47/46 BC after he accused her of defrauding him.[13] Theirs cannot have been the only relationship to suffer from the curse of extravagance when there was so much in the world of beauty and desirability.

That Sulla could now own one or two of these most desirable homes should surely have provided him with every excuse to leave Rome and begin to enjoy some relaxation. Unfortunately, constant hard work and pressure eventually become not only a habit but sometimes even a necessity. It would be a great pity if, at Sulla's time of life and with his failing health, he had not earned the chance for rest. He had surely done enough.

However, despite the preparations Sulla was undoubtedly making, he was still not quite ready to walk away from Rome. He must have still felt that he needed to put in place whatever safeguards he could in order to protect the constitution he had tried so hard to make.[14] These safeguards must have cost him just as much thought as the laws themselves.

He was very much aware that some people are always able to find ways around regulations and that many people are quite indifferent to justice and good order. There will always be those of criminal intent or merely selfish tendencies who are prepared to give no more than lip service to whatever laws are on the statute books, however conducive to general public benefit they may have been intended to be. He had never been a foolish man, he certainly knew that as soon as he stepped out of the public eye there would be many people only too eager to begin the dissection of all that he had worked for. That was just an inevitable, if very disheartening, fact of life.

Sulla was also quite intelligent enough to realize that even if his reforms were dismantled, it did not necessarily mean that they were bad or wrong, only that men are often short-sighted and cannot, or do not wish to, see the long term gain or the greater good. For many people, who would help to destroy his constitutional reforms as soon as he was no longer there to protect them, it would not necessarily even be a case of any personal animosity. Only that they would prefer to put their own requirements first, and did not intend to be constrained by any measures designed to inhibit their own freedom of action. It would be far more comfortable for them to simply slip back into the old, familiar ways and do as they wished, reverting to their thoughtless, selfish and grasping behaviour.

The Republic, in which Sulla believed whole heartedly, was actually already rotting from within. He had sincerely tried, from the depths of the reverence and respect he felt for the institution itself, to stop that rot, to reinvigorate and reinvent the republic, but it had already gone too far. The opportunity he had given the Romans to stop, or even slow down, the decline of the republic would not be enough. He had intended his work for posterity and posterity would eventually show that it did not want it, despite the feelings of a few men such as himself, who still believed in the republican ideal so emphatically.

He had, however, given Rome the means to protect itself. He still had his veterans situated around Italy, and more particularly in and around those towns where revolts had occurred before and whose loyalty might be suspect in the future. These veterans could still be relied upon to defend the constitution, which had given them their homes and their independence.[15] Even when Sulla was gone, there would be many men who would still revere and defend his name, let alone support his policies, against those of Cinnan sympathies. Naturally, those members of Sulla's party who had become the ruling nobility of Rome would also defend their rights and privileges, but the cohesion might reasonably be expected to splinter without its driving force, which was Sulla himself.

This would partly be due to the nature of Sulla's followers. The core of the party would certainly be derived from those officers and senators who had been his closest associates, including those men who had been obliged to flee to his side when he was in Greece. They had, of course, been joined over a period of time by the intelligent and sensible moderates, who had in their turn been sickened to be obliged to witness the excesses of the Cinnans. Those men had turned to Sulla in the desperate hope of basic stability, which he had always been at pains to provide. They should, in the true republican tradition, be grateful to him for his protection, while at the same time still considering themselves in every way his equals. There would also, however, naturally enough be a number of people who had turned to Sulla merely because they disliked the Cinnans even more, and theirs was the allegiance which was likely to become shaky once he was no longer there to demand their obedience. They were the very ones who might prefer to assist in the repeal of much of his legislation, as soon as it became inconvenient for them to continue with it. His legacy would eventually be that although his carefully thought out senatorial changes did not last long after his death, his administrative ones did.[16]

Sulla had intended that his close friends and supporters Quintus Lutatius Catulus and Mamercus Aemilius Lepidus to stand for election for the consulship of 78 BC. These were two of the men he could trust, forming an intimate circle, along with Decimus Junius Brutus, who could see and appreciate what Sulla was trying to do. They honestly believed that he was the republic's upholder and considered that his laws were beneficial for the state.[17]

Unfortunately, their election would not be without opposition, as Marcus Aemilius Lepidus also declared himself a candidate. Furthermore, he said openly that not only did he intend to stand, but that if he got in he would immediately repeal all of Sulla's new laws! To make things seem even worse, he appeared to have the backing of Gnaeus Pompeius Magnus. This must have been a real annoyance to Sulla, even though it did serve to confirm that his worst opinions of that perfidious young man had been correct. He had started to slide away from Sulla as soon as the tenuous marriage tie through Aemilia Scaura had broken, and although Sulla seems to have expected that to happen, it must have been particularly infuriating to then see him siding with his opponents. Pompeius Magnus did have a good deal of support, mainly due to his campaign successes, which always gave a man prominence, therefore he made a strong ally for Marcus Aemilius Lepidus at that time. So much so that the election results were to show that he successfully gained the senior consulship, while Catulus became his junior.

Sulla, who had been out of the city at the time, had rushed back into Rome on hearing of Magnus' defection in an attempt to help his friend and canvass support for him. When the election was over he rounded angrily on Pompeius Magnus, on coming face to face with him. It is reported that he said 'This is a fine piece of statesmanship of yours, young man, in getting Lepidus elected ahead of Catulus. When Catulus is the soundest man in the world, while Lepidus is the most likely to lose his head!'[18] This was a perfectly reasonable remark for him to have made at that time, knowing that his plans for Rome's security were dependent on having men to follow him who would play their part in that. Rather than those who wanted status for themselves alone, or, like Pompeius Magnus, changed sides merely out of pique and could not be relied upon. Sulla was, in fact, perfectly correct in his estimation of Lepidus and of Magnus himself, who was soon to turn against Lepidus after realizing that friendship with such a man would inevitably do him no favours and that he would do well to dissociate himself from him.[19] This was to show itself only too quickly, as Lepidus was soon to break off any attempt at working sensibly with Catulus, and also attempted to make fundamental changes to Sulla's constitution even before he died, but he was not to enjoy his success for long.

Incidentally, trouble was to erupt in Etruria just after Sulla's death when some dispossessed locals fought with Sulla's veterans who had been assigned to their lands. Both consuls were sent to deal with the matter but Lepidus, true to form, took the side of the locals against the Roman veterans. The Senate, alarmed at the idea of another civil war breaking out, made both consuls swear an oath not to continue their quarrel and in 77 BC Lepidus was sent to Gaul, as his province, with Marcus Junius Brutus as his legate. He would there make contact with the rebel Sertorius, who was still lurking in Spain and finally Lepidus was to march on Rome, accompanied by those men from Etruria whose side he had taken, leaving Brutus behind. The Senate then passed the 'Ultimate Decree' in an attempt to stop him and he was finally defeated and killed the same year at the Milvian Bridge, by no less than Catulus himself.[20] The irony of the situation may have escaped him, but Sulla's shade might have been laughing!

However, for Sulla at the time, having been right about Lepidus would have been very little consolation. It merely proved that he would not be able to retire fully for some time to come, and that his allies were likely to go on being in need of his support. He also knew that there would be a considerable amount of time required for his new legislation to become fully settled and accepted as the normal state of affairs before it could really be considered to be a permanent feature. He would have to continue working even if he already realized that a long amount of time was not likely to be granted to him.

If Sulla could have seen into the future, it might have amused him to know that his colonies would later be copied by the First Triumvirate which was to shortly follow after him. (Pompeius Magnus, Julius Caesar and Crassus were to form the First Triumvirate in 60 BC, an unfortunate coalition of at least two of Rome's slipperiest characters, contact with whom would do Caesar no favours.) Sulla had been called 'ruthless' because he deprived his enemies of their territories.[21] It must be remembered, as Sulla was often at pains to point out, that he was fighting the enemies of Rome, not personal foes, and that the recent Social War had caused the loss of many useful Romans, not to mention the effective bankruptcy of Rome itself. His enemies should, in those circumstances, have considered themselves very fortunate to be able to escape with their lives, let alone their property. It was to be proved that those people who were glad to use his ideas after his death (such as the Triumvirs) were to show themselves far more determined (and efficient) than he had ever been at grasping the land of opponents. They were to waste little time in making no less than twenty such new foundations of colonies of their own.[22]

Sulla still wanted, indeed needed, to find the leisure to write his memoirs. These would, in accordance with the practice in his time, be not merely the story of his life, but would also be his justification of acts performed and a reiteration of his work successfully completed. They would give him a final opportunity to make his point and have his opinions aired, but also to put right any misconceptions about him, and to refute any accusations made against him, such as the one claiming that he had stolen money from the Greek temples. This particular accusation obviously still rankled with him and he made the point of emphasizing that not only had he actually borrowed the money, not stolen it, but that he had also paid it back without delay, as soon as he was able.[23] Which was far more than Carbo did, when he 'borrowed' Rome's funds without any thought of repayment.

Sulla's memoirs would give him the chance to not only air his views about policy, but also about other commanders. He would be able to tell the truth as he saw it, without anyone being able to refute it to his face. He would also be able to deal with those aspects of his life which might be considered controversial and give reasons for his actions in a balanced way. Therefore, a man's memoirs were very important indeed and we know that he started work on them as soon as he was able to spend some time away from Rome. He was to write twenty-two books of his memories and experiences, giving in detail all of his work and ideas and his hopes for the republic. We know that he was still occupied with this work when he died. Most unfortunately, these most personal writings have largely failed to survive, except for small sections. We are, therefore, denied the chance to hear his own voice through his written words and form a clear picture of his intentions and ambitions, as we can with the writings of other prominent men, (for instance with Caesar's own 'Commentaries'), self-serving or vainglorious though they often are.

He may around this time have been informed that his young wife, Valeria Messala, was pregnant. Another irony for him, in that he would be unlikely to be allowed enough time to see any new child grow, and that his twins by Caecilia Metella were also still very young. He would be leaving behind him a family largely composed of babies, rather than the young man of promise, perhaps ready to begin to take on his father's work, that he could otherwise have hoped and planned for. It must have been at a time like this that the grief at the death of his elder son would come back to him most forcefully.

We do know, however, that he was able at this time to enjoy the company of his true friends. Many, if not most, of these unimportant people had always been considered highly unsuitable by the Roman elite, but with these more humble citizens he could be himself, relaxing perhaps in a way he could not with any others. This does not mean to say that he necessarily indulged in any particularly delinquent or promiscuous behaviour. There has never been any real evidence, despite many accusations, of what his 'debauchery' actually consisted. It must therefore be assumed that the mere fact of his bisexuality was enough for most historians to back away from the subject in horror, according to the prejudices of their own times, without troubling themselves to find any real evidence of what might otherwise be considered 'perversions'. He appears to have been fairly restrained compared to others we know of, whose predilections were notorious and errant behaviour was certainly not confined to members of the lower classes.

What we do know of these friendships is enough to show that these people liked him for himself, enjoyed his company, and that he esteemed and appreciated them in return. We know also that Sulla had always enjoyed the theatre, helping to write certain bawdy verses himself, as was fashionable at that time, and that he also liked to watch comedies. He was very likely able to laugh and joke with such theatrical and circus friends, or even get drunk with them, without having to worry that they might be making malicious fun of him or carrying licentious tales. His relationship with the actor Metrobius was in a similar vein, valuable to him particularly in that it had lasted through many years, despite them being apart for the vast majority of that time. Sulla would be able to take pleasure from the thought that these were people who actually loved and respected him as a man, quite separately from his military successes or his political influence, without them expecting anything from him in return, other than the enduring friendship itself.

It is to his credit that, despite all the criticism he had received on the subject, he still stayed loyal to these people, who were despised by those who considered themselves their superiors, while it is also to their credit that they, in their turn, stayed loyal to him. This ability to connect with ordinary people, as was shown in his close relationship with his soldiers, who were devoted to him to the last, is not to be easily discounted. It tells us clearly what the man was really like, and that he was far more than merely a general and a dictator. Many of them did not know him as such, but they knew him as a companion, and as such they loved him.

We are also told that Sulla enjoyed the gentle occupation of fishing when he had time to spare for relaxation at one of his villas. It is strange to think of him patiently waiting for a fish to bite, taking pleasure in that most placid of sports, but it forms yet another facet of this man's complex and fascinating character.

However, we also know that his last year of life could not be all relaxation and enjoying the company of friends, however well earned such times may have been. It would never be so simple for a man like Sulla. He was still working, not only on his memoirs, but also in his official position whenever he felt it was necessary to show that he was still able to protect his laws and reforms. He would certainly have also been thinking about the fate of his wife and children. With his young wife pregnant and his twins by Caecilia Metella still small and helpless, he would be aware that he would need to appoint a guardian for them all. It would need to be someone he could trust to take care of their interests, including looking after their inheritances, when Sulla was no longer available to protect them with his still imposing presence.

He chose Lucius Licinius Lucullus (118–50 BC) for this responsibility. This man was a nephew of Metellus Numidicus, so his son Metellus Pius (who had for a long time been a friend and political associate of Sulla's), was his first cousin. He was therefore from the close circle already around Sulla and was trusted by him. He had supported Sulla during the Social War and also had a long history with Sulla against Mithradates of Pontus. He was the man who had allowed Mithradates to escape the clutches of Fimbria, on Sulla's orders. Later he had taken Sulla on his ships to meet with Mithradates face to face to arrange their treaty. In 79 BC he held an aedileship with his brother. He was to show his friendship by accepting the guardianship, which Sulla asked of him, and was also to undertake the publishing of Sulla's memoirs after his death, again proving himself a good friend. He would later become propraetor in Africa in 77 BC and he went on to become Consul in 74 BC.[24]

Sulla's prophecy from the Chaldean seer many years before had told him that he would die at the height of his success and *felicitas*. He had already managed to achieve as much as any man could reasonably be expected to do, furthermore he had done it from very unpromising beginnings. He had good reason to be proud of his achievements, and it might have been obvious that he had already reached, if not passed, the pinnacle of his career. But although he was naturally and prudently making what preparations he could, he did not seem to have any intimation that his death might be imminent. He was working steadily on his memoirs, when he recounted that he had had one of his prophetic dreams. This one, however, was more poignant and disturbing than most.

He described seeing his elder son, the young man of hope and promise whose death must have caused him such grief. The young man called to him, and invited him to go with him, and to join him and Caecilia Metella, to live with them both in peace and quiet.[25]

Even with his religious sensibilities and his natural desire to be reunited with lost loved ones, such a warning from the 'other side' must have been something of a shock and brought to the forefront of Sulla's mind the knowledge that his time was now short.

However, apart from recounting his vision, he carried on with his normal routine.

One day in 78 BC Sulla heard that the settlers he had established at Puteoli were at odds with the original inhabitants there and he decided to visit them, using his authority as their patron, to give them a charter which was intended to end their arguments. He then heard, shortly after this, that one of the colony's magistrates, a man named Quintus Granius, was deliberately holding on to money which by rights belonged to the treasury of the colony and despite every approach he was refusing to pay it back.

The Granius family had for generations dominated the area, being the local bankers and shipping magnates. They no doubt considered themselves to be the most prominent and important family in the area, quite beyond the laws made for everyone else, and certainly beyond apprehension or any kind of punishment for ill-doing.[26] The town was in serious financial difficulties due to Granius' refusal to hand over the money he held, but he was intransigent and Sulla was asked to deal with him personally. Detesting peculation as he always had, and still concerned to uphold the rights of the ordinary people against the rich and powerful, Sulla ordered that this man be brought before him.

Despite Sulla's awe-inspiring presence and the possibility of real punishment Granius was still obdurate, refusing to hand over the money. Sulla, possibly tired out as well as angry, lost his temper with him. He was already getting old by Roman standards and had never spared himself effort. He was not perhaps in the best of health and may even have been miserably aware that his hold on things was beginning to slide. He may also have been far more unnerved by his recent disturbing dream about his son than he ever openly admitted. Illness and anxiety are not conducive to good temper, particularly in a man who was accustomed to being obeyed. He would certainly have been furious that a magistrate of one of his own colonies should dare to embezzle money openly in the way Granius had done, in direct contravention of all Sulla's laws. Sulla's unfortunate loss of temper on that day can easily be explained. However, its result was to be a disaster. He had demanded that Granius repay what he owed to the people of Puteoli, and the man had again refused when Sulla cried out angrily that he should be executed for his presumption.

Before anyone could make a move to obey his order, Sulla was taken suddenly ill. For a man whose main health problem until then had been the skin ailment, which had made his life difficult for so long, but which by then he may have grown almost accustomed to living with, this new and unexpectedly violent attack must have been a complete shock. He began to haemorrhage profusely from the mouth.

This is one of the classic signs of acute liver failure, due no doubt to the heavy drinking in which he had taken refuge, initially, years previously, in an attempt to minimize the effects of the painful shingles in his face, but which may by then have become habitual.

His illness caused panic among the people surrounding him and they must have started running in all directions, calling for doctors and doing their best to make him as comfortable as possible, but there was nothing they could do that would help him. In our time, if the condition had not progressed too far to benefit from surgery, something might have been done. For Sulla, suffering such a sudden collapse, indicative as it was that the condition had already become terminal, there could be no remedy. The toxins build up rapidly in the body and he would have quickly lapsed into delirium, which was probably a blessing. In such cases the end is not normally far off, despite all the doctors can do now to aid the patient, and in his time they would have been perfectly helpless. On reaching this stage, the patient normally expires within twenty-four hours.

Although it was mercifully a relatively short final illness, Sulla might be said to have died as hard as he had lived, fighting against greed and injustice, almost literally with his last breath. He was 60 years old.

There would be, of course, a state funeral. He was, after all, a man who had ruled the Roman world. It would also have to outshine even his great Triumph, but that was not to prove to be a problem. It was at this time that it became obvious just how many true friends Sulla had actually had. The people of Rome wished, indeed intended, to show their respects to him openly. His funeral pyre was to be enhanced by huge amounts of spices and unguents, which was customary. What did come as a surprise to those organizing the event was that these extremely expensive and luxurious items, ingredients which would cost literally a fortune, should be donated for the occasion by the women of Rome. They actually provided so much frankincense, myrrh, cinnamon, balsam and every other imaginable aromatic spice that there was plenty and to spare for the pyre itself. This was customary to disguise the aroma of cremation, but on this occasion there was also enough left over to allow the organizers to have a life-sized statue of Sulla, made entirely out of the remainder. Cost was obviously not to be considered by the donors, there was only their intense desire to do what they could to pay the proper tribute.

There is no evidence of hatred here. There is no evidence that the people of Rome wished to abuse or manhandle his body, as they had done with that of Pompeius Strabo before he could be buried. There was to be absolutely no disgrace for Sulla at the last. On the contrary, it was obvious that his burial was to be conducted with every possible dignity and with the full respect of the spectators.

It was customary for the body to be displayed, followed by wagons which also displayed his trophies and 'crowns' which were the golden wreaths given to him by towns and rulers from all over the world, as their tokens of esteem. Other floats depicted his life and achievements, and special ones would show actors, impersonating his ancestors, wearing wax images of their faces, to accompany him to his funeral, as if his real ancestors had come to life for the day to also show him honour. Particularly prominent at his funeral were his troops, who were conspicuous in their determination to attend in order to show all of Rome the extent of their continuing devotion to their commander.

The procession wound its way into the Forum, where Lucullus gave the eulogy from the rostra.[27] The whole circus then continued on to the Fontinalis Gate, heading for the Campus Martius. His tomb was intended to be on the Via Lata near to the area where the Centuriate Assembly met. It is said that when the torches were set to the pyre to light it, a strong wind blew up, causing the flames to roar into life. The body was consumed quickly surrounded by the sweet-smelling herbs and spices. The pyre is said to have burned so fiercely that the people watching began to be concerned that it would be difficult to douse the flames. However, as soon as the body was completely burned, it began to rain. The heavy downpour then quenched the flames without difficulty. It was as though Fortuna was staying by her especial favourite until the end.

Sulla's ashes were eventually deposited inside his tomb, which bore inscriptions with his name and rank, and gave details of his achievements. Along with these details, there was what might be taken to be his motto, which claimed that he was not only the fiercest enemy, but also the best and most faithful friend that anyone could have.[28] This declaration, undoubtedly true, proclaimed that he had always been a good friend to those who had befriended him and been trustworthy, and he had equally been a firm enemy to those who had opposed him or had shown themselves the enemies of his beloved Republic. Plutarch tells us that Sulla's tomb was still on the Campius Martius, with its inscriptions still perfectly readable, when he saw it two centuries later.

Sulla, throughout his life, had certainly proved that the Republic, in which he so firmly believed, could have had in him 'no better friend'.

Chapter Seventeen

Sulla's legacy was necessarily limited. History usually belongs to the last man standing and, unfortunately for the continuance of the Republic, Sulla was not the last man.

The men who would follow after him did not share his ideals and would not be so determined to protect the constitution he had tried so hard to make. On the contrary, once his strong hand was removed, there was again a melee of disorder, with each leading man trying to force himself to the top of the pile.

In 78/77 BC, after Pompeius and Catulus had defeated Lepidus, Pompeius was sent off to govern Spain. Even on his way to his new posting he dealt with another rebellion in Gaul. However, by the following year, Pompeius found himself being beaten by Sertorius, who had become very powerful in Spain with a great deal of support. He was even powerful enough to make an alliance with Mithradates of Pontus, who was always willing to help ferment trouble for Rome.[1]

By 75 BC Gaius Aurelius Cotta, the then Consul, passed a law once again allowing the tribunes to stand for higher office after they had completed their period of service. This was in direct contravention of the law Sulla had previously passed intending to prevent them from using the tribunate as a stepping stone to such higher offices. It was also mainly meant to curb the accompanying great temptation presented to them, which involved 'selling' their veto to the highest bidders in order to make their fortunes. Sulla's much-needed common sense measure, designed to prevent such customary misapplication of their powers, was therefore successfully cast out, leaving the tribunate once again wide open to exactly the sort of abuses that Sulla had attempted to prevent. The following year Nicomedes of Bithynia died, leaving his kingdom to the care of Rome. That did not, of course, prevent the ever-troublesome Mithradates from immediately declaring war on Rome and grasping at the opportunity of invading the unprotected Bithynia, before Rome could make a move to safeguard it.[2] Lucullus was obliged to go abroad in order to oppose him in his expansionist ambitions in Asia. At the same time, Antonius (then a praetor) was given a commission to deal with the pirates who were yet again infesting the Middle Sea, to the ruination of safe trading. Unfortunately, he was not able to make any really permanent satisfactory ending to the problem.

Between 73 and 71 BC attention shifted to the Italian mainland, where the escaped slave Spartacus was gathering men and leading a revolt. He had initially done well, probably due to his military training. (He had originally been in the army, but seemed to have a problem with accepting discipline and had been given the choice of becoming a gladiator or being severely punished for a number of offences.) He defeated Cassius Longinus and Mutina but he then roamed over Italy with his following horde as though he was unsure where he intended to go. He made camp for some time on the slopes of Vesuvius, as he knew the area well and his family originally came from there, but it was obvious that he could not stay in one place for too long. His group of followers was growing and there would have to be measures taken to prevent him from becoming any more of a problem.

He may have been intending to join Sertorius in Spain, but he could not know that by this time Sertorius had already been killed (in 73 BC) by the treachery of one Marcus Veiento Perperna.[3] This man had originally declined to join Sulla, then abandoned Sicily to Pompeius. He had taken Lepidus' army over to Spain and joined Sertorius there, but he eventually grew jealous of Sertorius' successes and attempted a takeover. Due to trickery he then succeeded in assassinating him. The following year he was in his turn completely overwhelmed by Pompeius and duly executed. Spartacus and his ever-growing band of followers were then left with no final destination. After some time of indecision, which forced them to move up and down the mainland, and after being defrauded out of their funds by pirates who had promised them safe passage to Sicily, they were finally brought to bay and were defeated by Crassus in Lucania. In the same year Lucullus was able to concentrate on settling Asia's debt problems.

By 70 BC Pompeius and Crassus, that most unlikely of combinations between two men who mutually disliked each other, were sharing the consulship. Full power was restored to the tribunate, giving them back not only the veto Sulla had considered them too corrupt to hold but all their old privileges too. Aurelius Cotta then reconstituted Sulla's criminal courts.

By 67 BC Pompeius Magnus was given full commission to rid the Middle Sea of the pirates nobody else seemed able to control. He did a wonderful job in a very short time, forcing them all into one area, where they were cleared up and executed. For the first time in many years the Middle Sea was open to proper trade without fear of the captures, outright thievery and illegal hostage taking which had become such a feature over the years.

In 66 BC Pompeius Magnus received full power from Gaius Manilius, then a tribune, who proposed the Manilian Law giving him permission to go abroad to finally crush Mithradates, replacing Lucullus. King Mithradates was finally defeated, and for the following couple of years Pompeius was to fight for Rome again, firstly against the Iberi and Albani and then in Syria, where he overthrew the Selucid monarch's power.

By 63 BC the young Gaius Julius Caesar, who was proving to be every bit as brilliantly charismatic and arrogantly ambitious as Sulla had always feared, became the Pontifex Maximus. Pompeius besieged Jerusalem in the same year, and finally Mithradates of Pontus died. He had been so much of a thorn in Rome's flesh for so many years that it must have been a relief to everyone to finally hear of his demise. Pompeius, consolidating his successes, made Syria, Cilicia and Bythinia into full provinces in the following year, and held his Triumph in 61 BC in Rome, while Caesar was governing Further Spain.

Pompeius Magnus had been married to Mucia Tertia, daughter of the lawyer Quintus Mucius Scaevola who had borne him his two sons, Gnaeus and Sextus and a daughter. On his return from the East Pompeius had divorced her, apparently for her adultery with Caesar![4] Caesar's liaisons with the married women of Rome were not only notorious but conducted quite openly. It can have been no consolation to the husbands concerned, when he was cutting a swathe through the virtues of their wives, to know that they were not the only ones suffering from the problem. It is surprising that none of them ever attempted to do anything about it, except in some cases divorce the lady concerned. However, Caesar now did his best to reconcile Pompeius to Crassus and by the year 60 BC the first (unofficial) Triumvirate was formed, bringing Caesar, Pompeius and Crassus himself into a coalition. These three men, heartily mistrustful of each other, had been well known to Sulla. In one way or another he had been deeply suspicious of them all, knowing them to be grasping and ambitious and in each case quite unscrupulous how they achieved their ends. They were together to form a most unlikely alliance.

Caesar then tried to do exactly what Sulla had done, in binding Magnus to him and his cause by the use of the marriage tie. He offered Pompeius Magnus his only daughter Julia and this became an unusual love match, given that Magnus was by then middle-aged and the girl thirty years his junior and it is said, very beautiful. She could potentially have married anyone, but Caesar needed Pompeius and successfully tied him down by using Julia. It was during the time of this marriage that Pompeius built his wonderful theatre, in an extensive complex on the Campus Martius, including a forum surrounded by one hundred columns, complete with senate house and temple of Venus. However, just like Sulla's stepdaughter Aemilia Scaura, Julia was to die young. Their marriage – so vital to Caesar at that time – had in fact lasted for six or seven years, but Julia had suffered a miscarriage or two and she eventually died in childbirth. (Pompeius seemed to be unlucky with his wives in that regard.) Caesar, though reported to have been very grieved at her death, as was Pompeius, quickly offered the widower another wife, in a desperate effort to keep him within the 'family' fold.[5] However, this time Pompeius was not tempted and refused the offer of a new bride who might benefit Caesar, preferring instead to marry Cornelia, daughter of Quintus Caecilius Metellus (known as Pius Scipio). He then threatened Caesar's position still further by making his new father-in-law his colleague for the remainder of that year.

Whatever the obvious differences between the three leaders, they managed to cling together long enough, so that in 56 BC their unholy alliance was extended for a further five years. However, they had never been really friends and once Julia Caesaris was dead Pompeius Magnus began to slip away from Caesar slowly but surely, in exactly the same way that he had some years earlier done with Sulla. He was again proving himself to be the sort of man who was very difficult to keep a firm hold of.

Caesar may have had a better relationship, certainly a longer lasting one, with Crassus. This was another man who had proved himself venal and from whom Sulla had preferred to dissociate himself, but Caesar seemed to get on fairly well with him, probably because he was still deeply in his debt. (Even as Pontifex Maximus Caesar had had to have Crassus stand as guarantor for him, before he could leave Rome, so enormous were his debts that the people to whom he owed money feared he would never be able to pay.) Crassus had the Midas touch when it came to making money, though his methods usually left a great deal to be desired morally. He was famous for his ability to lend almost any amount of money at short notice from his own vast funds, while refusing to charge interest, which might on the surface have made him the number-one favourite moneylender of the indigent in Rome. However, instead of interest being charged, he tended to demand a full return of the amount loaned without notice, merely at his request. This was generally impossible for men to manage, so instead he took possession of whatever estates they had. In this, and other equally unprincipled ways he had amassed an amazing fortune. Unfortunately, he was not to be able to enjoy it for too long, for in 53 BC he was defeated and killed at the battle of Carrhae fighting against the Parthians.[6]

Caesar and Pompeius Magnus now faced each other alone. Their relationship had already begun to slide, possibly through the jealousy of Magnus, who was by then on his third consulship, a position he held without a colleague for some months in 52 BC.

Caesar had by this realized that he would need to follow his governorship with a period of office in Rome, otherwise he would be open to prosecutions. He could not aim for his second consulship (which would protect him) until 48 BC. He therefore attempted to stand for the consulship as soon as he possibly could, but in absentia. Pompeius agreed to this, but at the same time he arranged that his own absentee governorship of Spain should be extended for a further five years. He hoped that a new provincial commander could be discussed as his replacement in March of 50 BC. However, Caesar, fully aware that he could not trust Pompeius, had also already taken steps to protect his own position. He by then had the backing of a new young tribune, Gaius Scribonius Curio. He was to prove just how sensible Sulla's previous measures in acting against the tribunes had been; purely by the way he proceeded to use his tribunate. He persistently vetoed any demands Pompeius made for a discussion regarding his own necessary replacement, and this impasse went on for so long that it became ridiculous. This extreme and obstructive behaviour was, of course, exactly what Sulla had tried to prevent when he took away the power of veto from the tribunes. Curio went on to suggest that Pompeius should resign his post, and that Caesar should resign his also, to end the impasse. The Senate agreed to this measure, but the diehards vetoed it yet again, resulting in further deadlock and delays.

The split between Julius Caesar and Pompeius Magnus was now complete, and in January of 49 BC the Senate passed the Ultimate Decree against the threat now presented by Caesar. Also in 49 BC Caesar crossed the Rubicon and became Dictator for just eleven days, before going on to win the siege of Massilia, while Curio was killed in Africa.[7] Caesar's march into Rome had been quite unlike Sulla's in that Sulla had intended to protect and strengthen the Senate and the Republic itself. In Caesar's case, the march was to strengthen his own position, which otherwise would have slipped away, and to entrench himself at the centre of affairs from which he would rule alone, a king in all but name. Caesar certainly had no problem with the idea of the rule of one man, as Sulla had truly had, always believing firmly in the role of the Senate as the supreme power, designed to prevent one man from becoming too strong and overtaking his peers.

Caesar, on the other hand, had enough belief in his own aristocratic birth, his own abilities, and even in that mythical spark of divinity that he was convinced he possessed, to be able to quite easily see himself as the ruler of the world. Even if for the time being it remained expedient to give lip service to the Republican ideal. If Rome was to have one ruler, even if he could not dare to officially call himself a king, so be it, so long as Caesar was to be that ruler, that one man to whom all others would defer. But even he would not dare to eventually lay down the power as Sulla had done, nor could he feel entirely safe in the position he had appropriated for himself. He would also, eventually, have to pay for his presumption with his life when the strong feeling against him reached such proportions that his assumption of power could no longer be tolerated.

The nation had fallen into another civil war, but unlike the war in which Sulla had been involved, this was not to save the Republic, which was already on its last legs, as the Triumvirate had already taken away all of its real power. The new civil war would also not be confined to the Italian peninsula alone but would eventually involve the empire itself. Pompeius had intended to fight Caesar abroad rather than in Italy, and he moved his troops to Macedonia, collecting a formidable army from all the eastern provinces to use against him. In the spring of 48 BC he beat Caesar at Dyrrachium but in the following August was routed in his turn by Caesar in a pitched battle at Pharsalus in Greece.[8] Disillusioned, he then left for Egypt with his wife, arriving there on 28 September 48 BC, but whatever hopes of refuge and a new life there he may have had were to come to nothing. Immediately on his arrival he was killed on the orders of the young King Ptolemy XIII, a weak and foolish boy who thought he was doing Caesar a favour by arranging the assassination of his enemy.

The death of Pompeius Magnus was to prove a catalyst for Rome, in that Caesar, with his victory at Pharsalus and Pompeius' death, was to take over Rome completely, but not entirely without opposition. Pompeius Magnus' sons and their followers were still to continue the struggle against Caesar, culminating in the great battle at Thapsus in April of 46 BC.

After Caesar's triumph there against the Pompeiians, 10,000 unarmed men attempted to surrender to Caesar, but he ordered that they should be killed. It must be remembered that these men were not barbarians or savages, but Romans like himself. Nonetheless, they were all executed. Also killed after the battle, on Caesar's orders and at the hand of Sittius, was Sulla's only surviving son Faustus Cornelius Sulla.[9]

In 44 BC Caesar became Dictator for Life. The Rome, which Sulla had spent all those years fighting to protect, the Republic in which he had believed so implicitly, was dead.

Caesar's own assassination was finally accomplished, after much plotting, in March of 44 BC and, ironically enough, was to take place in the very senate house built by Pompeius Magnus on the Campus Martius. Caesar's dead body, riddled with up to sixty stab wounds, is popularly supposed to have fallen at the feet of a statue of Pompeius Magnus. However, even this assassination could not restore what had been destroyed, simply because it had been arranged by men who did not share Sulla's ideals.

Sulla's surviving family members could not avoid being involved in the upheavals which took place in Rome during those years after his death. His elder son had, of course, predeceased him and his elder daughter Cornelia, by his first wife Julia, had been married early to Quintus Pompeius Rufus. Her daughter Pompeia, Sulla's granddaughter and a girl reputed to possess the Sulla family beauty, was in 68 BC to become Caesar's second wife. He was to divorce her in 61 BC after the scandal of the Bona Dea celebrations, during which Publius Clodius Pulcher, that young blood about town, was apprehended gate-crashing an important all-female festivity while he was thinly disguised as a dancing girl! The scandal made the festival a sacrilege and caused great worry to those of real religious feeling, as the Bona Dea was concerned with the luck of all of

Rome, not just its women, and his foolish action caused outrage, so much so that Clodius was put on trial.[10]

It was considered too serious a matter to ignore and some people were happy to believe that he had gone to the house to seduce Pompeia herself, rather than indulge in a silly prank. She was probably perfectly innocent but Caesar divorced her, making the famous remark about Caesar's wife being 'above suspicion'. What he really meant was that the wife of the Pontifex Maximus needed to remain above any suspicion. He may, of course, already have been indulging in a little of the feeling of exclusivity and hauteur which was to mark his later position, and perhaps also resented the idea that any man might attempt to do what he had already done so freely around the city. Whatever Caesar's real motive for divorcing Pompeia had been (and as she was childless, that may also have been a factor), Clodius was acquitted at his trial, but only because the jury had been bribed sufficiently by Crassus.

Clodius was later to be involved in the civil disturbances of the mid–century, while engaging in gang warfare against the followers of Milo. This disorder had gone on for quite some time, with each side employing mobs of roughs to not only protect them, but also to engage in street fighting whenever they met. In January of 52 BC he was apprehended by one of these mobs, employed by Milo, while he was travelling. Despite having some supporters with him he was outnumbered and was subsequently murdered by Milo's supporters at Bovillae.[11]

Fausta Sulla, the daughter of Sulla and Caecilia Metella, was married to Gaius Memmius after having been the ward of Lucullus, as Sulla had carefully arranged for his children's safety. However, Memmius had developed a hatred for the Lucullus family and Fausta suffered the fallout from that. In 54 BC Memmius divorced her. She went on to marry none other than Titus Annius Milo, whose family had held the hereditary priesthood at Lanuvium. In 53 BC he stood for office, aiming at the consulship of 52 BC. Also standing for election in that year was Publius Clodius Pulcher. Determined to succeed, Milo invested almost 1,000,000 sesterces into putting on wonderful games as an inducement to voters. However, due to the disorders taking place in Rome at that time, largely between the supporters of Clodius and Milo, no elections were held at all and in January 52 BC Milo's men went on to kill Clodius at Bovillae.

As Sulla's only surviving son, Faustus Cornelius Sulla must have felt his family responsibilities keenly. He was to try very hard to uphold his father's reputation despite Rome's teetering on the brink and despite also the destruction of most of what his father had tried too hard to accomplish. Even Sulla's little senate house, his Curia Hostilia, had burned down in 52 BC and Faustus took it upon himself to have it completely restored.[12]

He was to fight alongside the Pompeiians even after the death of Magnus in Egypt, then led by his son Sextus Pompeius Magnus Pius. No son of Sulla's could countenance the idea of Caesar, with his desire for dominance, being ultimately the victor, so his alliance with Pompeius' son was natural enough.

Sextus Pompeius had gone with his father in his flight to Egypt and seen him killed there. After that time he made his way to Africa. He was to fight at Thapsus in April of 46 BC along with all those of his father's followers who continued to oppose Caesar. Unlike Faustus Sulla, Sextus Pompeius had managed to escape from the field of Thapsus, eventually fleeing to Spain. Faustus, however, always as true a republican as his revered father had been, was captured after the battle. Perhaps Caesar saw something of his father in him that he would not be able to allow to live and fight on, as Sulla once, many years before, had remarked that he saw something of Marius in Caesar? Perhaps something of that intransigence which he knew would never give in to him? Whatever the reason, Caesar gave a specific order for the death of Faustus Sulla and he was executed. He was 40 years old.

Also executed after their defeat at Thapsus were the already mentioned 10,000 troops of the Pompeiian faction's supporters, even though they were unarmed and apparently attempting to surrender. If the proscriptions have stained Sulla's name forever, then that action at Thapsus, so much more extensive in its brutal scale, its lack of discrimination, and also so totally unnecessary, should certainly have stained Caesar's! It was something that Sulla, despite his blackened name and his so-called 'ruthless' streak, would never have permitted to happen.

Sulla's other work, however, lived on. His land allocations to his veterans, given not only as reward for services rendered to the republic, but also as an attempt to repopulate the areas concerned, had resulted in the eventual growth of prosperous colonies.[13] A relative of Sulla's, one Publius Cornelius Sulla, was to become prominent in that most Sullan of towns, the one whose charms Sulla had refused to allow to be destroyed, Pompeii. It became *Colonia Cornelia Venusia Pompeianorum* and there was a definite change in the constituent parts of its population, with new faces on its town council and many new businessmen achieving a high level of prosperity in the years ahead.[14] Other colonies were also to survive; Abellinum, Allifae, Ardea and of course Nola. There was Clusium, Arretum, Florentia, Faesulae and Interimna and last but certainly not the least, Praeneste itself, which held the huge temple to Fortuna Primagenia, the goddess Sulla revered.

The love and devotion of Sulla's troops was also still evident after his death. It is certainly enough to show what sort of man he was, when in contact with people who knew him well and had reason to trust him. With these men there was no standing on ceremony, except for the proper respect due him as their commander. Keeping oneself aloof from one's men would, in many of the situations they had shared, have been a grave and foolish mistake. No man will respect a leader who considers himself to be too superior to his men.

I remember reading an account given by a man who had served under Field Marshall Montgomery.[15] This veteran forcefully expressed his resentment at what he considered to be that famous leader's too casual attitude. His particular grievance centred on Montgomery's constant use of sporting metaphors to describe the difficulties they faced in battle. It was made clear that the ordinary soldiers were angered and offended by the fact that he seemed to consider the battle situation to be some game of sport. The man who wrote the later account emphasized that he and his fellow soldiers were always very conscious that their leaders seemed to cheerfully disregard the fact that it was actually men's lives on the line. It all meant far more to them than their leaders' ideas of 'a sporting chance' whether an action were successful or not, or that it was merely 'jolly bad luck' if they suffered too many casualties. A great pity that an otherwise competent leader should leave behind him such a sour memory of lack of consideration for the feelings of his men.

No soldier, unless he is a fanatic, wants to enter a battle zone expecting to be maimed or killed, even though he must be aware that the possibility is always present. He does need to be convinced that his leaders are not only competent in their respective duties, but also that they have some consideration for his welfare and safety. Without that, there can be no trust in him and his command is likely to fail under pressure. Sulla's men always knew that he had a concern for the ordinary soldier and that he could moreover be friendly and approachable. This mutual confidence was shown by the men offering him their own money when they knew he had little, which was surely a most unusual display of respect and trust. Also to be taken into consideration is the rapidity with which the troops of other commanders, not just once but several times, abandoned their leaders to desert to Sulla. They, too, must have been aware that he was a superior leader and also that he was a more reliable man.

This ability to connect with people of all different classes was something which must have been fairly unusual in Sulla's own time. In our own time everyone likes to imagine they have the 'common touch', from so-called celebrities who live a rarified lifestyle, to grinning politicians who pretend that they understand the problems of ordinary people. In Rome this pretence at understanding would hardly have been necessary. Upper class people would have had little to do with their inferiors and would not have considered it a requirement to consider their opinions. Sulla, despite his patrician birth, did not quite fit in with his peers. Partly due to his chronic lack of money, which prevented him from joining the young bloods of his own class in their amusements, but also partly because he formed friendships with people of the 'lower orders' of their society. This attachment to unsuitable friends would have been incomprehensible to them.

Unfortunately, this lack of any real bonding with so many people of his own class was to dog him all his life. It might even be said to have shown its face when he was Dictator and an Auger. His colleagues in the college of augers convinced him into forcing his then wife, Caecilia Metella, from his house, when her mortal illness made her 'unclean' in religious terms.[16]

He has been criticized for actually divorcing her when she was obviously dying, but we cannot possibly know what pressure he was under from his fellow augers to make the break open and final. Why would they do this? It is not too far-fetched to assume that even in the college of augers there were members who still felt a personal dislike or distaste for him. When a man chooses many of his closest friends from a different section of society it can be taken as a form of criticism of his own kind. This can be resented. If people are prevented from expressing their dislike openly, they can often do so in subtle and petty ways. By this behaviour they not only reduce the victim of their malice in their own eyes, but also boost themselves due to the power gained over him. Forcing Sulla to actually divorce a beloved wife under the guise of correct religious procedure would be a perfect example of this. They would know that, with Sulla's strong religious beliefs, he would be unable to refuse. He would not wish to offend the gods and would accede to their demands even if the decision would cause him personal pain. There is no evidence of personal malice in his action towards her. His true feelings towards the lady were surely shown by the generous, even extravagant, funeral which he then arranged for her.

On the other hand, Sulla's ability to form quite familiar relationships and attachments to other people was not confined only to personal friendships or even the respect he received from his troops. His own servants were also recipients of examples of his generous and familiar nature. Of course, in Rome, slavery was not quite always what we presume it to have been. Certainly, the poor victims on the large agricultural estates, probably bought in batches and worked to death, or the young girls sold into brothels, would have nothing good to say about it, and we must concur with the horror of one person owning another. However, many slaves were treated quite differently.

Many young Greeks sold themselves into slavery, often as tutors, in order to achieve a better lifestyle and in hope of a secure future. A good slave, well qualified, would be valued accordingly and would not only be well treated but also able to expect to either be freed eventually, or earn enough money to buy himself free.[17] Most households would have had a steward, trained in the running of the house and even in the administration of the accounts. Such people were often greatly trusted and essentially a part of the family. Unfortunately, Sulla had found that his own steward, Chrysogonus, was not trustworthy but not all examples were to prove so extreme. Many were treated as part of the family.

Later on, during the even more degenerate Empire, it became the expensive if pointless fashion to have slaves who were supposed to be specialists in one ridiculous aspect or another of domestic life. For instance, there could be a slave particularly trained to dust the marble busts which decorated the house, or one specially instructed in the care of togas, or the lady's jewels. These people, whose real talents may have been few, certainly brought extremely high prices, and would have been consequently treated well, if only to display to the world that their owners could afford the waste of money on trivia.

It was common in Rome to free slaves, giving them the family name and setting them up in some business. Of course, the patron would take a share of the profits of that business but the slave could still look forward to not only a reasonable prosperity (and some actually became rich) but more importantly he knew that his children would be born free. In the meantime, he had a patron to help and advise him and a steady and secure place in the world. One of Sulla's fortunate freedmen, taking Sulla's family name as was customary, was known as Lucius Cornelius Epicadus, and became well known as a writer.[18]

In another famous case Cicero's family slave, Tiro, was so highly regarded within that family that when he was finally freed, after many years of devoted service as a trusted steward, Cicero's brother complained that it should have been done years previously. This was due to the man being obviously far too good to be a servant, even such a highly paid and highly valued one, and they regarded him far more as an associate.[19]

Regarding Sulla's loss of good name, which he would personally have considered unfair, it is futile to pretend that the proscriptions Sulla instituted on his return to Rome and to personal power have not blackened that name and influenced the general perception of him as a man. However, it is equally futile to pretend that these incidents were in any way unusual, or that as a man he took any particular pleasure in such activities.

Gaius Marius certainly proscribed, turning Rome into something resembling the 'Terror' in eighteenth century France. Pompeius Magnus was known as the 'young butcher' by Helvius due to his enthusiasm in killing, probably drawn from a childhood and adolescence spent watching his father cut swathes through the population. He certainly had no compunction in ending the lives of innocent people. Neither did Caesar who followed in his footsteps.

Caesar certainly cannot be separated from his wonderful achievements as a general. He was one of those unusual men who not only had the knack of making his men like and respect him, but also possessed an amazing talent as a military leader. However, in his private life he was less impressive. He certainly believed that he was something special, and that he could therefore do largely as he wished. From one end of the empire to the other he killed efficiently, culminating in the appalling murder of so many Romans at Thapsus. These excesses were unfortunately all too common to the war leaders and would hardly have been considered a matter for shame, merely that a man was doing his duty in ridding the republic of people who would be its natural opponents in defiance of public order. Neither were the republican leaders alone in this, as such behaviour became even more common and even more extreme under the Empire.

Much later, in Byzantium, during the reign of Justinian, there was a revolt in which a large part of the city was destroyed. Order was 'restored' by Belisarius who trapped the crowds in the Hippdrome and simply waded in with his troops, killing more than 30,000 people on that day.[20] These examples are given merely to show that such subjugation of the people by force was not considered reprehensible, merely a necessary adjunct of ruling.

However, that a show of force is sometimes the only option is undoubted, although often regrettable. A purge could be required not only to restore order during times of anarchy, but also to rid society of disruptive elements likely to cause even more bloodshed in the future. Or it may necessitate the removal of people whose alternative ideas to the accepted norm may even be blocking the route to healthy prosperity for the majority of the people, whose requirements must be considered paramount.

Sulla's own purge had certainly been necessary in order to try to get Rome back on her feet, after a long period of conflict. He had to eventually attempt to eliminate those people who refused to accede to the need for basic common sense measures, knowing that they would never consent to settle down within the framework of law and constitution that he was attempting to put in place. That the funds of these people were then used to restore Rome, both in building work itself and to refill the empty treasuries, provided a chance for prosperity and security to be regained. These measures may well prove unfortunate, certainly to those who can be considered victims. However, if the body politic, just like a physical body, does not respond to normal procedures, then sometimes those more extreme measures may have to be tried, in order to preserve peace for the good of all the citizens. It is hardly democratic, or even basically sensible, to allow a disruptive element to take over, which would then destroy good order.

What Sulla never did, in marked contrast to other leaders, was to blame or punish the ordinary people. His measures were aimed at those whom he considered had behaved badly and he frequently made a point of ensuring that the lesser people were not to be harmed in any way. He never intended them to be held accountable for the crimes of their superiors, and in this regard he was very unusual indeed among his peers.

Despite the regular assertions that Sulla was soundly hated in his own time, there is actually little evidence of this, except reports of inflammatory talk.[21] Naturally, anyone who held a grievance might be inclined to believe in it and perhaps pass on their own feelings, with embellishments. But the general attitude of the people towards Sulla belies this. Not only the already mentioned personal friendships or the respect of his troops, but the attitude of the women of Rome who provided such amazing amounts of valuable ointments and spices at the time of his funeral. These actions must not be discounted, showing as they clearly do the desire of less powerful people to show their respect.

Sulla's ability to touch the sensibilities of the average Roman is also shown in his love of the theatre, with another group of firm friends being won by him due to his ability as a writer and versifier. It was fashionable to decry his associations with these theatrical circles, but his own peers were not averse to a little rough trade when the fancy took them. They certainly had no reason to consider themselves superior to him either in their friendships or in their sexual proclivities. There are no details of what he is supposed to have done, no rapes, no orgies, no recorded cruelties to account for it. Others in many cases far exceeded him in real debauchery and delinquency, well recorded.

These 'hatreds' seem to stem from something else entirely. The blackening of a foe's character, particularly after his death, is quite common. It not only makes those who come after him appear better in themselves (as we know, history belongs to the winners), and if they can feel, or claim, that the deceased is in some way wicked or evil, they are able to actually change history itself. An accusation, made often enough and not refuted firmly enough, tends to become accepted as being a correct and truthful account. How many times has an historical character been maligned, only for historians to later find that their real persona was quite different? The 'character' which comes down to us often bears little or no relation to the actual, living, person who was known to his intimates.

When Richard III was killed at Bosworth in 1485 the Tudors went out of their way to present a quite different picture of the man, than the one known to his friends and supporters. They also found it convenient to blame on him all the troubles they were responsible for, making him a very useful scapegoat.[22] Even when they went on to murder all the survivors of the old White Rose royal family, over a period of years, men and women alike, their efficient casting of opprobrium on the reputation of the defeated royal family ensured that their actions were accepted without open resistance.

Likewise, when Anne Boleyn was murdered by her husband Henry VIII in 1536 it was in his interests to have her shown as everything from an adulteress to a witch! Few people found themselves strong enough to stand out against the obvious injustice, and those few who did were ruthlessly eliminated.[23] Others found it safer to retire from court and say nothing. It did not mean that they privately agreed with the accounts of their masters.

It was not until much later that historians were able to show that in both these cases the real person was very far from being the individual depicted. Anne was not wicked, immoral, overly ambitious or avaricious, but a woman concerned with justice, and education and unwilling to see the immense sums raised from the dissolution of the monasteries being wasted on her husband's foolish extravagances. Richard was a decent man, loyal to his brother King Edward IV and a good soldier. He was greatly revered in Yorkshire for his good qualities and honest lawmaking and furthermore still is, the only King of England with a society dedicated to the preservation of his good name.[24]

In Sulla's case, it was also very much in the interests of those who succeeded him to portray him as a man who was evil and debauched in his personal life and cruel and murderous in his public one. That there was evidence to the contrary was irrelevant.

The voices of his friends, which may have been raised in protest, were unimportant and could easily be ignored. People generally soon forgot how things really were, as they always do, and the opinions of his genuine followers easily dismissed as bias.

Concentrating on the faults, or supposed faults, of the victim very nicely takes away attention from one's own actions, as well as using the possibility of being able to shift responsibility for crimes committed onto the memory of the deceased. Fear also plays its part in the desire to denigrate. People whose own sensibilities were less keen had good reason to fear Sulla's influence. Despite his obvious power during his life and his definite ability to coldly exert punishment for crimes against the state, he also held some disconcertingly modern ideas about justice, particularly towards those very people who would be unlikely to figure in many of his peers' minds at all.

It needs to be remembered that it was Pompeius Strabo who destroyed towns and murdered the inhabitants, and his son Magnus who cheerfully learned from his father and followed his example. It was Caesar who murdered unarmed foes after a battle, during a time of attempted surrender. It was Gaius Marius who gave the order against the people of Ostia, when they attempted to welcome him, and then carried that destruction into Rome itself. It was Crassus who made a study of the best ways to part men from their money and estates, when they had gone to him for help.[25] Not to forget his infamous 'fire brigade' in Rome, which brought him the cheap ownership of numerous properties by the simple expedient of buying up burning insulae before his men would put out the fires, to the endangerment of the lives of the residents trapped inside. Such considerations doubtless bothered him little. He may even have had the fires started in the first place; otherwise it is amazing how often his water carriers found themselves in the right place at the right time. These were examples of the men who infested Rome, who were totally unscrupulous, ambitious, avaricious and oblivious to the lives of others, not Sulla.

Casual cruelty was a fact of Roman life, which we in the present day may find hard to accept, even while we imagine it is not indulged in within our own times. Animal cruelty, child cruelty, serial murders, terrorism, the subjugation of women, and the casual killing of innocent civilians in conflicts are all habits of behaviour, from which we like to pretend we are now completely free. Such belief is a fallacy, and a dangerous one.

The facts give a different picture. We coined the appalling phrase 'collateral damage' as well as inventing fearsome weapons which would have amazed the Romans, efficient at warfare though they were. I won't even begin to describe the horrors of the First and Second World Wars, or the ears 'collected' by soldiers in Vietnam, sometimes very small ones! We tend to forget that we behave exactly as they did, if and when the necessity presents itself. At least the Romans had the firm belief that the punishment should fit the crime, which is something we have forgotten, resulting in much misery from recidivists which otherwise might be avoided. We are certainly little better than they were.

Sulla was a very rare man for his time, in that he preferred to keep his sights on the real culprits without making, or even enjoying, the opportunity to create havoc among the innocent or defenceless. That he fought so hard against the enemies of the republic was patriotism, not cruelty. Even in that he did not exceed his mandate, always taking his instructions from the senate, whose power and authority he respected, even if he did not always get on well with its members on a personal level. He fought tirelessly to strengthen and support that senate, even when the senators were not to be trusted to support him in return. Many of these people were able to work against his ideals after his death, while his true friends had no voice with which to defend his name.

The people who did respect and trust Sulla could do nothing to put right the wildest misconceptions about him, which were designed to ruin his reputation. If they belonged to the upper class (and he did still have friends there too), they would have had their own careers to consider. Too close a connection or even too vigorous a defence of him might prove disastrous when it became time for the distribution of offices. At the very least, it might engender some suspicion. If they belonged to the lower classes, then they might be free to mutter among themselves about any perceived injustice, but their dissatisfaction would go no further. They were already disregarded. The only man of standing who had considered them of any worth was gone and they had no voice except through him. They may well have not recognized the character which was emerging, brought to life by those who had a vested interest in playing down his better attributes, but there was little to be done to change the growing disrespect towards the man they had known.

Generally, people no longer wanted to know if he was a decent, civilized and cultured man, honest and fun loving, quick to do a friend a good turn as well as being loyal and devoted to the state. That he was kind and very fair to his respective wives, and even to Metrobius, or that he treated them all with courtesy and consideration, including the divorced Aelia, from whom he parted with thanks and with gifts.[26] It was moreover a courtesy and respect which they all returned, there being no ill feeling between them. However, this domestic amity was not what his detractors were looking for. Nor did they wish to be reminded that he had abhorred corruption and injustice of all kinds, detested self-seekers and self-promoters and all those who were too selfish to put Rome's welfare ahead of their own, in defence of which he had spent his life.

All these finer attributes of the man were easier and safer to simply push aside as being uninteresting. People are bored by the decent and suspicious of personal charm, which Sulla undoubtedly had in bucket loads, as is well testified by all those who came into personal contact with him. It is evil which attracts, degeneracy which holds interest. Evil is better remembered, not basic honesty, hard work or a genuine desire to do some good.

Sulla's desire to do what he could for Rome is what marks him out the most clearly. He was certainly not the only decent and right-minded man in the city at that time, but they were definitely growing fewer. The old ideals were being eroded and many men had become too corrupted, too easily tempted, to consider worthwhile the sacrifices that others had made, for the way of life they were casually preparing to cast aside. For the majority of men at that time, it must have seemed as if all the opportunities for self-gratification, in their political as well as their personal lives, had come at once. If grasping at a future on the other side of the present muddle meant throwing away the ideals and loyalties their forefathers had lived for, then so be it.

This is how important Sulla's life story actually is, not just the life of one man, even if he was still fighting what was essentially a doomed, but valiant, rearguard action to defend a dying republic, being supported by a few remaining moderate and sensible men. It is truly the story of the death of that republic itself. That ideal which had once been so powerful and so valuable, ever since the last king of Rome, Tarquinius Superbus, was expelled in 509 BC and replaced by the first consuls, Lucius Junius Brutus, and Lucius Tarquinius Collatinus.[27] It would have seemed incredible to those eminently honourable men, those first republicans, that even the Republic itself could become outmoded. Even if the men who would eventually come to call themselves 'Emperor', (derived from the generals' title of Imperator), would still never dare to use the title of 'King' so detested had it become. But even if they had difficulties with the title, they had none at all in assuming the power inherent in it, and usually holding on to it, grimly, to the death.

In that also was Sulla different. His real desire to do some good extended to Rome itself. He felt very strongly that he must do what he could to keep Rome strong – not just in her attitude towards foreign enemies, where he had already done his part, never having lost any campaign he undertook – but also in the need to keep the Senate itself strong. That was the bulwark between Rome's citizens and the incursions of men like Cinna, who could and would form their personal takeover bids. He hated the idea of kingship because of the injustices which came with it, inevitable in themselves when the rule of one man, supported by his favourites, was omnipotent.

In Sulla's opinion, the larger the Senate was, the more secure it also was, against attempts to undermine its authority. Simply due to its unwieldiness and the unlikelihood of just one man of ability being able to rule all its members at once. Ironically, in order to promote and support it, to bring it to such strength, Sulla was obliged to take on the 'rule of one man' himself, if only temporarily and ultimately for the good of all. Again, he was to show the clear difference between himself and other, lesser, men. He was to willingly lay down the power when it was at its height, with the entire Roman world at his feet, and I cannot think of any other man of his time who would have done that. Power is a very tempting thing to hold, and men always have difficulty in believing that another man can use it as well as themselves. Yet Sulla, having done the best he could, stepped down, even though he must have known that there was no other man to follow after him who would have done the same. There seems to have been no real desire in him to carry on to the bitter end, which is surely a desire that not even age and illness can destroy. Certainly most people would have been unable and very unwilling to take that courageous step.

He had brought in sensible and reasonable laws, designed to help Rome's financial situation and prevent the appalling waste, which was endemic among the wealthier classes, along with measures designed to curb the corruption always at the heart of the political world. He tried to ease out at least the worst of the abuses and excesses, so that Rome's substance could be used for the good of all.

Arthur Keaveney was absolutely correct in calling him 'the last Republican' for he truly was the last of those men, rare though they always are, who are capable of taking hold of the supreme power, without allowing it to take hold of them.[28] There were few who had many of the old loyalties left and the disorders which were to follow after his death were no more than the usual struggles of ambitious men who wanted to use that power for their own aggrandizement, rather than what it could do for Rome.

Crassus the Rich, in his ill-advised invasion of Parthia threw away not only his own life but also the lives of too many of his army. His demise also dissolved the Triumvirate (unofficial though it might have been), to reveal the open struggle between Caesar and Pompeius Magnus, bringing in its wake a succession of disastrous years for Rome itself. The stability which Sulla had worked so hard to ensure was already gone and the men who squabbled between themselves were too busy fighting to make any real attempt to put anything in its place. The murder of Clodius by the mob supporting Milo may have come as something as a relief to Pompeius Magnus, who had also had issues with Clodius and may have feared the thugs he also employed. Even a man like Magnus was not secure from assassination attempts. But the situation affected Caesar's position too, as he admitted in the seventh book of his *Commentaries*. When Vercingetorix surrendered to Caesar in the autumn of 52 BC there was no longer anything to stand in his way when he intended to return to Rome, even if that meant the crossing of the Rubicon and the march on the city.[29] He would certainly never have stood back, as Sulla had once done, patiently awaiting the deliberations of the Senate, after sending them a reasonable and considered letter expressing his grievances. Caesar then moved with amazing speed towards the city, taking towns as he went, and Pompeius Magnus had to either stand at bay or run. He ran. At least for a time, but eventually he would have to turn and fight and the struggle between those two men, with Pompeius now ageing in his turn, were to lead to his death in Egypt and the well attempted, but ultimately ill-fated, defence by his son at Thapsus.

Pompeius Magnus, probably always conscious of his own father's legacy as a hard-bitten fighter, had fought on valiantly, but had not been able to hold on as well as he had hoped. However, he certainly did not deserve to die at the hands of a stupid boy, even if he was King Ptolemy XIII. Albeit a mere puppet of others who was taking his instructions from his eunuch Pothinus, who in his turn had hoped to benefit from Caesar's approbation after his despicable action.[30] Fortunately even Caesar appeared disgusted at the result.

Caesar managed to force himself into the supreme position – king in all but name – but even he would not be able to hold it for long. For all his obvious charisma and fierce determination there were still too many others who wanted a share, and who resented him for his possession of it. These included Marcus Antonius, Caesar's second cousin, who might have been prepared to stand by as a supporter, but who had his own ideas on the subject of who Caesar's eventual successor ought to be. While Caesar was Dictator Antonius was Master of Horse, and even in that position he showed that he was more inclined to use bully-boy tactics than was practical. His loyalty was to be sorely tested when Caesar's many enemies finally overcame him, and Antonius found that he was not, after all, to have the honour of being Caesar's heir. He had been ousted in favour of Caesar's slight, weakly looking 18-year-old great-nephew, the son of Caesar's niece Atia Balba and her husband Gaius Octavius. That young man, despite his delicate appearance, was to prove more than a match for the more earthy Antonius. Their struggle was to continue until the foolish, and emotionally rather immature, Antonius finally threw in his lot with Egypt, and then paid for it at Actium in 31 BC.[31]

Octavius was sensible enough to realize that he was no war leader, but he was also clever enough to employ a man who was, Marcus Vipsanius Agrippa. Their association was to prove decisive and Agrippa's military ability competently propped up the ambitious and determined young man who was to prove himself perfectly capable of fulfilling all of Caesar's expectations, as he was able to hold together all the disparate elements in Rome.

He was to become the first real Emperor and despite it having been many unsettling years between Sulla's death and any man daring to actually claim that title, the Republic had been in its death throes throughout that time. Although the man who would call himself Augustus liked to claim that he created a balance between himself as ruler and the Senate itself, and even though that Senate appeared to have returned to something like its old position, there was no real doubt that it was Augustus who really ruled from then onwards. From then on it was Augustus alone who controlled Rome's foreign policy and had the power to make war and peace. The Republic was finally, obviously, dead. But this time there would be no attempt to revive it.

The last 150 years of the Republic had been a time when some of the greatest men (together with a few scintillating women), who ever lived walked one after the other across the world stage. There can surely have been no other such time, when so many truly distinguished people lived, many of them within reaching distance of each other, taking turns to step forward into history's spotlight for us to watch, fascinated, as their movements through their lives are recounted for us.

Sulla deserves to be counted among these great and noble people, these high achievers who accomplished so much, if often at so great a cost. He also deserves to be judged according to the standards of his own time, regarding many of his actions, rather than with a modern politically correct perspective. That flawed view would only be calculated to consider the proper Roman ideal of his time, which he personally fulfilled to the letter, to be no more than that of bloodthirsty fighters, enslavers and empire builders. The people of his own time did not view it in such a way. They knew that they were special, that they had created a society which could not only cast its net over the entire known world, but could lead that world in civilization, culture and knowledge. Their sensible laws, their calendar, architecture, building projects from aqueducts to amphitheatres, their language, their ideals and their ability to be flexible and to integrate and expand new ideas, have all come down to us. Furthermore, they lasted, far more than any other empire ever did. If anyone wishes to ask the old question 'What did the Romans do for us?' there can be only one answer. 'Everything!'

The only real benefit which Sulla is likely to achieve from being considered in a modern way, is that a modern viewpoint is more likely to accept that his relationship with Metrobius might be regarded without the horror and prejudice which so many writers have openly expressed. Unfortunately, many have been unable to see such an affection, however genuine and lasting, in any reasonable light. Likewise, his enduring friendships with the people of the lower classes might now hopefully be considered more equably, as being greatly to his credit rather than otherwise, and without the need to look for ulterior motives or bring such associations into disrepute. We, at least, should now be able to judge people for what they are, rather than for what they have.

Sulla may have only had one life to spend, like any other man. However, for some men history can extend that life beyond its normal span. He spent the time he had available to him in exerting every ounce of his physical and mental strength in attempts to defend and support the Republic, in which he honestly believed implicitly. This was often at great personal cost, without him ever having the prescience that it was already doomed.

It is a tragedy that such creditable attempts were to be so misrepresented after his death that his name became anathema. I have not found him to be merely that man of bloodshed and cruelty, of debauchery and vice who is usually portrayed. He certainly had his faults, like other men, and he freely admitted to them, openly and honestly. He had a quick temper, and exacted revenge when necessary, but he also had a ready humour, a disarming friendliness and a genuine desire for peace.

An opinion contrary to what is considered the norm might initially be something of a lone voice. It might even be supposed to have been expressed merely to appear controversial.

Controversy may be inescapable when there are so many centuries of malice to be overcome, but if controversy is not being sought for its own sake, neither will it be shied away from. These are genuinely held opinions. Contrary ideas may often provide an opportunity for a man's character, if automatically maligned, to instead be re-evaluated.

That is what I would wish for Lucius Cornelius Sulla. That his outstanding character and his achievements might be considered with more impartiality, more accuracy, and a good deal less bias. In short, that his memory should be treated with the respect, decency and justice which he would have wanted, and which he most certainly deserves.

Notes and References

Chapter Two

1. Regarding Sulla's immediate family. We know that a Publius Cornelius Sulla was active in Pompeii after the town became a colony in the 80's. He is referred to as a nephew by Stefano Giuntoli. There would therefore have to have been an elder brother of Sulla's to take the family praenomen of Publius and pass it to his own son. Why then did the stepmother not leave some of the inheritance to this elder brother? Was he already deceased? Arthur Keaveney does not mention siblings at all. The Publius Sulla in Pompeii may, of course, have been a cousin.

2. The grammaticus Lutatius Daphnis who was sold twice for 700,000 sesterces a time, was eventually manumitted by Quintus Catulus who was Consul for 102 BC. Prices for highly educated slaves are quoted by J.P.V.D. Balsdon.

3. Plutarch, *Sulla*.

4. Plutarch, *Sulla*.

5. Keaveney suggests that Sulla's first wife may have been a sister of Caesar Strabo. However the early closeness between Marius and Sulla suggests that a financial deal was likely to have been struck by Gaius Julius Caesar, with Gaius Marius, in order to benefit both his sons' political careers, together with providing dowries for his daughter(s). If so, this would have made Gaius Marius and Sulla direct brothers-in-law. It would settle the fortunes of Caesar's family completely, in return for which Gaius Marius achieved social acceptability. As an incidental, it also went some way towards giving Sulla the more respectable connections that he needed.

6. Plutarch, *Sulla*.

Chapter Three

1. King Micipsa's 'adopting' of Jugurtha is reported by Keaveney, together with the pressure he may well have been under from Rome to do so.

2. Keaveney reports on the old friendship between Jugurtha and Gaius Marius.

3. Beesley, regarding Jugurtha's popularity amongst his own people.

4. Stobart. Regarding suggestions of senatorial bribery.

5. Michael Grant tells us that Bocchus 'detested' his son-in-law Jugurtha.

6. Stobart. Regarding the power of the Plebian Assembly. Since 287 BC the Plebians had the right to have the resolutions of their council binding on the state, both Patricians and Plebians alike. Tribunes of the Plebs were protected by oath and their persons were considered sacred, giving them enormous power. Senatorial decrees had the force of custom and tradition, but not actual law. The ten Tribunes of the Plebs had the power to introduce a bill and speak on its behalf in the Comitia. Although the Senate

could also marshal speakers to oppose a bill, they would also have to be Plebian, not Patrician, or they would not have been able to speak in the Plebian Assembly. It was always possible to 'buy' oneself a co-operative Tribune of the Plebs, who would then raise support to push through a bill on your behalf. This is very likely what happened in the case of Gaius Marius being able to immediately replace Metellus in the command of the Jugurthan campaign. Indeed, this particular action set a precedent by referring to Metellus' replacement by name.

7. Social situation of the *capite censi* – Pierre Grimal.
8. Army reorganization under Gaius Marius – detailed by Lawrence Keppie.
9. Regarding Sulla's abilities. Keaveney.
10. Keaveney makes reference to Sulla's great charm and helpful attitude and his personal popularity among the men under his command.
11. Keaveney refers to Sulla's friendliness and courtesy towards King Bocchus and its effect on him. Bocchus was certainly impressed by Sulla and the friendship which grew between them was not only to last for a considerable time, but had a definite effect on the progress of the war. It is greatly to Sulla's credit that he took this line with a man who was notoriously difficult to pin down and had only recently been an attacker. There is, however, no evidence that it was mere expediency, as Sulla and Bocchus were still on friendly terms many years later, when Sulla had moved on.
12. Keaveney. Envoys manhandled and their credentials stolen from them.
13. Keaveney. Volux's suggestions regarding Jugurtha's presence in the vicinity.
14. Keaveney. Regarding Bocchus' reward at the end of the war.
15. Beesley. Death of Jugurtha. The form of punishment used.
16. Sulla being accosted and abused in the Forum is reported by Keaveney, but unattributed.
17. Balsdon reports that Bocchus donated a statue of Sulla. The friendship between the two of them seemed to last well beyond the end of the Jugurthine War. After the Battle of the Colline Gate when Sulla instituted his Victory Celebrations, the Ludi Victoriae Sullae, which were to take place yearly from 26 October to 1 November, King Bocchus sent him 100 lions for his inaugural games.

Chapter Four
1. Theodor Mommsen, *History of Rome Part IV.*
2. A.H. Beesley, *The Gracchi Marius and Sulla.*
3. Theodor Mommsen.
4. Livy in his 'Epitome' states that the barbarians asked for a domicile in the area and were refused, but that this request did not take place until *after* the battle. This seems very unlikely. Whereas Florus in *Roman History* tells us that the Cimbri requested that concession *before* the battle took place, and the refusal was the reason for the following engagement, which seems far more sensible.
5. Marcus Tullius Cicero.
6. Beesley.
7. Tacitus details the actions of Popillius Laenas.
8. Beesley describes the defeated legions 'passing under the yoke'.

9. J.P.V.D. Balsdon. Both in *Life and Leisure in Ancient Rome* and in his *Roman Women* he is invaluable for full details of the daily life of the period.

10. Mommsen.

11. Michael Grant, *History of Rome.*

12. Mommsen describes the foolish and extreme behaviour of Quintus Servilius Caepio at this time.

13. Mommsen.

14. Mommsen.

15. Livy. Book LXVII.

16. Mommsen.

17. Publius Rutilius Rufus, the Consul at that time, (quoted by Licinianus) stated that the basic number of casualties was probably around 70,000. This was, however, among the regular and lightly armed troops alone. That figure would therefore *not* include the auxiliaries and cavalry troops, or the non-combatants, whose numbers would very likely bring the total up to around 110,000 dead. This would also include the wounded that had to be left on the field, and were later killed by the barbarians. These figures, given by Publius Rutilius Rufus, are also quoted by Mommsen in his *History of Rome IV.*

18. Plutarch in his *Life of Marius* refers to the obvious fertility of the land on which the battle was fought. He attributes this to the amount of human decomposition in the area. He stated that the land was able to produce a great quantity of crops for many years afterwards.

19. Lawrence Keppie, *The making of the Roman Army.*

20. Plutarch in his *Life of Marius* gives full details of the prophetess of North Africa who told Gaius Marius that he would be elected Consul seven times. Her prophecy was well known and Gaius Marius certainly believed in it, going so far as to alter his actions to accommodate it, as when he later insisted on his seventh Consulship despite obvious ill health and inability after his second stroke. Plutarch states that her name was Martha and that she was a Syrian. Marius is described as making sacrifices as dictated by her and having her carried on a litter, even to the armies, where she was 'very much looked up to'. There is no record of her later life.

Chapter Five

1. Keith Richardson, *Daggers in the Forum,* for details of the struggle of the Graccchi.

2. Keaveney, *Sulla, the Last Republican,* regarding the death of King Jugurtha.

3. McCullough *Masters of Rome,* glossary, regarding details of the Lex Atinia.

4. Keaveney. Regarding Marius' troops wishing to remain in North Africa.

5. Pierre Grimal, *The Grandeur that was Rome.*

6. Michael Grant, *History of Rome.*

7. McCullough, *Masters of Rome,* glossary.

8. Keaveney, *Sulla.*

9. Plutarch, *Sulla.*

10. Keaveney and also Plutarch's *Sulla.*

11. Plutarch.

12. Keaveney.

13. P.F. Cagniart, *L.Cornelius Sulla's quarrel with G. Marius at the time of the Germanic Invasions, Athenaeum* (1989) for details of Sulla's *apparent* demotion.
14. Plutarch, *Sulla*.
15. Keaveney attributes to H. Barden the fact of Sulla's and Catulus' shared literary interests, and Sulla was already known for his friendship with actors and poets. Also in Donald Dudley's *Roman Society* there is a description of Catulus' deep cultural interests. He was a patron of Greek poets and wrote poetry himself, one or two examples of which still survive. He also wrote a history of his own times. He would later fight in the Social Wars and be driven to commit suicide in 87 BC due to the victory at that time of Marius' party. Cicero referred to him as a man of great culture and a patron of writers.
16. Keaveney.
17. Plutarch, *Marius*.
18. Re: Princeps Senatus. This high position was effectively the Leader of the House. The Censors (themselves elected every fifth year) would choose a patrician senator of unimpeachable dignitas and auctoritas to fulfil the role. The position could be reviewed every five years, as each new batch of Censors was elected. In the case of Marcus Aemilius Scaurus, the title was given to him while still actually serving as a Consul, in 115 BC although it was more usual for a man to have been a Censor before being eligible for the post. It may have been that it was a particular mark of honour for him, or simply that he was the most senior patrician available at that time. He did, in fact, hold the position until his death. (McCullough, *Masters of Rome*, Glossary.)
19. Sulla was to later marry Scaurus' widow, Caecilia Metella Dalmatica. She would, in my opinion, thereby become his *third* wife, not his fourth as many histories claim. My reasons for this assumption will be explained fully in Chapter Six.
20. Muir's Historical Atlas, for full details of the area concerned at that period.
21. Mommsen, *History of Rome*.
22. Lawrence Keppie, *The Making of the Roman Army*, for the details of the changes made by Gaius Marius to the pila, or throwing spears, as well as his other alterations to the kit and equipment of the ordinary soldier in the interests of efficiency.
23. Mommsen.
24. Geoffrey Richardson, *The Deceivers*, for details of the normal rituals of medieval kings before a battle, especially the 'morale boosting' in which a commander would habitually appear before his troops wearing his full decorations, or the crown itself in the case of a sovereign.
25. Mommsen.
26. Mommsen.
27. Donald Dudley's *Roman Society* for details of the commemoration of the site of Aquae Sextiae. He also shows an example of the 'centuriation' of the area around Ravenna. The land there is still very clearly marked by the narrow strips into which it was commonly divided to make the individual land appropriations for Marius' veteran legions, both there and in the other areas which Marius was to use. It is very similar in appearance to medieval strip farming.
28. Malcolm Todd, *The Barbarians, Goths, Franks and Vandals*.
29. Mommsen.

30. Mommsen.
31. Keaveney, for a discussion on Sulla's first forays into political office after his return to Rome with the conclusion of the Germanic Wars.

Chapter Six
1. Plutarch, *Sulla*.
2. Robert Maynard Hutchins, ed. Britannia Great Books. University of Chicago.
3. Plutarch, *Sulla*.
4. She was the daughter of the Princeps Senatus, Marcus Aemilius Scaurus and his then wife Caecilia Metella. At the time of her marriage to Gnaeus Pompeius she was Sulla's stepdaughter.
5. Keaveney, *Sulla*.
6. McCullough. Glossary. The centuriate assembly (*comitia centuriata*) marshalled the people in their classes, which were economic in nature, and means tested. It met to elect consuls, praetors and censors (every five years) and could also hear treason trials. The assembly of the people (*comitia populi tributa*) was convoked by a consul or a praetor and could formulate laws, as well as arrange the election of the curule aediles, quaestors and tribunes of the soldiers. It could also conduct trials.
7. McCullough, *Masters of Rome*, Glossary.
8. Keaveney, *Sulla*.
9. McCullough, *Masters of Rome*, Glossary. The praetor urbanus had duties of litigation and was responsible for the supervision of the courts within Rome. His imperium did not extend beyond the fifth milestone from Rome and he was not allowed to leave the city for more than ten days at a time. If both consuls were absent from Rome at the same time he was then temporarily the senior magistrate empowered to defend the city if necessary, or to summon the Senate. He could decide a legal matter between two litigants on his own authority, without the necessity for the full trial process. The praetor peregrinus dealt with lawsuits and other legal matters where one party was not a Roman citizen. While his duties were concerned with the dispensation of justice, they took him all over Italy, and sometimes even further afield. He was also responsible for the non-citizen cases within Rome.
10. Keaveney, *Sulla*.
11. J.P.V.D. Balsdon, *Life and Leisure in Ancient Rome*.
12. J.P.V.D. Balsdon, *Life and Leisure in Ancient Rome*.
13. Balsdon, 'Sulla Felix', *Journal of Roman Studies* (1951).
14. Keaveney, *Sulla*.
15. McCullough, *Masters of Rome*, Glossary.
16. John Hazel, *Who's Who in the Roman World*.
17. Keaveney, *Sulla*.
18. Keaveney, *Sulla*.
19. McCullough, *Masters of Rome*, Glossary.
20. John Hazel, *Who's Who in the Roman World*.
21. Plutarch, *Sulla*.
22. Balsdon, 'Sulla Felix', *Journal of Roman Studies*.

23. Balsdon, 'Sulla Felix', *Journal of Roman Studies*.
24. Keaveney, *Sulla*
25. John Hazel, *Who's Who in the Roman World*.
26. Ultimate Decree – the Senatus Consultum de Republica Defendenda – proclaimed the sovereignty of the Senate and the establishment of martial law. From the time of the brothers Gracchi it was used in civil emergencies allowing the Senate to then overrule all other bodies in government. It was used as a device to control difficult situations without being obliged to appoint a dictator.
27. 27. Keaveney, *Sulla*.

Chapter Seven
1. Pierre Grimal, *The Civilization of Rome*.
2. McCullough, *Masters of Rome*, Glossary.
3. McCullough.
4. John Hazel, *Who's Who in Ancient Rome*.
5. Keaveney, *Sulla*.
6. Plutarch, *Sulla*.
7. McCullough, *Masters of Rome*, Glossary.
8. Keaveney, *Sulla*.
9. Keaveney, *Sulla*.
10. McCullough, *Masters of Rome*, Glossary.
11. John Hazel, *Mithradates VI*.
12. John Hazel, *Sertorius*. Sertorius was awarded the Corona Graminea, or Grass Crown, sometimes called the Corona Obsidianalis. This was a purely private award given by the men of a legion to a commander they considered had saved the legion in battle on a specific day. This was different from the 'crowns' or wreaths of honour usually awarded by the State for valour. The highest of these official awards was the Corona Civica.
13. McCullough, *Masters of Rome*, glossary.
14. McCullough. Glossary.
15. John Hazel. Servilius Caepio – for assertion that he was killed by Silo personally.
16. John Hazel, *Who's Who In Ancient Rome*.
17. Michael Grant, *History of Rome*. Regarding the law promulgated by Lucius Julius Caesar at the end of his consulship in 90 BC. The law gave full citizenship to all Italians who had not taken up arms against Rome during the Social (sometimes called Marsic) War. It probably also gave full enfranchisement to the Latin communities. (McCullough. Glossary. Its full and correct title is the *Lex Julia de civitate Latinis et sociis danda*.)
18. Stobart, *The Grandeur that was Rome*. By laws passed in 90 and 89 BC some states received the desired franchise (all Italians south of the Po). However, it was dealt with very cleverly by confining all the new Roman citizens to only a few of the tribes, which meant that their votes became useless in any real sense. In the Roman voting system, there were 35 tribes, 31 rural and 4 urban. Each member of a particular tribe possessed just one vote in a Tribal Assembly, but his personal vote was not really significant, as the votes within each tribe were counted first, then a majority opinion was cast as being the ONE vote from that tribe. Therefore, however many members a tribe possessed

(i.e. including all the new citizens), it gave that tribe no real advantage, as it still only possessed its one majority vote. Voting details from McCullough Glossary, where she refers to Dr. L.R. Taylor's *Roman Voting Assemblies.*

19. Georgina Masson, *Republican Rome.*
20. Keaveney, *Sulla.*
21. Marcel Brion, *Pompeii & Herculaneum.*
22. Marcel Brion, *Pompeii & Herculaneum.*
23. Stefano Giuntoli, *Art & History of Pompeii.*
24. McCullough, *Masters of Rome,* Glossary.
25. Marcel Brion, *Pompeii & Herculaneum.*
26. Theodor Mommsen.
27. Hugh Chisholm, *Aeclanum.*
28. McCullough, Glossary. Augers were priests from the College of Augers, an official state body, and in Sulla's day there were twelve of these, six patrician and six plebian. Augers were not required to pretend to predict the future, or be in any way psychic, as there was a manual of interpretations from which they read, which explained what the proper signs should be, in order to obtain the approval of the gods. When on official business an auger wore a toga trabea (a toga striped in alternate red and purple) and carried a ceremonial staff (a lituus).

Chapter Eight
1. Plutarch, *Sulla.*
2. A.H.Beesley, *The Gracchi, Marius and Sulla.*
3. Keaveney, *Sulla.*
4. John Hazel, *Who's Who in Ancient Rome.*
5. Keaveney, *Sulla.*
6. McCullough, Glossary re: Leges Corneliae.
7. John Hazel.
8. Plutarch, *Sulla.*
9. R.M.Ogilvie, *The Romans and their Gods* re: Haruspex.
10. The haruspices were never an official priesthood in Rome. They did not hold the authority of the augers or pontifices. However, when a doubtful point of interpretation came up the haruspex could give an opinion, for a fee, in examining the entrails of the sacrificed animal. There is a bronze model of a liver, found at Piacenza, which must have been used as a model for instruction or practice. *The Journal of Roman Studies 36* (1946) describes it as 'divided into two halves, each containing eight regions, marked on the back "of the Sun" and "of the Moon" probably referring to day or night'.
11. Keaveney, *Sulla.*
12. Keaveney, *Sulla.*
13. R.M.Ogilvie, Re: *Bellona.* Bellona was actually the Roman goddess responsible for foreign wars. Perhaps in Sulla's dream she also represented the war against Mithradates?
14. Plutarch, *Sulla.*
15. Keaveney, *Sulla.*
16. Keaveney, *Sulla.*

17. Plutarch, *Sulla*.
18. 17. McCullough, Glossary, regarding the Leges Caecilia Didia. The first of these laws stipulated that three market days should elapse between the first *contio* (discussion) to promulgate a law and the vote which passed the bill into law. The second of these laws prevented the tacking together of unrelated matters to form one law in order to get unpopular measures passed more easily. These laws were passed by the consuls of 98 BC.
19. McCullough, Glossary, regarding the Leges Corneliae passed by Sulla in 88 BC. The first waived the provisions of the lex Caecilia Didia in order to bring in his new laws more quickly.

     The second commanded that 300 new members should be added to the Senate, which originally had contained only forty men. The new members would be appointed by the censors in the normal way. As the monetary fund designed to put those senators, who had been expelled for debt, back into the senate was working on their behalf, there was no reason why the censors could not reinstate senators to strengthen the Senate. It would also repair the losses caused by war.

     The third repealed the lex Hortensia. Under Sulla's law nothing could be brought before the tribal assemblies unless it had received the Senate's approval; this was intended to muzzle the Tribunes. If the Senate did not issue a senatus consultum the assemblies could not legislate. Nor could the assemblies alter the wording of any senatus consultum to suit themselves.

     The fourth lex Cornelia came down from the Senate to the people as a senatus consultum. It was to alter the top-heaviness of the centuries by removing later modifications it had undergone. Once again it gave the first class nearly fifty per cent of the available political power, strengthening both Senate and Ordo Equestor.

     The fifth declared that no discussion or voting of laws could in future take place in the tribal assemblies. All legislation must in future be passed by the centuriate assembly which allowed the Senate and Ordo Equestor total control. The Assembly of the People or the Plebian Assembly could elect magistrates but nothing else. It basically took power away from the tribes.

     The sixth and final law was a trial process, to indict twenty men on charges of treason. This was the perduellio or greater treason, which carried the death sentence. The men included Gaius Marius, his son Gaius Marius junior, Publius Sulpicius Rufus and several others by name. The sentence of death could be meted out on apprehension, no further formality being required.
20. Keaveney, *Sulla*.
21. Keaveney, *Sulla*.
22. Keaveney, *Sulla*.
23. Beesley, *The Gracchi, Marius and Sulla*.

Chapter Nine

  1. Keaveney, *Sulla*.
  2. J.P.V.D. Balsdon, *Life and Leisure in Ancient Rome*.
  3. John Hazel, *Who's Who In Ancient Rome*.
  4. Plutarch, *Marius*. Plutarch describes him as 'unwieldy of body' at this time.

5. Beesley, *The Gracchi, Marius and Sulla*.
6. Beesley.
7. Appian, *History of Rome*.
8. Beesley.
9. Beesley.
10. It is often stated that Marius suffered from pleurisy at the end of his life. I can only assume that such a belief is held by persons who have not seen a sufferer from this ailment. It is impossible, if suffering from this disease, to breathe normally, or sit or lie down in basic comfort, let alone indulge in the behaviour Marius did at this time. I contend, for reasons I have given in the text, that Marius died finally of a stroke, possibly after having suffered a minor event of the same nature at an earlier date.
11. The total numbers of victims in Rome at this time are not recorded, nor is it possible to identify the vast majority of them. Marius' slave army killed indiscriminately throughout the city, mainly innocent bystanders, while Marius concentrated on the deaths of the people he by then considered his personal enemies.
12. Beesley. Re Cinna's use of power.
13. Donald Dudley, *Roman Society*. Ironically, many of those killed were actually people of Greek descent from the southern half of Italy, where Greek families still predominated.
14. Keaveney, *Sulla*.
15. Appian. Re: Epiphradatos being 'the favourite of Aphrodite'.
16. Balsdon, 'Sulla Felix'. For a Sullan cult of Venus in Italy there is actually very little evidence. Even the use of her name on the new colony at Pompeii is probably due to there having been a large temple to her already in the city. However, for a Sullan cult of Aphrodite in the East there is plenty of evidence to be found. 'Sulla Felix' *Journal of Roman Studies* (1951).
17. Balsdon, 'Sulla Felix'.
18. Keaveney, *Sulla*.
19. Keaveney, *Sulla*. See also Appian's *Mithradates*.
20. Appian. For evidence that Sulla borrowed, not stole, money from the Greek temples. See also Plutarch who agrees on this subject. This is also covered by Keaveney who declares that Sulla also repaid the debts as soon as he possibly could.
21. Keaveney, *Sulla*.
22. Plutarch's *Sulla* and Appian's *Mithradates* for evidence of the people being obliged to search on the slopes of the Acropolis for whatever weeds could be found and also that they ate boiled leather from shoes and bags. Also that they sometimes were desperate enough to resort to cannibalism.
23. Plutarch, *Sulla*.
24. Keaveney, *Sulla*. Arthur Keaveney also refers here to Sherwin-White 1973 for evidence that Sulla did not indulge in conspicuous cruelty at this time. He emphasized that the commander was normally obliged to allow his men a period of licence in order for them to let off steam after a siege and that this prevented mutiny. It was normal procedure not only in ancient times but also more recently.

Chapter Ten

1. Balsdon. 'Sulla Felix' *Journal of Roman Studies*. Faustus and Fausta were effectively being named Fortune and Fortunata in recognition of Sulla's new and closer connection with the gods. He was already beginning to create a myth around himself and his family.

2. Balsdon, 'Sulla Felix'.

   (a) Balsdon states that Sulla's friends and soldiers used the name 'Felix' freely and with his approval as early as 86 BC although it was not granted to him officially until 82 BC.

   (b) Harry Ericsson in his article 'Sulla Felix' in *Eranos XLI* (1943) agrees, but considers that it was conferred by popular decree, rather than senatorial decree.

   (c) Appian also states that the new name was given officially in connection with the erection of a new gilded equestrian statue before the rostra, and to coincide with the voting of a Triumph at that time. This fits in with the ending of a chapter in his life, namely the suppression of the Marians in Rome, and the ending of the war in the east.

3. Mommsen, *History of Rome*. Mommsen states that the sons of patricians were commonly named on the ninth day after birth. Whether the daughter was also named at this time we cannot confirm but the naming of his new son while in Greece would be an affirmation of Sulla's belief in his future success and his confidence in his strong and devoted army.

4. Keaveney, *Sulla*.

5. Plutarch, *Sulla*. Most histories state categorically that Archelaus had three times as many men as Sulla, but if Plutarch's figures are correct it seems that the numbers were far less in Sulla's army and therefore even more unequal.

6. Keaveney, *Sulla*.

7. Plutarch, *Sulla*. Gives details of the disorder within the Pontic army.

8. Plutarch, *Sulla*. Plutarch states that the Romans, with shouts and laughter, called out to the charioteers as though they were watching a performance at the circus.

9. This man cannot have been aware of the use of a slave army by Gaius Marius in Rome. Only a short time previously there, Roman citizens had been killed by slaves.

10. Plutarch, *Sulla*. Plutarch here draws on Sulla's own writing of the *Commentarii Rerum Gestarum* of Sulla himself. Twenty-two books, on which Sulla worked until two days before his death. Plutarch quotes from this work sixteen times explicitly, on five occasions with regard to Sulla's references to his luck, dreams, or other supernatural happenings. Cicero also believed that the morale of troops depended greatly on their general having the knack of winning battles, especially if he also had the privilege of being in intimate contact with some supernatural agency. Three generals were considered to be supernaturally inspired, the elder Africanus, Sertorius and Sulla himself. Sulla wrote as if he had absolute belief in his supernatural assistance and protection by the gods.

11. Balsdon, 'Sulla Felix'. Balsdon refers to the monument, but also to Professor L. R. Farnell's book *Cults of the Greek States* in which he says that use of the name of Aphrodite there is probably due to her more warlike nature in the folklore of the area.

12. Keaveney, *Sulla*.

13. Keaveney, *Sulla*.

14. Plutarch, *Sulla*. Appian, *Mithradates*.
15. Keaveney, *Sulla*.
16. Plutarch, *Sulla*. Plutarch here states categorically that the relieving force was in excess of 80,000 men, a huge number to face when Sulla still had so few men.
17. Keaveney, *Sulla*.
18. Plutarch, *Sulla*. For the actual words Sulla is supposed to have used on that occasion.
19. Keaveney, *Sulla*.
20. Plutarch, *Sulla*. Plutarch states, 'The marshes were filled with blood, and the lake with dead bodies. Insomuch that to this day many bows, helmets, fragments of iron, breastplates, and swords of barbarian make continue to be found deep in mud, two hundred years after the fight.'
21. Plutarch, *Sulla*. Appian, *Mithradates*.
22. Keaveney, *Sulla*.

Chapter Eleven
1. Plutarch, *Sulla*.
2. Plutarch, *Sulla*.
3. Beesley, *The Gracchi, Marius and Sulla*.
4. Beesley.
5. Keaveney, *Sulla*.
6. Keaveney, *Sulla*. On the other hand, if he were so good a soldier why did his men desert to Sulla at the first opportunity? It could not have been only because of Sulla's reputation of being the 'beloved' of the gods. Given a choice, men will only entrust their lives to a commander they respect. It seems to me that they did not like Fimbria any more than they had Flaccus, and were glad enough to leave his service.
7. Plutarch, *Sulla*.
8. Plutarch, *Sulla*.
9. Keaveney, *Sulla*.
10. Keaveney, *Sulla*. Also references on this from Plutarch and Appian, *Mithradates*. Regarding the return of the captured Roman generals.
11. Beesley, *The Gracchi, Marius and Sulla*.
12. Plutarch, *Sulla*, regarding Sulla's desire to refute such accusations made against him.
13. Keaveney, *Sulla*.
14. Plutarch, *Sulla*, regarding Sulla's contempt of Mithradates' lack of personal involvement in the war he commanded. Also Appian's *Mithradates*.
15. Plutarch, *Sulla*, regarding Archelaus' melodramatic declaration of intent.
16. Appian, *Mithradates* and Plutarch, *Sulla*. Also Keaveney, in his *Sulla* quotes Licinianus, who says that there were two attempts made against the tribes of pirates. It was also left to L.Scipio to deal with them again later on.
17. Keaveney, *Sulla*.
18. Plutarch, *Sulla*.
19. Plutarch, *Sulla*.
20. Plutarch, *Sulla*.
21. Keaveney, *Sulla*.

22. Plutarch, *Sulla* and Appian, *Mithradates*.

23. Beesley, *The Gracchi, Marius and Sulla*.

24. Balsdon, 'Sulla Felix', *Journal of Roman Studies* (1951). Balsdon states that the dedications to Sulla and his wife Caecilia Metella are not dated, but certainly refer to the period when he was working in Greece. Inscriptions to him were known in Oropus, Helicarnassus and in Rhodes. One in Cos is later and names Sulla not only as Epiphradatos but also as 'Dictator' so it is more likely to have been erected around 81 BC in his honour.

25. Plutarch, *Sulla*, for references to Sulla's 'blotchy' complexion.

26. Christopher Robbins, *Household Herbal*, 1995.

27. *Blood Red Roses*, Oxbow 2000. Edited by Fiorato, Boylston and Knussel. The archaeology of a mass grave from the battle of Towton, AD 1461 particularly with regard to previous severe injuries which were well healed by medieval medicine.

28. Dieter Podlech, *Herbs and Healing Plants*, with reference to the types of plants available in the area and their various medicinal uses.

29. I have personally helped save the life of a pet dog, suffering a terrible post-operative infection, by use of a daily strong garlic poultice, when regular antibiotics prescribed by a veterinary professional failed to deal with the problem. She recovered fully.

30. Dr. Martin Scurr in an article published in the Daily Mail in June 2012.

31. Patricia Cornwell, *Portrait of a Killer* (2002). The investigation into the Ripper murders and references to the murderer's mutilation of his victims' faces, probably in order to negate personality.

32. Plutarch, *Sulla*, in which he refers to the 'scurrilous jesters in Athens' who made the verses on Sulla's appearance which said 'Sulla is a mulberry sprinkled with meal'.

33. Keaveney, *Sulla*.

34. Keaveney, *Sulla*.

35. Keaveney, *Sulla*, in which he gives details of the coins minted by Sulla at this time which showed his war trophies together with the figure of a flying victory.

Chapter Twelve

1. Keaveney, *Sulla*.

2. Keaveney, *Sulla*.

3. McCullough, *Masters of Rome*, for details of the pressure to conciliate.

4. Beesley, *The Gracchi, Marius and Sulla*.

5. Beesley, *The Gracchi, Marius and Sulla*.

6. Keaveney, *Sulla*.

7. Beesley, *The Gracchi, Marius and Sulla*. Also Plutarch's *Sulla*.

8. Keaveney, *Sulla*.

9. Beesley, *The Gracchi, Marius and Sulla*. Where he gives the wording of the centurion who is supposed to have refused the bribe. Plutarch also quotes it.

10. McCullough, *Masters of Rome*, refers to the possible consuls.

11. Keaveney, *Sulla*.

12. Keaveney, *Sulla*.

13. Keaveney, *Sulla*.

14. Plutarch, *Sulla*. Where the 'satyr' like creature is described along with Sulla's reaction to it when other people were afraid of the omens it may have represented.
15. Plutarch, *Sulla*. Where full details are given of the offer made by Sulla's troops in order to furnish him with sufficient funds.
16. Plutarch, *Sulla*, describes the omen received at the sacrifice.
17. Plutarch, *Sulla*, describes the possible omen of the fighting animals. Notes 16 and 17 are given by Plutarch, who in his turn attributes them to Sulla's own words, being taken by him from Sulla's memoirs.
18. Keaveney, *Sulla*, referring to exemption from the harbour tax.
19. McCullough, *Masters of Rome*. Glossary referring to the marital connections of Sulla. John Hazel in his *Who's Who in Ancient Rome* also describes the family connections of the Metella clan.
20. Keaveney, *Sulla*.
21. John Hazel, *Who's Who in Ancient Rome*.
22. John Hazel, *Who's Who in Ancient Rome*.
23. Keaveney, *Sulla*, referring to the destruction by burning of the Temple of Jupiter Optimus Maximus and the neighbouring temples on Capitol Hill.
24. McCullough, *Masters of Rome*. Glossary, giving details of the positions of the temples on the Capitol and the numinae (faceless) gods like Ops and Fides.
25. Balsdon, *Life and Leisure in Ancient Rome*, gives full details of the religious life of the Roman people and the offerings made to individual gods and goddesses.
26. The Senatus Consultum Utimum, the Ultimate Decree. In effect, martial law, used in times of extreme emergency.
27. Plutarch, *Sulla*. Plutarch suggests that young Marius, Gaius Marius' only son, may have been present at the battle.
28. Keaveney, *Sulla*, for the donation to the local goddess made in gratitude by Sulla.
29. Keaveney, *Sulla*.
30. John Hazel, *Who's Who in Ancient Rome*, gives full details of Quintus Sertorius and his reactions to the regime.
31. Keaveney, *Sulla*.
32. Plutarch, *Sulla* and Keaveney, *Sulla*, for the claim that Carbo may have been in the area when Sulla and Scipio were having talks. Keaveney suggests that it is more likely that Carbo was fighting against Gnaeus Pompeius Magnus at the time.
33. Keaveney, *Sulla*.
34. Keaveney, *Sulla*. And also John Hazel, *Who's Who in Ancient Rome*. Crassus' father had been allied to Marius in the Social War and was in favour of Drusus' reforms against Lucius Marcius Philippus.

Chapter Thirteen
1. Keaveney, *Sulla*.
2. Plutarch, *Pompeius Magnus*.
3. If he had done what the others did he would have gone to fight his war in the East with a far healthier war chest than the meagre 9,000 librae he actually started out with, and would not have had to borrow from Greece, which he was also blamed for.

4. Plutarch, *Pompeius Magnus*, referring to Magnus' bold character.
5. Keaveney, *Sulla*, refers to Gabba and Gardner. Salmon (1964) suggests Colleferro.
6. Plutarch, *Sulla*, describes the utter exhaustion of Sulla's troops at that time.
7. Plutarch, *Sulla*, for Sulla's soldiers' furious reaction to the ambush.
8. Plutarch, *Sulla*, refers to Fenestella regarding young Marius, claiming that he had slept throughout most of the action, missing it all rather than doing any of the fighting, and that he was only awakened by his defeated men fleeing for their lives.
9. Plutarch, *Sulla*, refers to Sulla's own words regarding the numbers captured.
10. Keaveney, *Sulla*.
11. Keaveney, *Sulla* and also John Hazel, *Who's Who in Ancient Rome*, for family relationships.
12. Keaveney, *Sulla*, regarding the deaths of the moderates in Rome at the hands of Sulla's enemies, before he could arrive in Rome to protect them.
13. Keaveney, *Sulla*.
14. Keaveney, *Sulla*, regarding the killing in a fury of Carbo's own cavalry after he blamed them for initiating the desertion of so many of his men to Sulla.
15. Plutarch, *Sulla*, regarding reports of the numbers involved.
16. Keaveney, *Sulla*, who also quotes Appian regarding another mass desertion.
17. Keaveney, *Sulla*, also Appian, who states that Norbanus fled to refuge in Rhodes.
18. Plutarch, *Sulla*.
19. Plutarch, *Sulla*, regarding the position of the camp in relation to the Gate.
20. Plutarch, *Sulla*, who states that it took place at the tenth hour.
21. Plutarch, *Crassus*, regarding Crassus' immediate success in the battle.
22. Balsdon, 'Sulla Felix', who gives full details of the image of Apollo usually carried by Sulla when about to go into battle, and to which he directed his prayers at that time.
23. Appian.
24. Plutarch, *Crassus*, gives details of the battle and the falling darkness.
25. Plutarch, *Sulla*. He could not enter the city as he was still proconsular.
26. Plutarch, *Sulla*, regarding the Senators' reactions to the sounds of punishment, along with Sulla's reply about the punishment of the men he considered criminals.

Chapter Fourteen
1. In much the same way as the heads and bodies of executed criminals were displayed in our own country up to the eighteenth century, supposedly for the deterrent of others.
2. Keaveney, *Sulla*.
3. As example, the Knights of St. John (Hospitallers) at Rhodes in 1522 when fighting the Turks. They surrendered Rhodes and were allowed to leave with honour. However, when they were fighting later, on Malta in 1565, also against the Turks, they refused to surrender the Island, fighting the besiegers to the end with appalling loss of life. Had they not finally managed to fight off their attackers, they could have expected to be killed to the last man, as the Turks had killed all the defenders of Fort St. Elmo. Ernle Bradford, *The Great Siege of Malta*, (1565).
4. Keaveney, *Sulla*.

5. Alternatively, he may also have been asked by Gaius Caecilius Metellus, who was one of his wife's relatives.

6. Keaveney, *Sulla*. Keaveney rightly points out that the idea (quoted by Plutarch) was unlikely to have been ordered by Publius Fursidius as he was not a member of the Senate and therefore lacked the rank to give such an order. However, I do not think that this prevented him from making the original suggestion to Sulla. It may have been seen as a sensible way of dealing with the situation before them, and Sulla was known to be on close terms with his officers, therefore might have listened to him.

7. A Public Horse was one which belonged to the State. It had originally been government policy to provide these mounts to the 1800 Knights and the 18 Senior Centuries, due to the prohibitive expense. The rights of their descendents to also receive a Public Horse were jealously guarded and it was considered a mark of honour. Even Pompeius Magnus always claimed his, though he could certainly have afforded to buy his own. The Public Horses were inspected officially at an annual ceremony where they were paraded as for show.

8. Plutarch, *Crassus*. Regarding Crassus (known as 'the rich') also John Hazel regarding Gaius Verres, another notoriously rapacious man. He was to eventually be proscribed in his turn and killed by Marcus Antonius in 43 BC.

9. An example here would be the Massacre of St. Bartholomew's which took place in Paris (then spreading to the remainder of France) in August of 1572. Originally intended as a means of removing religious opponents by the King, Charles IX, and his mother the Queen Regent, Catherine de'Medici, it spread to include the murders of many innocent people, due to their enemies grasping the opportunity to dispose of them, under cover of the general disorder.

10. Keaveney, *Sulla* and also Plutarch's *Crassus*. It is interesting to note that this man, whom Sulla considered unworthy, should rise to great prominence later, under Gaius Julius Caesar. He had become immensely rich and Caesar was in debt to him.

11. Keaveney, *Sulla*.

12. This lack of interest from the common people regarding the fate of the wealthy 'bankers' brings to mind the beginnings of the recession in 2008. Then ordinary citizens in New York, blaming the modern-day bankers for the crisis, congregated beneath their office windows bearing placards with the slogan 'Jump, you bastards!' That total lack of sympathy is very similar to the citizens of Rome during the proscription of many members of the Ordo Equestor. The common people in Rome had a good deal of respect for Sulla and may well have considered that he was correct in punishing the Equites for their misappropriation of Rome's wealth.

13. John Hazel, *Who's Who in Ancient Rome*, regarding the strange exploits of Lucius Sergius Catalina, right up to his famous legal battle with Cicero in 63 BC.

14. Keaveney, *Sulla*.

15. Plutarch, *Sulla*.

16. McCullough, *Masters of Rome*. Glossary. Re. the position of Flamen Dialis. There were 15 Flaminiates, the three most important of which were Dialis (for Jupiter Optimus Maximus), Martialis (for Mars), and Quirinalis (for Quirinus). None of them were particularly restrictive in their daily office, except for the Dialis. This had several taboos

(including one about not witnessing a death), which precluded the holder from taking up any kind of military life.

17. McCullough. The mother of Gaius Julius Caesar was Aurelia Cotta. She was the daughter of Lucius Aurelius Cotta and Rutilia, sister of Publius Rutilius Rufus. Aurelia's father died relatively young, and then her mother married her brother-in-law Marcus Aurelius Cotta, and had three more sons of the second marriage. Therefore, through his mother Caesar was very closely connected to the extensive Cottae clan.

18. Keaveney, *Sulla*. Keaveney rightly says that we should not be influenced by exaggerated figures. He quotes Hinard (1985) to illustrate the difficulty in making any real sense of the figures usually given.

19. Keaveney, *Sulla*.

20. Plutarch, *Sulla*. For details of Sulla's orders regarding the removal of the trophies of Gaius Marius, together with the indignity of his scattered ashes.

21. Balsdon, 'Sulla Felix'. *Journal of Roman Studies*. Balsdon quotes Carolina Lanzani in stating that there was a great deal of the mystic in Sulla's character. Certainly Sulla, in his own *Commentarii* showed his absolute belief in omens, portents and dreams as being a direct form of communication with divinities. Lanzani also notes Sulla's religious preference for Venus in this context.

22. Plutarch, *Sulla*. Plutarch reports that Sulla 'kept company with actors, musicians and dancers, along with the mime Sorex, and the player Metrobius, for whom he had professed a passionate fondness'. He was certainly close to Metrobius all his life.

23. Keaveney, *Sulla*. Regarding Gaius Marius' essential failure as a political figure.

24. Regarding the number of lictors used by magistrates. The lictors carried the bundles of rods, (the fasces). Outside of Rome's Pomerium the fasces had axes added to signify that the magistrate had the power to chastise. A Dictator was the only man whose lictors were allowed to carry the axes within the Pomerium. The number of lictors who accompanied a magistrate about his business indicated the degree of Imperium held by him. As state employees they had to be Roman citizens.

Aediles were allowed two, Praetors and Propraetors had six, Consuls or Proconsuls were allowed twelve. A Dictator might be expected to have more, due to his unique position, but Sulla did not do so, using only the customary twelve lictors assigned to Consuls.

25. Plutarch, *Sulla*. The motto 'No better friend, no worse enemy', or words to that effect, were carved on Sulla's tomb. Plutarch claimed to have seen it, stating 'it still stands on the Campus Martius'.

26. Plutarch, *Sulla* also Keaveney, *Sulla*. Keaveney quotes Sherwin White regarding Sulla's status as a properly constituted magistrate.

27. Balsdon, 'Sulla Felix', *Journal of Roman Studies*. Regarding Sulla's title of 'Epiphradatos' which was the cognomen adopted officially in early 81 BC. Appian in turn states that the order of events was the capture of Praeneste, the proscriptions, Sulla's ratification by the Senate, and then the voting of the equestrian statue for the Forum.

28. Balsdon, 'Sulla Felix'. Regarding the trophies belonging to Sulla, to which Gaius Marius had originally objected.

29. While Sulla's proconsular imperium prevented him from access to the city, keeping him officially outside the pomerium, it must be noted that it also prevented him from keeping too close an eye on everything that went on within the city walls.
30. The *mos maiorum* was the established custom, the way things were, but more than that. It also referred to the preferred way that things always should be, setting a precedent for correct behaviour.
31. Plutarch, *Sulla*.
32. Keaveney, *Sulla*.
33. Keaveney, *Sulla*. For explanation of the exact powers given to Sulla.
34. Keaveney, *Sulla*. Regarding the presidency of the then Interrex, Lucius Valerius Flaccus, the Princeps Senatus.
35. Appian. BC. For Sulla's aims during the period of his dictatorship and the need for one controlling hand (if only temporarily) to undo the damage done by the recent conflicts. See also Keaveney *Sulla* who confirms the need for one man to make the necessary constitutional changes and Sulla's promises to maintain and strengthen the Republic.

Chapter Fifteen
1. J.P.V.D. Balsdon, *Life and Leisure in Ancient Rome*.
2. J.P.V.D. Balsdon, *Life and Leisure in Ancient Rome*, for details of the inauguration of the Ludi Victoriae Sullae.
3. J.P.V.D. Balsdon, *Life and Leisure in Ancient Rome*, for full details of all the major celebrations in Rome and the running dates.
4. McCullough, *Masters of Rome*, Glossary.
5. McCullough. This remark of Sulla's regarding young Gaius Julius may be apocryphal, but in the words of one famous novelist (S.King) 'If it isn't true, then it certainly ought to be!'
6. Plutarch, *Sulla*.
7. Plutarch, *Sulla*. Plutarch does not actually give a date but puts the death of Sulla's elder son 'a little while' before that of his wife Caecilia Metella.
8. Regarding Metella's final illness. I have personal knowledge of a similar case where a young woman, recently a mother, was diagnosed with cancer shortly after the birth of her child. Presumably her doctors would have examined her before the child's birth and found nothing. Most unfortunately, she died six weeks later.
9. Balsdon, 'Sulla Felix', *Journal of Roman Studies*.
10. Plutarch, *Sulla*.
11. Plutarch, *Sulla*.
12. Keaveney, *Sulla*.
13. Keaveney, *Sulla*.
14. Plutarch, *Pompeius Magnus*.
15. Keaveney, *Sulla*.
16. Keaveney, *Sulla*.
17. Plutarch, *Sulla* and Appian *Mithradates*. Mithradates would in fact send yet another embassy to Rome in 78 BC although by that time Sulla was already dead and it was left to others in Rome to attempt to deal with the recalcitrant king.

18. McCullough, *Masters of Rome*, Glossary. Regarding *contiones*. These were the preliminary meetings of all the comitial assemblies. A *contio* could only be called by a magistrate having correct powers to convoke whichever assembly it was. A consul or praetor could convoke the centuriate assembly but only a tribune of the plebs could convoke a plebian assembly.
19. Keaveney, *Sulla*.
20. Keaveney, *Sulla*.
21. Keaveney, *Sulla*.
22. McCullough, *Masters of Rome*, Glossary. Re provinces and need for administrators.
23. Note – the case of Gaius Marius junior was probably on his mind at this point, as that young man had become a senior consul while still in his twenties, without having had any real experience of either military or political life. True, he was being used merely as a puppet leader at that time, but it still showed a fault in the system, in that it was possible to push a man up the ladder to higher office, even when he was obviously totally unfitted for the task.
24. McCullough, *Masters of Rome*, Glossary. Regarding curule offices. The senior magistracies were allowed to use a curule chair, made of ivory, which was reserved for the use of the senior ranks in the Senate.
25. Regarding the increase in the number of senators – anyone who has ever been a part of a large and unwieldy committee will be aware that the greater numbers do not make for greater efficiency. They actually slow down the decision-making process. However, they also divide the power between larger numbers and tend to prevent the emergence of a too-prominent person who might otherwise lead by nature of their strong opinions.
26. McCullough, *Masters of Rome*, Glossary. The meaning of the cognomen 'Caesar' is believed to refer to the holder having a fine head of hair. This was unfortunate in the case of Gaius Julius, as he was well-known for balding early.
27. Keaveney, *Sulla*.For details of Sulla's reformed courts I am particularly indebted to Arthur Keaveney.
28. As with the courtiers of Kings Louis XIV and Louis XV in eighteenth century France. They were conditioned to believe that being at court was to be at the centre of the world and that exile to their country estates meant social death.
29. Cicero. In Cicero's day there was a court dealing with embezzlement and it is likely that this was first instituted by Sulla.
30. Cicero for the use of Sulla's court system in his own day.
31. Keaveney, *Sulla*.
32. Balsdon, *Life and Leisure in Ancient Rome*. For descriptions of the Lusus Troiae which was a military tournament given by boys of the highest social level between the ages of twelve and sixteen. They paraded in armour and performed complicated drill movements before engaging in a mock battle. The event would be revived in Caesar's time.
33. Regarding funerals. Naturally Sulla was also guilty of this form of extravagance when he buried his wife Caecilia Metalla, spending lavishly on the ceremonies. It is however doubtful whether he appreciated the irony of it in his time of distress.
34. Keaveney, *Sulla*.

35. McCullough, *Masters of Rome*, Glossary regarding the provisions of the Lex Scantinia and attitudes towards personal irregularies in general.
36. Plutarch, *Crassus*.
37. Keaveney, *Sulla*.
38. Keaveney, *Sulla*.
39. McCullough, *Masters of Rome*, Glossary. In modern terms the iugurum of land was approximately five eighths of an acre, or one quarter of a hectare.
40. Keith Richardson, *Daggers in the Forum*, for the full story of the lives and deaths of the brothers Gracchi and what they had attempted to achieve with their opposition to the *latifundia* estates.

Chapter Sixteen

1. Plutarch, *Pompeius Magnus*.
2. J. Hazel, *Who's Who in Ancient Rome*, for family relationships.
3. At this period, there were only two types of gladiators, Thracians and Gauls. This did not refer to their nationality, but to their costumes and styles of fighting.
4. Pompeii had the first custom built ampitheatre, much earlier than that of Rome, erected in 80 BC. However, even now in Pompeii it is possible to see the double storey of pillars around the Forum, which suggests a public gallery area from which it was once intended to view games from above, taking place in the Forum itself. Incidentally, Pompeii's public thermae (baths) had open air sports grounds attached (palestrae), long before Rome's did.
5. Their cousin, Metellus Pius was consul for that year. The 'retired' Chief Vestal would not necessarily be an elderly lady, as Vestals entered the service around the ages of seven or eight years and served usually for thirty years. Therefore, they could and often did retire by the time they were in their late thirties. Their dowries would be intact, indeed invested on their behalf, so they could be financially independent.
6. Plutarch, *Sulla*.
7. J. Hazel's, *Who's Who in Ancient Rome*, is again invaluable for family relationships.
8. Keaveney, *Sulla*.
9. Keaveney, *Sulla*.
10. T.W. Potter, *Roman Italy*.
11. T.W. Potter, *Roman Italy*.
12. McCullough, *Masters of Rome*. Glossary. Despite being close by, they were not at that time considered to actually to be inside the boundaries of Rome.
13. J.Hazel, *Who's Who in Ancient Rome*, for details of Cicero's life.
14. Keaveney, *Sulla*.
15. Keaveney, *Sulla*.
16. Plutarch, *Sulla* and also Appian, *History of Rome*.
17. Keaveney, *Sulla*.
18. Plutarch, *Sulla* and Plutarch, *Pompeius Magnus*.
19. Plutarch, *Pompeius Magnus*.
20. J.Hazel, *Who's Who in Ancient Rome*.
21. T.W. Potter, *Roman Italy*.

22. T.W.Potter, *Roman Italy*.
23. Balsdon, 'Sulla Felix', *Journal of Roman Studies*.
24. Keaveney, *Lucullus, a Life* (1992). For details of the career of Lucullus after Sulla's death.
25. Plutarch, *Sulla*.
26. Keaveney, *Sulla*.
27. Keaveney, *Lucullus, a Life*.
28. Plutarch, *Sulla*. For his eyewitness account of Sulla's monument, still to be seen on the Campus Martius two centuries after his death.

Chapter Seventeen
1. Georgina Masson, *History of Republican Rome*.
2. Appian, *Mithradates*.
3. John Hazel, *Who's Who in Ancient Rome*, for family connections.
4. P.A.L. Greenhalgh, *Pompey, the Republican Prince* (1981).
5. Michael Grant, *Julius Caesar*.
6. Georgina Masson, *History of Republican Rome*.
7. Tom Holland, *Rubicon* (2003).
8. Michael Grant, *Julius Caesar*.
9. Plutarch, *Pompeius Magnus*.
10. John Hazel, *Who's Who in Ancient Rome*. Regarding the trial of Pub. Clodius Pulcher.
11. John Hazel, *Who's Who in Ancient Rome*. Regarding Clodius' death at Bovillae.
12. T.W.Potter, *Roman Italy*. Regarding the burning and rebuilding of Sulla's Curia.
13. T.W.Potter, *Roman Italy*. Regarding Sulla's colonies.
14. Colin Amery & Brian Curran Jnr., *Lost World of Pompeii*, regarding Pompeii's political life and the population changes due to the town becoming a colony.
15. James Lucas, *The Last Days of the Reich*, for personal discussions and eye-witness accounts of the latter days of World War II.
16. Plutarch, *Sulla*. Regarding Sulla forcing his wife Caecilia Metella Dalmatica from his house when she was terminally ill.
17. J.P.V.D. Balsdon, *Life and Leisure in Ancient Rome*. Regarding the value and lives of slaves and the possibilities of freedom for them, either from manumission or buying themselves free, together with their associations with their patrons.
18. J.P.V.D. Balsdon, *Life and Leisure in Ancient Rome*. For accounts of slaves who had improved their lot after being freed, including the fact that many did very well.
19. Plutarch, *Cicero*. Cicero's slave Tiro was highly regarded and the other members of the family, notably Cicero's brother, considered he should have been freed sooner.
20. Carlo Maria Franzeri, *The Life and Times of Theodora*. This gives accounts of the measures taken, particularly by Belisarius, to restore order in Byzantium.
21. Plutarch, *Sulla*. Refers to Sulla 'being hated' but gives no examples of what form this supposed hatred took. Certainly nobody attempted assassination of him, which might have been expected, and was unlikely to have been prevented, in such a case.
22. Geoffrey Richardson, *The Deceivers*. For full details in this and the four other books of his series of the *Wars of the Roses* in which he gives careful accounts of the plots against

the Yorkist royal family. He explains the motives of the plotters with accuracy and good sense, but without the fault of following any accepted 'line'.

23. Eric Ives, *Anne Boleyn*. Eric Ives provides the definitive biography of Queen Anne and shows exactly how she differed from the accepted character usually portrayed.

24. The Richard III Society is a worldwide organization devoted to the study of the life and times of King Richard Plantagenet.

25. Plutarch, *Crassus*. The ability of Marcus Licinius Crassus to make and keep money was phenomenal, although his methods were often immoral. He could be generous when he considered it politic to be so, and certainly paid Caesar's debts and loaned him money on several other occasions. However, there was always an underside to any generosity on his part and many people feared being obliged to fall into his hands, knowing of his ruthlessness in such matters.

26. Plutarch, *Sulla*. Plutarch makes it clear that although Sulla divorced Aelia due to her barrenness, and probably also because the lady he really wanted to marry, Caecilia Metella Dalmatica, had been widowed and was therefore available, he did not do so in a spirit of malice. On the contrary, he treated her well (though if a woman was divorced for barrenness the ex-husband was not legally obliged to return her dowry!). In this case, Sulla shows himself to be reasonable and kind beyond the norm, in giving the lady thanks for the years she had spent in bringing up his young children, and also presenting her with gifts and expressions of his respect.

27. Georgina Masson, *Republican Rome*.

28. Arthur Keaveney, *Sulla, the last Republican*.

29. Tom Holland, *Rubicon*.

30. Georgina Masson, *Republican Rome*.

31. J.Hazel, *Who's Who in Ancient Rome*. Details of the employment of Marcus Vipsanius Agrippa as a war leader, by Gaius Octavianus (Caesar's heir and adopted son), who was to become the first Emperor, Augustus.

Selected Bibliography

Albrecht-Gott, Dr, G. Kachel, M. Locher and Dr Mehling *Rome and Latium* (Phaidon Press, 1987).

Amery, Colin and Brian Curran jr, *The Lost World of Pompeii* (Ted Smart, 2002).

Balsdon, J.P.V.D., *Life and Leisure in Ancient Rome* (Phoenix, 1969).

Balsdon, J.P.V.D., *Roman Women* (Bodley Head, 1962).

Balsdon, J.P.V.D., 'Sulla Felix' *Journal of Roman Studies* (1951).

Balsdon, J.P.V.D., 'Consular Provinces under the Late Republic' *Journal of Roman Studies* (1939).

Beesley, A.H, *The Gracchi, Marius and Sulla* (Aeterna Press, 2010).

Birley, A, *Life in Roman Britain* (1964).

Bradford, Ernle, *The Great Siege, Malta 1565* (Hodder and Stoughton, 1961).

Butterworth, Alex and Ray Lawrence, *Pompeii, the Living City* (Phoenix Press, 2006).

Calza G and G. Becatti, *Ostia* (Instituto Poligrafico Della Stata. Roma. 3rd Edition).

Cavan, Brian, *The Punic Wars* (Weidenfeld and Nicolson, 1980).

Cornell, Tim and John Matthews, *Atlas of the Roman World* (Phaidon Press 1982).

Cowell, F.R, *Everyday Life in Ancient Rome* (1961).

Dudley, Donald, *Roman Society* (Pelican 1975).

Fiorato, Dr, Dr. Boylston and Dr. Knussel *Blood Red Roses* (Oxbow 2007).

Giuntoli, Stefano, *Art and History of Pompeii* (1989).

Grant, Michael, *History of Rome* (Weidenfeld and Nicolson, 1978).

Grant, Michael. *Cities of Vesuvius* (Book Club Associates, 1974).

Grant, Michael, *Julius Caesar* (Weidenfeld and Nicolson, 1979).

Grant, Michael, *Gladiators* (Penguin, 1967).

Greenhalgh, P.A.L., *Pompey, the Roman Alexander* (Weidenfeld and Nicolson, 1980).

Greenhalgh, P.A.L., *Pompey, the Republican Prince* (Weidenfield and Nicolson, 1981).

Grimal, Pierre, *The Civilisation of Rome* (George Allen & Unwin, 1963).

Goodenough, Simon, *Citizens of Rome* (Hamlyn, 1979).

Hazel, John, *Who's Who in the Roman World* (Routledge, 2002).

Holland, Tom, *Rubicon* (Abacus, 2005).

Holloway, R.Ross, *The Archaeology of Early Rome & Latium* (Routledge, 1996).

Keaveney, Arthur, *Sulla, the Last Republican* (Routledge, 2005).

Keaveney, Arthur, *Lucullus, a Life* (London 1992).

Keppie, Lawrence, *The Making of the Roman Army* (Batsford, 1987).

Lanzani, Christina, *Lucio Cornelio Silla, Dittatore* (Milan, 1930).

Leprohon, Pierre, *Rome* (Liber, 1981).

del Maso, Leonardo B, *Rome of the Caesars* (Rome 1981).

Masson, Georgina, *Republican Rome* (Thames and Hudson, 1974).

McCullough, Colleen, (Masters of Rome Series – Glossaries):

McCullough, Colleen, *The First Man in Rome* (Arrow, 1990)

McCullough, Colleen, *The Grass Crown* (Arrow, 1991).

McCullough, Colleen, *Fortune's Favourites* (Arrow, 1993).

Meier, Christian, *Caesar* (Harper Collins, 1995).

Mommsen, Theodor, *History of Rome Part IV*.

Muir's Historical Atlas (Book Club Associates, 1974).

Nappo, Salvatore, *Pompeii* (2004).

Nogueres, Henri, *The Massacre of St. Bartholomew* (George Allen & Unwin, 1959).

Ogilvie, R.M., *The Romans and their Gods* (Pimlico, 2000).

Plutarch's Lives, *Encyclopaedia Britannica* 'Sulla', 'Pompey', 'Crassus', 'Caesar'.

Pomeroy, Sarah, *Goddesses, Whores, Wives & Slaves* (Pimlico, 1994).

Potter, David, *Emperors of Rome* (Quercus, 2007).

Potter, Tim W., *Roman Italy* (British Museum Publications, 1987).

Richardson, Geoffrey, *The Deceivers* (Baildon Books, 1997).

Richardson, Keith, *Daggers in the Forum* (Cassell & Company, 1976).

Rickard, J., *Battle of Chaeronea in 86 bc* (2008).

Robbins, Christopher, *The Household Herbal* (Bantam, 1995).

Rodgers, Nigel, *The History and Conquests of Ancient Rome* (Hermes House 2010).

Scullard, H.H., *From the Gracchi to Nero* (Methuen, 1982).

Stobart, J.C., *The Grandeur that was Rome* (Sidgwick & Jackson, 1961).

Index

Explanatory Notes to the Index

It is appropriate at this point to clarify the matter of Roman names. As the reader is probably already aware, most of the distinguished families used a third name, in addition to their first and family names. The third name, or **cognomen**, differentiated them from other branches of their **gens** bearing the same name and was often in the nature of a nickname e.g. Pulcher (beautiful), Africanus (of Africa) or Vopiscus (the survivor of twins). In this index the cognomen has been used for identification where the person concerned is commonly known by it, for instance Sulla, Caesar, Caepio, Drusus and the Gracchi, etc.

The family name, or **nomen**, indicates the gens to which each belonged. The most famous ones are:

Aemilius, Antonius, Aurelius, Claudius, Cornelius, Flavius, Fulvius, Julius, Junius, Licinius, Livius, Octavius, Pompeius, Rutilius, Sempronius, Servilius, and so on. The term gens was actually feminine in gender, so in Latin it would properly be referred to as gens Julia, gens Cornelia, gens Aemilia, gens Servilia, and so on.

There was a limited number of first names, or **praenomen**, used by Roman families, and they tended to prefer only two or three, used repeatedly. These names, with their usual abbreviations, are as follows:

Ap.	Appius	P.	Publius
A.	Aulus	Q.	Quintus
C.	Gaius	Ser.	Servius
Cn.	Gnaeus	Sex.	Sextus
D.	Decimus	Sp.	Spurius
L.	Lucius	T.	Titus
M.	Marcus	Ti.	Tiberius
M'	Manius		

Discover Your History

Ancestors • Heritage • Memories

Each issue of *Discover Your History* presents special features and regular articles on a huge variety of topics about our social history and heritage – such as our ancestors, childhood memories, military history, British culinary traditions, transport history, our rural and industrial past, health, houses, fashions, pastimes and leisure ... and much more.

Historic pictures show how we and our ancestors have lived and the changing shape of our towns, villages and landscape in Britain and beyond.

Special tips and links help you discover more about researching family and local history. Spotlights on fascinating museums, history blogs and history societies also offer plenty of scope to become more involved.

Keep up to date with news and events that celebrate our history, and reviews of the latest books and media releases.

Discover Your History presents aspects of the past partly through the eyes and voices of those who were there.

FREE BOOK WHEN YOU SUBSCRIBE TO *Discover Your History*

UK only

Discover Your History is in all good newsagents and also available on subscription for six or twelve issues. For more details on how to take out a subscription and how to choose your free book, call 01778 392013 or visit **www.discoveryourhistory.net**